Dedication

For Pavle Bataveljic 1945–2008

Brief Table of Contents

Software Project Management

Fifth Edition

Software
Project
Management

Fifth Edition

Bob Hughes and Mike Cotterell

McGraw-Hill
Higher Education

London Boston Burr Ridge, IL Dubuque, IA Madison, WI New York San Francisco
St. Louis Bangkok Bogotá Caracas Kuala Lumpur Lisbon Madrid Mexico City
Milan Montreal New Delhi Santiago Seoul Singapore Sydney Taipei Toronto

Software Project Management, 5e
Bob Hughes and Mike Cotterell
ISBN-13 978-0-07-712279-9
ISBN-10 0-07-712279-8

 **McGraw-Hill Higher Education**

Published by McGraw-Hill Education
Shoppenhangers Road
Maidenhead
Berkshire
SL6 2QL
Telephone: 44 (0) 1628 502 500
Fax: 44 (0) 1628 770 224
Website: **www.mcgraw-hill.co.uk**

British Library Cataloguing in Publication Data
A catalogue record for this book is available from the British Library

Library of Congress Cataloguing in Publication Data
The Library of Congress data for this book has been applied for from the Library of Congress

Acquisitions Editor: Catriona Hoyle
Marketing Manager: Alice Duijser
Production Editor: Alison Holt

Text Design by Hardlines
Cover design by Ego-Creative
Printed and bound in the UK by Bell and Bain Ltd, Glasgow

ISBN-13 978-0-07-712279-9
ISBN-10 0-07-712279-8

The **McGraw·Hill** Companies

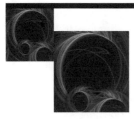

Detailed Table of Contents

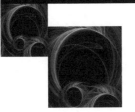

Preface

Preparing the fifth edition of this book has reminded us that project management is not just a crucial element in successful software and IT development, but is also a fascinating topic in its own right. It is an intriguing mixture of the technical and the very human, of the rational and also the intuitive. Initially we offered this topic as an ancillary discipline for software engineers and IT practitioners. We have, however, become increasingly convinced that the discipline should have a more central role: that the question of *how* systems are implemented is a vital one to be asked at the same time as that of *what* a system is to do.

Not many software books have lasted as long as this one. Clearly the principles of project management are less transient than those of software design and implementation, which have gone through some very major developments over recent years. However, project management has not been immune from change. One development has been the growth in project management bodies of knowledge such as those of the Project Management Institute (PMI) in the United States and the Association for Project Management (APM) in the United Kingdom. There has also been the development of project management standards such as PRINCE2. These developments are to be welcomed as externalizing and codifying good practice – indeed we have included an appendix on PRINCE2. However, we have resisted becoming a 'PMI' book or a 'PRINCE2' book. Partly this is because we believe that software project management, while incorporating all the key elements of generic project management, also has to deal with the peculiar problems associated with creating software. These include the relative intangibility of software, its extreme malleability, the intimate relationship it has with the systems within which it is embedded, and its sheer complexity. We also wanted to avoid means–end inversion where there was a focus on the recall of specific terminology and procedural detail at the expense of an understanding of underlying concepts and purpose.

One new development that has been taken on board has been the growing awareness that a project is rarely an isolated activity but is almost always part of a broader programme of work aimed at meeting organizational and business objectives. There are also agile approaches, such as extreme programming, which have been a timely reminder that software development is an intensely human activity. In contrast to this emphasis on the highly productive, highly interactive co-located team, there is also a growth of dispersed or virtual projects where all or part of the development team is in another country or even continent. We noted these developments in previous editions but have expanded their treatment in this one – this greater emphasis on development team dynamics has led to the creation of a chapter devoted solely to these topics.

One major problem has been the conflict between a desire to include all the topics that our reviewers would like to see and the desire for a concise volume that avoids 'bloating'. Sometimes there are topics and standards which appear to be current and of which one feels people should be aware. On closer inspection, the material for various reasons is less useful or relevant than one hoped. In this edition we have dropped an appendix on the British standard BS6079. This is because the new version of this has become what is essentially a general advisory guide on project management practice. As such it duplicates material already covered in this book. Some individual topics have also been dropped because it was felt that they really needed a deeper treatment better conveyed by a more specialist publication than this one: the internal rate of return (IRR) in project evaluation and the Hofstede analysis of national cultural characteristics are examples. In general, though, we have erred on the side of caution in retaining topics.

It seems a long time since the first, rather slim, edition published in 1995. As novice authors, Cotterell and Hughes were very indebted to Dave Hatter and Martin Campbell Kelly who had a huge influence on the style of the book. Dave Hatter in particular emphasized the need for each chapter to have clear learning objectives: ideally the reader should finish the chapter feeling they had learnt a new skill. He also instilled the need to explain things clearly – to feel confident in using simple words to explain things that might at first appear complicated. We are aware that we have not always lived up to these values – and have been taken to task by our students and teachers from other institutions who have kindly acted as reviewers. Many of the changes we have made in the new edition are as a result of this process.

Acknowledgements

During the course of preparing the four previous editions since 1995, we have received assistance from many people. These people have included: Ken I'Anson, Chris Claire, David Howe, Martin Campbell Kelly, Barbara Kitchenham (for permission to use a project data set shown in Chapter 5), Paul Radford and Robyn Lawrie of Charismatek Software Metrics in Melbourne, David Garmus and David Herron (the last four, all for material in Chapter 10), David Purves, David Wynne, Dick Searles, John Pyman, Jim Watson, Mary Shepherd, Sunita Chulani, David Wilson, David Farthing, Charlie Svahnberg, Henk Koppelaar and Ian McChesney.

We have made use of materials produced by Abdullah Al Shehab and David I. Shepherd in the chapter on risk. David also offered some advice on the developments in earned value analysis. Our colleague Marian Eastwood helped us out on some of the finer points of the Unified System Development Method.

We would also like to thank the team at McGraw-Hill. The role previously taken by Karen Mosman was taken over by Catriona Hoyle (née Watson) and Katy Hamilton who, among other good things, instilled the necessary disciplines of timeliness. We have already mentioned Dave Hatter who was our former editor at International Thomson Press and then at McGraw-Hill and we hope he continues to enjoy retirement in the groves and glades of Essex.

Guided tour

Objectives

Each chapter opens with a set of learning objectives, summarizing what the reader should learn from each chapter.

Margin notes

New ideas, terms and references are placed in the margin where appropriate. Margin notes also indicate the links to ideas and concepts covered elsewhere in the textbook.

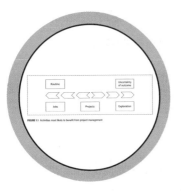

Figures and tables

Each chapter provides a number of figures to show the various models, project planning tools and charts.

Case study examples

Brief case studies run throughout the chapters to illustrate the application of project management techniques.

Exercises

Brief exercises are dotted throughout the chapters, to allow students to practise the techniques and apply the methodology to real-world situations.

Chapter conclusions

This briefly reviews and reinforces the main topics covered in each chapter to ensure that students have acquired a solid understanding of the key topics.

Further exercises

These questions encourage the reader to review and apply the knowledge acquired from each chapter and to explore further some of the ideas in the chapter.

Appendices

Appendix A at the end of the book explains PRINCE2. Appendix B, Answer pointers, provides guide answers to the questions and exercises set in the book.

Technology to enhance learning and teaching

*Visit **www.mcgraw-hill.co.uk/textbooks/hughes** today*

Online Learning Centre (OLC)

After completing each chapter, log on to the supporting Online Learning Centre website. Take advantage of the study tools offered to reinforce the material you have read in the text, and to develop your knowledge of project management in a fun and effective way.

Resources for lecturers include:

- *Power Point Slides*
- *Tutorial Exercises*
- *Artwork from Book*

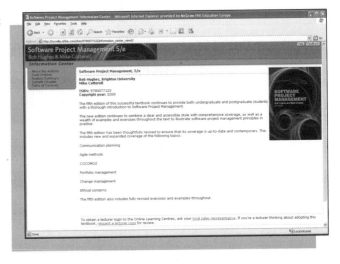

Custom Publishing Solutions: Let us help make our **content** your **solution**

At McGraw-Hill Education our aim is to help lecturers to find the most suitable content for their needs delivered to their students in the most appropriate way. Our **custom publishing solutions** offer the ideal combination of content delivered in the way which best suits lecturers and students.

Our custom publishing programme offers lecturers the opportunity to select just the chapters or sections of material they wish to deliver to their students from a database called Primis at **www.primisonline.com**.

Primis contains over two million pages of content from:

- textbooks
- professional books
- case books – Harvard Articles, Insead, Ivey, Darden, Thunderbird and BusinessWeek
- Taking Sides – debate materials

across the following imprints:

- McGraw-Hill Education
- Open University Press
- Harvard Business School Press
- US and European material

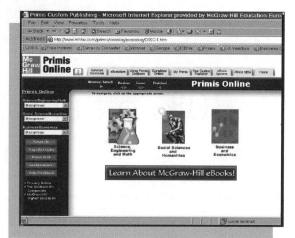

There is also the option to include additional material authored by lecturers in the custom product – this does not necessarily have to be in English.

We will take care of everything from start to finish in the process of developing and delivering a custom product to ensure that lecturers and students receive exactly the material needed in the most suitable way.

With a **Custom Publishing Solution**, students enjoy the best selection of material deemed to be the most suitable for learning everything they need for their courses – something of real value to support their learning. Teachers are able to use exactly the material they want, in the way they want, to support their teaching on the course.

Please contact **your local McGraw-Hill representative** with any questions or alternatively contact Warren Eels at **warren_eels@mcgraw-hill.com**.

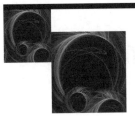
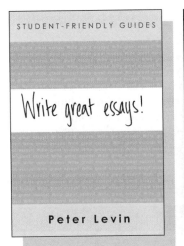

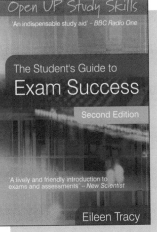

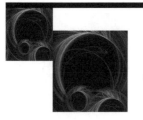

Acknowledgements

Our thanks go to the following reviewers for their comments at various stages in the text's development:

Christopher Procter, University of Salford

Darren Dalcher, Middlesex University

David Gustafos, Kansas State University

David Farthing, University of Glamorgan

Klaus Van den Berg, University of Twente

Miroslaw Staron, IT University of Goteborg

Every effort has been made to to trace and acknowledge ownership of copyright and to clear permission for material reproduced in this book. The publishers will be pleased to make suitable arrangements to clear permission with any copyright holders whom it has not been possible to contact.

Introduction to software project management

1.1 Introduction

This textbook is about 'software project management'. The first question is whether the management of *software* projects is really that different from that of other projects. To answer this, we need to look at some key ideas about the planning, monitoring and control of software projects. We will see that all projects are about meeting objectives. Like any other project, a software project must satisfy real needs. To do this we must identify the project's stakeholders and their objectives. Ensuring that their objectives are met is the aim of project management. However, we cannot know that a project will meet its objectives in the future unless we know the present state of the project.

1.2 Why is software project management important?

This book is for students of software engineering and computer science and also those studying business information systems. More technically oriented students can be impatient at having to study something which keeps them away from their code. So why is it important to become familiar with project management?

First, there is the question of money. A lot of money is at stake with ICT projects. In the United Kingdom during the financial year 2002–2003, the central government spent more on contracts for ICT projects than on contracts related to roads (about £2.3 billion as opposed to £1.4 billion). The biggest departmental spender was the Department for Work and Pensions, who spent over £800 million on ICT. Mismanagement of ICT projects means that there is less to spend on good things such as hospitals.

> The information in this paragraph comes from a National Audit Office report, Improving IT Procurement, November 2004.

Unfortunately, projects are not always successful. In a report published in 2003, the Standish Group in the United States analysed 13,522 projects and concluded that only a third of projects were successful; 82% of projects were late and 43% exceeded their budget.

> There has been some debate about the precise validity of the Standish findings but the key point about the prevalence of IT project failings remains clear.

The reason for these project shortcomings is often the management of projects. The National Audit Office in the UK, for example, among other factors causing project failure identified 'lack of skills and proven approach to project management and risk management'.

1.3 What is a project?

The dictionary definitions put a clear emphasis on the project being a *planned* activity.

> Dictionary definitions of 'project' include: 'A specific plan or design' 'A planned undertaking' 'A large undertaking: e.g. a public works scheme', *Longman Concise English Dictionary*, 1982.

The emphasis on being planned assumes we can determine how to carry out a task before we start. Yet with exploratory projects this might be difficult. Planning is in essence thinking carefully about something before you do it – even with uncertain projects this is worth doing as long as the resulting plans are seen as provisional. Other activities, such as routine maintenance, will have been performed so many times that everyone knows exactly what to do. In these cases, planning hardly seems necessary, although procedures might be documented to ensure consistency and to help newcomers.

The activities that benefit most from conventional project management are likely to lie between these two extremes – see Figure 1.1.

> Programme management is often used to coordinate activities on concurrent jobs.

There is a hazy boundary between the non-routine project and the routine job. The first time you do a routine task it will be like a project. On the other hand, a project to develop a system similar to previous ones that you have developed will have a large element of the routine.

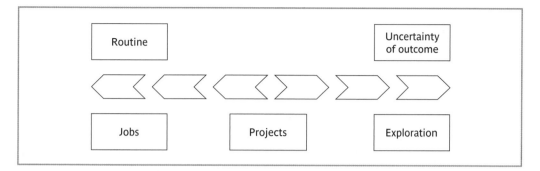

FIGURE 1.1 Activities most likely to benefit from project management

The following characteristics distinguish projects:

- non-routine tasks are involved;
- planning is required;
- specific objectives are to be met or a specified product is to be created;
- the project has a predetermined time span;
- work is carried out for someone other than yourself;
- work involves several specialisms;
- people are formed into a temporary work group to carry out the task;
- work is carried out in several phases;
- the resources that are available for use on the project are constrained;
- the project is large or complex.

The more any of these factors apply to a task, the more difficult that task will be. Project size is particularly important. The project that employs 20 developers is likely to be disproportionately more difficult than one with only 10 staff because of the need for additional coordination. The examples and exercises used in this book usually relate to smaller projects in order to make the techniques easier to grasp. However, the techniques and issues discussed are of equal relevance to larger projects.

EXERCISE 1.1

Consider the following:

- producing an edition of a newspaper;
- putting a robot vehicle on Mars to search for signs of life;
- getting married;
- amending a financial computer system to deal with a common European currency;

▶ ■ a research project into what makes a good human–computer interface;

■ an investigation into the reason why a user has a problem with a computer system;

■ a second-year programming assignment for a computing student;

■ writing an operating system for a new computer;

■ installing a new version of a word processing package in an organization.

Some seem more like real projects than others. Put them into an order most closely matching your ideas of what constitutes a project. For each entry in the ordered list, describe the difference between it and the one above which makes it less worthy of the term 'project'.

There is no one correct answer to this exercise, but a possible solution to this and the other exercises you will come across may be found at the end of the book.

For example, see Rolf A. Lundin and Andres Söderholm (1995) 'A theory of the temporary organization' *Scandinavian Journal of Management* 11(4) 437–55.

Some argue that projects are especially problematic as they are temporary sub-organizations. A group of people is brought together to carry out a task. The existence of this sub-organization cuts across the authority of the existing units within the organization. This has the advantage that a group containing various specialists is focused on a single important task. However, the project is likely to be seen as disruptive to others. Also, expertise built up during the project may be lost when the team is eventually dispersed at the end of the project.

1.4 Software projects versus other types of project

F. P. Brooks (1987). 'No silver bullet: essence and accidents of software engineering'. This essay has been included in *The Mythical Man-Month*, Anniversary Edition, Addison Wesley, 1995.

Many techniques in general project management also apply to software project management, but Fred Brooks identified some characteristics of software projects which make them particularly difficult:

Invisibility When a physical artefact such as a bridge is constructed the progress can actually be seen. With software, progress is not immediately visible. Software project management can be seen as the process of making the invisible visible.

Complexity Per dollar, pound or euro spent, software products contain more complexity than other engineered artefacts.

Conformity The 'traditional' engineer usually works with physical systems and materials like cement and steel. These physical systems have complexity, but are governed by consistent physical laws. Software developers have to conform to the requirements of human clients. It is not just that individuals can be inconsistent. Organizations, because of lapses in collective memory, in internal communication or in effective decision making, can exhibit remarkable 'organizational stupidity'.

Flexibility That software is easy to change is seen as a strength. However, where the software system interfaces with a physical or organizational system, it is expected that the software will change to accommodate the other components rather than vice versa. Thus software systems are particularly subject to change.

1.5 Contract management and technical project management

In-house projects are where the users and the developers of new software work for the same organization. However, increasingly organizations contract out ICT development to outside developers. Here, the client organization will often appoint a 'project manager' to supervise the contract who will delegate many technically oriented decisions to the contractors. Thus, the project manager will not worry about estimating the effort needed to write individual software components as long as the overall project is within budget and on time. On the supplier side, there will need to be project managers who deal with the more technical issues. This book leans towards the concerns of these 'technical' project managers.

1.6 Activities covered by software project management

Chapter 4 on project analysis and technical planning looks at some alternative life cycles.

A software project is not only concerned with the actual writing of software. In fact, where a software application is bought in 'off the shelf', there may be no software writing as such, but this is still fundamentally a software project because so many of the other activities associated with software will still be present.

Usually there are three successive processes that bring a new system into being – see Figure 1.2.

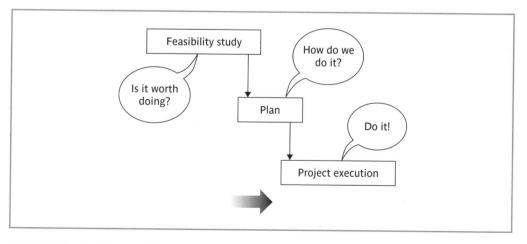

FIGURE 1.2 The feasibility study/plan/execution cycle

Chapter 2 explores some further aspects of programme management.

1 **The feasibility study** assesses whether a project is worth starting – that it has a valid *business case*. Information is gathered about the requirements of the proposed application. Requirements elicitation can, at least initially, be complex and difficult. The stakeholders may know the aims they wish to pursue, but not be sure about the means of achievement. The developmental and operational costs, and the value of the benefits of the new system, will also have to be estimated. With a large system, the feasibility study could be a project in its own right with its own plan. The study could be part of a strategic planning exercise examining a range of potential software developments. Sometimes an organization assesses a *programme* of development made up of a number of projects.

The PRINCE2 method, which is described in Appendix A, takes this iterative approach to planning. Annex 1 to this chapter has an outline of the content of a plan.

2 **Planning** If the feasibility study indicates that the prospective project appears viable, then project planning can start. For larger projects, we would not do all our detailed planning at the beginning. We create an outline plan for the whole project and a detailed one for the first stage. Because we will have more detailed and accurate project information after the earlier stages of the project have been completed, planning of the later stages is left to nearer their start.

3 **Project execution** The project can now be executed. The execution of a project often contains *design* and *implementation* sub-phases. Students new to project planning often find that the boundary between design and planning can be hazy. Design is making decisions about the form of the *products* to be created. This could relate to the external appearance of the software, that is, the user interface, or the internal architecture. The plan details the *activities* to be carried out to create these products. Planning and design can be confused because at the most detailed level, planning decisions are influenced by design decisions. Thus a software product with five major components is likely to require five sets of activities to create them.

Figure 1.3 suggests that these stages must be done strictly in sequence – we will see in Chapter 4 that other, iterative approaches can be adopted. However, the actual activities listed here would still be done.

Figure 1.3 shows the typical sequence of software development activities recommended in the international standard ISO 12207. Some activities are concerned with the *system* while others relate to *software*. The development of software will be only one part of a project. Software could be developed, for example, for a project which also requires the installation of an ICT infrastructure, the design of user jobs and user training.

■ *Requirements analysis* starts with *requirements elicitation* or requirements gathering which establishes what the potential users and their managers require of the new system. It could relate to a *function* – that the system should do something. It could be a quality requirement – how well the functions must work. An example of this is dispatching an ambulance in response to an emergency telephone call. In this case transaction time would be affected by hardware and software performance as well as the speed of human operation. Training to ensure that operators use the computer system efficiently is an example of a *system requirement* for the project, as opposed to a specifically

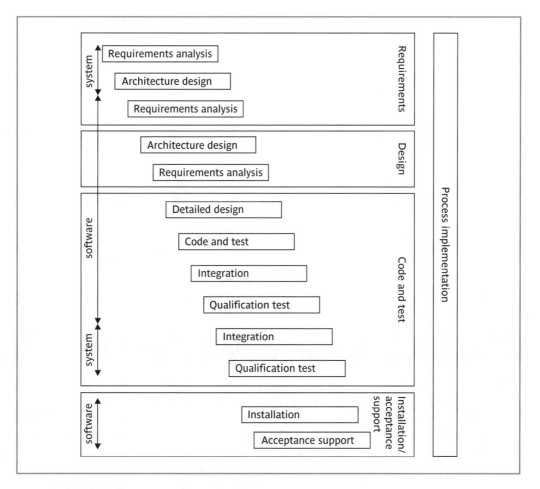

FIGURE 1.3 The ISO 12207 software development life cycle

software requirement. There would also be *resource requirements* that relate to application development costs.

- *Architecture design* The components of the new system that fulfil each requirement have to be identified. Existing components may be able to satisfy some requirements. In other cases, a new component will have to be made. These components are not only software: they could be new hardware or work processes. Although software developers are primarily concerned with software components, it is very rare that these can be developed in isolation. They will, for example, have to take account of existing legacy systems with which they will interoperate. The design of the *system architecture* is thus an input to the *software requirements*. A second architecture design process then takes place that maps the software requirements to *software components*.

- *Detailed design* Each software component is made up of a number of software units that can be separately coded and tested. The detailed design of these units is carried out separately.

- *Code and test* refers to writing code for each software unit. Initial testing to debug individual software units would be carried out at this stage.

- *Integration* The components are tested together to see if they meet the overall requirements. Integration could involve combining different software components, or combining and testing the software element of the system in conjunction with the hardware platforms and user interactions.

- *Qualification testing* The system, including the software components, has to be tested carefully to ensure that all the requirements have been fulfilled.

- *Installation* This is the process of making the new system operational. It would include activities such as setting up standing data (for example, the details for employees in a payroll system), setting system parameters, installing the software onto the hardware platforms and user training.

- *Acceptance support* This is the resolving of problems with the newly installed system, including the correction of any errors, and implementing agreed extensions and improvements. Software maintenance can be seen as a series of minor software projects. In many environments, most software development is in fact maintenance.

EXERCISE 1.2

Brightmouth College is a higher education institution which used to be managed by a local government authority but has now become autonomous. Its payroll is still administered by the local authority and pay slips and other output are produced in the local authority's computer centre. The authority now charges the college for this service. The college management are of the opinion that it would be cheaper to obtain an 'off-the-shelf' payroll package and do the payroll processing themselves.

What would be the main stages of the project to convert to independent payroll processing by the college? Bearing in mind that an off-the-shelf package is to be used, how would this project differ from one where the software was to be written from scratch?

1.7 Plans, methods and methodologies

A plan for an activity must be based on some idea of a *method* of work. For example, if you were asked to test some software, you may know nothing about the software to be tested, but you could assume that you would need to:

- analyse the requirements for the software;
- devise and write test cases that will check that each requirement has been satisfied;
- create test scripts and expected results for each test case;
- compare the actual results and the expected results and identify discrepancies.

While a *method* relates to a type of activity in general, a *plan* takes that method (and perhaps others) and converts it to real activities, identifying for each activity:

- its start and end dates;
- who will carry it out;
- what tools and materials – including information – will be needed.

The output from one method might be the input to another. Groups of methods or techniques are often grouped into *methodologies* such as object-oriented design.

EXERCISE 1.3

This should ideally be done in groups of about four, but you can think about how you would go about this exercise on your own if needs be. You are probably in a building that has more than one storey. From the point of view of this exercise, the bigger the building the better.

In a group of four, work out how you would obtain an accurate estimate of the height of the building. (If you happen to be in a single-storey building, you can estimate the floor area instead!) Plan how you would carry out any actions needed to obtain your estimate. Spend 20 minutes on this – you must remain in the same room for this planning phase. Once planning is complete, implement your plan, timing how long it takes to produce your final figure.

If there is more than one group carrying out this exercise, after completion of the task you can compare answers and also the approach you used when coming up with your answer.

1.8 Some ways of categorizing software projects

Projects may differ because of the different technical products to be created. Thus we need to identify the characteristics of a project which could affect the way in which it should be planned and managed. Other factors are discussed below.

Compulsory versus voluntary users

In workplaces there are systems that staff have to use if they want to do something, such as recording a sale. However, use of a system is increasingly voluntary, as in the case of computer games. Here it is difficult to elicit precise requirements from potential users as we could with a business system. What the game will do will thus depend much on the informed ingenuity of the developers, along with techniques such as market surveys, focus groups and prototype evaluation.

Information systems versus embedded systems

Embedded systems are also called real-time or industrial systems.

A traditional distinction has been between *information systems* which enable staff to carry out office processes and *embedded systems* which control machines. A stock control system would be an information system. An embedded, or process control, system might control the air conditioning equipment in a building. Some systems may have elements of both where, for example, the stock control system also controls an automated warehouse.

EXERCISE 1.4

Would an operating system on a computer be an information system or an embedded system?

Objectives versus products

Projects may be distinguished by whether their aim is to produce a *product* or to meet certain *objectives.*

A project might be to create a product, the details of which have been specified by the client. The client has the responsibility for justifying the product.

Service level agreements are becoming increasingly important as organizations contract out functions to external service suppliers.

On the other hand, the project requirement might be to meet certain objectives which could be met in a number of ways. An organization might have a problem and ask a specialist to recommend a solution.

Many software projects have two stages. First is an objective-driven project resulting in recommendations. This might identify the need for a new software system. The next stage is a project actually to create the software product.

This is useful where the technical work is being done by an external group and the user needs are unclear at the outset. The external group can produce a preliminary design at a fixed fee. If the design is acceptable the developers can then quote a price for the second, implementation, stage based on an agreed requirement.

EXERCISE 1.5

Would the project to implement an independent payroll system at the Brightmouth College described in Exercise 1.2 above be an objective-driven project or a product-driven project?

1.9 Stakeholders

These are people who have a stake or interest in the project. Their early identification is important as you need to set up adequate communication channels with them. Stakeholders can be categorized as:

- *Internal to the project team* This means that they will be under the direct managerial control of the project leader.
- *External to the project team but within the same organization* For example, the project leader might need the assistance of the users to carry out systems testing. Here the commitment of the people involved has to be negotiated.

B. W. Boehm and R. Ross, 'Theory 'W software project management: principles and examples', in B. W. Boehm (ed.) (1989) *Software Risk Management*, IEEE Computer Society Press.

- *External to both the project team and the organization* External stakeholders may be customers (or users) who will benefit from the system that the project implements. They may be contractors who will carry out work for the project. The relationship here is usually based on a contract.

Different types of stakeholder may have different objectives and one of the jobs of the project leader is to recognize these different interests and to be able to reconcile them. For example, end-users may be concerned with the ease of use of the new application, while their managers may be more focused on staff savings. The project leader therefore needs to be a good communicator and negotiator. Boehm and Ross proposed a 'Theory W' of software project management where the manager concentrates on creating situations where all parties benefit from a project and therefore have an interest in its success. (The 'W' stands for 'win–win'.)

The role and format of communication plans will be explained in greater detail in Chapter 11 on managing people in software environments.

Project managers can sometimes miss an important stakeholder group, especially in unfamiliar business contexts. These could be departments supplying important services that are taken for granted.

Given the importance of coordinating the efforts of stakeholders, the recommended practice is for a *communication plan* to be created at the start of a project.

EXERCISE 1.6

Identify the stakeholders in the Brightmouth College payroll project.

1.10 Setting objectives

Among all these stakeholders are those who actually own the project. They control the financing of the project. They also set the objectives of the project. The objectives should define what the project team must achieve for project success. Although different stakeholders have different motivations, the project objectives identify the shared intentions for the project.

Objectives focus on the desired outcomes of the project rather than the tasks within it – they are the 'post-conditions' of the project. Informally the objectives could be written as a set of statements following the opening words *'the project will be a success if. . . .'* Thus one statement in a set of objectives might be *'customers can order our products online'* rather than *'to build an e-commerce website'*. There is often more than one way to meet an objective and the more possible routes to success the better.

There may be several stakeholders, including users in different business areas, who might have some claim to project ownership. In such a case, a *project authority* needs to be explicitly identified with overall authority over the project.

> This committee is likely to contain user, development and management representatives.

This authority is often a *project steering committee* (or *project board* or *project management board*) with overall responsibility for setting, monitoring and modifying objectives. The project manager runs the project on a day-to-day basis, but regularly reports to the steering committee.

Sub-objectives and goals

> Defining sub-objectives requires assumptions about how the main objective is to be achieved.

An effective objective for an individual must be something that is within the control of that individual. An objective might be that the software application produced must pay for itself by reducing staff costs. As an overall business objective this might be reasonable. For software developers it would be unreasonable as any reduction in operational staff costs depends not just on them but on the operational management of the delivered system. A more appropriate *goal* or sub-objective for the software developers would be to keep development costs within a certain budget.

We can say that in order to achieve the objective we must achieve certain goals or sub-objectives first. These are steps on the way to achieving an objective, just as goals scored in a football match are steps towards the objective of winning the match. Informally this can be expressed as a set of statements following the words *'To reach objective . . . , the following must be in place . . .'.*

The mnemonic SMART is sometimes used to describe well-defined objectives:

■ *Specific* Effective objectives are concrete and well defined. Vague aspirations such as *'to improve customer relations'* are unsatisfactory. Objectives should be defined so that it is obvious to all whether the project has been successful.

> This still leaves a problem about the level at which the target should be set, e.g. why, say, a 50% reduction in complaints and not 40% or 60%?

■ *Measurable* Ideally there should be *measures of effectiveness* which tell us how successful the project has been. For example, *'to reduce customer complaints'* would be more satisfactory as an objective than *'to improve customer relations'*. The measure can, in some cases, be an answer to simple yes/no question, e.g. *'Did we install the new software by 1 June?'*

■ *Achievable* It must be within the power of the individual or group to achieve the objective.

■ *Relevant* The objective must be relevant to the true purpose of the project.

■ *Time constrained* There should be a defined point in time by which the objective should have been achieved.

EXERCISE 1.7

Bearing in mind the above discussion of objectives, comment on the appropriateness of the wording of each of the following 'objectives' for software developers:

(i)   to implement the new application on time and within budget;

(ii) to implement the new software application with the fewest possible software errors that might lead to operational failures;

(iii) to design a system that is user-friendly;

(iv) to produce full documentation for the new system.

Measures of effectiveness

These concepts are explained more fully in Chapter 13 on software quality.

Measures of effectiveness provide practical methods of checking that an objective has been met. 'Mean time between failures' (mtbf) might, for example, be used to measure reliability. This is a *performance* measurement and, as such, can only be taken once the system is operational. Project managers want to get some idea of the performance of the completed system as it is being constructed. They will therefore seek *predictive* measures. For example, a large number of errors found during code inspections might indicate potential problems with reliability later.

EXERCISE 1.8

Identify the objectives and sub-objectives of the Brightmouth College payroll project. What measures of effectiveness could be used to check the success in achieving the objectives of the project?

1.11 The business case

The business case should be established at the time of the project's feasibility study. Chapter 2 explains the idea of a business case in more detail.

Most projects need to have a justification or business case: the effort and expense of pushing the project through must be seen to be worthwhile in terms of the benefits that will eventually be felt. A cost–benefit analysis will often be part of the project's feasibility study. This will itemize and quantify the project's costs and benefits. The benefits will be affected by the completion date: the sooner the project is completed, the sooner the benefits can be experienced. The quantification of benefits will often require the formulation of a *business model* which explains how the new application can generate the claimed benefits.

A simple example of a business model is that a new web-based application might allow customers from all over the world to order a firm's products via the internet, increasing sales and thus increasing revenue and profits.

Any project plan must ensure that the business case is kept intact. For example:

- that development costs are not allowed to rise to a level which threatens to exceed the value of benefits;
- that the features of the system are not reduced to a level where the expected benefits cannot be realized;
- that the delivery date is not delayed so that there is an unacceptable loss of benefits.

1.12 Project success and failure

A good introduction to the issues discussed here can be found in A. J. Shenhar and O. Levy (1997) 'Mapping the dimensions of project success' *Project Management Journal* 28(2) 9–12.

The project plan should be designed to ensure project success by preserving the business case for the project. However, every non-trivial project will have problems, and at what stage do we say that a project is actually a failure? Because different stakeholders have different interests, some stakeholders in a project might see it as a success while others do not.

Broadly speaking, we can distinguish between *project objectives* and *business objectives*. The project objectives are the targets that the project team is expected to achieve. In the case of software projects, they can usually be summarized as delivering:

- the agreed functionality
- to the required level of quality
- on time
- within budget.

A project could meet these targets but the application, once delivered could fail to meet the business case. A computer game could be delivered on time and within budget, but might then not sell. A commercial website used for online sales could be created successfully, but customers might not use it to buy products, because they could buy the goods more cheaply elsewhere.

The assessment of the value of project benefits is explored in greater depth in Chapter 2.

We have seen that in business terms it can generally be said that a project is a success if the value of benefits exceeds the costs. We have also seen that while project managers have considerable control over development costs, the value of the benefits of the project deliverables is dependent on external factors such as the number of customers. Project objectives still have some bearing on eventual business success. As we will see in Chapter 2, increasing development costs reduce the chances of the delivered product being profitable. A delay in completion reduces the amount of time during which benefits can be generated and diminishes the value of the project.

A project can be a success on delivery but then be a business failure, On the other hand, a project could be late and over budget, but its deliverables could still, over time, generate benefits that outweigh the initial expenditure.

Some argue that the possible gap between project and business concerns can be reduced by having a broader view of projects that includes business issues. For example, the project management of an e-commerce website implementation could plan activities such as market surveys, competitor analysis, focus groups, prototyping, and evaluation by typical potential users – all designed to reduce business risks.

Because the focus of project management is, not unnaturally, on the immediate project, it may not be seen that the project is actually one of a sequence. Later projects benefit from the technical skills learnt on earlier projects. Technical learning will increase costs on the earlier projects, but later projects benefit as the learnt technologies can be deployed more quickly, cheaply and accurately. This expertise is often accompanied by additional software assets, for example reusable code. Where software development is outsourced, there may be immediate savings, but these longer-term benefits of increased expertise will be lost. Astute managers may assess which areas of technical expertise it would be beneficial to develop.

> For a wider discussion of the relationships between successive projects, see M. Engwall (2003) 'No project is an island: linking projects to history and context' *Research Policy* 32 789–808.

Customer relationships can also be built up over a number of projects. If a client has trust in a supplier who has done satisfactory work in the past, they are more likely to use that company again, particularly if the new requirement builds on functionality already delivered. It is much more expensive to acquire new clients than it is to retain existing ones.

1.13 What is management?

We have explored some of the special characteristics of software. We now look at the 'management' aspect of software project management. It has been suggested that management involves the following activities:

- planning – deciding what is to be done;
- organizing – making arrangements;
- staffing – selecting the right people for the job etc.;
- directing – giving instructions;
- monitoring – checking on progress;
- controlling – taking action to remedy hold-ups;
- innovating – coming up with new solutions;
- representing – liaising with clients, users, developer, suppliers and other stakeholders.

EXERCISE 1.9

Paul Duggan is the manager of a software development section. On Tuesday at 10.00 a.m. he and his fellow section heads have a meeting with their group manager about the staffing requirements for the coming year. Paul has already drafted a document 'bidding' for staff. This is based on the work planned for his section for the next year. The document is discussed at the meeting. At 2.00 p.m. Paul has a meeting with his senior staff about an important project his section is undertaking. One of the programming staff has just had a road accident and will be in hospital for some time. It is decided that the project can be kept on schedule by transferring another team member from less urgent work to this project. A temporary replacement is to be brought in to do the less urgent work but this may take a week or so to arrange. Paul has to phone both the human resources manager about getting a replacement and the user for whom the less urgent work is being done, explaining why it is likely to be delayed.

Identify which of the eight management responsibilities listed above Paul was responding to at different points during his day.

1.14 Management control

Management, in general, involves setting objectives for a system and then monitoring the performance of the system. In Figure 1.4 the 'real world' is shown as being rather formless. Especially in the case of large undertakings, there will be a lot going on about which management should be aware.

EXERCISE 1.10

An ICT project is to replace locally held paper-based records with a centrally organized database. Staff in a large number of offices that are geographically dispersed need training and will then have to use the new ICT system to set up the backlog of manual records on the new database. The system cannot be properly operational until the last record has been transferred. The new system will only be successful if new transactions can be processed within certain time cycles.

Identify the data that you would collect to ensure that during execution of the project things were going to plan.

This will involve the local managers in *data collection*. Bare details, such as 'location X has processed 2000 documents', will not be very useful to higher management: *data processing* will be needed to transform this raw *data* into useful *information*. This might be in such forms as 'percentage of records processed', 'average documents processed per day per person' and 'estimated completion date'.

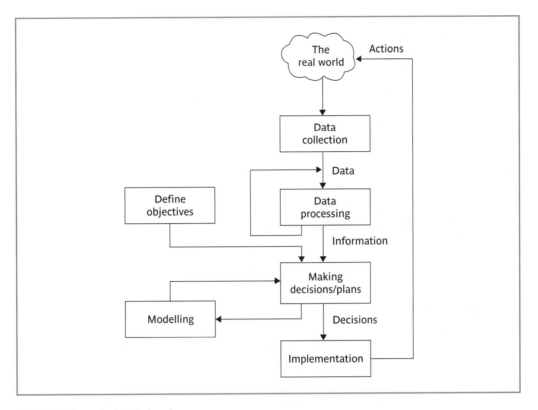

FIGURE 1.4 The project control cycle

In our example, the project management might examine the 'estimated completion date' for completing data transfer for each branch. These can be checked against the overall target date for completion of this phase of the project. In effect they are comparing actual performance with one aspect of the overall project objectives. They might find that one or two branches will fail to complete the transfer of details in time. They would then need to consider what to do (this is represented in Figure 1.4 by the box *Making decisions/plans*). One possibility would be to move staff temporarily from one branch to another. If this is done, there is always the danger that while the completion date for the one branch is pulled back to before the overall target date, the date for the branch from which staff are being moved is pushed forward beyond that date. The project manager would need to calculate carefully what the impact would be in moving staff from particular branches. This is *modelling* the consequences of a potential solution. Several different proposals could be modelled in this way before one was chosen for *implementation*.

Having implemented the decision, the situation needs to be kept under review by collecting and processing further progress details. For instance, the next time that progress is reported, a branch to which staff have been transferred could still be behind in transferring details. This might be because the reason why the branch has got behind in transferring details is because the manual records are incomplete and another department, for whom the project has a low priority, has to be involved in providing the missing information. In this case, transferring extra staff to do data inputting will not have accelerated data transfer.

It can be seen that a project plan is dynamic and will need constant adjustment during the execution of the project. Courses and books on project management (such as this one) often focus considerable attention on project planning. While this is to be expected, with nearly all projects much more time is spent actually doing the project rather than planning it. A good plan provides a foundation for a good project, but is nothing without intelligent execution. The original plan will not be set in stone but will be modified to take account of changing circumstances.

1.15 Conclusion

This chapter has laid a foundation for the remainder of the book by defining what is meant by various terms such as 'software project' and 'management'. Among some of the more important points that have been made are the following:

- Projects are by definition non-routine and therefore more uncertain than normal undertakings.
- Software projects are similar to other projects but have some attributes that present particular difficulties, e.g. the relative invisibility of many of their products.
- A key factor in project success is having clear objectives. Different stakeholders in a project, however, are likely to have different objectives. This points to the need for a recognized overall project authority.
- For objectives to be effective there must be practical ways of testing that the objectives have been met.
- Where projects involve many different people, effective channels of information have to be established. Having objective measures of success helps unambiguous communication between the various parties to a project.

Annex 1 Contents list for a project plan

The detail that goes into these sections will be explained in later chapters. For example, Chapter 7 relates to risk while Chapter 13 explains aspects of the management of quality.

- Introduction
- Background: including reference to the business case
- Project objectives
- Constraints – these could be included with project objectives
- Methods
- Project products: both deliverable products that the client will receive and intermediate products
- Activities to be carried out
- Resources to be used

- Risks to the project
- Management of the project, including
  - organizational responsibilities
  - management of quality
  - configuration management

1.16 Further exercises

1. List the problems you experienced when you carried out a recent ICT-related assignment. Try to put these problems into some order of magnitude. For each problem consider whether there was some way in which the problem could have been reduced by better organization and planning by yourself.

2. Identify the main types of personnel employed in an information systems department. For each stage of a typical IS development project, list the types of personnel who are likely to be involved.

3. A public library is considering the implementation of a computer-based system to help administer book loans at libraries. Identify the stakeholders in such a project. What might be the objectives of such a project and how might the success of the project be measured in practical terms?

4. A software house has developed a customized order processing system for a client. You are an employee of the software house that has been asked to organize a training course for the end-users of the system. At present, a user handbook has been produced, but no specific training material. A plan is now needed for the project which will set up the delivery of the training courses. The project can be assumed to have been completed when the first training course starts. Among the things that will need to be considered are the following:

   - training materials will need to be designed and created;
   - a timetable will need to be drafted and agreed;
   - date(s) for the course will need to be arranged;
   - the people attending the course will need to be identified and notified;
   - rooms and computer facilities for the course will need to be provided.

   A Identify the main stakeholders for this project.
   B Draw up objectives for this project.
   C For the objectives, identify the measures of effectiveness.
   D For each objective, write down sub-objectives or goals and the stakeholders who will be responsible for their achievement.

5. A manager is in charge of a sub-project of a larger project. The sub-project requires the transfer of paper documents into a computer-based document retrieval system and their subsequent indexing so that they can be accessed via key-words. Optical character readers are to be used for the initial transfer but the text then needs to be clerically checked and corrected by staff. The project is currently scheduled to take 12 months using permanent staff. A small budget is available to hire temporary staff in the case of

staff absences through holidays, sickness or temporary transfer to other, more urgent, jobs. Discuss the control system that will need to be in place to control that sub-project.

6   The idea behind a project is that students should be able to access details of available placements via an intranet. When there is a placement opportunity for which they wish to be considered, they would be able to apply for it electronically. This would cause a copy of their CV, which would also be held online, to be sent to the potential employer.

Details of interviews and placement offers would all be sent by e-mail. While some human intervention would be needed, the process would be automated as far as possible.

You are required to produce a business case report for such an application, which justifies the potential development by showing that the value of its potential benefits outweighs its development and operational costs.

Create lists of the main benefits and costs for the project. You do not have to specify actual figures, just the headings under which they would appear.

Project evaluation and programme management

2

❖ OBJECTIVES

When you have completed this chapter you will be able to:

- ❖ describe the contents of a typical business plan;

- ❖ explain project portfolio management;

- ❖ carry out an evaluation and selection of projects against strategic, technical and economic criteria;

- ❖ use a variety of cost–benefit evaluation techniques for choosing among competing project proposals;

- ❖ evaluate the business risk involved in a project;

- ❖ explain how individual projects can be grouped into programmes;

- ❖ explain how the implementation of programmes and projects can be managed so that the planned benefits are achieved.

2.1 Introduction

The first that many developers hear of an ICT project is when they are allocated to the project team. However, new projects do not appear out of thin air. There will be some process – varying in sophistication between organizations – that decides that the project is worth doing.

As we saw in Chapter 1, sometimes managers justify a commitment to a single project as the benefits will exceed the costs of the implementation and operation of the new application. In other cases, managers would not approve a project on its own, but can see that it enables the fulfilment of strategic objectives when combined with other projects.

Thus a project to establish an ICT infrastructure within an organization might not deliver a direct financial benefit, but could provide a platform for subsequent projects to do so.

It might not be possible to measure the benefits of a project in financial terms. If you create a system which allows the more accurate recording of data concerning the medical condition of patients, it might contribute to the alleviation of pain and the preservation of life, but it would be difficult to put a money value on these.

The last chapter emphasized that an ICT or software project needed a business case. In this chapter we explain what such a document might contain. A business case may be presented for several potential projects, but there may be money or staff time for only some of the projects. Managers need some way of deciding which projects to select. This is part of *portfolio management*. This chapter will discuss some ways in which projects can be evaluated and compared for inclusion in a project portfolio. The chapter finishes by discussing the way groups of projects which together contribute to a common business objective can be managed as *programmes* of projects.

2.2 A business case

The section on the business case draws on B. Hughes (2008) *Exploiting IT for business benefit.* British Computer Society.

Organizations may have different titles such as a *feasibility study* or a *project justification* for what we call the business case. Its objective is to provide a rationale for the project by showing that the benefits of the project outcomes will exceed the costs of development, implementation and operation (or production).

Typically a business case document might contain:

1 Introduction and background to the proposal

2 The proposed project

3 The market

4 Organizational and operational infrastructure

5 The benefits

6 Outline implementation plan

7 Costs

8 The financial case

9 Risks

10 Management plan

These sections will be now be described in more detail.

Introduction and background

This is a description of the current environment of the proposed project. A problem to be solved or an opportunity to be exploited is identified.

The proposed project

A brief outline of the proposed project is provided.

The market

In Section 2.3 we will explore further the difference between new product development and renewal projects.

This is needed when the project is to create new product or a new service capability. This would contain information like the estimated demand for the product or service and any likely competitors.

Organizational and operational infrastructure

This describes how the structure of the organization will be affected by the implementation of the project. This is of most relevance where the project is implementing or modifying an information system as part of a broader business change project. It would also be relevant if a tailored production or distribution system has to be set up when a new product is designed.

Benefits

Where possible, a financial value should be put on the benefits of the implemented project. For commercial organizations this could be related to increased profits caused either by increasing income or by making savings on costs. For not-for-profit organizations we would try to quantify the benefits even if we cannot quote a precise financial value. In an example we used earlier relating to an IT system that improved the diagnosis of a particular disease, an increase in the rate of diagnosis might be quoted.

Outline implementation plan

In addition to the ICT aspects of the project, activities such as marketing, promotion and operational and maintenance infrastructures need to be considered. One consideration will be which project activities can be outsourced, and which are best kept in-house.

This will also detail the management of the implementation. The responsibilities are allocated for the tasks identified in the outline implementation plan. Key decision points or milestones, where a health-check on the state of the implementation is taken, should be identified. As we will see, for a large implementation a number of projects may be needed which can be managed as a programme.

Costs

Having outlined the steps needed to set up the operations needed by the proposal, a schedule of expected costs associated with the planned approach can now be presented.

There will clearly be some uncertainties about some of the costs, especially as the details of the requirements have not yet been worked out.

The financial case

There are a number of ways in which the information on income and costs can be analysed and these will be the subject of the section on evaluation techniques later in this chapter.

Risks

Once again a more detailed discussion of risks will follow in a later section. We note here that many estimates of costs and, more particularly, benefits of the project will be speculative at this stage and the section on risk should take account of this. In the last chapter we distinguished between project and business objectives. We can similarly distinguish project risk – relating to threats to successful project execution – from business risk – relating to factors threatening the benefits of the delivered project. In the business case the main focus is on business risk.

2.3 Project portfolio management

Quite a good introduction to the concepts of portfolios can be found in B. De Reyck et al. 'The impact of project portfolio management on information technology projects' (2005) *International Journal of Project Management* 23 524–37.

Portfolio project management provides an overview of all the projects that an organization is undertaking or is considering. It prioritizes the allocation of resources to projects and decides which new projects should be accepted and which existing ones should be dropped.

The concerns of project portfolio management incude:

- identifying which project proposals are worth implementation;
- assessing the amount of risk of failure that a potential project has;
- deciding how to share limited resources, including staff time and finance, between projects – one problem can be that too many projects are started given the resources available so that inevitably some projects will miss planned completion dates;
- being aware of the dependencies between projects, especially where several projects need to be completed for an organization to reap benefits;
- ensuring that projects do not duplicate work;
- ensuring that necessary developments have not been inadvertently been missed.

The three key aspects of project portfolio management are *portfolio definition*, *portfolio management* and *portfolio optimization*. An organization would undertake portfolio definition before adopting portfolio management and then proceeding to optimization.

Project portfolio definition

An organization should record in a single repository details of all current projects. A decision will be needed about whether projects of all types are to be included. Should

Warren McFarlan's (1981) 'Portfolio approach to information systems' *Harvard Business Review* 59(5) 142–50 introduced the portfolio concept to information systems.

just ICT projects be included in the repository, or should other projects such as the setting up of a new warehouse also be included? One problem for many organizations is that projects can be divided into *new product developments* (NPD) where the project deliverable is a product, such as a computer game, that is sold to customers, and *renewal* projects which improve the way an organization operates – information systems projects are often like this. The distinction is not always clear-cut. For example, a new information system could be used to provide a customer service such as recording the details of people buying a new insurance product.

NPD projects are often more frequent in organizations which have a continuous development of new goods and services. Renewal projects may be less frequent and thus inherently more risky as there is less experience of these types of project. NPD projects find attracting funding easier with their clear relationship between the project and income. Where both types of project call upon the same pools of resources, including finance, the argument for a common portfolio is strong.

Project portfolio management

Once the portfolio has been established, more detailed costings of projects can be recorded. The value that managers hope will be generated by each project can also be recorded. Actual performance of projects on these performance indicators can then be tracked. This information can be the basis for the more rigorous screening of new projects.

Project portfolio optimization

The performance of the portfolio can be tracked by high-level managers on a regular basis. A better balance of projects may be achieved. Some projects could potentially be very profitable but could also be risky. In the case of an e-commerce site, for example, sales may not be as great as hoped because established competitors reduce prices. Other projects could have modest benefits, such as those cutting costs by automating processes, but have fewer risks. The portfolio ought to have a carefully thought-out balance between the two types of project.

Some problems with project portfolio management

Interesting insights into the practical problems of portfolios can be found in B. S. Blichfeldt and P. Eskerod (2008) 'Project portfolio

An important role of project portfolio management is sharing resources between projects. There can be problems because while apparently full-time staff are allocated to a project, they may effectively be part-time because they still have routine work to do. This is particularly so with users, and with developers who may on occasion be called away from project work to deal with support tasks.

The official project portfolio may not accurately reflect organizational activity if some projects are excluded. A formal decision may be made that only projects over a certain level of cost will be recorded in the portfolio.

management –
there's more to it
than management
enacts'
*International
Journal of Project
Management*
26 357–65.

The 'below the line' projects could in fact consume substantial staff effort and bleed away effort from the official projects. It can be argued that all projects should be included in the official portfolio.

However, there are advantages in allowing these tasks. It allows small ad hoc tasks to be done, such as quick fixes to systems to deal with externally imposed changes. They reduce work for higher management by saving them from having to process a large number of small work requests. Developers may find these small tasks rewarding: dealing with these small requests is an easy way to keep users happy. Thus when allocating resources to projects, a margin should be set to allow first-line managers some judgement in accepting non-planned work.

2.4 Evaluation of individual projects

We will now look more closely at how the feasibility of an individual project can be evaluated.

Technical assessment

Technical assessment of a proposed system consists of evaluating whether the required functionality can be achieved with current affordable technologies. Organizational policy, aimed at providing a consistent hardware/software infrastructure, is likely to limit the technical solutions considered. The costs of the technology adopted must be taken into account in the cost–benefit analysis.

Cost–benefit analysis

Any project aiming at a return on investment must, as a minimum, provide a greater benefit than putting that investment in, say, a bank.

Even where the estimated benefits will exceed the estimated costs, it is often necessary to decide if the proposed project is the best of several options. Not all projects can be undertaken at any one time and, in any case, the most valuable projects should get most resources.

Cost–benefit analysis comprises two steps:

- *Identifying all of the costs and benefits of carrying out the project and operating the delivered application* These include the development costs, the operating costs and the benefits expected from the new system. Where the proposed system is a replacement, these estimates should reflect the change in costs and benefits due to the new system. A new sales order processing system, for example, could only claim to benefit an organization by the increase in sales due to the use of the new system.

- *Expressing these costs and benefits in common units* We must express each cost and benefit – and the *net benefit* which is the difference between the two – in money.

Most direct costs are easy to quantify in monetary terms and can be categorized as:

The different types of benefits will be discussed in greater detail in the context of benefits management later in this chapter.

- *development costs*, including development staff costs;
- *setup costs*, consisting of the costs of putting the system into place, mainly of any new hardware but also including the costs of file conversion, recruitment and staff training;
- *operational costs* relating to operating the system after installation.

EXERCISE 2.1

Brightmouth College is considering the replacement of the existing payroll service, operated by a third party, with a tailored, off-the-shelf computer-based system. List some of the costs it might consider under the headings of:

- Development costs
- Setup costs
- Operational costs

List some of the benefits under the headings:

- Quantified and valued benefits
- Quantified but not valued
- Identified but not easily valued

For each cost or benefit, explain how, in principle, it might be measured in monetary terms.

Typically products generate a negative cash flow during their development followed by a positive cash flow over their operating life. There might be decommissioning costs at the end of a product's life.

The difficulty and importance of cash flow forecasting is evidenced by the number of companies that suffer bankruptcy because, although they are developing profitable

Cash flow forecasting

As important as estimating the overall costs and benefits of a project is producing a cash flow forecast which indicates when expenditure and income will take place (Figure 2.1).

We need to spend money, such as staff wages, during a project's development. Such expenditure cannot wait until income is received (either from using software developed in-house use or from selling it). We need to know that we can fund this development expenditure either from the company's own resources or by borrowing. A forecast is needed of when expenditure, such as the payment of salaries, and any income are to be expected.

Accurate cash flow forecasting is difficult, as it is done early in the project's life cycle (at least before any significant expenditure is committed) and many items to be estimated (particularly the benefits of using software) might be some years in the future.

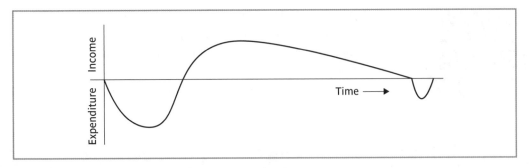

FIGURE 2.1 Typical product life cycle cash flow

> products or services, they cannot sustain an unplanned negative cash flow.

When estimating future cash flows, it is usual to ignore the effects of inflation. Forecasts of inflation rates tend to be uncertain. Moreover, if expenditure is increased due to inflation it is likely that income will increase proportionately.

2.5 Cost–benefit evaluation techniques

We now take a look at some methods for comparing projects on the basis of their cash flow forecasts.

Table 2.1 illustrates cash flow forecasts for four projects. In each case it is assumed that the cash flows take place at the end of each year. For short-term projects or where there are significant seasonal cash flow patterns, quarterly, or even monthly, cash flow forecasts could be appropriate.

EXERCISE 2.2

Consider the project cash flow estimates for four projects at IOE shown in Table 2.1. Negative values represent expenditure and positive values income.

Rank the four projects in order of financial desirability and make a note of your reasons for ranking them in that way before reading further.

Net profit

The net profit of a project is the difference between the total costs and the total income over the life of the project. Project 2 in Table 2.1 shows the greatest net profit but this is at the expense of a large investment. Indeed, if we had £1m to invest, we might undertake all of the other three projects and obtain an even greater net profit. Note also that all projects contain an element of risk and we might not be prepared to risk £1m. We shall look at the effects of risk and investment later in this chapter.

Year	Project 1	Project 2	Project 3	Project 4
0	−100,000	−1,000,000	−100,000	−120,000
1	10,000	200,000	30,000	30,000
2	10,000	200,000	30,000	30,000
3	10,000	200,000	30,000	30,000
4	20,000	200,000	30,000	30,000
5	100,000	300,000	30,000	75,000
Net profit	50,000	100,000	50,000	75,000

TABLE 2.1 Four project cash flow projections – figures are end of year totals (£)

Cash flows take place at the end of each year. The year 0 represents the initial investment made at the start of the project.

Moreover, the simple net profit takes no account of the timing of the cash flows. Projects 1 and 3 each have a net profit of £50,000 and therefore, according to this selection criterion, would be equally preferable. The bulk of the income occurs late in the life of project 1, whereas project 3 returns a steady income throughout its life. Having to wait for a return has the disadvantage that the investment must be funded for longer. Add to that the fact that, other things being equal, estimates in the more distant future are less reliable than short-term estimates and we can see that the two projects are not equally preferable.

Payback period

The *payback period* is the time taken to break even or pay back the initial investment. Normally, the project with the shortest payback period will be chosen on the basis that an organization will wish to minimize the time that a project is 'in debt'.

EXERCISE 2.3

Consider the four project cash flows given in Table 2.1 and calculate the payback period for each of them.

The advantage of the payback period is that it is simple to calculate and is not particularly sensitive to small forecasting errors. Its disadvantage as a selection technique is that it ignores the overall profitability of the project – in fact, it totally ignores any income (or expenditure) once the project has broken even. Thus the fact that projects 2 and 4 are, overall, more profitable than project 3 is ignored.

Return on investment

The *return on investment* (ROI), also known as the *accounting rate of return* (ARR), provides a way of comparing the net profitability to the investment required. There are some variations on the formula used to calculate the return on investment but a straightforward common version is:

$$ROI = \frac{average\ annual\ profit}{total\ investment} \times 100$$

EXERCISE 2.4

Calculating the ROI for project 1, the net profit is £50,000 and the total investment is £100,000. The return on investment is therefore calculated as

$$ROI = \frac{average\ annual\ profit}{total\ investment} \times 100$$

$$= \frac{50,000/5}{100,000} \times 100 = 10\%$$

Calculate the ROI for each of the other projects shown in Table 2.1 and decide which, on the basis of this criterion, is the most worthwhile.

The return on investment provides a simple, easy-to-calculate measure of return on capital. Unfortunately, it suffers from two severe disadvantages. Like the net profitability, it takes no account of the timing of the cash flows. More importantly, this rate of return bears no relationship to the interest rates offered or charged by banks (or any other normal interest rate) since it takes no account of the timing of the cash flows or of the compounding of interest. It is therefore, potentially, very misleading.

Net present value

Net present value (NPV) and internal rate of return (IRR) are collectively known as discounted cash flow (DCF) techniques.

The calculation of *net present value* is a project evaluation technique that takes into account the profitability of a project and the timing of the cash flows that are produced. This is based on the view that receiving £100 today is better than having to wait until next year to receive it. We could, for example, invest the £100 in a bank today and have £100 plus the interest in a year's time. If we say that the *present value* of £100 in a year's time is £91, we mean that £100 in a year's time is the equivalent of £91 now.

Note that this example uses approximate figures.

The equivalence of £91 now and £100 in a year's time means we are discounting the future income by approximately 10%. If we received £91 now and invested it for a year at an annual interest rate of 10%, it would be worth £100 in a year's time. The annual rate by which we

A rate of 10% may be unrealistic but is used here for ease of calculation.

discount future earnings is known as the *discount rate* – 10% in the above example.

Similarly, £100 received in two years' time would have a present value of approximately £83 – in other words, £83 invested at an interest rate of 10% would yield approximately £100 in two years' time.

The present value of any future cash flow may be obtained by applying the following formula

$$Present\ value = \frac{value\ in\ year\ t}{(1 + r)^t}$$

More extensive or detailed tables may be constructed using the formula *discount factor* = $\frac{1}{(1 + r)^t}$ for various values of *r* (the discount rate) and *t* (the number of years from now).

where *r* is the discount rate, expressed as a decimal value, and *t* is the number of years into the future that the cash flow occurs.

Alternatively, and rather more easily, the present value of a cash flow may be calculated by multiplying the cash flow by the appropriate discount factor. A small table of discount factors is given in Table 2.2.

The NPV for a project is obtained by discounting each cash flow (both negative and positive) and summing the discounted values. It is normally assumed that any initial investment takes place immediately (indicated as year 0) and is not discounted. Later cash flows are normally assumed to take place at the end of each year and are discounted by the appropriate amount.

	Discount rate (%)					
Year	5	6	8	10	12	15
1	0.9524	0.9434	0.9259	0.9091	0.8929	0.8696
2	0.9070	0.8900	0.8573	0.8264	0.7972	0.7561
3	0.8638	0.8396	0.7938	0.7513	0.7118	0.6575
4	0.8227	0.7921	0.7350	0.6830	0.6355	0.5718
5	0.7835	0.7473	0.6806	0.6209	0.5674	0.4972
6	0.7462	0.7050	0.6302	0.5645	0.5066	0.4323
7	0.7107	0.6651	0.5835	0.5132	0.4523	0.3759
8	0.6768	0.6274	0.5403	0.4665	0.4039	0.3269
9	0.6446	0.5919	0.5002	0.4241	0.3606	0.2843
10	0.6139	0.5584	0.4632	0.3855	0.3220	0.2472
15	0.4810	0.4173	0.3152	0.2394	0.1827	0.1229
20	0.3769	0.3118	0.2145	0.1486	0.1037	0.0611
25	0.2953	0.2330	0.1460	0.0923	0.0588	0.0304

TABLE 2.2 NPV discount factors

EXERCISE 2.5

A ssuming a 10% discount rate, the NPV for project 1 (Table 2.1) would be calculated as in Table 2.3. The net present value for project 1, using a 10% discount rate, is therefore £618. Using a 10% discount rate, calculate the net present values for projects 2, 3 and 4 and decide which, on the basis of this, is the most beneficial to pursue.

Year	Project 1 cash flow (£)	Discount factor @ 10%	Discounted cash flow (£)
0	−100,000	1.0000	−100,000
1	10,000	0.9091	9,091
2	10,000	0.8264	8,264
3	10,000	0.7513	7,513
4	20,000	0.6830	13,660
5	100,000	0.6209	62,090
Net Profit:	£50,000	NPV: £618	

TABLE 2.3 Applying the discount factors to project 1

It is interesting to note that the net present values for projects 1 and 3 are significantly different – even though they both yield the same net profit and both have the same return on investment. The difference in NPV reflects the fact that, with project 1, we must wait longer for the bulk of the income.

The main difficulty with NPV for deciding between projects is selecting an appropriate discount rate. Some organizations have a standard rate but, where this is not the case, then the discount rate should be chosen to reflect available interest rates (borrowing costs where the project must be funded from loans) plus some premium to reflect the fact that software projects are normally more risky than lending money to a bank. The exact discount rate is normally less important than ensuring that the same discount rate is used for all projects being compared. However, it is important to check that the ranking of projects is not sensitive to small changes in the discount rate – have a look at the following exercise.

EXERCISE 2.6

C alculate the net present value for each of the projects A, B and C shown in Table 2.4 using each of the discount rates 8%, 10% and 12%.

For each of the discount rates, decide which is the best project. What can you conclude from these results?

Year	Project A (£)	Project B (£)	Project C (£)
0	−8,000	−8,000	−10,000
1	4,000	1,000	2,000
2	4,000	2,000	2,000
3	2,000	4,000	6,000
4	1,000	3,000	2,000
5	500	9,000	2,000
6	500	−6,000	2,000
Net Profit	4,000	5,000	6,000

TABLE 2.4 Three estimated project cash flows

Alternatively, the discount rate can be thought of as a target rate of return. If, for example, we set a target rate of return of 15% we would reject any project that did not display a positive net present value using a 15% discount rate. Any project that displayed a positive NPV would be considered for selection – perhaps by using an additional set of criteria where candidate projects were competing for resources.

Internal rate of return

One disadvantage of NPV as a measure of profitability is that, although it may be used to compare projects, it might not be directly comparable with earnings from other investments or the costs of borrowing capital. Such costs are usually quoted as a percentage interest rate. The internal rate of return (IRR) attempts to provide a profitability measure as a percentage return that is directly comparable with interest rates. Thus, a project that showed an estimated IRR of 10% would be worthwhile if the capital could be borrowed for less than 10% or if the capital could not be invested elsewhere for a return greater than 10%.

The IRR is calculated as that percentage discount rate that would produce an NPV of zero. It is most easily calculated using a spreadsheet or other computer program that provides functions for calculating the IRR. Microsoft Excel, for example, provides IRR functions which, provided with an initial guess or seed value (which may be zero), will search for and return an IRR.

One deficiency of the IRR is that it does not indicate the absolute size of the return. A project with an NPV of £100,000 and an IRR of 15% can be more attractive than one with an NPV of £10,000 and an IRR of 18% – the return on capital is lower but the net benefits greater.

Another objection to the internal rate of return is that, under certain conditions, it is possible to find more than one rate that will produce a zero NPV. However, if there are multiple solutions, it is always appropriate to take the lowest value and ignore the others.

NPV and IRR are not, however, a complete answer to economic project evaluation.

- A total evaluation must also take into account the problems of funding the cash flows – will we, for example, be able to repay the interest on any borrowed money at the appropriate time?
- While a project's IRR might indicate a profitable project, future earnings from a relatively risky project might be far less reliable than earnings from, say, investing with a bank. We might undertake a more detailed risk analysis as described below.
- We must also consider any one project within the financial and economic framework of the organization as a whole – if we fund this one, will we also be able to fund other worthy projects?

2.6 Risk evaluation

Every project involves risk. We have already noted that *project* risks, which prevent the project from being completed successfully, are different from the *business* risk that the delivered products are not profitable. Project risks will be discussed in Chapter 7. Here we focus on business risk.

Risk identification and ranking

In any project evaluation we should identify the risks and quantify their effects. One approach is to construct a project risk matrix utilizing a checklist of possible risks and classifying risks according to their relative importance and likelihood. Importance and likelihood need to be separately assessed – we might be less concerned with something that, although serious, is very unlikely to occur than with something less serious that is almost certain. Table 2.5 illustrates a basic project risk matrix listing some of the business risks for a project, with their importance and likelihood classified as high (H), medium (M), low (L) or exceedingly unlikely (—). So that projects may be compared, the list of risks must be the same for each project assessed. It is likely, in reality, that it would be longer than shown and more precise.

The project risk matrix may be used as a way of evaluating projects (those with high risks being less favoured) or as a means of identifying and ranking the risks for a specific project.

Risk	Importance	Likelihood
Client rejects proposed look and feel of site	H	—
Competitors undercut prices	H	M
Warehouse unable to deal with increased demand	M	L
Online payment has security problems	M	M
Maintenance costs higher than estimated	L	L
Response times deter purchasers	M	M

TABLE 2.5 A fragment of a basic project/business risk matrix for an e-commerce application

Risk and net present value

Where a project is relatively risky it is common practice to use a higher discount rate to calculate net present value. This risk premium might, for example, be an additional 2% for a reasonably safe project or 5% for a fairly risky one. Projects may be categorized as high, medium or low risk using a scoring method and risk premiums designated for each category. The premiums, even if arbitrary, provide a consistent method of taking risk into account.

Cost–benefit analysis

A rather more sophisticated approach to the evaluation of risk is to consider each possible outcome and estimate the probability of its occurring and the corresponding value of the outcome. Rather than a single cash flow forecast for a project, we will then have a set of cash flow forecasts, each with an associated probability of occurring. The value of the project is then obtained by summing the cost or benefit for each possible outcome weighted by its corresponding probability. Exercise 2.7 illustrates how this may be done.

EXERCISE 2.7

BuyRight, a software house, is considering developing a payroll application for use in academic institutions and is currently engaged in a cost–benefit analysis. Study of the market has shown that, if BuyRight can target it efficiently and no competing products become available, it will obtain a high level of sales generating an annual income of £800,000. It estimates that there is a 1 in 10 chance of this happening. However, a competitor might launch a competing application before its own launch date and then sales might generate only £100,000 per year. It estimates that there is a 30% chance of this happening. The most likely outcome, it believes, is somewhere in between these two extremes – it will gain a market lead by launching before any competing product becomes available and achieve an annual income of £650,000. BuyRight has therefore calculated its expected sales income as in Table 2.6.

Sales	Annual sales income (£)	Probability	Expected value (£)
	i	p	$i \times p$
High	800,000	0.1	80,000
Medium	650,000	0.6	390,000
Low	100,000	0.3	30,000
Expected Income			500,000

TABLE 2.6 BuyRight's income forecasts

▶
Development costs are estimated at £750,000. Sales levels are expected to be constant for at least four years. Annual costs of marketing and product maintenance are estimated at £200,000, irrespective of the market share. Would you advise going ahead with the project?

This approach is frequently used to evaluate large projects such as the building of motorways, where variables such as traffic volumes, and hence the total benefit of shorter journey times, are uncertain. The technique, of course, relies on being able to assign probabilities of occurrence to each scenario, which requires extensive research.

When used to evaluate a single major project, the cost–benefit approach, by 'averaging out' the negative and positive outcomes of the different scenarios, does not take full account of 'worst-case scenarios'. Because of this, it is more appropriate for the evaluation of a portfolio of projects where overall profitability is the primary concern, more successful projects can offset the impact of less successful ones.

Risk profile analysis

An approach which attempts to overcome some of the objections to cost–benefit averaging is the construction of risk profiles using sensitivity analysis.

This involves varying each of the parameters that affect the project's cost or benefits to ascertain how sensitive the project's profitability is to each factor. We might, for example, vary one of our original estimates by plus or minus 5% and recalculate the expected costs and benefits for the project. By repeating this exercise for each of our estimates in turn we can evaluate the sensitivity of the project to each factor.

By studying the results of a sensitivity analysis we can identify those factors that are most important to the success of the project. We then need to decide whether we can exercise greater control over them or otherwise mitigate their effects. If neither is the case, then we must live with the risk or abandon the project.

Using decision trees

The approaches to risk analysis discussed previously rather assume that we are passive bystanders allowing nature to take its own course – the best we can do is to reject over-risky projects or choose those with the best risk profile. There are many situations, however, where we can evaluate whether a risk is important and, if it is, decide a suitable course of action.

Such decisions will limit or affect future options and, at any point, it is important to be able to assess how a decision will affect the future profitability of the project.

As an example, say a successful company is considering when to replace its sales order processing system. The decision largely rests upon the rate at which its business expands – if its market share significantly increases (which it believes will happen if rumours of a competitor's imminent bankruptcy are fulfilled) the existing system might need to be replaced within two years. Not replacing the system in time could be an expensive option as it could lead to lost revenue if it cannot cope with increased sales. Replacing the system immediately will, however, be expensive as it will mean deferring other projects already scheduled.

It is calculated that extending the existing system will have an NPV of £75,000, although if the market expands significantly, this will be turned into a loss with an NPV of −£100,000 due to lost revenue. If the market does expand, replacing the system now has an NPV of £250,000 due to the benefits of being able to handle increased sales and other benefits such as improved management information. If sales do not increase, however, the benefits will be severely reduced and the project will suffer a loss with an NPV of −£50,000.

The company estimate the likelihood of the market increasing significantly at 20% – and, hence, the probability that it will not increase as 80%. This scenario can be represented as a tree structure as shown in Figure 2.2.

The analysis of a decision tree consists of evaluating the expected benefit of taking each path from a decision point (denoted by D in Figure 2.2). The expected value of each path is the sum of the value of each possible outcome multiplied by its probability of occurrence. The expected value of extending the system is therefore £40,000 (75,000 × 0.8 − 100,000 × 0.2) and the expected value of replacing the system £10,000 (250,000 × 0.2 − 50,000 × 0.8). The company should therefore choose the option of extending the existing system.

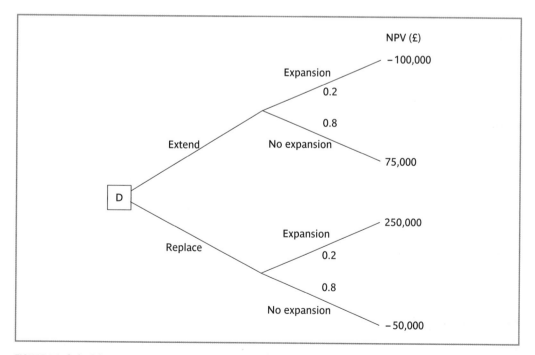

FIGURE 2.2 A decision tree

2.7 Programme management

Ferns' paper appeared in the *International Journal of Project Management* August 1991.

It should now have been made clear that there will be an element of risk with any single project. Even where projects produce real financial benefits, the precise size of those benefits will often be uncertain at the start of the project. This makes it important for organizations to take a broad view of all its projects to ensure that while some projects may disappoint, organizational developments overall will generate substantial benefits.

We introduced project portfolios in Section 2.3. We will now examine how careful management of programmes of projects can provide benefits. D. C. Ferns defined a programme as '*a group of projects that are managed in a coordinated way to gain benefits that would not be possible were the projects to be managed independently*'.

Programmes can exist in different forms, as can be seen below.

Business cycle programmes

The collection of projects that an organization undertakes within a particular planning cycle has already been discussed under the topic of project portfolios. We have seen that many organizations have a fixed budget for ICT development. Decisions have to be made about which projects to implement within that budget within the accounting period, which often coincides with the financial year.

Strategic programmes

Several projects together can implement a single strategy. For example, the merging of two organizations' computer systems could require several projects each dealing with a particular application area. Each activity could be treated as a distinct project, but would be coordinated as a programme.

Infrastructure programmes

Organizations can have various departments which carry out distinct, relatively self-contained, activities. In a local authority, one department might have responsibilities for the maintenance of highways, another for refuse collection, and another for education. These distinct activities will probably require distinct databases and information systems. In such a situation, the central ICT function would have responsibility for setting up and maintaining the ICT infrastructure, including the networks, workstations and servers upon which these distinct applications run. In these circumstances, a infrastructure programme could refer to the activities of identifying a common ICT infrastructure and its implementation and maintenance.

Research and development programmes

Truly innovative companies, especially those that are trying to develop new products for the market, are well aware that projects will vary in terms of their risk of failure and the potential returns that they might eventually reap. Some development projects will be relatively safe, and result in the final planned product, but that product might not be radically different from existing ones on the market. Other projects might be extremely risky, but the end result, if successful, could be a revolutionary technological breakthrough that meets some pressing but previously unsatisfied need.

Alan Webb (2001) 'When project management doesn't work' *Project Management Today* May.

A successful portfolio would need to be a mixture of 'safe projects' with relatively low returns and some riskier projects that might fail, but if successful would generate handsome profits which will offset the losses on the failures.

Innovative partnerships

Companies sometimes come together to work collaboratively on new technologies in a 'pre-competitive' phase. Separate projects in different organizations need to be coordinated and this might be done as a programme.

2.8 Managing the allocation of resources within programmes

We are now going to examine in more detail programmes where resources have to be shared between concurrent projects. Typically, an ICT department has pools of particular types of expertise, such as software developers, database designers and network support staff, and these might be called upon to participate in a number of concurrent projects.

The comparison is based on G. Reiss (1996) *Programme Management Demystified*, Chapman & Hall.

In these circumstances, programme managers will have concerns about the optimal use of specialist staff. These concerns can be contrasted with those of project managers – see Table 2.7.

The project managers are said to have an 'impersonal relationship' with resource types because, essentially, they require, for example, a competent systems analyst and who fills that role does not matter. The programme manager has a number of individual systems analysts under his or her control whose deployment has to be planned.

When a project is planned, at the stage of allocating resources, programme management will be involved. Some activities in the project might have to be delayed

Programme manager	Project manager
Many simultaneous projects	One project at a time
Personal relationship with skilled resources	Impersonal relationship with resource type
Need to maximize utilization of resources	Need to minimize demand for resources
Projects tend to be similar	Projects tend to be dissimilar

TABLE 2.7 Programme managers versus project managers

until the requisite technical staff are freed from work on other projects. Where expensive technical staff are employed full-time, then you would want to avoid them having short periods of intense activity interspersed with long periods of idleness, during which they are still being paid. It is most economic when the demand for work is evenly spread from month to month.

As will be seen in Chapter 9 on monitoring and control, when a project is executed activities can take longer (or sometimes even less time) than planned. Delays can mean that specialist staff are prevented from moving on to their next project. Hence it can be seen that programme management needs continually to monitor the progress of projects and the use of resources.

2.9 Strategic programme management

A different form of programme management is where a portfolio of projects all contribute to a common objective. Take, for example, a business which carries out maintenance work for clients. A customer's experience of the organization might be found to be very variable and inconsistent. The employee who records the customer's requirements is different from the people who actually carry out the work and different again from the clerk who deals with the accounts. Often a customer has to explain to one company employee a problem that has already been discussed at length with some other employee. A business objective might be to present a consistent and uniform front to the client. This objective might require changes to a number of different systems which until now have been largely self-contained. The work to reorganize each individual area could be treated as a separate project, coordinated at a higher level as a programme.

Recall that OGC is the Office of Government Commerce which was formerly the Central Computing and Telecommunications Agency or CCTA.

These types of programme are most often needed by large organizations which have a large and complicated organizational structure. Government departments are typical examples and it is not surprising that the OGC, the United Kingdom government agency which was responsible (as the CCTA) for the introduction of PRINCE2 project management standards, has directed its attention to guidelines for effective programme management. The approach now described is based on the OGC guidelines.

2.10 Creating a programme

The programme mandate

The OGC envisages that the planning of a programme will be triggered by the creation of an agreed *programme mandate*. Ideally this should be a formal document describing:

- the new services or capabilities the programme should deliver;
- how the organization will be improved by use of the new services or capability;
- how the programme fits with corporate goals and any other initiatives.

At this point, a *programme director* ought to be appointed to provide initial leadership for the programme. To be successful, the programme needs a champion who is in a prominent position within the organization. This will signal the seriousness with which the organization takes the programme.

The progamme brief

A *programme brief* is now produced which outlines the business case for the programme. It will have sections setting out:

- a preliminary *vision statement* which describes the new capacity that the organization seeks – it is described as 'preliminary' because this will later be elaborated;
- the *benefits* that the programme should create – including when they are likely to be generated and how they might be measured;
- risks and issues;
- estimated costs, timescales and effort.

The vision statement

The programme brief should give the sponsors enough information to decide whether to request a more detailed definition of the programme. This stage would justify the setting up of a small team. A *programme manager* with day-to-day responsibility for the programme would be appointed.

This group takes the vision statement from the project brief and refines and expands it. It should describe in detail the new capability that the programme will give the organization. If estimates for costs, performance and service levels cannot be provided, then there should at least be an indication of how they might be measured; for example, one might be able to say that repeat business will be increased, even if the precise size of the increase cannot be provided.

The blueprint

The achievement of the improved capability described in the vision statement can come only through changes to the structure and operations of the organization. These are detailed in the *blueprint*. This should contain:

- business models outlining the new processes required;
- organizational structure – including the numbers of staff required in the new systems and the skills they will need;
- the information systems, equipment and other, non-staff, resources that will be needed;
- data and information requirements;
- costs, performance and service level requirements.

To return to the example of the organization which wants to present a consistent interface to its customers: while this aspiration might be stated in the vision statement, the way that it is to be achieved would have to be stated in the blueprint. This might, for example, suggest:

- the appointment of 'account managers' who could act as a point of contact for the client throughout their business transactions with the company;
- a common computer interface allowing the account manager to have access to all the information relating to a particular client or job, regardless of the computer system from which it originates.

The blueprint is supported by *benefit profiles* which estimate when the expected benefits will be experienced following implementation of the enhanced capability. One principle is that a programme should deliver tangible benefits. Being provided with a capability does not guarantee that it will be used to obtain the benefits envisaged. For example, as a part of the programme above, the marketing department might be provided with sales and demographic information which allows them to target potential customers more accurately. This should improve the ratio of sales revenue to advertising costs. However, just because this information is available does not mean that the marketing staff will necessarily make effective use of it. Hence the need for evidence of actual business benefits. The timing of the benefits needs to be carefully considered. Thus marketing campaigns that target particular customers might take time to plan and organize and the benefits in increased sales and/or lower advertising costs could take some months to become apparent.

The management structure needed to drive this programme forward would also need to be planned and organized.

A preliminary list of the projects needed to achieve the programme objectives will be created with estimated timescales. This *programme portfolio* will be presented to the programme sponsors.

A major risk is that some of those whose work will be affected by the programme will not be drawn into the programme effectively. A *stakeholder map* identifying the groups of people with an interest in the project and its outcomes and their particular interests could be drawn up. This can be used to write a *communications strategy* and *plan* showing how the appropriate information flows between stakeholders can be set up and maintained.

> Communication plans are considered in more detail in Chapter 12.

We noted back in Chapter 1 that with conventional project planning, it is not usually possible to plan all the phases of a project at the outset, as much of the information needed to produce the detailed plans will not be available. This is more so with programmes. However, at the initial programme planning stage, a preliminary plan can be produced containing:

- the project portfolio;
- cost estimates for each project;
- the benefits expected (including the appropriate benefits profile);
- risks identified;
- the resources needed to manage, support and monitor the programme.

This information allows a *financial plan* to be created. This enables higher management to put in place the budget arrangements to meet the expected costs at identified points in time. These will be tied to points in the programme when higher management review progress and authorize further expenditure.

2.11 Aids to programme management

Dependency diagrams

There will often be physical and technical dependencies between projects. For example, a project to relocate staff from one building to another cannot start until the project to construct the new building has been completed. Dependency diagrams, which are very similar to activity networks at project level, can show these dependencies. However, where projects run concurrently in a programme and products interchange, the dependency diagrams could become quite complicated.

Figure 2.3 shows a dependency diagram for a programme to merge two organizations, the constituent parts of which are explained below.

A *Systems study/design* A project is carried out which examines the various existing IT applications in the two old organizations, analyses their functionality, and makes recommendations about how they are to be combined.

> There will be interdependencies between C and D that will need to be managed.

B *Corporate image design* Independently of Project A, this project is designing the corporate image for the new organization. This would include design of the new logo to be put on company documents.

C *Build common systems* Once Project A has been completed, work can be triggered on the construction of the new common ICT applications.

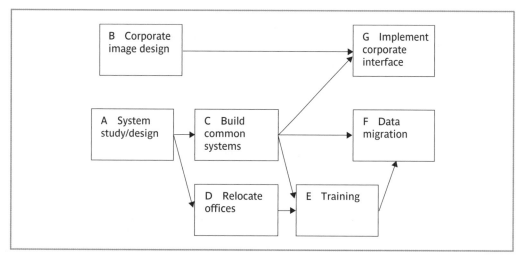

FIGURE 2.3 An example of a dependency diagram

D *Relocate offices* This is the project that plans and carries out the physical co-location of the staff in the two former organizations. In this scenario, this has to wait until the completion of Project A because that project has examined how the two sets of applications for the previous organizations could be brought together, and this has repercussions on the departmental structure of the new merged organization.

E *Training* Once staff have been brought together, perhaps with some staff being made redundant, training in the use of the new systems can begin.

F *Data migration* When the new, joint, applications have been developed and staff have been trained in their use, data can be migrated from existing databases to the new consolidated database.

G *Implement corporate interface* Before the new applications can 'go live', the interfaces, including the documentation generated for external customers, must be modified to conform to the new company image.

Delivery planning

The creation of a delivery dependency diagram would typically lead to the definition of *tranches* of projects. A tranche is a group of projects that will deliver their products as one step in the programme. The projects in a tranche should combine to provide a coherent new capability or set of benefits for the client. A consideration in scheduling a tranche will be the need to avoid contention for scarce resources.

Figure 2.4 shows how the programme's portfolio of projects can be organized into tranches, each of which delivers some tangible benefits to the user.

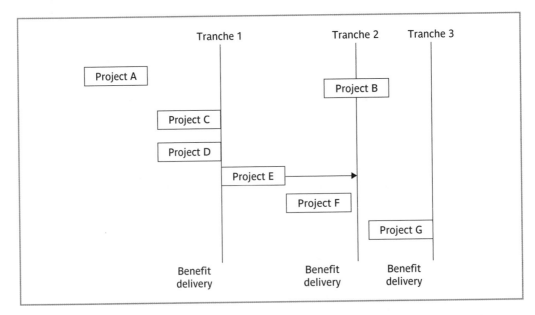

FIGURE 2.4 Delivering tranches of project deliverables

At this point, the planning of individual projects can be considered. This could be initiated by the writing of *project briefs*, defining the scope and objectives of each project.

2.12 Some reservations about programme management

Some writers on project management have expressed reservations about the way they see the ideas of programme management being presented. It is argued that approaches like the one we have described above focus on *structure* – for example, who reports to whom – at the expense of *process* – for example, the basis on which decisions are made.

The main concern is that the programme may be seen as some kind of 'super-project'. This could lead to two problems: first, that programme management may exert an unnecessary control over the subordinate projects, leading to bureaucratic obstruction. The second is that programmes should be seen as the means by which the objectives of the business are converted into action at the level of projects. The business environment is constantly changing and as a consequence programmes need to evolve and be modified during the course of their execution. If the super-project idea predominates then too much planning at the beginning plus a reluctance to change the scope of the programme may lead to inflexibility.

As we have seen in the case of the company merger programme, the projects within a programme may be very different from one another. Also, some programmes – for example where engineering integration is important – may need to be quite tightly coordinated, whereas other programmes could afford a more flexible regime.

The main lessons here seem to be:

■ programme management is *not* simply a scaled-up project management;
■ different forms of programme management may be appropriate for different types of project.

2.13 Benefits management

Thomas K. Landauer (1995) *The Trouble with Computers: Usefulness, Usability and Productivity*, MIT Press, explores the issues of the 'productivity paradox' in IT.

We have already noted that providing a capability does not guarantee that the capability will be used to deliver the planned benefits. Businesses have become aware of the lack of evidence of some investments in ICT increasing the productivity of organizations. Even with *business process re-engineering* (BPR), the radical reorganization of businesses to deliver improvements in efficiency and effectiveness, there are many reported cases where the expected benefits have not materialized.

Benefits management is an attempt to remedy this. It encompasses the identification, optimization and tracking of the expected benefits from a business change in order to ensure that they are actually achieved.

To do this, you must:

- define the expected benefits from the programme;
- analyse the balance between costs and benefits;
- plan how the benefits will be achieved and measured;
- allocate responsibilities for the successful delivery of the benefits;
- monitor the realization of the benefits.

Benefits can be of many different types, including;

- *Mandatory compliance* Governmental or European legislation might make certain changes mandatory.
- *Quality of service* An insurance company, for example, might want to settle claims by customers more quickly.
- *Productivity* The same, or even more, work can be done at less cost in staff time.

- *More motivated workforce* This might be because of an improved rewards system, or through job enlargement or job enrichment.

Job enlargement and enrichment will be discussed in Chapter 11.

- *Internal management benefits* (for instance, better decision making) To take an insurance example again, better analysis of insurance claims could pinpoint those categories of business which are most risky and allow an insurance company to adjust premiums to cover this.

- *Risk reduction* The insurance example might also be applicable here, but measures to protect an organization's networks and databases from intrusion and external malicious attack would be even more pertinent.
- *Economy* The reduction of costs, other than those related to staff – procurement policies might be put in place which encourage the consolidation of purchasing in order to take advantage of bulk-buying at discount.
- *Revenue enhancement/acceleration* The sooner bills reach customers, the sooner they can pay them.
- *Strategic fit* A change might not directly benefit a particular group within the organization but has to be made in order to obtain some strategic advantage for the organization as a whole.

A change could have more than one of these types of benefit. In fact, benefits are often inter-linked. An example of this is an insurance company which introduced a facility whereby when settling claims for damage to property, they directly arranged for contractors to carry out the remedial work. This improved quality of service for customers as it saved them the trouble of locating a reputable contractor, reduced costs to the insurance company because they could take advantage of the bulk purchase of services, and improved staff morale because of the goodwill generated between the insurance company's front-line staff and the customer.

Quantifying benefits

We have already seen that benefits can be:

- quantified and valued – that is, a direct financial benefit is experienced;
- quantified but not valued – for example, a decrease in the number of customer complaints;
- identified but not easily quantified – for example, public approval of the organization in the locality where it is based.

A particular activity might also have *disbenefits*. For example, increased sales might mean that more money has to be spent on expensive overtime working.

There can be controversy over a whether a business change will lead to the particular benefits claimed for it, for example that a new company logo will improve staff morale. Some key tests have been suggested in order to sound out whether a putative benefit is likely to be genuine:

- Can you explain in precise terms why this benefit should result from this business change?
- Can you identify the ways in which we will be able to see the consequences of this benefit?
- If the required outcomes do occur, can they be attributed directly to the change, or could other factors explain them?
- Is there any way in which the benefits can be measured?

We mentioned earlier the need for *benefit profiles* that estimate when and how benefits will be experienced. Specific staff have to be allocated responsibility for ensuring that the planned benefits actually materialize. These will often be *business change managers*.

Benefits cannot normally be monitored in a purely project environment because the project will almost certainly have been officially closed before the benefits start to filter through.

In our view, benefits management brings to the fore the powerful idea that developers and users are *jointly* responsible for ensuring the delivery of the benefits of projects.

2.14 Conclusion

Some of the key points in this chapter are:

- Projects must be evaluated on strategic, technical and economic grounds.
- Many projects are not justifiable on their own, but are as part of a broader programme of projects that implement an organization's strategy.
- Not all benefits can be precisely quantified in financial values.
- Economic assessment involves the identification of all costs and income over the lifetime of the system, including its development and operation and checking that the total value of benefits exceeds total expenditure.

- Money received in the future is worth less than the same amount of money in hand now, which may be invested to earn interest.

- The uncertainty surrounding estimates of future returns lowers their real value measured now.

- Discounted cash flow techniques may be used to evaluate the present value of future cash flows taking account of interest rates and uncertainty.

- Cost–benefit analysis techniques and decision trees provide tools for evaluating expected outcomes and choosing between alternative strategies.

2.15 Further exercises

1   Identify the major risks that could affect the success of the Brightmouth College payroll project and try to rank them in order of importance.

2   Explain why discounted cash flow techniques provide better criteria for project selection than net profit or return on investment.

3   An insurance company has examined the way that it settles house insurance claims. It decides to introduce a new computer-based claims settlement system which will reduce the time taken to settle claims. This reduction in effort is partly achieved by enabling the claims clerk to obtain the information needed directly, rather than having to go through other departments. Also, as part of the new process, new repair work will be allocated by the insurance company to authorized builders, decorators, plumbers etc., rather than the claimant having to make arrangements to get estimates and so on.

    a   Explain the possible benefits and disbenefits that might be generated by this application. Note that the benefits could come under the following headings:

        Mandatory compliance
        Quality of service
        Productivity
        More motivated workforce
        Internal management benefits
        Risk reduction
        Economy
        Revenue enhancement/acceleration
        Strategic fit

    How could the actual benefit be assessed in each case?

    b   When the application is implemented, some of the claims staff at the insurance company complain about the additional stress of dealing with irate customers grumbling about tradespeople being slow to do repair work or about poor quality workmanship. Also, in some places there are shortages of qualified repair people leading to delays in getting work done.

        Which projected benefits are being affected by these developments?
        How would you deal with these problems?
        How would you assess your success in dealing with these problems?

CHAPTER

3

An overview of project planning

❖ OBJECTIVES

When you have completed this chapter you will be able to:

❖ approach project planning in an organized step-by-step manner;

❖ see where the techniques described in other chapters fit into an overall planning approach;

❖ repeat the planning process in more detail for sets of activities within a project as the time comes to execute them.

3.1 Introduction to Step Wise project planning

This chapter describes a framework of basic steps in project planning upon which the following chapters build. Many different techniques can be used in project planning and this chapter gives an overview of the points at which these techniques can be applied during project planning. Chapter 4 will illustrate how different projects may need different technical approaches, but the overall framework should always apply to the planning process.

The framework described is called the Step Wise method to help to distinguish it from other methods such as PRINCE2. PRINCE2 is a set of project management standards that were originally sponsored by what is now the Office of Government Commerce (OGC) for use on British government ICT and business change projects. The standards are now also widely used on non-government projects in the United Kingdom. Step Wise

The OGC was previously the CCTA (Central Computing and Telecommunications Agency).

Appendix A adds some further details about the PRINCE2 approach.

should be compatible with PRINCE2. It should be noted, however, that Step Wise covers only the planning stages of a project and not monitoring and control.

In order to illustrate the Step Wise approach and how it might have to be adapted to deal with different circumstances, two parallel examples are used. Let us assume that there are two former Computing and Information Systems students who now have several years of software development experience under their belts.

CASE STUDY EXAMPLE A: A BRIGHTMOUTH COLLEGE PAYROLL

Brigette has been working for the Management Services department of a local authority when she sees an advertisement for the position of Information Systems Development Officer at Brightmouth College. She is attracted to the idea of being her own boss, working in a relatively small organization and helping them to set up appropriate information systems from scratch. She applies for the job and gets it. One of the first tasks that confronts her is the implementation of independent payroll processing. (This scenario has already been used as the basis of some examples in Chapter 1.)

CASE STUDY EXAMPLE B: INTERNATIONAL OFFICE EQUIPMENT ANNUAL MAINTENANCE CONTRACTS

Amanda works for International Office Equipment (IOE), which assembles, supplies, installs and services various items of high-technology office equipment. An expanding area of their work is the maintenance of ICT equipment. They have now started to undertake maintenance of equipment of which they were not the original suppliers. An existing application built by the in-house ICT department allows sales staff to input and generate invoices for completed work. A large organization might have to call out IOE several times during a month to deal with problems with equipment. Each month a batch run of the system generates monthly statements for customers so that only one payment a month needs to be made. The management of IOE would like to provide a service where for a single annual payment customers would get free servicing and problem resolution for a pre-specified set of equipment. Amanda has been given her first project management role, the task of implementing this extension to the IOE maintenance jobs billing system.

The enhanced application will need a means of recording the details of the items of equipment to be covered by a customer's annual maintenance contract. The annual fee will depend on the numbers of each type of equipment item that is to be covered. Even though the jobs done under this contract will not be charged for, the work will be recorded to allow for an analysis of costs and the profitability of each customer and each type of equipment. This will provide information which will allow IOE to set

▶

future contract prices at an optimally profitable level. At the moment, job details are only recorded after job completion so that invoices can be generated. The new system will allow a central coordinator to allocate jobs to engineers and the system to notify engineers of urgent jobs automatically via their mobile phones.

In Table 3.1 we outline the general approach that might be taken to planning these projects. Figure 3.1 provides an outline of the main planning activities. Steps 1 and 2 'Identify project scope and objectives' and 'Identify project infrastructure' could be tackled in parallel in some cases. Steps 5 and 6 will need to be repeated for each activity in the project.

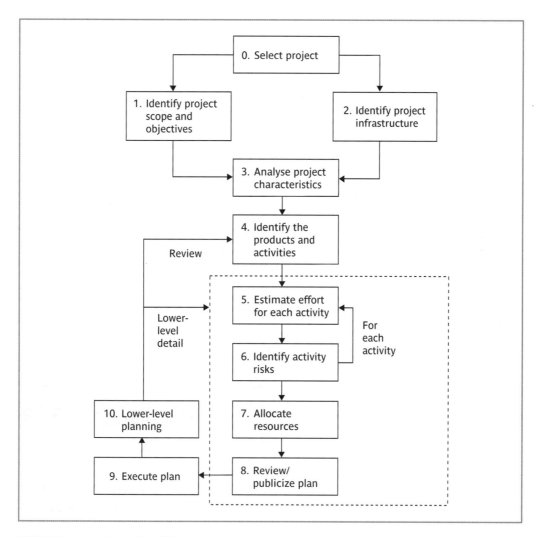

FIGURE 3.1 An overview of Step Wise

Step	Activities within step
0	Select project
1	Identify project scope and objectives
	1.1 Identify objectives and measures of effectiveness in meeting them
	1.2 Establish a project authority
	1.3 Identify stakeholders
	1.4 Modify objectives in the light of stakeholder analysis
	1.5 Establish methods of communication with all parties
2	Identify project infrastructure
	2.1 Establish relationship between project and strategic planning
	2.2 Identify installation standards and procedures
	2.3 Identify project team organization
3	Analyse project characteristics
	3.1 Distinguish the project as either objective- or product-driven
	3.2 Analyse other project characteristics
	3.3 Identify high-level project risks
	3.4 Take into account user requirements concerning implementation
	3.5 Select general life-cycle approach
	3.6 Review overall resource estimates
4	Identify project products and activities
	4.1 Identify and describe project products (including quality criteria)
	4.2 Document generic product flows
	4.3 Recognize product instances
	4.4 Produce ideal activity network
	4.5 Modify ideal to take into account need for stages and checkpoints
5	Estimate effort for each activity
	5.1 Carry out bottom-up estimates
	5.2 Revise plan to create controllable activities
6	Identify activity risks
	6.1 Identify and quantify activity-based risks
	6.2 Plan risk reduction and contingency measures where appropriate
	6.3 Adjust plans and estimates to take account of risks
7	Allocate resources
	7.1 Identify and allocate resources
	7.2 Revise plans and estimates to take account of resource constraints
8	Review/publicize plan
	8.1 Review quality aspects of project plan
	8.2 Document plans and obtain agreement
9/10	Execute plan/lower levels of planning
	This may require the reiteration of the planning process at a lower level

TABLE 3.1 An outline of Step Wise planning activities

A major principle of project planning is to plan in outline first and then in more detail as the time to carry out an activity approaches. Hence the lists of products and activities that are the result of Step 4 will be reviewed when the tasks connected with a particular phase of a project are considered in more detail. This will be followed by a more detailed iteration of Steps 5 to 8 for the phase under consideration.

3.2 Step 0: Select project

Chapter 2 has already discussed these issues in some detail.

This is called Step 0 because in a way it is outside the main project planning process. Proposed projects do not appear out of thin air – some process must decide to initiate this project rather than some other. While a feasibility study might suggest that there is a business case for the project, it would still need to be established that it should have priority over other projects. This evaluation of the merits of projects could be part of project portfolio management.

3.3 Step 1: Identify project scope and objectives

The activities in this step ensure that all the parties to the project agree on the objectives and are committed to the success of the project. We have already looked at the importance of the correct definition of objectives in Chapter 1.

Step 1.1: Identify objectives and practical measures of the effectiveness in meeting those objectives

CASE STUDY EXAMPLES: PROJECT OBJECTIVES

The project objectives for the Brightmouth College payroll project have already been discussed in Exercise 1.8.

Amanda at IOE has the objectives clearly laid down for her in the recommendations of a business case report which have been accepted by IOE management. The main objectives are to allow:

- details of annual maintenance contracts to be recorded;
- details of maintenance work covered by these contracts to be recorded;
- analysis of costs to be carried out so that the optimal level of maintenance contract fees may be identified;
- recording of job requests and notification of jobs to engineers via mobile phones.

Other objectives are laid down that refer to expected timescales and the resources that might be used.

Step 1.2: Establish a project authority

We have already noted in Chapter 1 that a single overall project authority needs to be established so that there is unity of purpose among all those concerned.

Step 1.3: Stakeholder analysis – identify all stakeholders in the project and their interests

Recall that this was the basis of a discussion in Chapter 1. Essentially all the parties who have an interest in the project need to be identified. In that chapter we listed as an example the stakeholders in the Brightmouth College payroll project.

EXERCISE 3.1

What important stakeholders outside the IOE organization might be considered in the case of the IOE annual maintenance contracts system?

CASE STUDY EXAMPLES: PROJECT AUTHORITIES

Throughout the text we use capitalized initial letters to indicate a term that has a precise meaning in the PRINCE2 standards, e.g. Project Board.

Amanda finds that her manager and the main user management have already set up a Project Board which will have overall direction of the project. She is a little concerned as the equipment maintenance staff are organized with different sections dealing with different types of equipment. This means that a customer could have work done by several different sections. Not all the sections are represented on the Project Board and Amanda is aware that there are some differences of opinion between some sections. It is left to the user representatives on the board to resolve those differences and to present an agreed policy to the systems developers.

Brigette finds that effectively she has two different clients for the payroll system: the finance and human resources departments. To help resolve conflicts, it is agreed that the managers of both departments should attend a monthly meeting with the vice-principal which Brigette has arranged in order to steer the project.

Step 1.4: Modify objectives in the light of stakeholder analysis

Compare this with the 'Theory W' of Boehm and Ross mentioned in Chapter 1.

In order to gain the full cooperation of all concerned, it might be necessary to modify the project objectives. This could mean adding new features to the system which give a benefit to some stakeholders as a means of assuring their commitment to the project. This is potentially dangerous as the system size may be increased and the original objectives obscured. Because of these dangers, it is suggested that this process be done consciously and in a controlled manner.

CASE STUDY EXAMPLES: MODIFIED PROJECT OBJECTIVES

The IOE maintenance staff are to be given the extra task of entering data about completed jobs. As no customer charges are generated by visits under annual maintenance contracts, engineers may feel that completing cost details is unnecessary bureaucracy, and start to do this in a careless and inaccurate manner. To give some benefit to the engineers, the system is to be extended to reorder spare parts automatically when required. It will also automatically capture timesheet details which previously had to be completed by hand.

At Brightmouth College, the human resources department has a lot of work preparing payroll details for finance. It would be tactful to agree to produce some management information reports for human resources from the payroll details held on the computer.

Step 1.5: Establish methods of communication with all parties

For internal staff this should be fairly straightforward, but a project leader implementing a payroll system would need to find a contact point with BACS (Bankers Automated Clearing Scheme), for instance. This step could lead to the first draft of a *communications plan* – to read more about these, see Chapter 12.

3.4 Step 2: Identify project infrastructure

Projects are never carried out in a vacuum. There is usually some kind of existing infrastructure into which the project must fit. Where project managers are new to the organization, they must find out the precise nature of this infrastructure. This could be the case where the project manager works for an outside organization carrying out the work for a client.

B. Iyer and R. Gottlieb (2004) 'The Four-Domain Architecture: an approach to support enterprise architecture design' *IBM Systems Journal* 43(3) 587–97 provides a good introduction to enterprise architecture concepts.

Step 2.1: Identify relationship between the project and strategic planning

We saw in Chapter 2 how project portfolio management supported the selection of the projects to be carried out by an organization. Also, how programame management can ensure that a group of projects contribute to a common organizational strategy. There is also a technical framework within which the proposed new systems are to fit. Hardware and software standards, for example, are needed so that various systems can communicate with each other. These technical strategic decisions should be documented as part of an *enterprise architecture* process. Compliance with the enterprise architecture should ensure that successive ICT projects create software and other components compatible with those created by previous projects and also with the existing hardware and software platforms.

CASE STUDY EXAMPLES: ROLE OF EXISTING STRATEGIC PLANS

A manda finds at IOE that there is a well-defined rolling strategic plan which has identified her annual maintenance contracts subsystem as an important required development. Because it is an extension of an existing system, the hardware and software platforms upon which the application are to run are dictated.

Enterprise Resource Planning (ERP) systems are integrated software applications usually acquired as off-the-shelf packages that require considerable customization. They integrate all the standard financial and trading applications common to most businesses.

Brigette at Brightmouth College finds that there is an overall College strategic plan which describes new courses to be developed, and so on, and mentions in passing the need for 'appropriate administrative procedures' to be in place. There is a recommendation in a consultant's report concerning the implications of financial autonomy that independent payroll processing be implemented as just one module in an ERP system which would cover all the college's financial processing needs. Although the college has quite a lot of ICT equipment for teaching purposes, there is no machine set aside for payroll processing and the intention is that the hardware to run the payroll will be acquired at the same time as the software.

Step 2.2: Identify installation standards and procedures

See discussion of the ISO/IEC 12207 standard in Chapter 1.

Any organization that develops software should define their development procedures. As a minimum, the normal stages in the software life cycle to be carried out should be documented along with the products created at each stage.

Change control and *configuration management* standards should be in place to ensure that changes to requirements are implemented in a safe and orderly way.

See Chapter 9 on monitoring and control.

The procedural standards may lay down the quality checks that need to be done at each point of the project life cycle or these may be documented in a separate *quality standards and procedures* manual.

The organization, as part of its monitoring and control policy, may have a *measurement programme* in place which dictates that certain statistics have to be collected at various stages of a project.

Finally the project manager should be aware of any *project planning and control standards*. These will relate to how the project is controlled: for example, the way that the hours spent by team members on individual tasks are recorded on timesheets.

CASE STUDY EXAMPLES: IDENTIFYING STANDARDS

Amanda at IOE finds that there is a very weighty volume of development standards which, among other things, specifies that a specific structured systems analysis and design method be used. She finds that a separate document has been prepared which lays down quality procedures. This specifies when the reviews of work will be carried out and describes detailed procedures governing how the reviews are to be done. Amanda also finds a set of project management guidelines modelled on PRINCE2.

Brigette finds no documents of the nature that Amanda found at IOE except for some handouts for students that have been produced by different lecturers at different times and which seem to contradict each other.

As a stop-gap measure, Brigette writes a brief document which states what the main stages of a 'project' (perhaps 'job for the user' would be a better term in this context) should be. This happens to be very similar to the list given in Chapter 1. She stresses that:

- no job of work to change a system or implement a new one is to be done without there being a detailed specification first;
- the users must record agreement to each specification in writing before the work is carried out.

She draws up a simple procedure for recording all changes to user requirements.

Brigette, of course, has no organizational quality procedures, but she dictates that each person in the group (including herself) has to get someone else to check through their work when they finish a major task and that, before any new or amended software is handed over to the users, someone other than the original developer should test it. She sets up a simple system to record errors found in system testing and their resolution. She also creates a log file of reported user problems with operational systems.

Brigette does not worry about timesheets but arranges an informal meeting with her colleagues each Monday morning to discuss how things are going and also arranges to see the vice-principal, who is her official boss, and the heads of the finance and human resources sections each month to review progress in general terms.

Step 2.3: Identify project team organization

| Some of these issues will be discussed in Chapter 12 on working in teams. | Project leaders, especially in the case of large projects, might have some control over the way that their project team is to be organized. Often, though, the organizational structure will be dictated to them. For example, a high-level managerial decision might have been taken that software developers and business analysts will be in different groups, or that the development of business-to-consumer web applications |

will be done within a separate group from that responsible for 'traditional' database applications.

If the project leader does have some control over the project team organization then this would best be considered at a later stage (see Step 7: Allocate resources).

CASE STUDY EXAMPLES: PROJECT ORGANIZATION

At IOE, there are groups of business analysts set up as teams which deal with individual user departments. Hence the users always know whom they should contact within the information systems department if they have a problem. Software developers, however, work in a 'pool' and are allocated to specific projects on an ad hoc basis.

At Brightmouth College, a software developer has been seconded to Brigette from the technicians supporting the computing courses in the college. She is also allowed to recruit a trainee analyst/programmer. She is not unduly worried about the organizational structure needed.

3.5 Step 3: Analyse project characteristics

Chapter 4 elaborates on the process of analysing project characteristics.

The general purpose of this part of the planning operation is to ensure that the appropriate methods are used for the project.

Step 3.1: Distinguish the project as either objective- or product-driven

This has already been discussed in the first chapter. As development of a system advances it tends to become more product-driven, although the underlying objectives always remain and must be respected.

Step 3.2: Analyse other project characteristics (including quality-based ones)

For example, is an information system to be developed or a process control system, or will there be elements of both? Will the system be safety critical, where human life could be threatened by a malfunction?

Step 3.3: Identify high-level project risks

Consideration must be given to the risks that threaten the successful outcome of the project. Generally speaking, most risks can be attributed to the operational or development environment, the technical nature of the project or the type of product being created.

We have already noted that Amanda has raised concerns about the possibility that engineers lack the motivation to complete with due care and attention the cost details for jobs done under annual contracts. Another risk relates to the software functionality which will produce cost analysis reports used for the future pricing of annual contracts. If the analysis is incorrect IOE could suffer financially. Amanda decides therefore that the analysis functionality will be produced using an iterative approach where an IOE marketing analyst will look at versions of the reports produced and suggest improvements to the methods of calculation and presentation before the system is finally made operational.

Brigette at Brightmouth College considers the application area to be very well defined. There is a risk, however, that there may be no package on the market that caters for the way that things are done at the moment. Brigette, therefore, decides that an early task in the project is to obtain information about the features of the main payroll packages that are available.

Step 3.4: Take into account user requirements concerning implementation

The clients may have their own procedural requirements. For example, an organization might mandate the use of a particular development method.

Step 3.5: Select development methodology and life-cycle approach

The development methodology and project life cycle to be used for the project will be influenced by the issues raised above. The idea of a methodology, that is, the group of methods to be used in a project, was discussed in Chapter 1. For many software developers, the choice of methods will seem obvious: they will use the ones that they have always used in the past. In Chapter 4 we recommend caution in assuming that the current project is really similar to previous ones.

Chapter 4 discusses life cycles in more detail.

As well as the methods to be used, there are generic ways of structuring projects, such as the use of the waterfall life cycle outlined in Chapter 4, that need to be considered. While the setting of objectives involves identifying the problems to be solved, this part of planning is working out the ways in which these problems are to be solved. For a project that is novel to the planner, some research into the methods typically used in the problem domain is worthwhile. For example, sometimes, as part of a project, a questionnaire survey has to be conducted. There are lots of books on the techniques used in such surveys and a wise move would be to look at one or two of them at the planning stage.

Chapter 5 goes into more detail on this topic. Function points are an attempt to measure system size without using lines of code.

Step 3.6: Review overall resource estimates

Once the major risks have been identified and the broad project approach has been decided upon, this would be a good point at which to re-estimate the effort and other resources required to implement the project. Where enough information is available an estimate based on function points might be appropriate.

3.6 Step 4: Identify project products and activities

The more detailed planning of the individual activities now takes place. The longer-term planning is broad and in outline, while the more immediate tasks are planned in some detail.

Step 4.1: Identify and describe project products (or deliverables)

In general, there can be no project products that do not have activities that create them. Wherever possible, we ought also to ensure the reverse: that there are no activities that do not produce a tangible product. Identifying all the things the project is to create helps us to ensure that all the activities we need to carry out are accounted for. Some of these products will be handed over to the client at the end of the project – these are *deliverables*. Other products might not be in the final configuration, but are needed as *intermediate* products used in the process of creating the deliverables.

These products will include a large number of *technical* products, such as training material and operating instructions. There will also be products to do with the *management* and the *quality* of the project. Planning documents would, for example, be management products.

The products will form a hierarchy. The main products will have sets of component products which in turn may have sub-component products and so on. These relationships can be documented in a Product Breakdown Structure (PBS) – see Figure 3.2. In this example the products have been grouped into those relating to the system as a whole, and those related to individual modules. A third 'group', which happens to have only one product, is called 'management products' and consists of progress reports. The asterisk in the progress reports indicates that there will be new instances of the entity 'progress report' created repeatedly throughout the project.

PRINCE2 suggests that the PBS be presented as a hierarchy diagram. In practice it may be more convenient to produce a structured list.

Note that in Figure 3.2 the only boxes that represent tangible products are those at the bottom of the hierarchy that are not further subdivided. Thus there are only six individual product types shown in the diagram. The boxes that are higher up – for example 'module products' – are simply the names of groups of items.

Some products are created from scratch, for example new software components. A product could quite easily be a document, such as a software design document. It might be a modified version of something that already exists, such as an amended piece of code. A product could even be

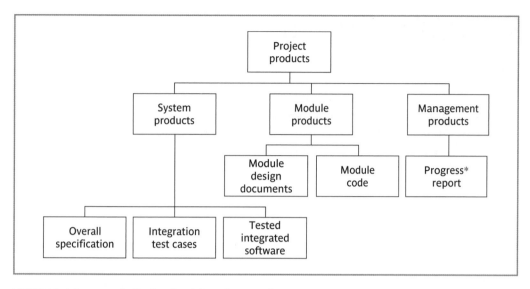

FIGURE 3.2 A fragment of a Product Breakdown Structure for a system development task
* indicates that further progress reports can be added during the course of the project.

a person, such as a 'trained user', a product of the process of training. Always remember that a product is the result of an activity. A common error is to identify as products things that are really activities, such as 'training', 'design' and 'testing'. Specifying 'documentation' as a product should also be avoided – by itself this term is just too vague.

This part of the planning process draws heavily on the standards laid down in PRINCE2. These specify that products at the bottom of the PBS should be documented by *Product Descriptions* which contain:

- the *name/identity* of the product;
- the *purpose* of the product;
- the *derivation* of the product (that is, the other products from which it is derived);
- the *composition* of the product;
- the *form* of the product;
- the relevant *standards*;
- the *quality* criteria that define whether the product is acceptable.

EXERCISE 3.2

At Brightmouth College, Brigette has decided that the finance department at the college should carry out acceptance testing of the new payroll system. This type of testing ensures that the application has been set up in a way that allows the users to carry out their jobs accurately using the new system. As the finance department staff are not sure what test case documents should look like, Brigette draws up a product description of a test case. Write the content for this product description.

At IOE, Amanda finds that there is a standard PBS that she can use as a checklist for her own project.

Brigette at Brightmouth College has no installation standard PBS, although she can, of course, refer to various books for standard checklists. She decides that one part of the PBS should contain the products needed to help select the appropriate hardware and software for the payroll application (Figure 3.3).

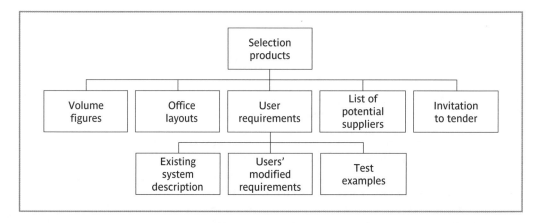

FIGURE 3.3 A Product Breakdown Structure (PBS) for the products needed to produce an invitation to tender (ITT)

Step 4.2: Document generic product flows

> The PFD effectively documents, in outline, the method (see Chapter 1) for the project.

Some products will need one or more other products to exist first before they can be created. For example, a program design must be created before the program can be written and the program specification must exist before the design can be commenced. These relationships can be portrayed in a *Product Flow Diagram* (PFD). Figure 3.4 gives an example. Note that the 'flow' in the diagram is assumed to be from top to bottom and left to right. In the example in Figure 3.4, 'user requirements' is in an oval which means that it is used by the project but is not created by it. It is often convenient to identify an overall product at the bottom of the diagram, in this case 'integrated/tested software', into which all the other products feed.

PFDs should not have links between products which loop back iteratively. This is emphatically *not* because iterations are not recognized. On the contrary, the PFD allows for looping back at any point. For example, in the PFD shown in Figure 3.4, say that during integration testing it was found that a user requirement had been missed in the overall system specification. If we go back to overall system specification and change it we can see from the PFD that all the products that follow it might need to be reworked. A new

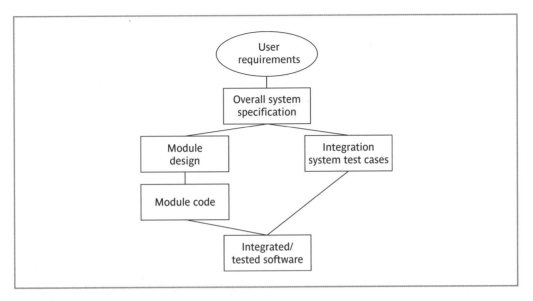

FIGURE 3.4 A fragment of a Product Flow Diagram (PFD) for a software development task

module might need to be designed and coded, test cases would need to be added to check that the new requirements had been successfully incorporated, and the integration testing would need to be repeated.

The form that a PFD takes will depend on assumptions and decisions about how the project is to be carried out. These decisions may not be obvious from the PFD and so a textual description explaining the reasons for the structure can be helpful.

CASE STUDY EXAMPLES: IOE HAS STANDARD PFD

At IOE, Amanda has an installation standard PFD for software development projects. This is because a recognized software development method is used which lays down a sequence of documents that have to be produced. This sequence of products can be straightforwardly documented as a PFD.

EXERCISE 3.3

Draw up a possible Product Flow Diagram (PFD) based on the Product Breakdown Structure (PBS) shown in Figure 3.3. This identifies some of the products of the Brightmouth payroll project, particularly those generated when gathering information to be presented to potential suppliers of the hardware as part of an 'invitation to tender'. The volume figures are such things as the number of employees for whom records will have to be maintained.

This may be delayed to later in the project when more information is known.

Step 4.3: Recognize product instances

Where the same generic PFD fragment relates to more than one instance of a particular type of product, an attempt should be made to identify each of those instances. In the example in Figure 3.2, it could be that in fact there are just two component software modules in the software to be built.

Step 4.4: Produce ideal activity network

In order to generate one product from another there must be one or more activities that carry out the transformation. By identifying these activities we can create an activity network which shows the tasks that have to be carried out and the order in which they have to be executed.

CASE STUDY EXAMPLES: ACTIVITY NETWORK FOR IOE MAINTENANCE ACCOUNTS

Part of the initial activity network developed from the PFD in Figure 3.4 for the software development task might look like Figure 3.5.

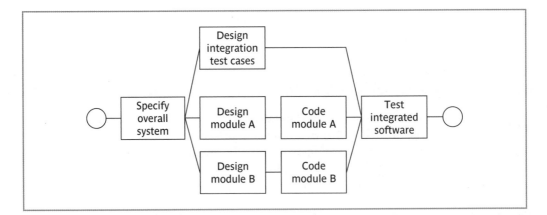

FIGURE 3.5 An example of an activity network

EXERCISE 3.4

Draw up an activity network for the Product Flow Diagram that you created in Exercise 3.3 (or the PFD given in the solution if you prefer!).

The activity networks are 'ideal' in the sense that no account has been taken of resource constraints. For example, in Figure 3.5, it is assumed that resources are available for both software modules to be developed in parallel. A good rule is that activity networks are never amended to take account of resource constraints.

Step 4.5: Modify the ideal to take into account need for stages and checkpoints

The approach to sequencing activities described above encourages the formulation of a plan which will minimize the overall duration, or 'elapsed time', for the project. It assumes that an activity will start as soon as the preceding ones upon which it depends have been completed.

> Strictly, a milestone is a dummy activity with no duration that indicates the start or end of a group of activities. The milestone would therefore be *after* the checkpoint activity.

There might, however, be a need to modify this by dividing the project into stages and introducing checkpoint activities. These are activities which draw together the products of preceding activities to check that they are compatible. This could potentially delay work on some elements of the project – there has to be a trade-off between efficiency and quality.

The people to whom the project manager reports could decide to leave the routine monitoring of activities to the project manager. However, there could be some key activities, or *milestones*, which represent the completion of important stages of the project of which they would want to take particular note. Checkpoint activities are often useful milestones.

EXERCISE 3.5

In the example in Figure 3.5, it has been decided that the designs for modules A and B are to be checked for consistency by 'dry-running' them against the integration test cases before committing staff to software coding. Redraw the activity network to reflect this.

3.7 Step 5: Estimate effort for each activity

Step 5.1: Carry out bottom-up estimates

Some overall estimates of effort, cost and duration will already have been done (see Step 3.6).

> Chapter 5 on software effort estimation deals with this topic in more detail.

At this point, estimates of the staff effort required, the probable elapsed time and the non-staff resources needed for each activity will need to be produced. The method of arriving at each of these estimates will vary depending on the type of activity.

The difference between *elapsed time* and *effort* should be noted. Effort is the amount of work that needs to be done. If a task requires three members of staff to work for two full days each, the effort expended is six days. Elapsed time is the time between the start and end of a task. In our example above, if the three members of staff start and finish at the same time then the elapsed time for the activity would be two days.

The individual activity estimates of effort should be summed to get an overall bottom-up estimate which can be reconciled with the previous top-down estimate.

The activities on the activity network can be annotated with their elapsed times so that the overall duration of the project can be calculated.

Step 5.2: Revise plan to create controllable activities

The estimates for individual activities could reveal that some are going to take quite a long time. Long activities make a project difficult to control. If an activity involving system testing is to take 12 weeks, it would be difficult after six weeks to judge accurately whether 50 per cent of the work is completed. It would be better to break this down into a series of smaller subtasks.

> ### CASE STUDY EXAMPLES: IOE ANNUAL MAINTENANCE CONTRACTS – CARRY OUT BOTTOM-UP ESTIMATES
>
> At IOE, Amanda has to estimate the lines of code for each of the software modules. She looks at programs that have been coded for similar types of application at IOE in the past to get some idea of the size of the new modules. She then refers to some conversion tables that the information systems development department at IOE have produced which convert the lines of code into estimates of effort. Other tables allow her to allocate the estimated effort to the various stages of the project.
>
> Although Brigette is aware that some additional programs might have to be written to deal with local requirements, the main software is to be obtained 'off the shelf' and so estimating based on lines of code would clearly be inappropriate. Instead, she looks at each individual task and allocates a time. She realizes that in many cases these represent 'targets' as she is uncertain at the moment how long these tasks will really take (see Step 6 below).

There might be a number of activities that are important, but individually take up very little time. For a training course, there might be a need to book rooms and equipment, notify those attending, register students on the training system, order refreshments, copy training materials and so on. In a situation like this it would be easier to bundle the activities into a single merged activity 'make training course arrangements' which could be supplemented with a checklist.

In general, try to make activities about the length of the reporting period used for monitoring and controlling the project. If you have a progress meeting every two weeks, then it would convenient to have activities of two weeks' duration on average, so that progress meetings would normally be made aware of completed tasks each time they are held.

3.8 Step 6: Identify activity risks

Step 6.1: Identify and quantify activity-based risks

Chapter 7 on risk touches on this topic in more detail. Risks inherent in the overall nature of the project have already been considered in Step 3. We now want to look at each activity in turn and assess the risks to its successful outcome. Any plan is always based on certain assumptions. Say the design of a component is planned to take five days. This is based on the assumption that the client's requirement is clear and unambiguous. If it is not then additional effort to clarify the requirement would be needed. The possibility that an assumption upon which a plan is based is incorrect constitutes a risk. In this example, one way of expressing the uncertainty would be to express the estimate of effort as a range of values.

As will be seen in Chapter 7, a simple way of dealing with uncertainty is to have a 'most likely' estimate for where everything works with no problems (such as users changing their requirements) and a second estimate that includes a safety margin so that it has an estimated 95 per cent chance of being met.

A project plan will be based on a huge number of assumptions, and so some way of picking out the risks that are most important is needed. The damage that each risk could cause and the likelihood of it occurring have to be gauged. This assessment can draw attention to the most serious risks. The usual effect if a problem materializes is to make the task longer or more costly.

Step 6.2: Plan risk reduction and contingency measures where appropriate

It may be possible to avoid or at least reduce some of the identified risks. On the other hand, *contingency plans* specify action that is to be taken if a risk materializes. For example, a contingency plan could be to use contract staff if a member of the project team is unavailable at a key time because of serious illness.

Step 6.3: Adjust overall plans and estimates to take account of risks

We may change our plans, perhaps by adding new activities which reduce risks. For example, a new programming language might mean we schedule training courses and time for the programmers to practise their new programming skills on some non-essential work.

CASE STUDY EXAMPLES: IDENTIFYING RISKS

As well as the new software modules that will have to be written, Amanda has identified several existing modules that will need to be amended. The ease with which the modules can be amended will depend upon the way that they were originally written. There is therefore a risk that they may take longer than expected to modify.

Amanda takes no risk reduction measures as such but notes a pessimistic elapsed time for the amendment activity.

Brigette identifies as a risk the possible absence of key staff when investigating the user requirements, as this activity will take place over the holiday period. To reduce this risk, she adds a new activity, 'arrange user interviews', at the beginning of the project. This will give her advance notice of any likely problems of this nature.

3.9 Step 7: Allocate resources

Step 7.1: Identify and allocate resources

Chapter 8 on resource allocation covers this topic in more detail.

The type of staff needed for each activity is recorded. The staff available for the project are identified and are provisionally allocated to tasks.

Step 7.2: Revise plans and estimates to take into account resource constraints

Some staff may be needed for more than one task at the same time and, in this case, an order of priority is established. The decisions made here may have an effect on the overall duration of the project when some tasks are delayed while waiting for staff to become free.

Gantt charts are named after Henry Gantt and 'Gantt' should therefore not be written in capital letters as if it stood for something!

Ensuring someone is available to start work on an activity as soon as the preceding activities have been completed might mean that they are idle while waiting for the job to start and are therefore used inefficiently.

The product of Steps 7.1 and 7.2 would typically be a Gantt chart – see Figure 3.6. The Gantt chart gives a clear picture of when activities will actually take place and highlights which ones will be executed at the same time. Activity networks can be misleading in this respect.

CASE STUDY EXAMPLES: TAKING RESOURCE CONSTRAINTS INTO ACCOUNT

Amanda has now identified three new major software modules plus an existing software module that will need extensive amendment. At IOE the specification of modules is carried out by the lead systems analyst for the project (who in this case is Amanda) assisted by junior analyst/designers. Four analyst/programmers are available to carry out the design, coding and unit testing of the individual modules. After careful consideration and discussion with her manager, Amanda decides to use only three analyst/programmers so as to minimize the risk of staff waiting between tasks and thus reduce staff costs. It is accepted that this decision, while reducing the cost of the project, will delay its end.

Brigette finds that she herself will have to carry out many important activities. She can reduce the workload on herself by delegating some work to her two colleagues, but she realizes that she will have to devote more time to specifying exactly what they will have to do and to checking their work. She adjusts her plan accordingly.

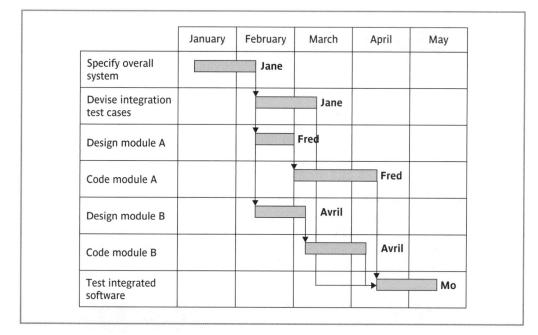

FIGURE 3.6 Gantt chart showing when staff will be carrying out tasks

3.10 Step 8: Review/publicize plan

Step 8.1: Review quality aspects of the project plan

A danger when controlling any project is that an activity can reveal that an earlier activity was not properly completed and needs to be reworked. This, at a stroke, can transform a project that appears to be progressing satisfactorily into one that is badly out of control. It is important to know that when a task is reported as completed, it really is – hence the importance of quality reviews. Each task should have *quality criteria*. These are quality checks that have to be passed before the activity can be 'signed off' as completed.

CASE STUDY EXAMPLES: IOE EXISTING QUALITY STANDARDS

Amanda finds that at IOE, the Quality Standards and Procedures Manual lays down quality criteria for each type of task. For example, all module design documentation for any group of modules that interact with one another has to be reviewed by a group of colleagues before the coding can commence. This is to reduce the likelihood of integration problems when the components are finally executed together. Amanda adds an activity to her plan to deal with this.

EXERCISE 3.6

Brigette has no installation standards to help her apart from the minimal ones she has written herself. What quality checks might Brigette introduce to ensure that she has understood the users' requirements properly?

Step 8.2: Document plans and obtain agreement

It is important that the plans be carefully documented and that all the parties to the project understand and agree to the commitments required of them in the plan. This may sound obvious, but it is amazing how often this is not done. Chapter 12 describes the use of a *communications plan* to ensure appropriate communications between stakeholders at the right points in the project.

EXERCISE 3.7

At the end of Chapter 1 the main sections of a project plan document were listed. Draw up a table showing which Step Wise activities provide material for which sections of the project plan.

3.11 Steps 9 and 10: Execute plan/lower levels of planning

Once the project is under way, plans will need to be drawn up in greater detail for each activity as it becomes due. Detailed planning of the later stages will need to be delayed because more information will be available nearer the start of the stage. Of course, it is necessary to make provisional plans for the more distant tasks, because thinking about what needs to be done can help unearth potential problems, but sight should not be lost of the fact that these plans are provisional.

CASE STUDY EXAMPLES: LOWER-LEVEL PLANNING

While work is going on with the specification of the individual modules, Amanda has some time to start planning the integration tests in some detail. She finds that one of the modules – the one that deals with recording job requests – does not actually communicate directly with the other new modules and can therefore be reviewed independently of the others. She schedules an earlier review of this module as this allows coding of the module to be started earlier.

When Brigette comes to consider the activity 'draft invitation to tender', she has to familiarize herself with the detailed institutional rules and procedures that govern this process. She finds that in order to draft this document she will need to obtain some additional pieces of information from the users.

3.12 Conclusion

This chapter has presented a framework into which the techniques described in the other parts of the book should slot. It is suggested that any planning approach should have the following elements:

- the establishment of project objectives;
- the analysis of the characteristics of the project;
- the establishment of an infrastructure consisting of an appropriate organization and set of standards, methods and tools;
- the identification of the products of the project and the activities needed to generate those products;
- the allocation of resources to activities;
- the establishment of quality controls.

Project planning is an iterative process. As the time approaches for particular activities to be carried out they should be replanned in more detail.

3.13 Further exercises

1 List the products created by the Step Wise planning process.

2 What products must exist before the activity 'test program' can take place? What products does this activity create?

3 An employee of a training organization has the task of creating case study exercises and solutions for a training course which teaches a new systems analysis and design method. The person's work plan has a three-week task 'learn new method'. A colleague

suggests that this is unsatisfactory as a task as there are no concrete deliverables or products from the activity. What can be done about this?

4 In order to carry out usability tests for a new word processing package, the software has to be written and debugged. User instructions have to be available describing how the package is to be used. These have to be scrutinized in order to plan and design the tests. Subjects who will use the package in the tests will need to be selected. As part of this selection process, they will have to complete a questionnaire giving details of their past experience of, and training in, typing and using word processing packages. The subjects will carry out the required tasks using the word processing package. The tasks will be timed and any problems the subjects encounter with the package will be noted. After the test, the subjects will complete another questionnaire about what they felt about the package. All the data from the tests will be analysed and a report containing recommendations for changes to the package will be drawn up. Draw up a Product Breakdown Structure, a Product Flow Diagram and a preliminary activity network for the above.

5 Question 4 in the further exercises for Chapter 1 refers to a scenario relating to a training exercise. Using that scenario, draw up a Product Breakdown Structure, a Product Flow Diagram and a preliminary activity network.

CHAPTER 4

Selection of an appropriate project approach

❖ *OBJECTIVES*

When you have completed this chapter you will be able to:

❖ evaluate situations where software applications could be acquired off-the-shelf rather than being built specially;

❖ take account of the characteristics of the system to be developed when planning a project;

❖ select an appropriate process model;

❖ make best use of the waterfall process model where appropriate;

❖ reduce some risks by the creation of appropriate prototypes;

❖ reduce other risks by implementing the project in increments;

❖ identify where unnecessary organizational obstacles can be removed by using agile development methods.

4.1 Introduction

The development of software in-house usually means that:

■ the developers and the users belong to the same organization;

■ the application will slot into a portfolio of existing computer-based systems;

■ the methodologies and technologies are largely dictated by organizational standards and policies, including the existing enterprise architecture.

However, a software supplier could carry out successive development projects for a variety of external customers. They would need to review the methodologies and

B. Fitzgerald, N. L. Russo and T. O'Kane (2003). 'Software development method tailoring at Motorola' *Communications of the ACM* 46(4) 65–70 provides a good insight into how method tailoring works in practice.

technologies to be used for each individual project. This decision-making process has been called *technical planning* by some, although here we use the term *project analysis*. Other terms for this process are *methods engineering* and *methods tailoring*. Even where development is in-house, any characteristics of the new project requiring a different approach from previous projects need to be considered. A wide range of system development methods exists, but many organizations get along without using any of the recognized approaches. Where methods are used, 'means–end inversion' can happen: developers focus on the means – the procedures and intermediate products of a prescribed method – at the expense of the 'end', the actual required outcomes of the work. These issues are the subject of this chapter.

The relevant part of the Step Wise approach is Step 3: *Analyse project characteristics*. The selection of a particular process model could add new products to the Project Breakdown Structure or new activities to the activity network. This will generate inputs for Step 4: Identify the products and activities of the project (see Figure 4.1).

In the remainder of this chapter we will look at how the characteristics of a project's environment and the application to be delivered influence the shape of the plan of a project. We will then look at some of the most common *process models*, namely the waterfall approach, prototyping and incremental delivery. Some of the ideas of prototyping and incremental delivery have been further developed and made part of *agile methods*. We will have a look at how these *lightweight* processes have been designed to remove what have been seen as the bureaucratic obstacles created by more formal, *heavyweight* methods.

4.2 Build or buy?

The communication challenges of geographically dispersed projects are discussed in Chapter 12 on working in teams.

Software development can be seen from two differing viewpoints: that of the developers and that of the clients or users. With *in-house development*, the developers and the users are in the same organization. Where the development is *outsourced*, they are in different organizations. In these days of global system development, the different organizations could be on different continents. These factors will affect the way that a project is organized.

The development of a new IT application within an organization would often require the recruitment of technical staff who, once the project has been completed, will no longer be required. Because this project is a unique new development for the client organization there may be a lack of executives qualified to lead the effort. Contracting the project out to an external IT development company may be attractive in these circumstances. The contracting company will have technical and project expertise not readily available to the client. However, there would still be considerable management effort needed by the client to establish and manage the contract and this is the subject of Chapter 10 on managing contracts.

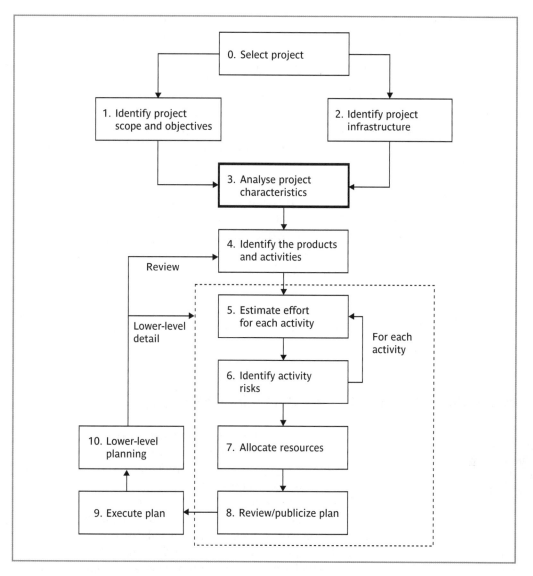

FIGURE 4.1 Project analysis is the subject of Step 3

Whether in-house or outsourced, software development is still involved. An option which is increasingly taken – as in the case of the Brightmouth College payroll scenario – is to obtain a licence to run off-the-shelf software. The advantages of such an approach include:

■ the supplier of the application can spread the cost of development over a large number of customers and thus the cost per customer should be reduced;

■ the software already exists and so
  ● it can be examined and perhaps even trialed before acquisition,
  ● there is no delay while the software is being built;

- where lots of people have already used the software, most of the bugs are likely to have been reported and removed, leading to more reliable software.

However, there are disadvantages, which include the following.

- As you have the same application as everyone else, there is no competitive advantage.
- Modern off-the-shelf software tends to be very customizable: the characteristics of the application can be changed by means of various parameter tables. However, this flexibility has limits and you may end up having to change your office procedures in order to fit in with the computer system.
- You will not own the software code. This may rule out making modifications to the application in response to changes in the organization or its environment.
- Once you have acquired your off-the-shelf system, your organization may come to be very reliant upon it. This may create a considerable barrier to moving to a different application. The supplier may be in a position to charge inflated licence fees because you are effectively a captive customer.

We will explore these issues further in Chapter 10 on managing contracts. In the remainder of this chapter we focus on situations where new software is being developed, whether in-house or outsourced.

4.3 Choosing methodologies and technologies

Strictly speaking, methodology should refer to the 'study of methods'.

In the context of ICT system development and software engineering, the term *methodology* describes a collection of *methods*. We introduced 'method' in Chapter 1 as a general way of carrying out a specific task that could be applicable to any project needing to do that task. *Techniques* and methods are sometimes distinguished. Techniques tend to involve the application of scientific, mathematical or logical principles to resolve a particular kind of problem. They often require the practice of particular personal skills (the word 'technique' is derived from the Greek for skilful) – software design is a good example. Methods often involve the creation of *models*. A model is a representation of a system which abstracts certain features but ignores others. For example, an entity relationship diagram (ERD) is a model of the structure of the data used by a system. What can be confusing is that a software development life cycle itself is a type of system. Features of life cycles can therefore be abstracted and represented as 'models' as we will see later in this chapter. Some of these models can thus start to look a bit like methods.

Project analysis should select the most appropriate methodologies and technologies for a project. Methodologies include approaches like the Unified Software Development Process (USDP), Structured Systems Analysis and Design Method (SSADM) and Human-Centred Design, while technologies might include appropriate application-building and automated testing environments. The analysis identifies the methodology, but also selects the methods within the methodology that are to be deployed.

As well as the products and activities, the chosen methods and technologies will affect:

- the training requirements for development staff;
- the types of staff to be recruited;
- the development environment – both hardware and software;
- system maintenance arrangements.

We are now going to describe some of the steps of project analysis.

Identify project as either objective-driven or product-driven

In Chapter 1 we distinguished between *objective-driven* and *product-driven* projects. A product-driven project creates products defined before the start of the project. An objective-driven project will often have come first which will have defined the general software solution that is to be implemented.

The project manager's dream is to have well-defined objectives but as much freedom as possible about how those objectives are to be satisfied. An objective might be to pay staff in a start-up company reliably, accurately and with low administrative costs. The company does not have to specify the use of a particular packaged software solution at the outset – but as we will see, there can be exceptions to this.

> The soft systems approach is described in P. Checkland and J. Scholes (1999) *Soft Systems Methodology in Action*, John Wiley and Sons.

Sometimes the objectives of the project are uncertain or are the subject of disagreement. People might be experiencing problems but no one knows exactly how to solve these problems. ICT specialists might provide help with some problems but assistance from other specialisms might be needed with others. In these kinds of situation a *soft systems* approach might be considered.

Analyse other project characteristics

The following questions can be usefully asked.

> We first introduced the difference between information systems and embedded systems in Chapter 1.

- *Is a data-oriented or process-oriented system to be implemented? Data-oriented* systems generally mean information systems that will have a substantial database. *Process-oriented* systems refer to embedded control systems. It is not uncommon to have systems with elements of both. Some writers suggest that the OO approach is more suitable for process-oriented systems where control is important than for systems dominated by a relational database.

- *Will the software that is to be produced be a general tool or application specific?* An example of a general tool would be a spreadsheet or a word processing package. An application-specific package could be, for example, an airline seat reservation system.

- *Are there specific tools available for implementing the particular type of application?* For example:

Note that here we are talking about writing the software tool, not its use.

– *does it involve concurrent processing?* – the use of techniques appropriate to the analysis and design of such systems would be considered;

– *will the system to be created be knowledge-based?* – expert systems have rules which result in some 'expert advice' when applied to a problem, and specific methods and tools exist for developing such systems; or

– *will the system to be produced make heavy use of computer graphics?*

■ *Is the system to be created safety critical?* For instance, could a malfunction in the system endanger human life? If so, among other things, testing would become very important.

■ *Is the system designed primarily to carry out predefined services or to be engaging and entertaining?* With software designed for entertainment, design and evaluation will need to be carried out differently from more conventional software products.

■ *What is the nature of the hardware/software environment in which the system will operate?* The environment in which the final software will operate could be different from that in which it is to be developed. Embedded software might be developed on a large development machine which has lots of supporting software tools such as compilers, debuggers and static analysers, but then be downloaded to a small processor in the target configuration. A standalone desktop application needs a different approach to one for a mainframe or a client–server environment.

EXERCISE 4.1

How would you categorize each of the following systems according to the classification above?

(a) a payroll system;

(b) a system to control a bottling plant;

(c) a system which holds details of the plans of plant used by a water company to supply water to consumers;

(d) a software package to support project managers;

(e) a system used by lawyers to access case law relating to company taxation.

Identify high-level project risks

Chapter 2 has already touched on some aspects of risk which are developed further in Chapter 7.

At the beginning of a project, some managers might expect elaborate plans even though we are ignorant of many important factors affecting the project. For example, until we have analysed the users' requirements in detail we cannot estimate the effort needed to build a system to meet those requirements. The greater the uncertainties at the beginning, the greater the risk that the project will be unsuccessful. Once we recognize an area of uncertainty we can, however, take steps to reduce its uncertainty.

One suggestion is that uncertainty can be associated with the *products, processes,* or *resources* of a project.

■ *Product uncertainty* How well are the requirements understood? The users themselves could be uncertain about what a proposed information system is to do. The government, say, might introduce a new form of taxation but its detailed operation might not be known until case law has been built up. Some environments change so quickly that a seemingly precise and valid statement of requirements rapidly becomes out of date.

Extreme programming will be discussed in Section 4.13.

■ *Process uncertainty* The project under consideration might be the first where an organization is using an approach like extreme programming (XP) or a new application-building tool. Any change in the way that the systems are developed introduces uncertainty.

Of course, some risk factors can increase both uncertainty and complexity.

■ *Resource uncertainty* The main area of uncertainty here is likely to be the availability of staff of the right ability and experience. The larger the number of resources needed or the longer the duration of the project, the more inherently risky it will be.

Some factors – such as continually changing requirements – increase *uncertainty*, while others – for instance, software size – increase *complexity*. Different strategies are needed to deal with the two distinct types of risks.

EXERCISE 4.2

At IOE, Amanda has identified possible user resistance as a risk to the annual maintenance contracts project. Would you classify this as a product, process or resource risk? It may be that it does not fit into any of these categories and some other is needed.

Brigette at Brightmouth College has identified as a risk the possibility that no suitable payroll package would be available on the market. What other risks might be inherent in the Brightmouth College payroll project?

Take into account user requirements concerning implementation

We suggested earlier that staff planning a project should try to ensure that unnecessary constraints are not imposed on the way that a project's objectives are to be met. The example given was the specification of the exact payroll package to be deployed. Sometimes, such constraints are unavoidable. International conglomerates have found that imposing uniform applications and technologies throughout all their component parts can save time and money. Obtaining IT services for the whole organization from a single supplier can mean that large discounts can be negotiated.

Chapter 13 on software quality discusses BS EN ISO 9001.

A client organization often lays down standards that have to be adopted by any contractor providing software for them. Sometimes organizations specify that suppliers of software have BS EN ISO 9001:2000 or TickIT accreditation. This will affect the way projects are conducted.

Select general life-cycle approach

- *Control systems* A real-time system will need to be implemented using an appropriate methodology. Real-time systems that employ concurrent processing may have to use techniques such as Petri nets.

> SSADM as a named methodology is now rarely used, but many of methods within it are still in wide use – sometimes under the general name of business system development (BSD) techniques.

- *Information systems* Similarly, an information system will need a methodology, such as SSADM or Information Engineering, that matches that type of environment. SSADM would be especially appropriate where the project employs a large number of development staff whose work will need to be coordinated: the method lays down in detail the activities and products needed at each step. Team members would therefore know exactly what is expected.

- *Availability of users* Where the software is for the general market rather than application and user specific, then a methodology which assumes that identifiable users exist who can be quizzed about their needs would have to be thought about with caution. Some business systems development methods assume an existing clerical system which can be analysed to yield the logical features of a new, computer-based, system. In these cases a marketing specialist may act as a surrogate user.

- *Specialized techniques* For example, expert system shells and logic-based programming languages have been invented to expedite the development of *knowledge-based systems*. Similarly, a number of specialized techniques and standard components are available to assist in the development of *graphics-based systems*.

- *Hardware environment* The environment in which the system is to operate could put constraints on the way it is to be implemented. The need for a fast response time or restricted computer memory might mean that only low-level programming languages can be used.

> OCL stands for Object Constraint Language.

- *Safety-critical systems* Where safety and reliability are essential, this might justify the additional expense of a formal specification using a notation such as OCL. Extremely critical systems could justify the cost of having independent teams develop parallel systems with the same functionality. The operational systems can then run concurrently with continuous cross-checking. This is known as *n-version programming*.

> The implications of prototyping and the incremental approach are explored later in the chapter.

- *Imprecise requirements* Uncertainties or a *novel hardware/software platform* mean that a prototyping approach should be considered. If the environment in which the system is to be implemented is a rapidly changing one, then serious consideration would need to be given to *incremental delivery*. If the users have *uncertain objectives* in connection with the project, then a *soft systems* approach might be desirable.

> ### EXERCISE 4.3
>
> What, in broad outline, would be the most suitable approach for each of the following?
>
> (a) a system which calculates the amount of a drug that should be administered to a patient who has a particular complaint;
>
> (b) a system to administer a student loans scheme;
>
> (c) a system to control trains in the Channel Tunnel.

4.4 Choice of process models

The word 'process' emphasizes the idea of a system *in action.* In order to achieve an outcome, the system will have to execute one or more activities: this is its process. This applies to the development of computer-based applications. A number of interrelated activities have to be undertaken to create a final product. These activities can be organized in different ways and we can call these *process models.*

The planner selects methods and specifies how they are to be applied. Not all parts of a methodology such as USDP or SSADM will be compulsory. Many student projects have the rather basic failing that at the planning stage they claim that, say, SSADM is to be used: in the event all that is produced are a few SSADM fragments such as a top-level data flow diagram and a preliminary logical data structure diagram. If this is all the particular project requires, it should be explicitly stated.

4.5 Structure versus speed of delivery

The principle behind structured methods is 'get it right first time'.

Although some 'object-oriented' specialists might object(!), we include the OO approach as a structured method – after all, we hope it is not unstructured. Structured methods consist of sets of steps and rules which, when applied, generate system products such as use case diagrams. Each of these products is carefully defined. Such methods are more time consuming and expensive than more intuitive approaches. The pay-off, it is hoped, is a less error prone and more maintainable final system. This balance of costs and benefits is more likely to be justified on a large project involving many developers and users. Because of the additional effort needed and their greater applicability to large and complex projects, these are often called *heavyweight* methods.

It might be thought that users would generally welcome the more professional approach that structured methods imply. However, customers for software are concerned with getting working applications delivered quickly and at less cost and often see structured methods as unnecessarily bureaucratic and slow. One response to this has been *rapid application development* (RAD) which puts the emphasis on quickly producing prototypes of the software for users to evaluate.

Joint Application Development by Jane Wood and Denise Silver, Wiley and Sons, 1995, is a useful introduction to JAD.

The RAD approach does not preclude the use of some elements of structured methods such as the drafting of logical data structure diagrams but also adopts tactics such as *joint application development* (JAD) workshops. In these workshops, developers and users work together intensively for, say, three to five days and identify and agree fully documented system requirements. Often these workshops are conducted away from the normal business and development environments in *clean rooms*, special conference rooms free from outside interruption and suitably furnished with whiteboards and other aids to communication. Advocates of JAD believe that these hot-house conditions can speed up communication and negotiation that might otherwise take several weeks or months.

Use of JAD does not mean that the project is not structured. The definition of the scope of the project, the initial research involving the interviewing of key personnel and the creation of preliminary data and process models would need to planned and executed before the JAD sessions were organized. The results of JAD sessions could be implemented using quite conventional methods.

Another way of speeding up delivery is simply to deliver less. This can be done by breaking a large development into a series of small increments, each of which delivers a small amount of useful functionality quickly.

Two competing pressures can be seen. One is to get the job done as quickly and cheaply as possible, and the other is to make sure that the final product has a robust structure which will be able to meet evolving needs. Later in this chapter and in Chapter 12 we will discuss the increasingly important topic of agile methods which focuses on lightweight processes. There is, however, a contrasting approach which is the attempt to create *model-driven architectures* (MDA). System development using MDA involves creating a platform-independent model (PIM) which specifies system functionality using UML diagrams supplemented by additional information recorded in the Object Constraint Language (OCL). A PIM is the logical structure that should apply regardless of the software and hardware environment in which the system is to implemented. This can be transformed into a platform-specific model (PSM) that takes account of a particular development and implementation environment. A PSM can then be transformed into executable code to implement a working system. The goal is that once a PIM had been created the creation of PSMs and executable code will be automated. At present, the automation of these transformation processes is still being developed.

4.6 The waterfall model

This is the 'classical' model of system development that is also known as the *one-shot* or *once-through* model. As can be seen from the example in Figure 4.2, there is a sequence of activities working from top to bottom. The diagram shows some arrows pointing upwards and backwards. This indicates that a later stage may reveal the need for some extra work at an earlier stage, but this should definitely be the exception rather than the rule. After all, the flow of a waterfall should be downwards, with the possibility of just a little splashing back. The limited scope for iteration is in fact one of the strengths of this

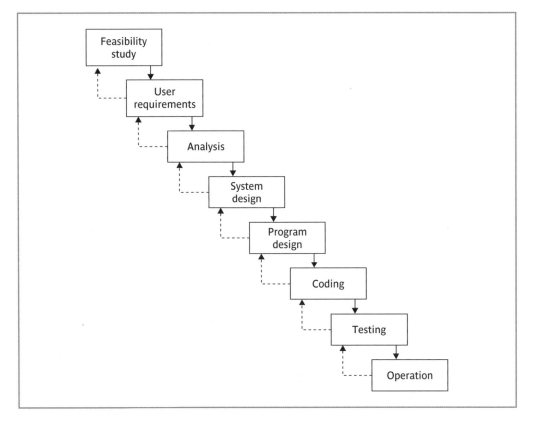

FIGURE 4.2 The waterfall model

The first description of this approach is said to be that of H. D. Bennington in 'Production of Large Computer Programs' in 1956. This was reprinted in 1983 in *Annals of the History of Computing* 5(4).

process model. With a large project you want to avoid reworking tasks previously thought to be completed. Having to reopen completed activities plays havoc with promised completion dates.

The waterfall approach may be favoured by some managements because it creates natural milestones at the end of each phase. At these points, managers can review project progress to see whether the business case for the project is still valid. This is sometimes referred to as the stage-gate model. As we will see, stage-gates are compatible with process models other than the waterfall, but higher management may have to accept that activities may have to be grouped in different ways with these alternative approaches.

Even though writers often advocate alternative models, there is nothing intrinsically wrong with the waterfall approach in the right place. It is the ideal for which the project manager strives. Where the requirements are well defined and the development methods are well understood, the waterfall approach allows project completion times to be forecast with some confidence, allowing the effective control of the project. However, where there is uncertainty about how a system is to be implemented, and unfortunately there very often is, a more flexible, iterative, approach is required.

The waterfall model can expanded into the **V-process model** which is further explored in Section 13.10 on testing. This expansion is done by expanding the testing process into different types of testing which check the executable code against the products of each of the activities in the project life cycle leading up to the coding. For example, the code may seem to execute correctly, but may be at variance with the expected design. This is explained further in Chapter 13.

4.7 The spiral model

> The original ideas behind the spiral model can be found in B. W. Boehm's 1988 paper 'A spiral model of software development and enhancement' in *IEEE Computer* 21(5).

It could be argued that this is another way of looking at the waterfall model. In the waterfall model, it is possible to escape at the end of any activity in the sequence. A feasibility study might decide that the implementation of a proposed system would be beneficial. The management therefore authorize work on the detailed analysis of user requirements. Some analysis, for instance the interviewing of users, might already have taken place at the feasibility stage, but a more thorough investigation is now launched. This could reveal that the costs of implementing the system would be higher than projected benefits and lead to a decision to abandon the project.

A greater level of detail is considered at each stage of the project and a greater degree of confidence about the probability of success for the project should be justified. This can be portrayed as a loop or a spiral where the system to be implemented is considered in more detail in each sweep. Each sweep terminates with an evaluation before the next iteration is embarked upon. Figure 4.3 illustrates how SSADM can be interpreted in such a way.

A key point here is that uncertainty about a project is usually because of a lack of knowledge about some aspect. We can spend money on activities at the start of the project that buy knowledge and reduce that uncertainty.

4.8 Software prototyping

This is one way in which we can buy knowledge and reduce uncertainty. A prototype is a working model of one or more aspects of the projected system. It is constructed and tested quickly and inexpensively in order to test out assumptions.

Prototypes can be classified as throw-away or evolutionary.

- *Throw-away prototypes* The prototype tests out some ideas and is then discarded when the true development of the operational system is commenced. The prototype could be developed using a different software or hardware environment. For example, a desktop application builder could be used to evolve an acceptable user interface. A procedural programming language is then used for the final system where machine-efficiency is important.

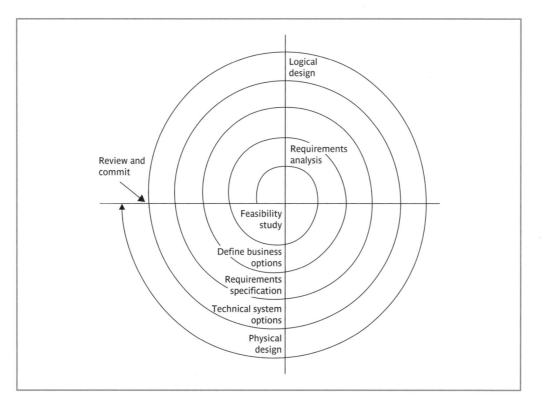

FIGURE 4.3 The application of the spiral model to SSADM version 4

- *Evolutionary prototypes* The prototype is developed and modified until it is finally in a state where it can become the operational system. In this case the standards that are used to develop the software have to be carefully considered.

Some of the reasons that have been put forward for prototyping follow.

- *Learning by doing* We can usually look back on a task and see where we have made mistakes.
- *Improved communication* Users do not get a feel for how the system is likely to work in practice from a specification.
- *Improved user involvement* The users can be more actively involved in design decisions.
  - *Clarification of partially known requirements* Where there is no existing system to mimic, users can often get a better idea of what might be useful to them by trying out prototypes.
  - *Demonstration of the consistency and completeness of a specification* Any mechanism that attempts to implement a specification on a computer is likely to uncover ambiguities and omissions. The humble spreadsheet can, for instance, check that calculations have been specified correctly.

> The most important justification for a prototype is the need to reduce uncertainty by conducting an experiment.

> Some may argue,
> however, that this is
> a very dangerous
> suggestion.

- *Reduced need for documentation* Because a working prototype can be examined there is less need for detailed documentation of requirements.

- *Reduced maintenance costs* If the user is unable to suggest modifications at the prototyping stage they are more likely to ask for changes to the operational system. This reduction of maintenance costs is the core of the financial case for prototypes.

- *Feature constraint* If an application-building tool is used, then the prototype will tend to have features that are easily implemented by that tool. A paper-based design might suggest features that are expensive to implement.

- *Production of expected results* The problem with creating test cases is generally not the creation of the test input but the accurate calculation of the expected results. A prototype can help here.

Software prototyping is not without its drawbacks and dangers, however.

- *Users can misunderstand the role of the prototype* For example, they might expect the prototype to have as stringent input validation or as fast a response as the operational system, although this was not intended.

- *Lack of project standards possible* Evolutionary prototyping could just be an excuse for a sloppy 'hack it out and see what happens' approach.

- *Lack of control* It can be difficult to control the prototyping cycle if the driving force is the users' propensity to try out new things.

- *Additional expense* Building and exercising a prototype will incur additional expenses. However, this should not be over-estimated as many analysis and design tasks have to be undertaken whatever the approach.

- *Machine efficiency* A system built through prototyping, while sensitive to the users' needs, might not be as efficient in machine terms as one developed using more conventional methods.

- *Close proximity of developers* Prototyping could mean that code developers have to be sited close to the users. One trend is for organizations in developed countries to transfer software development to developing countries with lower costs such as India. Prototyping might prevent this.

4.9 Other ways of categorizing prototypes

What is being learnt?

The most important reason for prototyping is a need to learn about an area of uncertainty. Thus it is essential to identify at the outset what is to be learnt from the prototype.

Computing students often realize that the software that they are to write as part of their final-year project could not safely be used by real users. They therefore call the software a 'prototype'. However, if it is a real prototype then they must:

- specify what they hope to learn from the prototype;
- plan how the prototype is to be evaluated;
- report on what has actually been learnt.

Prototypes can be used to find out about new development techniques, by using them in a pilot project. Alternatively, the development methods might be well known, but the nature of the application uncertain.

Different projects will have uncertainties at different stages. Prototypes can therefore be used at different stages. A prototype might be used, for instance, at the requirements gathering stage to pin down requirements that seem blurred and shifting. A prototype might, on the other hand, be used at the design stage to test out the users' ability to navigate through a sequence of input screens.

To what extent is the prototyping to be done?

It would be unusual for the whole of the application to be prototyped. The prototyping usually simulates only some aspects of the target application. For example there might be:

- *Mock-ups* As when copies of input screens are shown to the users on a terminal, but the screens cannot actually be used.

- *Simulated interaction* For example, the user can type in a request to access a record and the system will show the details of a record, but the details shown are always the same and no access is made to a database.

- Partial working model:
  - *Vertical* Some, but not all, features are prototyped fully.
  - *Horizontal* All features are prototyped but not in detail – perhaps there is not full validation of input.

What is being prototyped?

- *The human–computer interface* With business applications, business process requirements have usually been established at an early stage. Prototyping tends, therefore, to be confined to the nature of operator interaction. Here the physical vehicle for the prototype should be as similar as possible to the operational system.

- *The functionality of the system* Here the precise way the system should function internally is not known. For example, a computer model of some real-world phenomenon is being developed. The algorithms used might need to be repeatedly adjusted until they satisfactorily imitate real-world behaviour.

EXERCISE 4.4

At what stage of a system development project (for example, feasibility study, requirements analysis etc.) would a prototype be useful as a means of reducing the following uncertainties?

(a) There is a proposal that the senior managers of an insurance company have personal access to management information through an executive information system installed on personal computers located on their desks. Such a system would be costly to set up and there is some doubt about whether the managers would actually use the system.

(b) A computer system is to support sales office staff taking phone calls from members of the public enquiring about motor insurance and giving quotations over the phone.

(c) The insurance company is considering implementing the telephone sales system using the system development features supplied by Microsoft Access. They are not sure, at the moment, that it can provide the kind of interface that would be needed and are also concerned about the possible response times of a system developed using Microsoft Access.

Controlling changes during prototyping

A major problem with prototyping is controlling changes to the prototype following suggestions by the users. One approach has been to categorize changes as belonging to one of three types:

- *Cosmetic* (often about 35% of changes)
  These are simple changes to the layout of the screens or reports. They are:
  (a) implemented;
  (b) recorded.

  | Inspections are discussed in Chapter 13. |

- *Local* (often about 60% of changes)
  These change the way that a screen or report is processed but do not affect other parts of the system. They are:
  (a) implemented;
  (b) recorded;
  (c) backed-up so that they can be removed at a later stage if necessary;
  (d) inspected retrospectively.

- *Global* (about 5% of changes)
  These are changes that affect more than one part of the processing. All changes here have to be the subject of a design review before they can be implemented.

4.10 Incremental delivery

This approach breaks the application down into small components which are then implemented and delivered in sequence. Each component delivered must give some benefit to the user. Figure 4.4 gives a general idea of the approach.

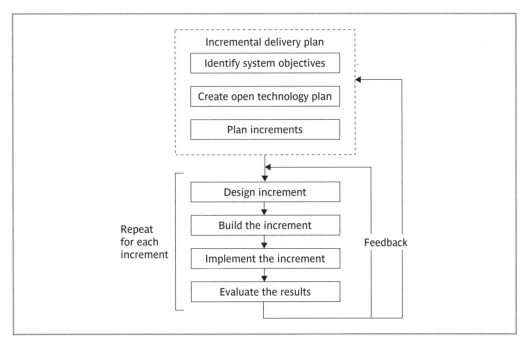

FIGURE 4.4 Intentional incremental delivery

Time-boxing is often associated with an incremental approach. Here the scope of deliverables for an increment is rigidly constrained by an agreed deadline. This deadline has to be met, even at the expense of dropping some of the planned functionality. Omitted features can be transferred to later increments.

Advantages of this approach

These are some of the justifications given for the approach.

Tom Gilb, whose *Principles of Software Engineering Management* was published by Addison-Wesley in 1988, is a prominent advocate of this approach.

- The feedback from early increments improves the later stages.
- The possibility of changes in requirements is reduced because of the shorter time span between the design of a component and its delivery.
- Users get benefits earlier than with a conventional approach.
- Early delivery of some useful components improves cash flow, because you get some return on investment early on.
- Smaller sub-projects are easier to control and manage.
- *Gold-plating*, that is, the requesting of features that are unnecessary and not in fact used, is less as users know that if a feature is not in the current increment then it can be included in the next.
- The project can be temporarily abandoned if more urgent work emerges.

■ Job satisfaction is increased for developers who see their labours bearing fruit at regular, short, intervals.

Disadvantages

On the other hand, these disadvantages have been put forward.

■ Later increments might require modifications to earlier increments. This is known as *software breakage.*

■ Software developers may be more productive working on one large system than on a series of smaller ones.

This quotation is from Grady Booch (1996) *Object Solutions: Managing the Object Oriented Project*, Addison-Wesley.

■ Grady Booch, an authority on OO, suggests that with what he calls 'requirements driven' projects (which equate to incremental delivery) *'Conceptual integrity sometimes suffers because there is little motivation to deal with scalability, extensibility, portability or reusability beyond what any vague requirements might imply.'* Booch also suggests there could be a tendency towards a large number of discrete functions with little common infrastructure.

The process of planning the increments of a project as described by Gilb has similarities with strategic planning described in Chapter 2.

The incremental delivery plan

The nature and order of each increment to be delivered to the users have to be planned at the outset.

This process is similar to strategic planning but at a more detailed level. Attention is given to increments of a user application rather than whole applications. The elements of the incremental plan are the *system objectives, incremental plan* and the *open technology plan.*

System objectives

Recall that earlier we suggested that project planners ideally want well-defined objectives, but as much freedom as possible about how these are to be met. These overall objectives can be expanded into more specific functional goals and quality goals.

Functional goals will include:

■ objectives it is intended to achieve;

■ jobs the system is to do;

■ computer/non-computer functions to achieve them.

Chapter 13 discusses software quality characteristics.

In addition, measurable quality characteristics should be defined, such as reliability, response and security. If this is done properly these overarching quality requirements can go some way to meeting the concerns, expressed by Grady Booch, that these might get lost with the concentration on the requirements at increment level. It also reflects Tom Gilb's concern that system developers always keep sight of the objectives that they are trying to achieve on behalf of their clients. In the changing environment of an application individual requirements could change over the course of the project, but the objectives should not.

Open technology plan

If the system is to be able to cope with new components being continually added then it needs to be extendible, portable and maintainable.

As a minimum this will require the use of:

- a standard high-level language;
- a standard operating system;
- small modules;
- variable parameters, for example items such as the names of an organization and its departments, charge rates and so on are held in a parameter file that can be amended without programmer intervention;
- a standard database management system.

These are all things that might be expected as a matter of course in a modern software development environment.

Although Gilb does not suggest this, following Booch's hints it would be desirable to draw up an initial logical data model or object model for the whole system. It is difficult to see how the next stage of planning the scope and order of each increment could be done without this foundation.

Incremental plan

Having defined the overall objectives and an open technology plan, the next stage is to plan the increments using the following guidelines:

- Steps typically should consist of 1–5% of the total project.
    - Non-computer steps should be included.
    - An increment should, ideally, not exceed one month and should not, at worst, take more than three months.

> A non-computer step could be something like a streamlined clerical procedure.

    - Each increment should deliver some benefit to the user.
    - Some increments will be physically dependent on others.
    - In other cases value-to-cost ratios may be used to decide priorities (see below).

A new system might be replacing an old computer system and the first increments could use parts of the old system. For example, the data for the database of the new system could initially be obtained from the old system's standing files.

Which steps should be first? Some steps will be prerequisites because of physical dependencies but others can be in any order. Value-to-cost ratios (see Table 4.1) can be used to establish the order in which increments are to be developed. The customer is asked to rate the value of each increment with a score in the range 1–10. The developers also rate the cost of developing each of the increments with a score in the range 0–10. This might seem rather crude, but people are often unwilling to be more precise. Dividing the value rating by the cost rating generates a ratio which indicates the relative 'value for money' of each increment.

A zero cost would mean that the change can be implemented without software development – some costs might be incurred by users in changing procedures.

The value to cost ratio = V/C where V is a score 1–10 representing value to customer and C is a score 0–10 representing cost.

Step	Value	Cost	Ratio	Rank
Profit reports	9	1	9	(2nd)
Online database	1	9	0.11	(6th)
Ad hoc enquiry	5	5	1	(4th)
Production sequence plans	2	8	0.25	(5th)
Purchasing profit factors	9	4	2.25	(3rd)
Clerical procedures	0	7	0	(7th)
Profit-based pay for managers	9	0	∞	(1st)

TABLE 4.1 Ranking by value-to-cost ratio

An incremental example

Tom Gilb describes a project where a software supplier negotiated a fixed-price contract with a three-month delivery time with the Swedish government to supply a system to support map-making. It later became apparent that the original estimate of effort upon which the bid was based was probably about half the real effort.

The project was replanned and divided into ten increments, each supplying something of use to the customer. The final increments were not available until three months after the contract's delivery date. The customer was not in fact unhappy about this as the most important parts of the application had actually been delivered early.

4.11 Agile methods

Agile methods are designed to overcome the disadvantages we have noted with heavyweight implementation methodologies. There are various agile approaches, including:

- Crystal technologies
- Atern (formerly DSDM)
- Feature-driven development
- Scrum
- Extreme Programming (XP)

The Agile Manifesto is available at http://www. agilealliance.org

Some of the leading proponents of these approaches came together in 2001 to issue an Agile Manifesto which stated that their various methods shared four core values:

- individuals and interaction over processes and tools;
- working together over comprehensive documentation;
- customer collaboration over contract negotiation;
- responding to change over following a plan.

See S. Nerur, R. Mahapatra and G. Mangalara (2005) 'Challenges of migrating to agile methodologies' *Communications of the ACM* 48(5) 73–8.

There is an argument that the agile approach would represent a revolutionary step for many organizations. Sridhar Nerur and colleagues have written, for example, '*Neither culture nor the mindsets of people can easily be changed which makes the move to agile methodologies all the more formidable for many organizations*'.

An alternative argument is that that agile practices represent simply a development from good practices that have been evolving for many years. As Hikka Merisalo-Rananen and colleagues suggest '. . . *XP canonizes, and to a certain extent formalizes, the good practices used by these exceptional individuals and teams, which is fine.*'

See H. Merisalo-Rantanen, T. Tuure and M. Rossi (2005) 'Is extreme programming just old wine in new bottles?' *Journal of Database Management* 16(4) 41–61.

In the remainder of this chapter we will examine two agile approaches: first, Atern, as DSDM is now called, which illustrates how agile practices are based on elements discussed earlier, such as iterations and increments. We will also look at Extreme Programming as perhaps the most well known of the remaining practice sets. Agile concepts are very closely tied to ideas about effective team communication and working, which are the main concerns of Chapter 12 where we will be looking at Scrum from this point of view.

4.12 Atern/Dynamic Systems Development Method

In the United Kingdom, SSADM (Structured Systems Analysis and Design Method) has until recently been a predominant methodology. In no small part, this has been because of sponsorship by the United Kingdom government. More recently, however, it has lost some favour, partly because it has been perceived as overly bureaucratic and prescriptive. In contrast, there has been an increased interest in the iterative and incremental approaches we have outlined above. As a consequence, a consortium has developed guidelines for the use of such techniques and packaged the overall approach as the Dynamic Systems Development Method (DSDM). This has been re-badged as Atern. It is possible to attend courses on the method and to become an accredited Atern practitioner.

Eight core Atern principles have been enunciated.

1 *Focus on business need.* Every decision in the development process should be taken with a view to best satisfying business needs. Effectively this is emphasizing the need to avoid means–end inversion that we described in Section 4.1, that is, focusing on the detail of a procedure to the detriment of satisfactory project deliverables.

2 *Deliver on time.* Time-boxing is applied. Every deadline will see the delivery of valuable products, even if some less valuable ones are held over. This is better than delivery dates being pushed back until a delivery of all scheduled products can made.

3 *Collaborate.* A one-team culture should be promoted, where user representatives are integrated into the delivery team.

4 *Never compromise quality.* Realistic quality targets are set early in the project. A process of continuously testing developing products starting as soon as possible is adopted.

5 *Develop iteratively.* The prototyping approach described in Section 4.8 would be example of how this might be done.

6 *Build incrementally from firm foundations.* The incremental delivery approach as described in Section 4.10 is embraced.

> JAD, Joint
> Application
> Development,
> was discussed in
> Section 4.5.

7 *Communicate continuously.* In the case of users this could, for example, be done via workshops and the demonstration of prototypes.

8 *Demonstrate control.* Atern methodology has a range of plans and reports that can be used to communicate project intentions and outcomes to project sponsors and other management stakeholders.

Figure 4.5 outlines the general approach. The main life-cycle phases are shown:

- *Feasibility/foundation.* Among the activities undertaken here is derivation of a business case of the sort discussed in Chapter 2 and general outlines of the proposed architecture of the system to be developed.
- *Exploration cycle.* This investigates the business requirements. These requirements are translated into a viable design for the application. This could be an iterative process that could involve the creation of exploratory prototypes. A large project could be decomposed into smaller increments to assist the design process.

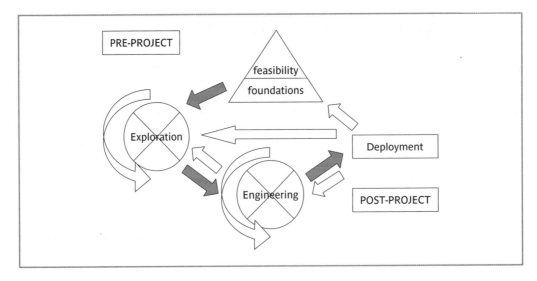

FIGURE 4.5 Atern process model

- *Engineering cycle.* This takes the design generated in the exploration cycle and converts it into usable components of the final system that will be used operationally. Once again this could be done using incremental and evolutionary techniques.
- *Deployment.* This gets the application created in the engineering cycle into actual operational use.

Not only can there be iterations within the exploration and engineering cycles, but an increment could involve requirements investigation followed by the building of the functionality.

Atern encourages the use of time-boxes. It is suggested that these should typically be between two and six weeks in order to make participants focus on real needs. It will be recalled that in order to meet the deadline imposed by a time-box, the implementation of less important features may be held over to later increments (or even dropped altogether). The relative importance of requirements can be categorized using the 'MoSCoW' classification:

> Time-boxes were discussed in Section 4.10 on incremental delivery.

- *Must have*: that is, essential features.
- *Should have*: these would probably be mandatory if you were using a conventional development approach – but the system can operate without them.
- *Could have*: these requirements can be delayed with some inconvenience.
- *Won't have*: these features are wanted, but their delay to a later increment is readily accepted.

The possibility of requirements being reallocated to different increments means that project plans will need to be constantly updated if the project is to be successfully controlled.

4.13 Extreme programming (XP)

The primary source of information on XP is Kent Beck's *Extreme programming explained: embrace change,* first published in 1999 and updated in 2004. The description here is based on the first edition, with some comments where the ideas have been developed further in the second.

> See Kent Beck (with Cynthia Andreas), *Extreme Programming Explained: Embrace Change*, Addison-Wesley, 1st edition 1999, 2nd edition 2004. 'Extreme programming' is sometimes shown with a capital 'X' i.e. 'eXtreme Programming'.

The ideas were largely developed on the C3 payroll development project at Chrysler. The approach is called 'extreme programming' because, according to Beck, '*XP takes commonsense principles to extreme levels*'. Four core values are presented as the foundations of XP.

1 **Communication and feedback.** It is argued that the best method of communication is face-to-face communication. Also, the best way of communicating to the users the nature of the software under production is to provide them with frequent working increments. Formal documentation is avoided.

2 **Simplicity.** The simplest design that implements the users' requirements should always be adopted. Effort should not be spent trying to cater for future possible needs – which in any case might never actually materialize.

3 **Responsibility.** The developers are the ones who are ultimately responsible for the quality of the software – not, for example, some system testing or quality control group.

4 **Courage.** This is the courage to throw away work in which you have already invested a lot of effort, and to start with a fresh design if that is what is called for. It is also the courage to try out new ideas – after all, if they do not work out, they can always be scrapped. Beck argues that this attitude is more likely to lead to better solutions.

Among the *core practices* of XP are the following.

The planning exercise

> In the second edition of his book, Beck favours iterations of one week on the grounds that people tend to work naturally in weekly cycles.

Previously, when we talked about 'increments' we meant components of the system that users could actually use. XP refers to these as *releases*. Within these releases code is developed in *iterations*, periods of one to four weeks' duration during which specific features of the software are created. Note that these are not usually 'iterations' in the sense that they are new, improved, versions of the same feature – although this is a possibility. The planning game is the process whereby the features to be incorporated in the next release are negotiated. Each of the features is documented in a short textual description called a *story* that is written on a card. A process similar to value-to-cost ratio analysis discussed earlier in Section 4.10 or Atern's MoSCoW rating is carried out in order to give priorities to the features. At the time of the next code release, any features that have not been completed will be held over – that is, time-boxing is employed.

Small releases

The time between releases of functionality to users should be as short as possible. Beck suggests that releases should ideally take a month or two. This is compatible with Tom Gilb's recommendation of a month as the ideal time for an increment, with a maximum of three months.

Metaphor

The system to be built will be software code that reflects things that exist and happen in the real world. A payroll application will calculate and record payments to employees. The terms used to describe the corresponding software elements should, as far as possible, reflect real-world terminology – at a very basic level this would mean using meaningful names for variables and procedures such as 'hourly_rate' and 'calculate_gross_pay'. Beck suggests that what he calls the use of metaphor can do the job that 'system architecture' does on conventional projects. In this context 'architecture' refers to the use of system models such as class and collaboration diagrams to describe the system. The astute reader might point out that the use of the term 'architecture' is itself a metaphor.

Simple design

This is the practical implementation of the value of simplicity that was described above.

Testing

Testing is done at the same time as coding. The test inputs and expected results should be scripted so that the testing can be done using automated testing tools. These test cases can then be accumulated so that they can be used for regression testing to ensure that later developments do not insert errors into existing working code. This idea can be extended so that the tests and expected results are actually created before the code is created. Working out what tests are needed to check that a function is correct can itself help to clarify requirements. Two types of testing are needed: unit testing which focuses on the code a developer has just written, and function testing which is user-oriented and checks the correctness of a particular feature and which may involve several code units.

Refactoring

A threat to the target of striving to have always the simplest design is that over time, as modifications are made to code, the structure tends to become more spaghetti-like. The answer to this is to have the courage to resist the temptation to make changes that affect as little of the code as possible and be prepared to rewrite whole sections of code if this will keep the code structured. The repository of past test cases – see the section immediately above – can be executed to ensure that the refactoring has not introduced bugs into the application.

Pair programming

All software code is written by pairs of developers, one actually doing the typing and the other observing, discussing and making comments and suggestions about what the other is doing. At intervals, the developers can swap roles. The ideal is that you are constantly changing partners so that you get to know about a wide range of features that are under development. It follows from this that office environments need to be designed carefully to allow this type of working, and that developers will generally need to keep the same office hours.

Helen Sharp of the Open University has studied XP in practice. One of her observations is that the social nature of the development process encourages a rhythm of group meetings, pair working and daily 'builds' when new code is integrated that helps to give the project momentum. Interestingly, this rhythm of activity and review acting as a heart-beat of the project has also been noted in a successful dispersed project.

Collective ownership

This is really the corollary of pair programming. The team as a whole take collective responsibility for the code in the system. A unit of code does not 'belong' to just one programmer who is the only one who can modify it.

Continuous integration

This is another aspect of testing practice. As changes are made to software units, integrated tests are run regularly – at least once a day – to ensure that all the components work together correctly.

Forty-hour weeks

Chapter 11 discusses, among other issues, the question of stress. It points out that working excessive hours (in some cases 60 hours or more a week) can lead to ill-health and be generally counterproductive. The principle is that normally developers should not work more than 40 hours a week. It is realistic to accept that sometimes there is a need for overtime work to deal with a particular problem – but in this case overtime should not be worked for two weeks in a row. Interestingly, in some case studies of the application of XP, the 40-hour rule was the only one not adhered to.

On-site customers

Fast and effective communication with the users is achieved by having a user domain expert on-site with the developers.

Coding standards

If code is genuinely to be shared, then there must be common, accepted, coding standards to support the understanding and ease of modification of the code.

Limitations of XP

The successful use of XP is based on certain conditions. If these do not exist, then its practice could be difficult. These conditions include the following.

- There must be easy access to users, or at least a customer representative who is a domain expert. This may be difficult where developers and users belong to different organizations.
- Development staff need to be physically located in the same office.
- As users find out about how the system will work only by being presented with working versions of the code, there may be communication problems if the application does not have a visual interface.
- For work to be sequenced into small iterations of work, it must be possible to break the system functionality into relatively small and self-contained components.

- Large, complex systems may initially need significant architectural effort. This might preclude the use of XP.

XP does also have some intrinsic potential problems – particularly with regard to its reliance on tacit expertise and knowledge as opposed to externalized knowledge in the shape of documentation.

- There is a reliance on high-quality developers which makes software development vulnerable if staff turnover is significant.

- Even where staff retention is good, once an application has been developed and implemented, the tacit, personal, knowledge of the system may decay. This might make it difficult, for example, for maintenance staff without documentation to identify which bits of the code to modify to implement a change in requirements.

- Having a repository of comprehensive and accurate test data and expected results may not be as helpful as might be expected if the rationale for particular test cases is not documented. For example, where a change is made to the code, how do you know which test cases need to be changed?

- Some software development environments have focused on encouraging code reuse as a means of improving software development productivity. Such a policy would seem to be incompatible with XP.

4.14 Managing iterative processes

This discussion of agile methods might be confusing as it seems to turn many of our previous planning concepts on their head.

Approaches like XP correctly emphasize the importance of communication and of removing artificial barriers to development productivity. XP to many might seem to be simply a 'licence to hack'. However, a more detailed examination of the techniques of XP shows that many (such as pair programming and installation standards) are conscious techniques to counter the excesses of hacking and to ensure that good maintainable code is written.

Booch suggests that there are two levels of development: the macro process and the micro process. The macro process is closely related to the waterfall process model. At this level, a range of activities carried out by a variety of specialist groups has to be coordinated. We need to have some dates when we know that major activities will be finished so that we know when we will need to bring in staff to work on subsequent activities. Within this macro process there will be micro process activities which might involve iterative working. Systems testing has always been one. Figure 4.6 illustrates how a sequential macro process can be imposed on a number of iterative sub-processes. With iterative micro processes, the use of time-boxes is needed to control at the macro level.

There are cases where the macro process itself can be iterative. It might be that a prototype for a complex technical system is produced in two or three successive versions, each taking several months to create and evaluate. In these circumstances, each iteration should be treated as a project in its own right.

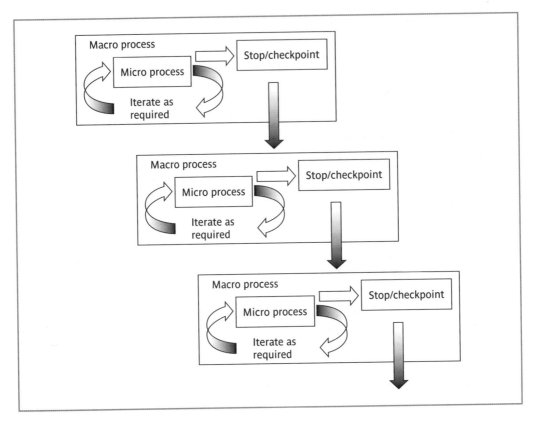

FIGURE 4.6 A macro process containing three iterative micro processes

D. Karlström and
P. Runeson (2005).
'Combining agile
methods with
stage-gate project
management' *IEEE
Software* May/June.

The packaging of micro processes within larger macro processes means that it is possible for agile projects using XP practices to exist within a more traditional stage-gate project environment (see Section 4.6) which has formal milestones where the business case for the project is reviewed. Agile projects might even contribute helpfully to this process as their progress is more visible.

4.15 Selecting the most appropriate process model

*C*onstruction of an application can be distinguished from its *installation*. It is possible to use different approaches for these two stages. For example, an application could be constructed using a waterfall or one-shot strategy but then be released to its users in increments. The only combinations of construction and installation strategies that are not feasible are the evolutionary installation with any construction approach other than evolutionary.

Where uncertainty is high then an evolutionary approach is to be favoured. An example of uncertainty would be where the users' requirements are not clearly defined.

Where the requirements are relatively certain but there are many complexities, as with a large embedded system needing a large amount of code, then an incremental approach is favoured. Where deadlines are tight, then either an evolutionary or an incremental approach is favoured over a one-shot strategy, as both tactics should allow at least something to be delivered at the deadline, even if it is not all that was originally promised. Students about to plan final-year projects would do well to note this.

4.16 Conclusion

This chapter has stressed the need to examine each project carefully to see if it has characteristics which suggest a particular approach or process model. These characteristics might suggest the addition of specific activities to the project plan.

The classic waterfall process model, which attempts to minimize iteration, should lead to projects that are easy to control. Unfortunately, many projects do not lend themselves to this structure. Prototyping may be able to reduce project uncertainties by allowing knowledge to be bought through experimentation. The incremental approach encourages the execution of a series of small, manageable, 'mini-projects' but does have some costs.

4.17 Further exercises

1 A building society has a long history of implementing computer-based information systems to support the work of its branches. It uses a proprietary structured systems analysis and design method. It has been decided to create a computer model of the property market. This would attempt, for example, to calculate the effect of changes of interest rates on house values. There is some concern that the usual methodology used for IS development would not be appropriate for the new project.
    (a) Why might there be this concern and what alternative approaches should be considered?
    (b) Outline a plan for the development of the system which illustrates the application of your preferred methodology for this project.

2 A software package is to be designed and built to assist in software cost estimation. It will input certain parameters and produce initial cost estimates to be used at bidding time.
    (a) It has been suggested that a software prototype would be of value in these circumstances. Explain why this might be.
    (b) Discuss how such prototyping could be controlled to ensure that it is conducted in an orderly and effective way and within a specified time span.

3 An invoicing system is to have the following transactions: amend invoice, produce invoice, produce monthly statements, record cash payment, clear paid invoices from database, create customer records, delete customer.
    (a) What physical dependencies govern the order in which these transactions are implemented?

(b) How could the system be broken down into increments which would be of some value to the users (hint – think about the problems of taking existing details onto a database when a system is first implemented)?

4 In Section 4.9 the need was stressed of defining what is to be learnt from a prototype and the way that it will be evaluated to obtain the new knowledge. Outline the learning outcomes and evaluation for the following.

(a) A final-year degree student is to build an application that will act as a 'suggestions box' in a factory. The application will allow employees to make suggestions about process improvements, and will track the subsequent progress of the suggestion as it is evaluated. The student wants to use a web-based front-end with a conventional database. The student has not previously developed any applications using this mix of technologies.

(b) An engineering company has to maintain a large number of different types of document relating to current and previous projects. It has decided to evaluate the use of a computer-based document retrieval system and wishes to try it out on a trial basis.

(c) A business which specializes in 'e-solutions', that is, the development of business applications that exploit the World Wide Web, has been approached by the computing school of a local university. The school is investigating setting up a special website for its former students. The website's core will be information about job and training opportunities and it is hoped that this will generate income through advertising. It is agreed that some kind of pilot to evaluate the scheme is needed.

5 In a college environment, an intranet for students that holds information about courses, such as lecture programmes, reading lists and assignment briefs, is often set up. As a 'real' exercise, plan, organize and carry out a JAD session to design (or improve the design of) an intranet facilty.

This will require:

- preliminary interviews with representative key stakeholders (for example, staff who might be supplying information for the intranet);
- creation of documents for use in the JAD proceedings;
- recording of the JAD proceedings;
- creating a report which will present the findings of the JAD session.

CHAPTER 5

Software effort estimation

❖ OBJECTIVES

When you have completed this chapter you will be able to:

- ❖ avoid the dangers of unrealistic estimates;
- ❖ understand the range of estimating methods that can be used;
- ❖ estimate projects using a bottom-up approach;

- ❖ estimate the effort needed to implement software using a procedural programming language;
- ❖ count the function points for a system;
- ❖ understand the COCOMO II approach to developing effort models.

5.1 Introduction

A successful project is one delivered '*on time, within budget and with the required quality*'. This implies that targets are set which the project manager then tries to meet. This assumes that the targets are reasonable – no account is taken of the possibility of project managers achieving record levels of productivity from their teams, but still not meeting a deadline because of incorrect initial estimates. Realistic estimates are therefore crucial.

A project manager like Amanda has to produce estimates of *effort*, which affect costs, and of activity *durations*, which affect the delivery time. These could be different, as in the case where two testers work on the same task for the same five days.

> In Chapter 1, the special characteristics of software identified by Brooks i.e. complexity, conformity, changeability and invisibility, were discussed.

Some of the difficulties of estimating arise from the complexity and invisibility of software. Also, the intensely human activities which make up system development cannot be treated in a purely mechanistic way. Other difficulties include:

- *Subjective nature of estimating* For example, some research shows that people tend to underestimate the difficulty of small tasks and over-estimate that of large ones.

> The possibility of the different groups with stakes in a project having different and possibly conflicting objectives was discussed in Chapter 1.

- *Political implications* Different groups within an organization have different objectives. The IOE information systems development managers may, for example, want to generate work and will press estimators to reduce cost estimates to encourage higher management to approve projects. As Amanda is responsible for the development of the annual maintenance contracts subsystem, she will want to ensure that the project is within budget and timescale, otherwise this will reflect badly on herself. She might therefore try to increase the estimates to create a 'comfort zone'. To avoid these 'political' influences, one suggestion is that estimates be produced by a specialist estimating group, independent of the users and the project team. Not all agree with this, as developers will be more committed to targets they themselves have set.

- *Changing technology* Where technologies change rapidly, it is difficult to use the experience of previous projects on new ones.

- *Lack of homogeneity of project experience* Even where technologies have not changed, knowledge about typical task durations may not be easily transferred from one project to another because of other differences between projects.

> The ISO 12207 standard, touched upon in Chapter 1, is an attempt to address this problem by standardizing on some of the terms used.

It would be very difficult on the basis of this information to advise a project manager about what sort of productivity to expect, or about the probable distribution of effort between the phases of design, coding and testing that could be expected from a new project.

Using existing project data for estimating is also difficult because of uncertainties in the way that various terms can be interpreted. For example, what exactly is meant by the term 'testing'? Does it cover the activities of the software developer when debugging code?

EXERCISE 5.1

Calculate the productivity (i.e. SLOC per work month) of each of the projects in Table 5.1 and also for the organization as a whole. If the project leaders for projects a and d had correctly estimated the source number of lines of code (SLOC) and then used the average productivity of the organization to calculate the effort needed to complete the projects, how far out would their estimates have been from the actual effort?

The figures are taken from B. A. Kitchenham and N. R. Taylor (1985) 'Software project development cost estimation' *Journal of Systems and Software (5)*. The abbreviation SLOC stands for 'source lines of code'. SLOC is one way of indicating the size of a system.

Project	Design wm	Design (%)	Coding wm	Coding (%)	Testing wm	Testing (%)	Total wm	Total SLOC
a	3.9	(23)	5.3	(32)	7.4	(44)	16.7	6050
b	2.7	(12)	13.4	(59)	6.5	(26)	22.6	8363
c	3.5	(11)	26.8	(83)	1.9	(6)	32.2	13334
d	0.8	(21)	2.4	(62)	0.7	(18)	3.9	5942
e	1.8	(10)	7.7	(44)	7.8	(45)	17.3	3315
f	19.0	(28)	29.7	(44)	19.0	(28)	67.7	38988
g	2.1	(21)	7.4	(74)	0.5	(5)	10.1	38614
h	1.3	(7)	12.7	(66)	5.3	(27)	19.3	12762
i	8.5	(14)	22.7	(38)	28.2	(47)	59.5	26500

TABLE 5.1 Some project data – effort in work months (as percentage of total effort in brackets)

5.2 Where are estimates done?

Estimates are carried out at various stages of a software project for a variety of reasons.

Chapter 2 discussed project portfolio management in some detail.

- *Strategic planning* Project portfolio management involves estimating the costs and benefits of new applications in order to allocate priorities. Such estimates may also influence the scale of development staff recruitment.

- *Feasibility study* This confirms that the benefits of the potential system will justify the costs.

- *System specification* Most system development methodologies usefully distinguish between the definition of the users' requirements and the design which shows how those requirements are to be fulfilled. The effort needed to implement different design proposals will need to be estimated. Estimates at the design stage will also confirm that the feasibility study is still valid.

- *Evaluation of suppliers' proposals* In the case of the IOE annual maintenance contracts subsystem, for example, IOE might consider putting development out to tender. Potential contractors would scrutinize the system specification and produce estimates as the basis of their bids. Amanda might still produce her own estimates so that IOE could question a proposal which seems too low in order to ensure that the proposer has properly understood the requirements. The cost of bids could also be compared to in-house development.

<table>
<tr><td>

The estimate at this stage cannot be based only on the user requirement: some kind of technical plan is also needed – see Chapter 4.

</td></tr>
</table>

- *Project planning* As the planning and implementation of the project becomes more detailed, more estimates of smaller work components will be made. These will confirm earlier broad-brush estimates, and will support more detailed planning, especially staff allocations.

As the project proceeds, so the accuracy of the estimates should improve as knowledge about the project increases. At the beginning of the project the user requirement is of paramount importance and premature consideration of the possible physical implementation is discouraged. However, in order to produce an estimate, there will need to be speculation about the eventual shape of the application.

To set estimating into the context of the Step Wise framework (Figure 5.1) presented in Chapter 3, re-estimating could take place at almost any step, but specific provision is

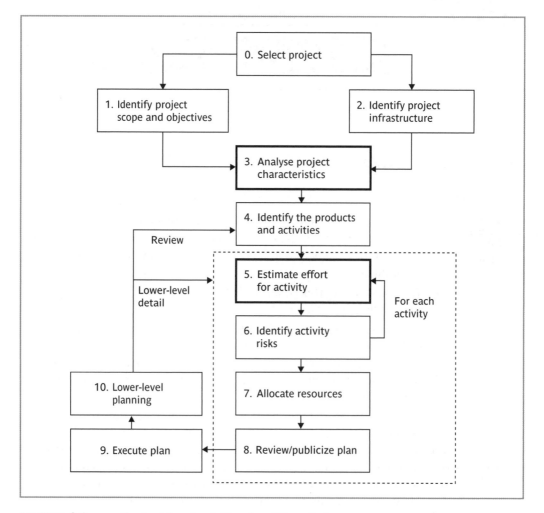

FIGURE 5.1 Software estimation takes place in Steps 3 and 5 in particular

made for the production of a relatively high-level estimate at Step 3, 'Analyse project characteristics', and for each individual activity in Step 5. As Steps 5–8 are repeated at progressively lower levels, so estimates will be done at a finer degree of detail. As we will see later in this chapter, different methods of estimating are needed at these different planning steps.

5.3 Problems with over- and under-estimates

A project leader such as Amanda will need to be aware that an over-estimate may cause the project to take longer than it would otherwise. This can be explained by the application of two 'laws'.

Parkinson's law was originally expounded in C. Northcote Parkinson's tongue-in-cheek book *Parkinson's Law*, John Murray, 1957. Brooks' law comes from *The Mythical Man-month* which has been referred to already.

- *Parkinson's Law* 'Work expands to fill the time available', that is, given an easy target staff will work less hard.

- *Brooks' Law* The effort of implementing a project will go up disproportionately with the number of staff assigned to the project. As the project team grows in size, so will the effort that has to go into management, coordination and communication. This has given rise, in extreme cases, to the notion of Brooks' Law: '*putting more people on a late job makes it later*'. If there is an over-estimate of the effort required, this could lead to more staff being allocated than needed and managerial overheads being increased.

See, for example, T. K. Hamid and S. E. Madnick (1986) 'Impact of schedule estimation on software project behaviour' *IEEE Software* July 3(4) 70–5.

Some have suggested that while the under-estimated project might not be completed on time or to cost, it might still be implemented in a shorter time than a project with a more generous estimate.

The danger with the under-estimate is the effect on quality. Staff, particularly those with less experience, could respond to pressing deadlines by producing work that is substandard. This may be seen as a manifestation of Weinberg's zeroth law of reliability: '*if a system does not have to be reliable, it can meet any other objective*'. Substandard work might only become visible at the later, testing, phases of a project which are particularly difficult to control and where extensive rework can easily delay project completion.

EXERCISE 5.2

How do agile methods such as XP – see Chapter 4 – attempt to address the problems with estimates described above?

Research has found that motivation and morale are enhanced where targets are achievable. If, over time, staff become aware that the targets set are unattainable and that projects routinely miss targets, motivation is reduced. People like to think of themselves as

Barry Boehm devised the COCOMO estimating models which are described later in this chapter.

winners and there is a general tendency to put success down to our own efforts and blame failure on the organization.

An estimate is not really a prediction, it is a *management goal*. Barry Boehm has suggested that if a software development cost is within 20% of the estimated cost for the job then a good manager can turn it into a self-fulfilling prophecy. A project leader like Amanda will work hard to make the actual performance conform to the estimate.

5.4 The basis for software estimating

The need for historical data

Details of the work of the International Software Benchmarking Standards Group can be found at http://isbsg.org

Most estimating methods need information about past projects. However, care is needed when applying past performance to new projects because of possible differences in factors such as programming languages and the experience of staff. If past project data is lacking, externally maintained datasets of project performance data can be accessed. One well-known international database is that maintained by the International Software Benchmarking Standards Group (ISBSG), which currently contains data from 4800 projects.

Measure of work

R. E. Park has devised a standard for counting source statements that has been widely adopted – see *Software Size Measurement: A Framework for Counting Source Statements*, Software Engineering Institute, 1992.

Direct calculation of costs or time is difficult at the early planning stage. The time to complete software will depend on the individual capability and experience of staff not yet identified. Implementation time and costs will also depend on the particular technologies selected. The usual practice is therefore to start by expressing work size independently of effort using a measure such as source lines of code (SLOC), sometimes expressed as KLOC (thousands of lines of code). The estimation of SLOC is of course itself problematic and may not be relevant when parameter-driven application-builders are used. Alternative size measures have been proposed, such as function points which are explained in more detail later in this chapter. It can also be argued that SLOC counts do not take account of the complexity of the code to be produced.

5.5 Software effort estimation techniques

See B. W. Boehm (1981) *Software Engineering Economics*, Prentice-Hall.

Barry Boehm, in his classic work on software effort models, identified the main ways of deriving estimates of software development effort as:

- *algorithmic models*, which use 'effort drivers' representing characteristics of the target system and the implementation environment to predict effort;

- *expert judgement*, based on the advice of knowledgeable staff;
- *analogy*, where a similar, completed, project is identified and its actual effort is used as the basis of the estimate;
- *Parkinson*, where the staff effort available to do a project becomes the 'estimate';
- *price to win*, where the 'estimate' is a figure that seems sufficiently low to win a contract;
- *top-down*, where an overall estimate for the whole project is broken down into the effort required for component tasks;
- *bottom-up*, where component tasks are identified and sized and these individual estimates are aggregated.

> This is also the principle behind the concept of time-boxing discussed in Chapter 4 in the context of incremental delivery.

Clearly, the 'Parkinson' method is not really an effort prediction method, but a method of setting the scope of a project. Similarly, 'price to win' is a way of identifying a price and not a prediction. Although Boehm rejects them as prediction techniques, they have value as management techniques. There is, for example, a perfectly acceptable engineering practice of *'design to cost'*.

We will now look at some of these techniques more closely. First we will examine the difference between top-down and bottom-up estimating.

5.6 Bottom-up estimating

With the bottom-up approach the estimator breaks the project into its component tasks. With a large project, the process of breaking it down into tasks is iterative: each task is decomposed into its component subtasks and these in turn could be further analysed. It is suggested that this is repeated until you get tasks an individual could do in a week or two. Why is this not a 'top-down approach'? After all, you start from the top and work down. Although this top-down analysis is an essential precursor to bottom-up estimating, it is really a separate process – that of producing a work breakdown schedule (WBS). The bottom-up part comes in adding up the calculated effort for each activity to get an overall estimate.

The bottom-up approach is best at the later, more detailed, stages of project planning. If this method is used earlier, assumptions about the characteristics of the final system and project work methods will have to be made.

Where a project is completely novel or there is no historical data available, the estimator would be forced to use the bottom-up approach.

EXERCISE 5.3

Brigette at Brightmouth College has been told that there is a requirement, once the payroll system has been successfully installed, to create a subsystem that analyses the staffing costs for each course. Details of the pay that each member of staff receives may be

▶

obtained from the payroll standing data. The number of hours that each member of staff spends teaching on each course may be obtained from standing files in a computer-based timetabling system.

What tasks would have to be undertaken to implement this requirement? Try to identify tasks that would take one person about 1 or 2 weeks.

Which tasks are the ones whose durations are most difficult to estimate?

A procedural code-oriented approach

The bottom-up approach described above works at the level of activities. In software development a major activity is writing code. Here we describe how a bottom-up approach can be used at the level of software components.

(a) **Envisage the number and type of software modules in the final system**
   Most information systems, for example, are built from a small set of system operations, e.g. Insert, Amend, Update, Display, Delete, Print. The same principle should equally apply to embedded systems, albeit with a different set of primitive functions.

(b) **Estimate the SLOC of each identified module**

> 'Software module' here implies a component that can be separately compiled and executed.

One way to judge the number of instructions likely to be in a program is to draw up a program structure diagram and to visualize how many instructions would be needed to implement each identified procedure. The estimator may look at existing programs which have a similar functional description to assist in this process.

(c) **Estimate the work content, taking into account complexity and technical difficulty**
   The practice is to multiply the SLOC estimate by a factor for complexity and technical difficulty. This factor will depend largely on the subjective judgement of the estimator. For example, the requirement to meet particular highly constrained performance targets can greatly increase programming effort.

(d) **Calculate the work-days effort**
   Historical data can be used to provide ratios to convert weighted SLOC to effort.

Note that the steps above can be used to derive an estimate of lines of code that can be used as an input to one of the COCOMO models which are described later.

EXERCISE 5.4

The IOE annual maintenance contracts subsystem for which Amanda is responsible will have a transaction which sets up details of new annual maintenance contract customers.

▶

The operator will input:

> Customer account number
>
> Customer name
>
> Address
>
> Postcode
>
> Customer type
>
> Renewal date

All this information will be set up in a CUSTOMER record on the system's database. If a CUSTOMER account already exists for the account number that has been input, an error message will be displayed to the operator.

Draw up an outline program structure diagram for a program to do the processing described above. For each box on your diagram, estimate the number of lines of code needed to implement the routine in a programming language that you are familiar with, such as Java.

5.7 The top-down approach and parametric models

The top-down approach is normally associated with *parametric* (or *algorithmic*) *models*. These may be explained using the analogy of estimating the cost of rebuilding a house. This is of practical concern to house-owners who need insurance cover to rebuild their property if destroyed. Unless the house-owner is in the building trade he or she is unlikely to be able to calculate the numbers of bricklayer-hours, carpenter-hours, electrician-hours and so on required. Insurance companies, however, produce convenient tables where the house-owner can find estimates of rebuilding costs based on such *parameters* as the number of storeys and the floor space of a house. This is a simple parametric model.

Project effort relates mainly to variables associated with characteristics of the final system. A parametric model will normally have one or more formulae in the form:

$$effort = (system\ size) \times (productivity\ rate)$$

For example, system size might be in the form 'thousands of lines of code' (KLOC) and have the specific value of 3 KLOC while the productivity rate was 40 days per KLOC. These values will often be matters of judgement.

A model to forecast software development effort therefore has two key components. The first is a method of assessing the amount of the work needed. The second assesses the rate of work at which the task can be done. For example, Amanda at IOE may estimate that the first software module to be constructed is 2 KLOC. She may then judge that if Kate undertook the development of the code, with her expertise she could work at a rate of 40 days per KLOC per day and complete the work in 2 × 40 days, i.e. 80 days, while Ken, who is less experienced, would need 55 days per KLOC and take 2 × 55, i.e. 110 days to complete the task. In this case KLOC is a *size driver* indicating the amount of work to be done, while developer experience is a productivity driver influencing the productivity or work rate.

If you have figures for the effort expended on past projects (in work-days for instance) and also the system sizes in KLOC, you should be able to work out a productivity rate as

$$productivity = effort/size$$

A more sophisticated way of doing this would be by using the statistical technique *least squares regression* to derive an equation in the form:

$$effort = constant_1 + (size \times constant_2)$$

Some parametric models, such as that implied by function points, are focused on system or task size, while others, such are COCOMO, are more concerned with productivity factors. Those particular models are described in more detail later in this chapter.

EXERCISE 5.5

Students on a course are required to produce a written report on an ICT-related topic each semester. If you wanted to create a model to estimate how long it should take a student to complete such an assignment, what measure of work content would you use? Some reports might be more difficult to produce than others: what factors might affect the degree of difficulty?

> At the earlier stages of a project, the top-down approach would tend to be used, while at later stages the bottom-up approach might be preferred.

Having calculated the overall effort required, the problem is then to allocate proportions of that effort to the various activities within that project.

The top-down and bottom-up approaches are not mutually exclusive. Project managers will probably try to get a number of different estimates from different people using different methods. Some parts of an overall estimate could be derived using a top-down approach while other parts could be calculated using a bottom-up method.

5.8 Expert judgement

This is asking for an estimate of task effort from someone who is knowledgeable about either the application or the development environment. This method is often used when estimating the effort needed to change an existing piece of software. The estimator would have to examine the existing code in order to judge the proportion of code affected and from that derive an estimate. Someone already familiar with the software would be in the best position to do this.

See R. T. Hughes (1996) 'Expert judgement as an estimating method' *Information and Software Technology* 38(3) 67–75.

Some have suggested that expert judgement is simply a matter of guessing, but our own research has shown that experts tend to use a combination of an informal analogy approach where similar projects from the past are identified (see below), supplemented by bottom-up estimating.

There may be cases where the opinions of more than one expert may need to be combined. The Delphi technique described in Section 12.3 tackles group decision-making.

5.9 Estimating by analogy

This is also called *case-based reasoning*. The estimator identifies completed projects (*source cases*) with similar characteristics to the new project (the *target case*). The effort recorded for the matching source case is then used as a base estimate for the target. The estimator then identifies differences between the target and the source and adjusts the base estimate to produce an estimate for the new project.

See M. Shepperd and C. Schofield (1997) 'Estimating software project effort using analogies' *IEEE Transactions in Software Engineering* SE-23(11) 736–43.

This can be a good approach where you have information about some previous projects but not enough to draw generalized conclusions about what might be useful drivers or typical productivity rates.

A problem is identifying the similarities and differences between applications where you have a large number of past projects to analyse. One attempt to automate this selection process is the ANGEL software tool. This identifies the source case that is nearest the target by measuring the Euclidean distance between cases. The Euclidean distance is calculated as:

$$distance = square\text{-}root\ of\ ((target\_parameter_1 - source\_parameter_1)^2 + \dots (target\_parameter_n - source\_parameter_n)^2)$$

EXAMPLE 5.1

Say that the cases are being matched on the basis of two parameters, the number of inputs to and the number of outputs from the application to be built. The new project is known to require 7 inputs and 15 outputs. One of the past cases, project A, has 8 inputs and 17 outputs. The Euclidean distance between the source and the target is therefore the square-root of $((7 - 8)^2 + (17 - 15)^2)$, that is 2.24.

EXERCISE 5.6

Project B has 5 inputs and 10 outputs. What would be the Euclidean distance between this project and the target new project being considered above? Is project B a better analogy with the target than project A?

The above explanation is simply to give an idea of how Euclidean distance may be calculated. The ANGEL package uses rather more sophisticated algorithms based on this principle.

5.10 Albrecht function point analysis

See A. J. Albrecht and J. E. Gaffney Jr., 'Software function, source lines of code, and development effort prediction: a software science validation', in M. Shepperd (ed.) (1993) *Software Engineering Metrics* (Vol. 1), McGraw-Hill.

This is a top-down method that was devised by Allan Albrecht when he worked for IBM. Albrecht was investigating programming productivity and needed to quantify the functional size of programs independently of their programming languages. He developed the idea of function points (FPs).

The basis of function point analysis is that information systems comprise five major components, or '*external user types*' in Albrecht's terminology, that are of benefit to the users.

- *External input types* are input transactions which update internal computer files.

- *External output types* are transactions where data is output to the user. Typically these would be printed reports, as screen displays would tend to come under external inquiry types (see below).

- *External inquiry types* – note the US spelling of inquiry – are transactions initiated by the user which provide information but do not update the internal files. The user inputs some information that directs the system to the details required.

- *Logical internal file types* are the standing files used by the system. The term 'file' does not sit easily with modern information systems. It refers to a group of data items that is usually accessed together. It may be made up of one or more *record types*. For example, a purchase order file may be made up of a record type PURCHASE-ORDER plus a second which is repeated for each item ordered on the purchase order – PURCHASE-ORDER-ITEM. In structured systems analysis, a logical internal file would equate to a datastore, while record types would equate to relational tables or entity types.

Albrecht also dictates that outgoing external interface files should be double counted as logical internal file types as well.

- *External interface file types* allow for output and input that may pass to and from other computer applications. Examples of this would be the transmission of accounting data from an order processing system to the main ledger system or the production of a file of direct debit details on a magnetic or electronic medium to be passed to the Bankers Automated Clearing System (Bacs). Files shared between applications would also be counted here.

The analyst identifies each instance of each external user type in the application. Each component is then classified as having either high, average or low complexity. The counts of each external user type in each complexity band are multiplied by specified weights (see Table 5.2) to get FP scores which are summed to obtain an overall FP count which indicates the information processing size.

External user type	Multiplier		
	Low	Average	High
External input type	3	4	6
External output type	4	5	7
External inquiry type	3	4	6
Logical internal file type	7	10	15
External interface file type	5	7	10

TABLE 5.2 Albrecht complexity multipliers

EXERCISE 5.7

The task for which Brigette has been made responsible in Exercise 5.3 needs a program which will extract yearly salaries from the payroll file, and hours taught on each course by each member of staff and the details of courses from two files maintained by the timetabling system. The program will produce a report showing for each course the hours taught by each member of staff and the cost of those hours.

Using the method described above, calculate the Albrecht function points for this subsystem assuming that the report is of high complexity, but that all the other elements are of average complexity.

The International FP User Group (IFPUG) have developed and published extensive rules governing FP counting. Hence Albrecht FPs are now often referred to as IFPUG FPs.

With FPs as originally defined by Albrecht, the question of whether the external user type was of high, low or average complexity was intuitive. The International FP User Group (IFPUG) has now promulgated rules on how this is assessed. For example, in the case of logical internal files and external interface files, the boundaries shown in Table 5.3 are used to decide the complexity level. Similar tables exist for external inputs and outputs.

Number of record types	Number of data types		
	<20	20–50	>50
1	Low	Low	Average
2 to 5	Low	Average	High
>5	Average	High	High

TABLE 5.3 IFPUG file type complexity

EXAMPLE 5.2

Alogical internal file might contain data about purchase orders. These purchase orders might be organized into two separate record types: the main PURCHASE-ORDER details, namely purchase order number, supplier reference and purchase order date, and then details for each PURCHASE-ORDER-ITEM specified in the order, namely the product code, the unit price and number ordered. The number of record types for that file would therefore be 2 and the number of data types would be 6. According to Table 5.3, this file type would be rated as 'low'. This would mean that according to Table 5.2, the FP count would be 7 for this file.

Function point analysis recognizes that the effort required to implement a computer-based information system relates not just to the number and complexity of the features provided but also to the operational environment of the system.

Further details on TCA can be found in the Albrecht and Gaffney paper.

Fourteen factors have been identified which can influence the degree of difficulty associated with implementing a system. The list that Albrecht produced related particularly to the concerns of information system developers in the late 1970s and early 1980s. Some technology which was then new and relatively threatening is now well established.

The technical complexity adjustment (TCA) calculation has had many problems. Some have even found that it produces less accurate estimates than using the unadjusted function point count. Because of these difficulties, we omit further discussion of the TCA.

The COCOMO II Model Definition Manual A contains a table of suggested conversion rates and can be downloaded from http://sunset.usc.edu/csse

Tables have been calculated to convert the FPs to lines of code for various languages. For example, it is suggested that 53 lines of Java are needed on average to implement an FP, while for Visual C++ the figure is 34. You can then use historical productivity data to convert the lines of code into an effort estimate, as previously described in Section 5.7.

EXERCISE 5.8

In the case of the subsystem described in Exercise 5.7 for which Brigette is responsible at Brightmouth HE College, how many lines of Java code should be needed to implement this subsystem, according to the standard conversion? Assuming a productivity rate of 50 lines of code a day, what would be the estimate of effort?

5.11 Function points Mark II

This method has came into the public domain with the publication of the book by Charles R. Symons (1991) *Software Sizing and Estimating – Mark II FPA*, John Wiley and Sons.

The Mark II method was originally sponsored by what was then the CCTA (Central Computer and Telecommunications Agency, now the Office of Government Commerce or OGC), which lays down standards for UK government projects. The 'Mark II' label implies an improvement and replacement of the Albrecht method. The Albrecht (now IFPUG) method, however, has had many refinements made to it and FPA Mark II remains a minority method used mainly in the United Kingdom.

As with Albrecht, the information processing size is initially measured in unadjusted function points (UFPs) to which a technical complexity adjustment can then be applied (TCA). The assumption is that an information system comprises transactions which have the basic structure shown in Figure 5.2.

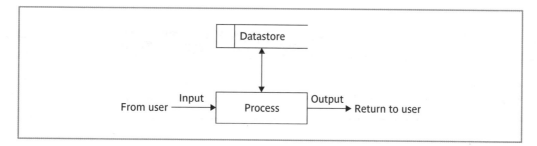

FIGURE 5.2 Model of a transaction

For each transaction the UFPs are calculated:

$$W_i \times (\textit{number of input data element types}) +$$

$$W_e \times (\textit{number of entity types referenced}) +$$

$$W_o \times (\textit{number of output data element types})$$

The only reason why 2.5 was adopted here was to produce FP counts similar to the Albrecht equivalents.

W_i, W_e, and W_o are weightings derived by asking developers the proportions of effort spent in previous projects developing the code dealing respectively with inputs, accessing and modifying stored data and processing outputs.

The proportions of effort are then normalized into ratios, or weightings, which add up to 2.5. This process for calculating weightings is time consuming and most FP counters use industry averages which are currently 0.58 for W_i, 1.66 for W_e and 0.26 for W_o.

EXAMPLE 5.3

A cash receipt transaction in the IOE maintenance accounts subsystem accesses two entity types – INVOICE and CASH-RECEIPT.

The data inputs are:

Invoice number

Date received

Cash received

If an INVOICE record is not found for the invoice number then an error message is issued. If the invoice number is found then a CASH-RECEIPT record is created. The error message is the only output of the transaction. The unadjusted function points, using the industry average weightings, for this transaction would therefore be:

$(0.58 \times 3) + (1.66 \times 2) + (0.26 \times 1) = 5.32$

EXERCISE 5.9

Calculate the number of unadjusted Mark II function points for the transaction described previously for Exercise 5.4, using the industry average weightings.

Mark II FPs follow the Albrecht method in recognizing that one system delivering the same functionality as another may be more difficult to implement (but also more valuable to the users) because of additional technical requirements. For example, the incorporation of additional security measures would increase the amount of effort to deliver the system. The identification of further factors to suit local circumstances is encouraged.

Symons is very much against the idea of using function points to estimate SLOC rather than effort. One finding by Symons is that productivity, that is, the effort per function point to implement a system, is influenced by the size of the project. In general, larger projects, up to a certain point, are more productive because of economies of scale. However, beyond a certain size they tend to become less productive because of additional management overheads.

Some of the rules and weightings used in FP counting, especially in the case of the Albrecht flavour, are rather arbitrary and have been criticized by academic writers on this account. FPs, however, have been found useful as a way of calculating the price for extensions to existing systems, as will be seen in Chapter 10 on managing contracts.

5.12 COSMIC full function points

COSMIC-FFP stands for Common Software Measurement Consortium – Full Function Points.

While approaches like that of IFPUG are suitable for information systems, they are not helpful when it comes to sizing real-time or embedded applications. This has resulted in the development of another version of function points – the COSMIC FFP method.

The full function point (FFP) method has its origins in the work of two interlinked research groups in Québec, Canada. At the start, the developers were at pains to stress that this method should be seen as simply an extension to the IFPUG method for real-time systems. The original work of FFPs has been taken forward by the formation of the Common Software Measurement Consortium (COSMIC) which has involved not just the original developers in Canada, but others from many parts of the world, including Charles Symons, the originator of Mark II function points. Interestingly, there has been little participation by anyone from the United States.

The argument is that existing function point methods are effective in assessing the work content of information systems where the size of the internal procedures mirrors the number of external features. With a real-time, or embedded, system, its features will be hidden because the software's user will probably not be a human but a hardware device or another software component.

COSMIC deals with this by decomposing the system architecture into a hierarchy of software *layers*. The software component to be sized can receive requests for services from layers above and can request services from those below it. At the same time there could be separate software components at the same level that engage in *peer-to-peer communication*. This identifies the boundary of the software component to be assessed and thus the points at which it receives inputs and transmits outputs. Inputs and outputs are aggregated into *data groups*, where each group brings together data items that relate to the same object of interest.

Data groups can be moved about in four ways:

- *entries* (E), which are effected by subprocesses that move the data group into the software component in question from a 'user' outside its boundary – this could be from another layer or another separate software component in the same layer via peer-to-peer communication;

- *exits* (X), which are effected by subprocesses that move the data group from the software component to a 'user' outside its boundary;

- *reads* (R), which are data movements that move data groups from persistent storage (such as a database) into the software component;

- *writes* (W), which are data movements that transfer data groups from the software component into persistent storage.

EXERCISE 5.10

A small computer system controls the entry of vehicles to a car park. Each time a vehicle pulls up before an entry barrier, a sensor notifies the computer system of the vehicle's presence. The system examines a count that it maintains of the number of vehicles that are currently in the car park. This count is kept on backing storage so that it will still be available if the system is temporarily shut down, for example because of a power cut. If the count does not exceed the maximum allowed then the barrier is lifted and the count is incremented. When a vehicle leaves the car park, a sensor detects the exit and reduces the count of vehicles.

There is a system administration system that can set the maximum number of cars allowed, and which can be used to adjust or replace the count of cars when the system is restarted.

Identify the entries, exits, reads and writes in this application.

The overall FFP count is derived by simply adding up the counts for each of the four types of data movement. The resulting units are *Cfsu* (COSMIC functional size units). The method does not take account of any processing of the data groups once they have been moved into the software component. The framers of the method do not recommend its use for systems involving complex mathematical algorithms, for example, but there is provision for the definition of local versions for specialized environments which could incorporate counts of other software features.

COSMIC FFPs have been incorporated into an ISO standard – ISO/IEC 19761:2003. Prior to this there were attempts to produce a single ISO standard for 'functional size measurement' and there is an ISO document – ISO/IEC 14143–1:1998 – which lays down some general principles. ISO has decided, diplomatically, that it is unable to judge the relative merits of the four main methods in the field: IFPUG, Mark II, NESMA and COSMIC-FFP, and all four have been allowed to submit their methods as candidates to become ISO standards and then to 'let the market decide'.

> The NESMA FP method has been developed by the Netherlands Software Measurement Association.

5.13 COCOMO II: a parametric productivity model

> Because there is now a newer COCOMO II, the older version is now referred to as COCOMO81.

Boehm's COCOMO (COnstructive COst MOdel) is often referred to in the literature on software project management, particularly in connection with software estimating. The term COCOMO really refers to a group of models.

Boehm originally based his models in the late 1970s on a study of 63 projects. Of these only seven were business systems and so the models could be used with applications other than information systems. The basic model was built around the equation

System type	c	k
Organic	2.4	1.05
Semi-detached	3.0	1.12
Embedded	3.6	1.20

TABLE 5.4 COCOMO81 constants

$$(effort) = c(size)^k$$

where *effort* was measured in *pm* or the number of 'person-months' consisting of units of 152 working hours, *size* was measured in *kdsi*, thousands of delivered source code instructions, and *c* and *k* were constants.

The first step was to derive an estimate of the system size in terms of *kdsi*. The constants, *c* and *k* (see Table 5.4), depended on whether the system could be classified, in Boehm's terms, as 'organic', 'semi-detached' or 'embedded'. These related to the technical nature of the system and the development environment.

Generally, information systems were regarded as organic while real-time systems were embedded.

- *Organic mode* This would typically be the case when relatively small teams developed software in a highly familiar in-house environment and when the system being developed was small and the interface requirements were flexible.

- *Embedded mode* This meant that the product being developed had to operate within very tight constraints and changes to the system were very costly.

- *Semi-detached mode* This combined elements of the organic and the embedded modes or had characteristics that came between the two.

The exponent value *k*, when it is greater than 1, means that larger projects are seen as requiring disproportionately more effort than smaller ones. This reflected Boehm's finding that larger projects tended to be less productive than smaller ones because they needed more effort for management and coordination.

The detailed COCOMO II Model Definition Manual has been published by the Center for Software Engineering, University of Southern California.

Over the years, Barry Boehm and his co-workers have refined a family of cost estimation models of which the key one is COCOMO II. This approach uses various multipliers and exponents the values of which have been set initially by experts. However, a database containing the performance details of executed projects has been built up and periodically analysed so that the expert judgements can be progressively replaced by values derived from actual projects. The new models take into account that there is now a wider range of process models in common use than previously. As we noted earlier, estimates are required at different stages in the system life cycle and COCOMO II has been designed to accommodate this by having models for three different stages.

- *Application composition* Here the external features of the system that the users will experience are designed. Prototyping will typically be employed to do this. With small applications that can be built using high-productivity application-building tools, development can stop at this point.

- *Early design* Here the fundamental software structures are designed. With larger, more demanding systems, where, for example, there will be large volumes of transactions and performance is important, careful attention will need to be paid to the architecture to be adopted.

- *Post architecture* Here the software structures undergo final construction, modification and tuning to create a system that will perform as required.

See R. D. Banker, R. Kauffman and R. Kumar (1992) 'An empirical test of object-based output measurement metrics' *Journal of MIS*, 8(3).

To estimate the effort for *application composition*, the counting of *object points* is recommended by the developers of COCOMO II. This follows the function point approach of counting externally apparent features of the software. It differs by focusing on the physical features of the application, such as screens and reports, rather than 'logical' ones such as entity types. This is seen as being more useful where the requirements are being elicited via prototypes.

At the *early design* stage, FPs are recommended as the way of gauging a basic system size. An FP count may be converted to a LOC equivalent by multiplying the FPs by a factor for the programming language that is to be used – see Section 5.10.

The following model can then be used to calculate an estimate of person-months.

$$pm = A(size)^{(sf)} \times (em_1) \times (em_2) \times \ldots \times (em_n)$$

where *pm* is the effort in 'person-months', *A* is a constant (which was set in 2000 at 2.94), *size* is measured in *kdsi* (which may have been derived from an FP count as explained above), and *sf* is exponent scale factor.

The scale factor is derived thus:

$$sf = B + 0.01 \times \Sigma \text{ (exponent driver ratings)}$$

where *B* is a constant currently set at 0.91. The effect of the exponent ('. . . to the power of . . .') scale factor is to increase the effort predicted for larger projects, that is, to take account of diseconomies of scale which make larger projects less productive.

The qualities that govern the exponent drivers used to calculate the scale factor are listed below. Note that the less each quality is applicable, the bigger the value given to the exponent driver. The fact that these factors are used to calculate an exponent implies that the lack of these qualities increases the effort required disproportionately more on larger projects.

- *Precedentedness (PREC)* This quality is the degree to which there are precedents or similar past cases for the current project. The greater the novelty of the new system, the more uncertainty there is and the higher the value given to the exponent driver.

Driver	Very low	Low	Nominal	High	Very high	Extra high
PREC	6.20	4.96	3.72	2.48	1.24	0.00
FLEX	5.07	4.05	3.04	2.03	1.01	0.00
RESL	7.07	5.65	4.24	2.83	1.41	0.00
TEAM	5.48	4.38	3.29	2.19	1.10	0.00
PMAT	7.80	6.24	4.68	3.12	1.56	0.00

TABLE 5.5 COCOMO II Scale factor values

- *Development flexibility (FLEX)* This reflects the number of different ways there are of meeting the requirements. The less flexibility there is, the higher the value of the exponent driver.

- *Architecture/risk resolution (RESL)* This reflects the degree of uncertainty about the requirements. If they are liable to change then a high value would be given to this exponent driver.

- *Team cohesion (TEAM)* This reflects the degree to which there is a large dispersed team (perhaps in several countries) as opposed to there being a small tightly knit team.

- *Process maturity (PMAT)* Chapter 13 on software quality explains the process maturity model. The more structured and organized the way the software is produced, the lower the uncertainty and the lower the rating will be for this exponent driver.

Each of the scale factors for a project is rated according to a range of judgements: very low, low, nominal, high, very high, extra high. There is a number related to each rating of the individual scale factors – see Table 5.5. These are summed, then multiplied by 0.01 and added to the constant 0.91 to get the overall exponent scale factor.

EXERCISE 5.11

A new project has 'average' novelty for the software supplier that is going to execute it and is thus given a nominal rating on this account for precedentedness. Development flexibility is high, but requirements may change radically and so the risk resolution exponent is rated very low. The development team are all located in the same office and this leads to team cohesion being rated as very high, but the software house as a whole tends to be very informal in its standards and procedures and the process maturity driver has therefore been given a rating of 'low'.

(i) What would be the scale factor (*sf*) in this case?

(ii) What would the estimate of effort if the size of the application was estimated as in the region of 2000 lines of code?

Code	Effort modifier	Extra low	Very low	Low	Nominal	High	Very high	Extra high
RCPX	Product reliability and complexity	0.49	0.60	0.83	1.00	1.33	1.91	2.72
RUSE	Required reusability			0.95	1.00	1.07	1.15	1.24
PDIF	Platform difficulty			0.87	1.00	1.29	1.81	2.61
PERS	Personnel capability	2.12	1.62	1.26	1.00	0.83	0.63	0.50
PREX	Personnel experience	1.59	1.33	1.12	1.00	0.87	0.74	0.62
FCIL	Facilities available	1.43	1.30	1.10	1.00	0.87	0.73	0.62
SCED	Schedule pressure		1.43	1.14	1.00	1.00	1.00	

TABLE 5.6 COCOMO II Early design effort multipliers

In the COCOMO II model the *effort multipliers* (*em*) adjust the estimate to take account of productivity factors, but do not involve economies or diseconomies of scale. The multipliers relevant to early design are in Table 5.6 and those used at the post architecture stage in Table 5.7. Each of these multipliers may, for a particular application, be given a

Modifier type	Code	Effort modifier
Product attributes	RELY	Required software reliability
	DATA	Database size
	DOCU	Documentation match to life-cycle needs
	CPLX	Product complexity
	REUSE	Required reusability
Platform attributes	TIME	Execution time constraint
	STOR	Main storage constraint
	PVOL	Platform volatility
Personnel attributes	ACAP	Analyst capabilities
	AEXP	Application experience
	PCAP	Programmer capabilities
	PEXP	Platform experience
	LEXP	Programming language experience
	PCON	Personnel continuity
Project attributes	TOOL	Use of software tools
	SITE	Multisite development
	SCED	Schedule pressure

TABLE 5.7 COCOMO II Post architecture effort multipliers

rating of very low, low, nominal, high or very high. Each rating for each effort multiplier has an associated value. A value greater than 1 increases development effort, while a value less than 1 decreases it. The nominal rating means that the multiplier has no effect. The intention is that the values that these and other ratings use in COCOMO II will be refined over time as actual project details are added to the database.

EXERCISE 5.12

A software supplier has to produce an application that controls a piece of equipment in a factory. A high degree of reliability is needed as a malfunction could injure the operators. The algorithms to control the equipment are also complex. The product reliability and complexity are therefore rated as very high. The company would like to take the opportunity to exploit fully the investment that they made in the project by reusing the control system, with suitable modifications, on future contracts. The reusability requirement is therefore rated as very high. Developers are familiar with the platform and the possibility of potential problems in that respect is regarded as low. The current staff are generally very capable and are rated in this respect as very high, but the project is in a somewhat novel application domain for them so experience is rated as nominal. The toolsets available to the developers are judged to be typical for the size of company and are rated as nominal, as is the degree of schedule pressure to meet a deadline.

Given the data in Table 5.6,

(i) What would be the value for each of the effort multipliers?

(ii) What would be the impact of all the effort multipliers on a project estimated as taking 200 staff-months?

At a later stage of the project, detailed design of the application will have been completed. There will be a clearer idea of application size in terms of lines of code, and the factors influencing productivity will be better known. A revised estimate of effort can be produced based on the broader range of effort modifiers seen in Table 5.7. The method of calculation is the same as for early design. Readers who wish to apply the model using the post architecture effort multipliers are directed to the COCOMO II Model Definition Manual which is available from the University of Southern California website http://sunset.usc.edu/csse/research/COCOMOII/COCOMO_main.html.

5.14 Conclusion

To summarize some key points:

- Estimates are really management targets.
- Collect as much information about previous projects as possible.
- Use more than one method of estimating.

- Top-down approaches will be used at the earlier stages of project planning while bottom-up approaches will be more prominent later on.
- Be careful about using other people's historical productivity data as a basis for your estimates, especially if it comes from a different environment (this includes COCOMO).
- Seek a range of opinions.
- Document your method of doing estimates and record all your assumptions.

5.15 Further exercises

1   The size (that is, the effort needed to complete it) of any task will depend on its characteristics. The units into which the work is divided will also differ. Identify the factors affecting the size of the task and work units for the following activities:

- installing computer workstations in a new office;
- transporting assembled personal computers from the factory where they were assembled to warehouses distributed in different parts of the country;
- typing in and checking the correctness of data that is populating a new database;
- system testing a newly written software application.

2   If you were asked as an expert to provide an estimate of the effort needed to make certain changes to an existing piece of software, what information would you like to have to hand to assist you in making that estimate?

3   A small application maintains a telephone directory. The database for the application contains the following data types:

- Staff reference
- Surname
- Forenames
- Title
- Department code
- Room number
- Telephone extension
- E-mail address
- Fax number

Transactions are needed which:

(i)   set up new entries;
(ii) amend existing entries;
(iii) delete entries;
(iv) allow enquirers to list online the details for a particular member of staff;
(v)   produce a complete listing of the telephone directory entries in alphabetical order.

(a)   Use this scenario to produce an estimated Mark II FP count. List all the assumptions you will need to make.
(b)   Another requirement could be to produce the listing in (v) in departmental order. In your view, should this increase FP count and if so by how much?

4 The following details are held about previously developed software modules.

Module	Inputs	Entity types accessed	Outputs	Days
a	1	2	10	2.60
b	10	2	1	3.90
c	5	1	1	1.83
d	2	3	11	3.50
e	1	3	20	4.30

A new module has 7 inputs, 1 entity type access and 7 outputs. Which of the modules a to e is the closest analogy in terms of Euclidean distance?

5 Using the data in further exercise 4 above, calculate the Symons Mark II FPs for each module. Using the results, calculate the effort needed for the new module described in further exercise 4. How does this estimate compare to the one based on analogy?

6 Given the project data below:

Project	Inputs	Outputs	Entity accesses	System users	Programming language	Developer days
1	210	420	40	10	x	30
2	469	1406	125	20	x	85
3	513	1283	76	18	y	108
4	660	2310	88	200	y	161
5	183	367	35	10	z	22
6	244	975	65	25	z	42
7	1600	3200	237	25	y	308
8	582	874	111	5	z	62
X	180	350	40	20	y	
Y	484	1190	69	35	y	

(a) What items are size drivers?
(b) What items are productivity drivers?
(c) What are the productivity rates for programming languages x, y and z?
(d) What would be the estimated effort for projects X and Y using a Mark II function point count?
(e) What would be the estimated effort for X and Y using an approximate analogy approach?
(f) What would have been the best estimating method if the actual effort for X turns out to be 30 days and for Y turns out to be 120 days? Can you suggest why the results are as they are and how they might be improved?

7   A report in a college timetabling system produces a report showing the students who should be attending each timetabled teaching activity. Four files are accessed: the STAFF file, the STUDENT file, the STUDENT-OPTION file and the TEACHING-ACTIVITY file. The report contains the following information:

Teaching activity reference
Topic name
Staff forenames
Staff surname
Title
Semester (1 or 2)
Day of week
Time
Duration
Location
For each student:
    student forename
    student surnames

Calculate the Mark II FPs that this transaction would generate. What further information would you need to create an estimate of effort?

CHAPTER 6

Activity planning

6.1 Introduction

In earlier chapters we looked at methods for forecasting the effort required for a project – both for the project as a whole and for individual activities. A detailed plan for the project, however, must also include a schedule indicating the start and completion times for each activity. This will enable us to:

- ensure that the appropriate resources will be available precisely when required;
- avoid different activities competing for the same resources at the same time;
- produce a detailed schedule showing which staff carry out each activity;
- produce a detailed plan against which actual achievement may be measured;
- produce a timed cash flow forecast;
- replan the project during its life to correct drift from the target.

To be effective, a plan must be stated as a set of targets, the achievement or non-achievement of which can be unambiguously measured. The activity plan does this by providing a target start and completion date for each activity (or a window within which each activity may be carried out). The starts and completions of activities must be clearly visible and this is one of the reasons why it is advisable to ensure that each and every project activity produces some tangible product or 'deliverable'.

Monitoring the project's progress is then, at least in part, a case of ensuring that the products of each activity are delivered on time.

Project monitoring is discussed in more detail in Chapter 9.

As a project progresses it is unlikely that everything will go according to plan. Much of the job of project management concerns recognizing when something has gone wrong, identifying its causes and revising the plan to mitigate its effects. The activity plan should provide a means of evaluating the consequences of not meeting any of the activity target dates and guidance as to how the plan might most effectively be modified to bring the project back to target. We shall see that the activity plan may well also offer guidance as to which components of a project should be most closely monitored.

6.2 The objectives of activity planning

In addition to providing project and resource schedules, activity planning aims to achieve a number of other objectives which may be summarized as follows.

- *Feasibility assessment* Is the project possible within required timescales and resource constraints? In Chapter 5 we looked at ways of estimating the effort for various project tasks. However, it is not until we have constructed a detailed plan that we can forecast a completion date with any reasonable knowledge of its achievability. The fact that a project may have been estimated as requiring two work-years' effort might not mean that it would be feasible to complete it within, say, three months were eight people to work on it – that will depend upon the availability of staff and the degree to which activities may be undertaken in parallel.

- *Resource allocation* What are the most effective ways of allocating resources to the project. When should the resources be available? The project plan allows us to investigate the relationship between timescales and resource availability (in general, allocating additional resources to a project shortens its duration) and the efficacy of additional spending on resource procurement.

- *Detailed costing* How much will the project cost and when is that expenditure likely to take place? After producing an activity plan and allocating specific resources, we can obtain more detailed estimates of costs and their timing.

Chapter 11 discusses motivation in more detail.

- *Motivation* Providing targets and being seen to monitor achievement against targets is an effective way of motivating staff, particularly where they have been involved in setting those targets in the first place.

This coordination will normally form part of Programme Management.

- *Coordination* When do the staff in different departments need to be available to work on a particular project and when do staff need to be transferred between projects? The project plan, particularly with large projects involving more than a single project team, provides an effective vehicle for communication and coordination among teams. In situations where staff may need to be transferred between project teams (or work concurrently on more than one project), a set of integrated project schedules should ensure that such staff are available when required and do not suffer periods of enforced idleness.

Activity planning and scheduling techniques place an emphasis on completing the project in a minimum time at an acceptable cost or, alternatively, meeting a set target date at minimum cost. These are not, in themselves, concerned with meeting quality targets, which generally impose constraints on the scheduling process.

One effective way of shortening project durations is to carry out activities in parallel. Clearly we cannot undertake all the activities at the same time – some require the completion of others before they can start and there are likely to be resource constraints limiting how much may be done simultaneously. Activity scheduling will, however, give us an indication of the cost of these constraints in terms of lengthening timescales and provide us with an indication of how timescales may be shortened by relaxing those constraints. If we try relaxing precedence constraints by, for example, allowing a program coding task to commence before the design has been completed, it is up to us to ensure that we are clear about the potential effects on product quality.

6.3 When to plan

Planning is an ongoing process of refinement, each iteration becoming more detailed and more accurate than the last. Over successive iterations, the emphasis and purpose of planning will shift.

During the feasibility study and project start-up, the main purpose of planning will be to estimate timescales and the risks of not achieving target completion dates or keeping within budget. As the project proceeds beyond the feasibility study, the emphasis will be placed upon the production of activity plans for ensuring resource availability and cash flow control.

Throughout the project, until the final deliverable has reached the customer, monitoring and replanning must continue to correct any drift that might prevent meeting time or cost targets.

6.4 Project schedules

On a large project, detailed plans for the later stages will be delayed until information about the work required has emerged from the earlier stages.

Before work commences on a project or, possibly, a stage of a larger project, the project plan must be developed to the level of showing dates when each activity should start and finish and when and how much of each resource will be required. Once the plan has been refined to this level of detail we call it a project schedule. Creating a project schedule comprises four main stages.

The first step in producing the plan is to decide what activities need to be carried out and in what order they are to be done. From this we can construct an *ideal activity plan* – that is, a plan of when each activity

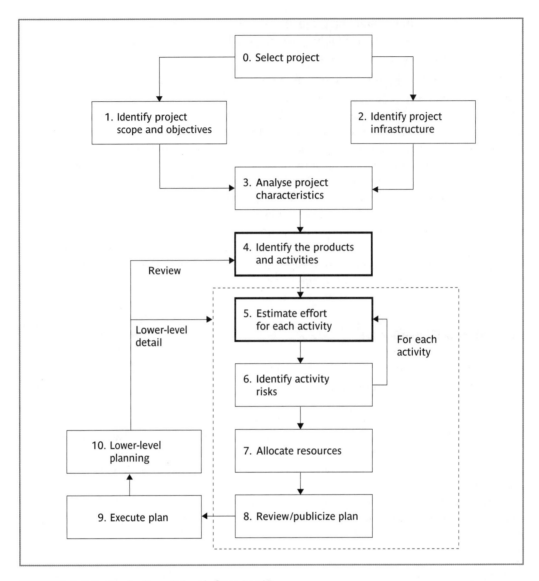

FIGURE 6.1 Activity planning is carried out in Steps 4 and 5

would ideally be undertaken were resources not a constraint. It is the creation of the ideal activity plan that we shall discuss in this chapter. This activity plan is generated by Steps 4 and 5 of Step Wise (Figure 6.1).

The ideal activity plan will then be the subject of an activity risk analysis, aimed at identifying potential problems. This might suggest alterations to the ideal activity plan and will almost certainly have implications for resource allocation. Activity risk analysis is the subject of Chapter 7.

The third step is *resource allocation*. The expected availability of resources might place constraints on when certain activities can be carried out, and our ideal plan might need to be adapted to take account of this. Resource allocation is covered in Chapter 8.

The final step is *schedule production*. Once resources have been allocated to each activity, we will be in a position to draw up and publish a project schedule, which indicates planned start and completion dates and a resource requirements statement for each activity. Chapter 9 discusses how this is done and the role of the schedule in managing a project.

6.5 Projects and activities

Defining activities

Before we try to identify the activities that make up a project it is worth reviewing what we mean by a project and its activities and adding some assumptions that will be relevant when we start to produce an activity plan.

> Activities must be defined so that they meet these criteria. Any activity that does not meet these criteria must be redefined.

- A project is composed of a number of interrelated activities.
- A project may start when at least one of its activities is ready to start.
- A project will be completed when all of the activities it encompasses have been completed.
- An activity must have a clearly defined start and a clearly defined end-point, normally marked by the production of a tangible deliverable.
- If an activity requires a resource (as most do) then that resource requirement must be forecastable and is assumed to be required at a constant level throughout the duration of the activity.
- The duration of an activity must be forecastable – assuming normal circumstances, and the reasonable availability of resources.
- Some activities might require that others are completed before they can begin (these are known as *precedence requirements*).

Identifying activities

Essentially there are three approaches to identifying the activities or tasks that make up a project – we shall call them the *activity-based approach, the product-based approach* and the *hybrid approach.*

The activity-based approach

The activity-based approach consists of creating a list of all the activities that the project is thought to involve. This might require a brainstorming session involving the whole project team or it might stem from an analysis of similar past projects. When listing activities, particularly for a large project, it might be helpful to subdivide the project into the main life-cycle stages and consider each of these separately.

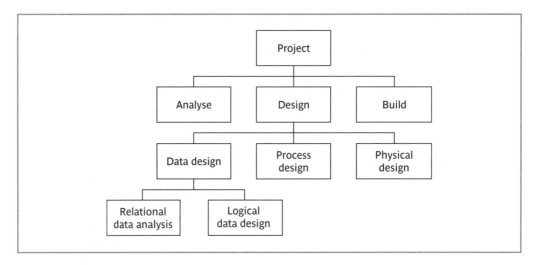

FIGURE 6.2 A fragment of an activity-based Work Breakdown Structure

WBSs are advocated by BS 6079, the British Standards Institution's *Guide to Project Management.*

Rather than doing this in an ad hoc manner, with the obvious risks of omitting or double-counting tasks, a much favoured way of generating a task list is to create a *Work Breakdown Structure* (WBS). This involves identifying the main (or high-level) tasks required to complete a project and then breaking each of these down into a set of lower-level tasks. Figure 6.2 shows a fragment of a WBS where the design task has been broken down into three tasks and one of these has been further decomposed into two tasks.

Activities are added to a branch in the structure if they contribute directly to the task immediately above – if they do not contribute to the parent task, then they should not be added to that branch. The tasks at each level in any branch should include everything that is required to complete the task at the higher level.

When preparing a WBS, consideration must be given to the final level of detail or depth of the structure. Too great a depth will result in a large number of small tasks that will be difficult to manage, whereas a too shallow structure will provide insufficient detail for project control. Each branch should, however, be broken down at least to a level where each leaf may be assigned to an individual or responsible section within the organization.

A complete task catalogue will normally include task definitions along with task input and output products and other task-related information.

Advantages claimed for the WBS approach include the belief that it is much more likely to result in a task catalogue that is complete and is composed of non-overlapping activities. Note that it is only the leaves of the structure that comprise the list of activities in the project – higher-level nodes merely represent collections of activities.

The WBS also represents a structure that may be refined as the project proceeds. In the early part of a project we might use a relatively high-level or shallow WBS, which can be developed as information becomes available, typically during the project's analysis and specification phases.

Once the project's activities have been identified (whether or not by using a WBS), they need to be sequenced in the sense of deciding which activities need to be completed before others can start.

The product-based approach

The product-based approach, used in PRINCE2 and Step Wise, has already been described in Chapter 3. It consists of producing a Product Breakdown Structure and a Product Flow Diagram. The PFD indicates, for each product, which other products are required as inputs. The PFD can therefore be easily transformed into an ordered list of activities by identifying the transformations that turn some products into others. Proponents of this approach claim that it is less likely that a product will be left out of a PBS than that an activity might be omitted from an unstructured activity list.

This approach is particularly appropriate if using a methodology such as SSADM or USDP (Unified Software Development Process), which clearly specifies, for each step or task, each of the products required and the activities required to produce it. For example, the SSADM Reference Manual provides a set of generic PBSs for each stage in SSADM, which can be used as a basis for generating a project specific PBS.

See I. Jacobson, G. Booch and J. Rumbaugh (1999) *The Unified Software Development Process*, Addison-Wesley.

In the USDP, products are referred to as *artifacts* – see Figure 6.3 – and the sequence of activities needed to create them is called a *workflow* – see Figure 6.4 for an example. Some caution is needed in drawing up an activity network from these workflows. USDP emphasizes that processes are iterative. This means that it may not be possible to map a USDP process directly onto a single activity in a network. In Section 4.15 we saw how one or more iterated processes could be hidden in the single execution of a larger activity. All projects, whether they contain iterations or not, will need to have some fixed milestones or time-boxes if progress towards a planned delivery date is to be maintained. These larger activities with the fixed completion dates would be the basis of the activity network.

The hybrid approach

BS 6079 states that WBSs may be product-based, cost-centre-based, task-based or function-based but that product-based WBSs are preferred.

Not all of the products in this activity structuring will be final products. Some will be further refined in subsequent steps.

The WBS illustrated in Figure 6.2 is based entirely on a structuring of activities. Alternatively, and perhaps more commonly, a WBS may be based upon the project's products as illustrated in Figure 6.5, which is in turn based on a simple list of final deliverables and, for each deliverable, a set of activities required to produce that product. Figure 6.5 illustrates a flat WBS and it is likely that, in a project of any size, it would be beneficial to introduce additional levels – structuring both products and activities. The degree to which the structuring is product-based or activity-based might be influenced by the nature of the project and the particular development method adopted. As with a purely activity-based WBS, having identified the activities we are then left with the task of sequencing them.

A framework dictating the number of levels and the nature of each level in the structure may be imposed on a WBS. For example, in their MITP methodology, IBM recommend that the following five levels should be used in a WBS:

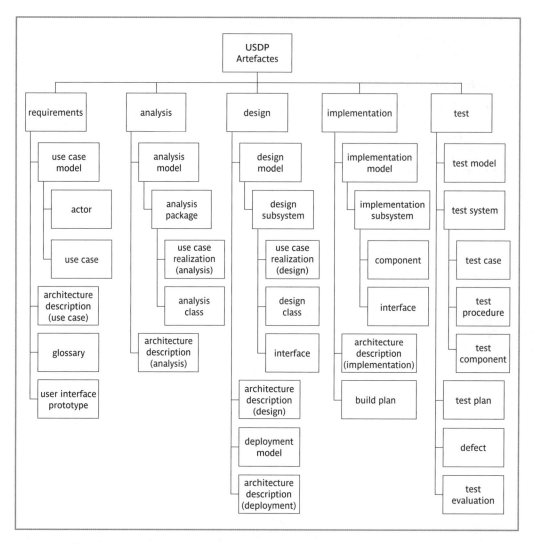

FIGURE 6.3 USDP product breakdown structure based on artefacts identified in Jacobson, Booch and Rumbaugh (1999)

- *Level 1: Project.*
- *Level 2: Deliverables* such as software, manuals and training courses.
- *Level 3: Components,* which are the key work items needed to produce deliverables, such as the modules and tests required to produce the system software.
- *Level 4: Work-packages,* which are major work items, or collections of related tasks, required to produce a component.
- *Level 5: Tasks,* which are tasks that will normally be the responsibility of a single person.

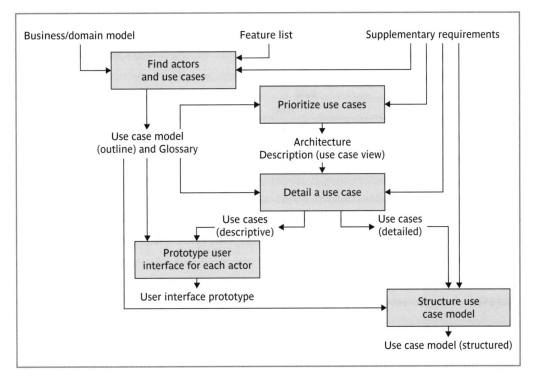

FIGURE 6.4 A structuring of activities for the USDP requirements capture workflow based on Jacobson, Booch and Rumbaugh (1999)

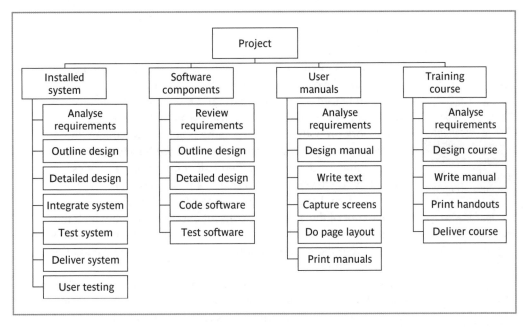

FIGURE 6.5 A hybrid Work Breakdown Structure based on deliverables and activities

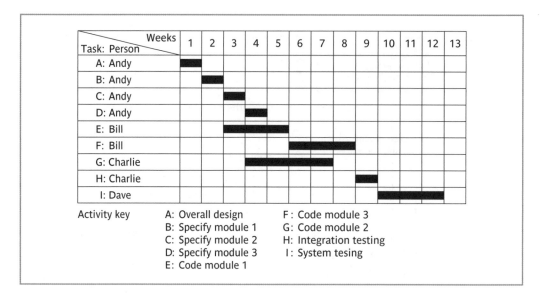

FIGURE 6.6 A project plan as a bar chart

6.6 Sequencing and scheduling activities

Throughout a project, we will require a schedule that clearly indicates when each of the project's activities is planned to occur and what resources it will need. We shall be considering scheduling in more detail in Chapter 8, but let us consider in outline how we might present a schedule for a small project. One way of presenting such a plan is to use a bar chart as shown in Figure 6.6.

The chart shown has been drawn up taking account of the nature of the development process (that is, certain tasks must be completed before others may start) and the resources that are available (for example, activity C follows activity B because Andy cannot work on both tasks at the same time). In drawing up the chart, we have therefore done two things – we have sequenced the tasks (that is, identified the dependencies among activities dictated by the development process) and scheduled them (that is, specified when they should take place). The scheduling has had to take account of the availability of staff and the ways in which the activities have been allocated to them. The schedule might look quite different were there a different number of staff or were we to allocate the activities differently.

In the case of small projects, this combined sequencing–scheduling approach might be quite suitable, particularly where we wish to allocate individuals to particular tasks at an early planning stage. However, on larger projects it is better to separate out these two

> The bar chart does not show why certain decisions have been made. It is not clear, for example, why activity H is not scheduled to start until week 9. It could be that it cannot start until activity F has been completed or it might be because Charlie is going to be on holiday during week 8.

> Separating the logical sequencing from the scheduling may be

activities: to sequence the tasks according to their logical relationships and then to schedule them taking into account resources and other factors.

likened to the principle in systems analysis of separating the logical system from its physical implementation.

Approaches to scheduling that achieve this separation between the logical and the physical use networks to model the project and it is these approaches that we will consider in subsequent sections of this chapter.

6.7 Network planning models

CPM was developed by the DuPont Chemical Company which published the method in 1958, claiming that it had saved them $1 million in its first year of use.

These project scheduling techniques model the project's activities and their relationships as a network. In the network, time flows from left to right. These techniques were originally developed in the 1950s – the two best known being CPM (Critical Path Method) and PERT (Program Evaluation Review Technique).

Both of these techniques used an *activity-on-arrow* approach to visualizing the project as a network where activities are drawn as arrows joining circles, or nodes, which represent the possible start and/or completion of an activity or set of activities. More recently a variation on these techniques, called *precedence networks*, has become popular. This method uses *activity-on-node* networks where activities are represented as nodes and the links between nodes represent precedence (or sequencing) requirements. This latter approach avoids some of the problems inherent in the activity-on-arrow representation and provides more scope for easily representing certain situations. It is this method that is adopted in the majority of computer applications currently available. These three methods are very similar and it must be admitted that many people use the same name (particularly CPM) indiscriminately to refer to any or all of the methods.

In the following sections of this chapter, we will look at the critical path method applied to precedence (activity-on-node) networks followed by a brief introduction to activity-on-arrow networks – a discussion of PERT will be reserved for Chapter 7 when we look at risk analysis.

CASE STUDY EXAMPLES

In Chapter 2 we saw how Amanda identified that three new software components would need to be developed and a further component would need to be rewritten. Figure 6.7 shows the fragment of a network that she has developed as an activity-on-node network. Figure 6.8 shows how this network would look represented as an activity-on-arrow network. Study each of the networks briefly to verify that they are, indeed, merely different graphical representations of the same thing.

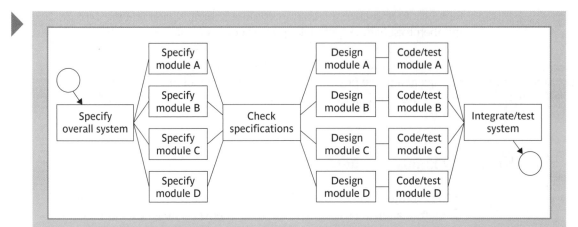

FIGURE 6.7 The IOE annual maintenance contracts project activity network fragment with a checkpoint activity added

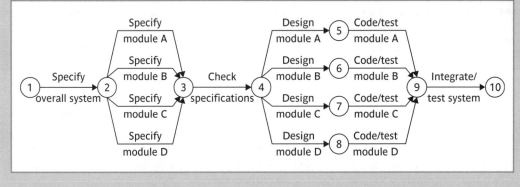

FIGURE 6.8 The IOE annual maintenance contracts project activity network fragment represented as a CPM network

6.8 Formulating a network model

The first stage in creating a network model is to represent the activities and their interrelationships as a graph. In activity-on-node we do this by representing activities as nodes (boxes) in the graph – the lines between nodes represent dependencies.

Constructing precedence networks

Before we look at how networks are used, it is worth spending a few moments considering some rules for their construction.

A project network should have only one start node Although it is logically possible to draw a network with more than one starting node, it is undesirable to do so as it is a potential source of confusion. In such cases (for example, where more than one activity can start immediately the project starts) it is normal to invent a 'start' activity which has zero duration but may have an actual start date.

A project network should have only one end node The end node designates the completion of the project and a project may finish only once! Although it is possible to draw a network with more than one end node, it will almost certainly lead to confusion if this is done. Where the completion of a project depends upon more than one 'final' activity it is normal to invent a 'finish' activity.

A node has duration A node represents an activity and, in general, activities take time to execute. Notice, however, that the network in Figure 6.7 does not contain any reference to durations. This network drawing merely represents the logic of the project – the rules governing the order in which activities are to be carried out.

> Later we will look at the possibility of 'lag' between activities.

Links normally have no duration Links represent the relationships between activities. In Figure 6.9 installation cannot start until program testing is complete. Program testing cannot start until both coding and data take-on have been completed.

Precedents are the immediate preceding activities In Figure 6.9, the activity 'Program test' cannot start until both 'Code' and 'Data take-on' have been completed and activity 'Install' cannot start until 'Program test' has finished. 'Code' and 'Data take-on' can therefore be said to be precedents of 'Program test', and 'Program test' is a precedent of 'Install'. Note that we do not speak of 'Code' and 'Data take-on' as precedents of 'Install' – that relationship is implicit in the previous statement.

Time moves from left to right If at all possible, networks are drawn so that time moves from left to right. It is rare that this convention needs to be flouted but some people add arrows to the lines to give a stronger visual indication of the time flow of the project.

A network may not contain loops Figure 6.10 demonstrates a loop in a network. A loop is an error in that it represents a situation that cannot occur in practice. While loops, in the sense of iteration, may occur in practice, they cannot be directly represented in a

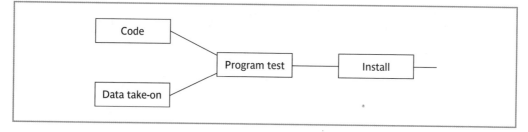

FIGURE 6.9 Fragment of a precedence network

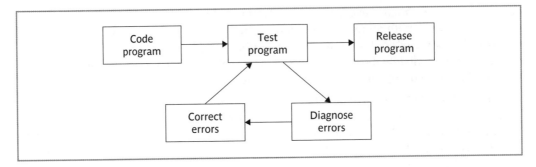

FIGURE 6.10 A loop represents an impossible sequence

project network. Note that the logic of Figure 6.10 suggests that program testing cannot start until the errors have been corrected.

If we know the number of times we expect to repeat a set of activities, a test–diagnose–correct sequence, for example, then we can draw that set of activities as a straight sequence, repeating it the appropriate number of times. If we do not know how many times a sequence is going to be repeated then we cannot calculate the duration of the project unless we adopt an alternative strategy such as redefining the complete sequence as a single activity and estimating how long it will take to complete it.

Although it is easy to see the loop in this simple network fragment, very large networks can easily contain complex loops which are difficult to spot when they are initially constructed. Fortunately, all network planning applications will detect loops and generate error messages when they are found.

A network should not contain dangles A dangling activity such as 'Write user manual' in Figure 6.11 should not exist as it is likely to lead to errors in subsequent analysis. Indeed, in many cases dangling activities indicate errors in logic when activities are added as an afterthought. If, in Figure 6.11, we mean to indicate that the project is complete once the software has been installed *and* the user manual written then we should redraw the network with a final completion activity – which, at least in this case, is probably a more accurate representation of what should happen. The redrawn network is shown in Figure 6.12.

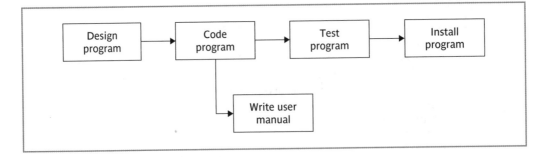

FIGURE 6.11 A dangle

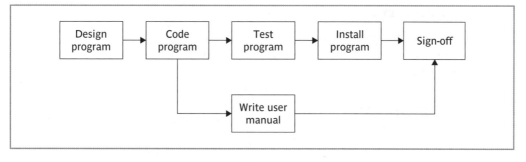

FIGURE 6.12 Resolving the dangle

Representing lagged activities

We might come across situations where we wish to undertake two activities in parallel so long as there is a lag between the two. We might wish to document amendments to a program as it is being tested – particularly if evaluating a prototype. In such a case we could designate an activity 'test and document amendments'. This would, however, make it impossible to show that amendment recording could start, say, one day after testing had begun and finish a little after the completion of testing.

Where activities can occur in parallel with a time lag between them, we represent the lag with a duration on the linking arrow as shown in Figure 6.13. This indicates that documenting amendments can start one day after the start of prototype testing and will be completed two days after prototype testing is completed.

Documenting amendments may take place alongside prototype testing so long as it starts at least one day later and finishes two days later.

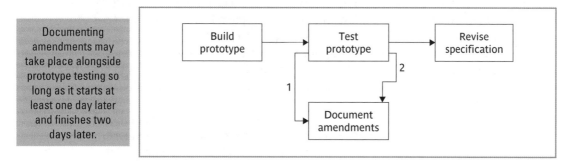

FIGURE 6.13 Indicating lags

Hammock activities

Hammock activities are activities which, in themselves, have zero duration but are assumed to start at the same time as the first 'hammocked' activity and to end at the same time as the last one. They are normally used for representing overhead costs or other resources that will be incurred or used at a constant rate over the duration of a set of activities.

Labelling conventions

There are a number of differing conventions that have been adopted for entering information on an activity-on-node network. The one adopted here is shown on the left and is based on the British Standard BS 4335.

Earliest start	Duration	Earliest finish
Activity label, activity description		
Latest start	Float	Latest finish

The activity label is usually a code developed to uniquely identify the activity and may incorporate a project code (for example, IoE/P/3 to designate one of the programming activities for IOE's annual maintenance contract project). The activity description will normally be a brief activity name such as 'Test take-on module'. The other items in our activity node will be explained as we discuss the analysis of a project network.

6.9 Adding the time dimension

Having created the logical network model indicating what needs to be done and the interrelationships between those activities, we are now ready to start thinking about when each activity should be undertaken.

The critical path approach is concerned with two primary objectives: planning the project in such a way that it is completed as quickly as possible; and identifying those activities where a delay in their execution is likely to affect the overall end date of the project or later activities' start dates.

The method requires that for each activity we have an estimate of its duration. The network is then analysed by carrying out a *forward pass*, to calculate the earliest dates at which activities may commence and the project be completed, and a *backward pass*, to calculate the latest start dates for activities and the *critical path*.

In practice we would use a software application to carry out these calculations for anything but the smallest of projects. It is important, though, that we understand how the calculations are carried out in order to interpret the results correctly and understand the limitations of the method.

The description and example that follow use the small example project outlined in Table 6.1 – a project composed of eight activities whose durations have been estimated as shown in the table. Brigette at Brightmouth College has completed the software package evaluation and a software package has been chosen and approved. Now that the application software is known, the hardware needed as a platform can be acquired. Another task will be 'system configuration' – there are a number of parameters that will have to set in the application so that it runs satisfactorily for Brightmouth College. Once the parameters have been set, details of the employees who are to be paid will have to be set up on the new system. Enough information about the new system will now be available so that office procedures can be devised and documented. There are currently no staff currently dedicated to payroll administration so a payroll officer is to be recruited and then trained.

Activity		Duration (weeks)	Precedents
A	Hardware selection	6	
B	System configuration	4	
C	Install hardware	3	A
D	Data migration	4	B
E	Draft office procedures	3	B
F	Recruit staff	10	
G	User training	3	E, F
H	Install and test system	2	C, D

TABLE 6.1 An example project specification with estimated activity durations and precedence requirements

EXERCISE 6.1

Figure 6.14 illustrates the network for the project specified in Table 6.1.

Draw an activity network using precedence network conventions for the project specified in Table 6.1. When you have completed it, compare your result with that shown in Figure 6.14.

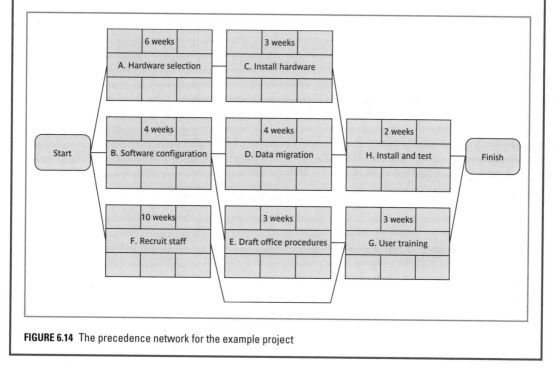

FIGURE 6.14 The precedence network for the example project

6.10 The forward pass

The forward pass is carried out to calculate the earliest dates on which each activity may be started and completed.

Where an actual start date is known, the calculations may be carried out using actual dates. Alternatively we can use day or week numbers and that is the approach we shall adopt here. By convention, dates indicate the end of a period and the project is therefore shown as starting at the end of week zero (or the beginning of week 1).

The forward pass and the calculation of earliest start dates are carried out according to the following reasoning.

> During the forward pass, earliest dates are recorded as they are calculated.

- Activities A, B and F may start immediately, so the earliest date for their start is zero.

- Activity A will take 6 weeks, so the earliest it can finish is week 6.

- Activity B will take 4 weeks, so the earliest it can finish is week 4.

- Activity F will take 10 weeks, so the earliest it can finish is week 10.

- Activity C can start as soon as A has finished so its earliest start date is week 6. It will take 3 weeks so the earliest it can finish is week 9.

> The forward pass rule: the earliest start date for an activity is the earliest finish date for the preceding activity. Where there is more than one immediately preceding activity we take the *latest* of the *earliest finish dates* for those activities.

- Activities D and E can start as soon as B is complete so the earliest they can each start is week 4. Activity D, which will take 4 weeks, can therefore finish by week 8 and activity E, which will take 3 weeks, can therefore finish by week 7.

- Activity G cannot start until both E and F have been completed. It cannot therefore start until week 10 – the later of weeks 7 (for activity E) and 10 (for activity F). It takes 3 weeks and finishes in week 13.

- Similarly, Activity H cannot start until week 9 – the later of the two earliest finish dates for the preceding activities C and D.

- The project will be complete when both activities H and G have been completed. Thus the earliest project completion date will be the later of weeks 11 and 13 – that is, week 13.

The results of the forward pass are shown in Figure 6.15.

6.11 The backward pass

The second stage in the analysis of a critical path network is to carry out a backward pass to calculate the latest date at which each activity may be started and finished without delaying the end date of the project. In calculating the latest dates, we assume that the latest finish date for the project is the same as the earliest finish date – that is, we wish to complete the project as early as possible.

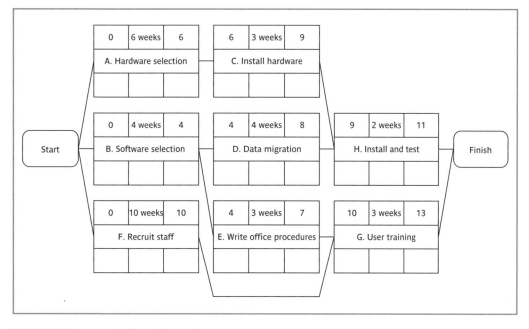

FIGURE 6.15 The network after the forward pass

Figure 6.16 illustrates our network after carrying out the backward pass. The latest activity dates are calculated as follows.

■ The latest completion date for activities G and H is assumed to be week 13.

■ Activity H must therefore start at week 11 at the latest (13 − 2) and the latest start date for activity G is week 10 (13 − 3).

■ The latest completion date for activities C and D is the latest date at which activity H must start – that is, week 11. They therefore have latest start dates of week 8 (11 − 3) and week 7 (11 − 4) respectively.

■ Activities E and F must be completed by week 10 so their earliest start dates are weeks 7 (10 − 3) and 0 (10 − 10) respectively.

■ Activity B must be completed by week 7 (the latest start date for both activities D and E) so its latest start is week 3 (7 − 4).

■ Activity A must be completed by week 8 (the latest start date for activity C) so its latest start is week 2 (8 − 6).

■ The latest start date for the project start is the earliest of the latest start dates for activities A, B and F. This is week zero. This is, of course, not very surprising since it tells us that if the project does not start on time it won't finish on time.

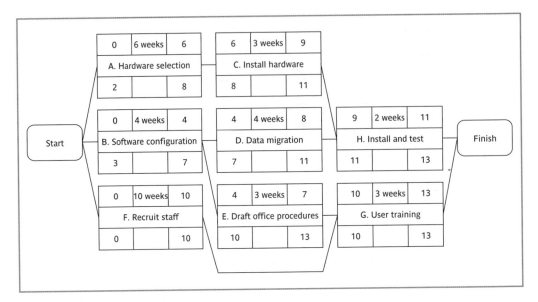

FIGURE 6.16 The network after the backward pass

6.12 Identifying the critical path

There will be at least one path through the network (that is, one set of successive activities) that defines the duration of the project. This is known as the *critical path*. Any delay to any activity on this critical path will delay the completion of the project.

The difference between an activity's earliest start date and its latest start date (or, equally, the difference between its earliest and latest finish dates) is known as the activity's *float* – it is a measure of how much the start or completion of an activity may be delayed without affecting the end date of the project. Any activity with a float of zero is critical in the sense that any delay in carrying out the activity will delay the completion date of the

project as a whole. There will always be at least one path through the network joining those critical activities – this path is known as the critical path and is shown bold in Figure 6.17.

The significance of the critical path is two-fold.

■ In managing the project, we must pay particular attention to monitoring activities on the critical path so that the effects of any delay or resource unavailability are detected and corrected at the earliest opportunity.

■ In planning the project, it is the critical path that we must shorten if we are to reduce the overall duration of the project.

Figure 6.17 also shows the *activity span*. This is the difference between the earliest start date and the latest finish date and is a measure of the maximum time allowable for the activity. However, it is subject to the same conditions of interpretation as activity float, which is discussed in the next section.

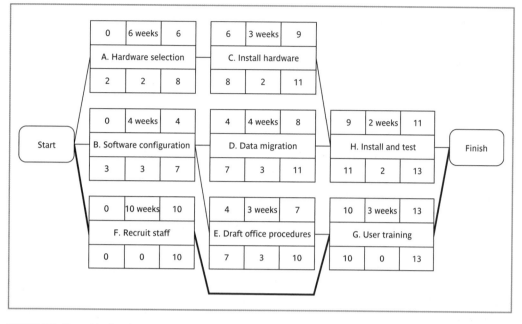

FIGURE 6.17 The critical path

EXERCISE 6.2

Refer back to Amanda's CPM network illustrated in Figure 6.7.

Using the activity durations given in Table 6.2, calculate the earliest completion date for the project and identify the critical path on your network.

Activity	Estimated duration (days)	Activity	Estimated duration (days)
Specify overall system	34	Design module C	4
Specify module A	20	Design module D	4
Specify module B	15	Code/test module A	30
Specify module C	25	Code/test module B	28
Specify module D	15	Code/test module C	15
Check specification	2	Code/test module D	25
Design module A	7	System integration	6
Design module B	6		

TABLE 6.2 Estimated activity durations for Amanda's network

6.13 Activity float

> Total float may only
> be used once.

Although the total float is shown for each activity, it really 'belongs' to a path through the network. Activities A and C in Figure 6.17 each have 2 weeks' total float. If, however, activity A uses up its float (that is, it is not completed until week 8) then activity B will have zero float (it will have become critical). In such circumstances it may be misleading and detrimental to the project's success to publicize total float!

There are a number of other measures of activity float, including the following:

- *Free float:* the time by which an activity may be delayed without affecting any subsequent activity. It is calculated as the difference between the earliest completion date for the activity and the earliest start date of the succeeding activity. This might be considered a more satisfactory measure of float for publicizing to the staff involved in undertaking the activities.

- *Interfering float:* the difference between total float and free float. This is quite commonly used, particularly in association with the free float. Once the free float has been used (or if it is zero), the interfering float tells us by how much the activity may be delayed without delaying the project end date – even though it will delay the start of subsequent activities.

EXERCISE 6.3

Calculate the free float and interfering float for each of the activities shown in the activity network (Figure 6.17).

6.14 Shortening the project duration

If we wish to shorten the overall duration of a project we would normally consider attempting to reduce activity durations. In many cases this can be done by applying more resources to the task – working overtime or procuring additional staff, for example. The critical path indicates where we must look to save time – if we are trying to bring forward the end date of the project, there is clearly no point in attempting to shorten non-critical activities. Referring to Figure 6.17, it can be seen that we could complete the project in week 12 by reducing the duration of activity F by one week (to 9 weeks).

As we reduce activity times along the critical path we must continually check for any new critical path emerging and redirect our attention where necessary.

There will come a point when we can no longer safely, or cost-effectively, reduce critical activity durations in an attempt to bring forward the project end date. Further savings, if needed, must be sought in a consideration of our work methods and by questioning the logical sequencing of activities. Generally, time savings are to be found by increasing the amount of parallelism in the network and the removal of bottlenecks (subject always, of course, to resource and quality constraints).

EXERCISE 6.4

Referring to Figure 6.17, suppose that the duration for activity F is shortened to 8 weeks. Calculate the end date for the project.

What would the end date for the project be if activity F were shortened to 7 weeks? Why?

6.15 Identifying critical activities

For a more in-depth discussion of the role of the critical path in project monitoring, see Chapter 9.

The critical path identifies those activities which are critical to the end date of the project; however, activities that are not on the critical path may become critical. As the project proceeds, activities will invariably use up some of their float and this will require a periodic recalculation of the network. As soon as the activities along a particular path use up their total float then that path will become a critical path and a number of hitherto non-critical activities will suddenly become critical.

It is therefore common practice to identify *near-critical* paths – those whose lengths are within, say, 10–20% of the duration of the critical path or those with a total float of less than, say, 10% of the project's uncompleted duration.

The importance of identifying critical and near-critical activities is that it is they that are most likely to be the cause of delays in completing the project. We shall see, in the next three chapters, that identifying these activities is an important step in risk analysis, resource allocation and project monitoring.

6.16 Activity-on-arrow networks

The developers of the CPM and PERT methods both originally used activity-on-arrow networks. Although now less common than activity-on-node networks, they are still used and introduce an additional useful concept – that of events. We will therefore take a brief look at how they are drawn and analysed using the same project example shown in Table 6.1.

In activity-on-arrow networks activities are represented by links (or arrows) and the nodes represent events of activities (or groups of activities) starting or finishing. Figure 6.18 illustrates our previous example (see Figure 6.14) drawn as an activity-on-arrow network.

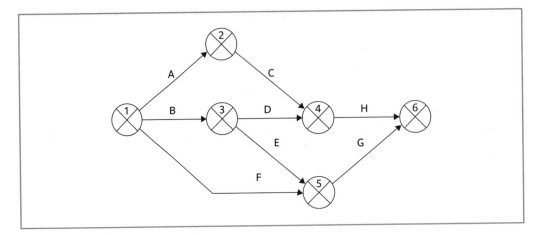

FIGURE 6.18 An activity-on-arrow network

Activity-on-arrow network rules and conventions

A project network may have only one start node This is a requirement of activity-on-arrow networks rather than merely desirable as is the case with activity-on-node networks.

A project network may have only one end node Again, this is a requirement for activity-on-arrow networks.

A link has duration A link represents an activity and, in general, activities take time to execute. Notice, however, that the network in Figure 6.18 does not contain any reference to durations. The links are not drawn in any way to represent the activity durations. The network drawing merely represents the logic of the project – the rules governing the order in which activities are to be carried out.

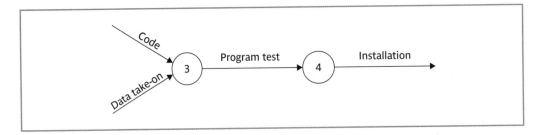

FIGURE 6.19 Fragment of a CPM network

Nodes have no duration Nodes are events and, as such, are instantaneous points in time. The source node is the event of the project becoming ready to start and the sink node is the event of the project becoming completed. Intermediate nodes represent two simultaneous events – the event of all activities leading in to a node having been completed and the event of all activities leading out of that node being in a position to be started.

In Figure 6.19, node 3 is the event that both 'coding' and 'data take-on' have been completed and activity 'program test' is free to start. 'Installation' may be started only when event 4 has been achieved, that is, as soon as 'program test' has been completed.

Time moves from left to right As with activity-on-node networks, activity-on-arrow networks are drawn, if at all possible, so that time moves from left to right.

Nodes are numbered sequentially There are no precise rules about node numbering but nodes should be numbered so that head nodes (those at the 'arrow' end of an activity) always have a higher number than tail events (those at the 'non-arrow' end of an activity). This convention makes it easy to spot loops.

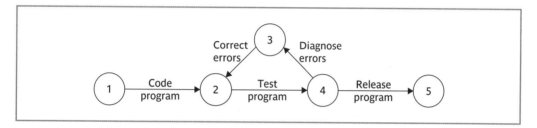

FIGURE 6.20 A loop represents an impossible sequence

A network may not contain loops Figure 6.20 demonstrates a loop in an activity-on-arrow network. As discussed in the context of precedence networks, loops are either an error of logic or a situation that must be resolved by itemizing iterations of activity groups.

A network may not contain dangles A dangling activity, such as 'Write user manual' in Figure 6.21, cannot exist, as it would suggest there are two completion points for the project. If, in Figure 6.21, node 5 represents the true project completion point and there are no activities dependent on activity 'Write user manual', then the network should be redrawn so that activity 'Write user manual' starts at node 2 and terminates at node 5 – in practice, we would need to insert a dummy activity between nodes 3 and 5. In other words, all events, except the first and the last, must have at least one activity entering them and at least one activity leaving them and all activities must start and end with an event.

> Dangles are not allowed in activity-on-arrow networks.

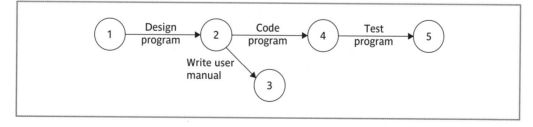

FIGURE 6.21 A dangle

EXERCISE 6.5

Take a look at the networks in Figure 6.22. State what is wrong with each of them and, where possible, redraw them correctly.

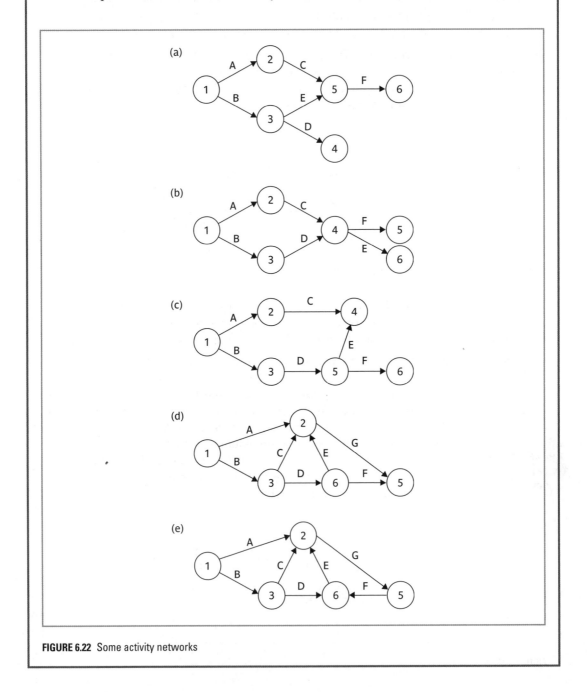

FIGURE 6.22 Some activity networks

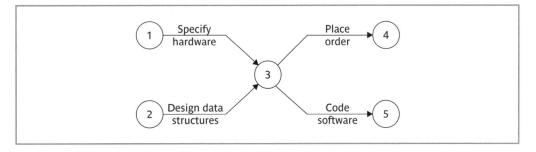

FIGURE 6.23 Two paths with a common node

Using dummy activities

When two paths within a network have a common event although they are, in other respects, independent, a logical error such as that illustrated in Figure 6.23 might occur.

Suppose that, in a particular project, it is necessary to specify a certain piece of hardware before placing an order for it and before coding the software. Before coding the software it is also necessary to specify the appropriate data structures, although clearly we do not need to wait for this to be done before the hardware is ordered.

Figure 6.23 is an attempt to model the situation described above, although it is incorrect in that it requires both hardware specification and data structure design to be completed before either an order may be placed or software coding may commence.

We can resolve this problem by separating the two (more or less) independent paths and introducing a dummy activity to link the completion of 'specify hardware' to the start of the activity 'code software'. This effectively breaks the link between data structure design and placing the order and is shown in Figure 6.24.

Dummy activities, shown as dotted lines on the network diagram, have a zero duration and use no resources. They are often used to aid in the layout of network drawings as in Figure 6.25. The use of a dummy activity where two activities share the same start and end nodes makes it easier to distinguish the activity end-points.

These are problems that do not occur with activity-on-node networks.

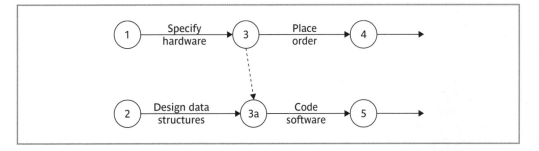

FIGURE 6.24 Two paths linked by a dummy activity

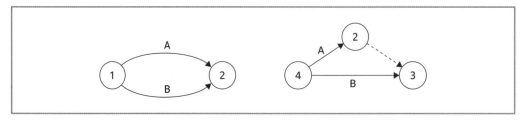

FIGURE 6.25 Another use of a dummy activity

EXERCISE 6.6

Take another look at Brigette's college payroll activity network fragment, which related to the earlier software selection process and which you developed in Exercise 3.4 (or take a look at the model answer in Figure B.2). Redraw this as an activity-on-arrow network.

Representing lagged activities

Activity-on-arrow networks are less elegant when it comes to representing lagged parallel activities. We need to represent these with pairs of dummy activities as shown in Figure 6.26. Where the activities are lagged because a stage in one activity must be completed before the other may proceed, it is likely to be better to show each stage as a separate activity.

Activity labelling

There are a number of differing conventions that have been adopted for entering information on an activity-on-arrow network. Typically the diagram is used to record information about the events rather than the activities – activity-based information

Where parallel activities have a time lag we may show this as a 'ladder' of activities: documentation may proceed alongside prototype testing so long as it starts at least a day later and will finish two days after the completion of prototype testing.

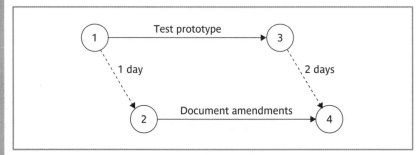

FIGURE 6.26 Using the ladder technique to indicate lags

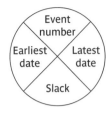

(other than labels or descriptions) is generally held on a separate activity table.

One of the more common conventions for labelling nodes, and the one adopted here, is to divide the node circle into quadrants and use those quadrants to show the event number, the latest and earliest dates by which the event should occur, and the event slack (which will be explained later).

Network analysis

Analysis proceeds in the same way as with activity-on-node networks, although the discussion places emphasis on the events rather than activity start and completion times.

> During the forward pass, earliest dates are recorded as they are calculated. For events, they are recorded on the network diagram and for activities they are recorded on the activity table.

The forward pass The forward pass is carried out to calculate the earliest date on which each event may be achieved and the earliest dates on which each activity may be started and completed. The earliest date for an event is the earliest date by which all activities upon which it depends can be completed. Using Figure 6.18 and Table 6.1, the calculation proceeds according to the following reasoning.

- Activities A, B and F may start immediately, so the earliest date for event 1 is zero and the earliest start date for these three activities is also zero.

- Activity A will take 6 weeks, so the earliest it can finish is week 6 (recorded in the activity table). Therefore the earliest we can achieve event 2 is week 6.

- Activity B will take 4 weeks, so the earliest it can finish and the earliest we can achieve event 3 is week 4.

- Activity F will take 10 weeks, so the earliest it can finish is week 10 – we cannot, however, tell whether or not this is also the earliest date that we can achieve event 5 since we have not, as yet, calculated when activity E will finish.

> The forward pass rule: the earliest date for an event is the earliest finish date for all the activities terminating at that event. Where more than one activity terminates at a common event we take the latest of the earliest finish dates for those activities.

- Activity E can start as early as week 4 (the earliest date for event 3) and, since it is forecasted to take 3 weeks, will be completed, at the earliest, at the end of week 7.

- Event 5 may be achieved when both E and F have been completed, that is, week 10 (the later of 7 and 10).

- Similarly, we can reason that event 4 will have an earliest date of week 9. This is the later of the earliest finish for activity D (week 8) and the earliest finish for activity C (week 9).

- The earliest date for the completion of the project, event 6, is therefore the end of week 13 – the later of 11 (the earliest finish for H) and 13 (the earliest finish for G).

The results of the forward pass are shown in Figure 6.27 and Table 6.3.

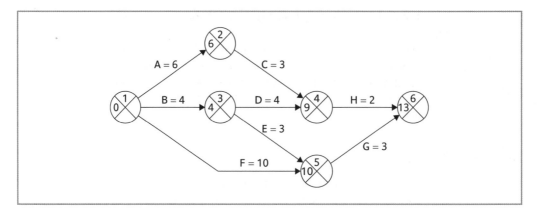

FIGURE 6.27 A CPM network after the forward pass

Activity	Duration (weeks)	Earliest start date	Latest start date	Earliest finish date	Latest finish date	Total float
A	6	0		6		
B	4	0		4		
C	3	6		9		
D	4	4		8		
E	3	4		7		
F	10	0		10		
G	3	10		13		
H	2	9		11		

TABLE 6.3 The activity table after the forward pass

> The backward pass rule: the latest date for an event is the latest start date for all the activities that may commence from that event. Where more than one activity commences at a common event we take the earliest of the latest start dates for those activities.

The backward pass The second stage is to carry out a backward pass to calculate the latest date at which each event may be achieved, and each activity started and finished, without delaying the end date of the project. The latest date for an event is the latest date by which all immediately following activities must be started for the project to be completed on time. As with activity-on-node networks, we assume that the latest finish date for the project is the same as the earliest finish date – that is, we wish to complete the project as early as possible.

Figure 6.28 illustrates our network and Table 6.4 the activity table after carrying out the backward pass – as with the forward pass, event dates are recorded on the diagram and activity dates on the activity table.

Identifying the critical path The critical path is identified in a way similar to that used in activity-on-node networks. We do, however, use a different concept, that of *slack*, in identifying the path. Slack is the difference between the earliest date and the latest date for an event – it is a measure of how late an event may be without affecting the end date of the project. The critical path is the path joining all nodes with a zero slack (Figure 6.29).

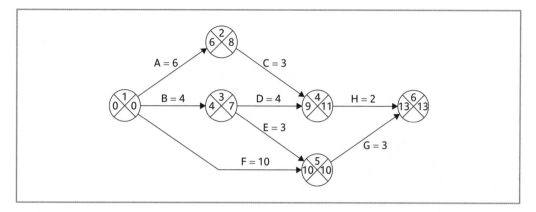

FIGURE 6.28 The CPM network after the backward pass

Activity	Duration (weeks)	Earliest start date	Latest start date	Earliest finish date	Latest finish date	Total float
A	6	0	2	6	8	
B	4	0	3	4	7	
C	3	6	8	9	11	
D	4	4	7	8	11	
E	3	4	7	7	10	
F	10	0	0	10	10	
G	3	10	10	13	13	
H	2	9	11	11	13	

TABLE 6.4 The activity table following the backward pass

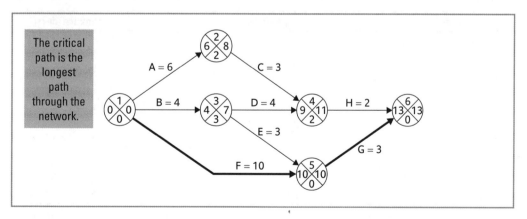

FIGURE 6.29 The critical path

6.17 Conclusion

In this chapter, we have discussed the use of the critical path method and precedence networks to obtain an ideal activity plan. This plan tells us the order in which we should execute activities and the earliest and latest we can start and finish them.

These techniques help us to identify which activities are critical to meeting a target completion date.

In order to manage the project we need to turn the activity plan into a schedule that will specify precisely when each activity is scheduled to start and finish. Before we can do this, we must consider what resources will be required and whether or not they will be available at appropriate times. As we shall see, the allocation of resources to an activity may be affected by how we view the importance of the task and the risks associated with it. In the next two chapters we look at these aspects of project planning before we consider how we might publish a schedule for the project.

6.18 Further exercises

1 Draw an activity network using either activity-on-node or activity-on-arrow network conventions for each of the following projects:
   - redecorating a room;
   - choosing and purchasing a desktop computer;
   - organizing and carrying out a survey of users' opinions of an information system.

2 If you have access to a project planning application, use it to produce a project plan for the IOE annual maintenance contracts project. Base your plan on that used for Exercise 6.2 and verify that your application reports the same information as you calculated manually when you did the exercise.

3 Based on your answer to Exercise 6.2, discuss what options Amanda might consider if she found it necessary to complete the project earlier than day 104.

4 Create a precedence activity network using the following details:

Activity	Depends on	Duration (days)
A		5
B	A	7
C	B	6
D	A	5
E	D	10
F	B	15
G	B	8
H	G	8
I	C	4
J	G	4
K	E, F	5
L	I, H	3

5   Calculate the earliest and latest start and end dates and the float associated with each activity in the network you have created for further exercise 4 above. From this identify the critical path.

6   Draw up a precedence activity network for the following scenario:
The specification of an ICT application is estimated as likely to take two weeks to complete. When this activity has been completed, work can start on three software modules, A, B and C. Design/coding of the modules will need 5, 10 and 10 days respectively. Modules A and B can only be unit-tested together as their functionality is closely associated. This joint testing should take about two weeks. Module C will need eight days of unit testing. When all unit testing has been completed, integrated system testing will be needed, taking a further three weeks. This testing will be based on the functionality described in the specification and will need 10 days of planning.

7   For the activity network in further exercise 6 above, derive the earliest and latest start dates for each activity and the earliest and latest finish dates. Work out the shortest project duration. If only two software developers were available for the design and coding of modules, what effect would this have on the project duration?

8   What are the limitations of the precedence and CPM activity network notations?

CHAPTER 7

Risk management

❖ **OBJECTIVES**

When you have completed this chapter you will be able to:

❖ identify the factors putting a project at risk;

❖ categorize and prioritize actions for risk elimination or containment;

❖ quantify the likely effects of risk on project timescales.

7.1 Introduction

In Chapter 6 we saw how, at IOE, Amanda planned how the software for the new annual maintenance contracts application was to be produced. This included estimating how long each task would take – see Figure 6.7 and Table 6.2. Her plan was based on the assumption that three experienced programmers were available for the coding of modules A, B, C and D. However, suppose two developers then left for better-paid jobs, and so far only one replacement has been recruited, who happens to be a trainee.

In the case of Brigette and the Brightmouth payroll implementation project, imagine that a payroll package has been purchased. However, a new requirement emerges that the payroll database should be accessed by a new application that calculates the staff costs for each course delivered by the college. Unfortunately, the purchased payroll application does not allow this access.

Amanda and Brigette will have to deal with these *problems* as part of the monitoring and control process that will be outlined in Chapter 9. In this chapter we consider whether the two project leaders could have

In some work environments 'problems' in this context are referred to as 'issues'.

162

foreseen that these problems were likely to occur and made plans to deal with them. In other words, could these problems have been identified as *risks*?

7.2 Risk

PM-BOK stands for Project Management Body of Knowledge, a project management standard published by the Project Management Institute in the USA.

PM-BOK defines risk as '*an uncertain event or condition that, if it occurs, has a positive or negative effect on a project's objectives*'. PRINCE2, the UK government-sponsored project management standard, defines risk as '*the chance of exposure to the adverse consequences of future events*'. The two definitions differ, as the first includes situations where a future uncertainty actually works in our favour and presents us with an opportunity. We will return to this later in the chapter.

The key elements of a risk follow.

■ *It relates to the future* The future is inherently uncertain. Some things which seem obvious when a project is over, for example that the costs were under-estimated or that a new technology was overly difficult to use, might not have been so obvious during planning.

The ISPL risk model (formerly Euromethod) refers to hazards as 'situational factors'.

■ *It involves **cause** and **effect*** For example, a 'cost over-run' might be identified as a risk, but 'cost over-run' describes some damage, but does not say what causes it. Is it, for example, an inaccurate estimate of effort, the use of untrained staff, or a poor specification? Both the cause (or *hazard*), such as 'inexperienced staff', and a particular type of negative outcome, such as 'lower productivity', should be defined for each risk.

EXERCISE 7.1

Match the following causes – a to d – to their possible effects – i to iv. The relationships are not necessarily one-to-one. Explain the reasons for each match.

Causes
(a) staff inexperience;
(b) lack of top management commitment;
(c) new technology;
(d) users uncertain of their requirements.

Effects
(i) testing takes longer than planned;
(ii) planned effort and time for activities exceeded;
(iii) project scope increases;
(iv) time delays in getting changes to plans agreed.

The boundary between risk management and 'normal' software project management is hazy. For example, when we were selecting the best general approach to a project – see Chapter 4 – one consideration was the possible consequences of future adverse events. As will be seen in Chapter 13, most of the techniques used to assure the quality of software, such as reviews and testing, are designed to reduce the risk of faults in project deliverables. Risk management is not a self-contained topic within project management. The key role of risk management is considering uncertainty remaining after a plan has been formulated. Every plan is based on assumptions and risk management tries to plan for and control the situations where those assumptions become incorrect. Risk planning is carried out in Steps 3 and 6 (Figure 7.1).

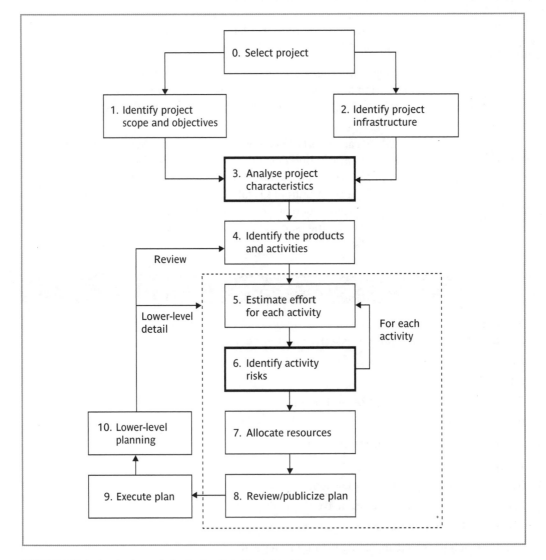

FIGURE 7.1 Risk planning is carried out primarily in Steps 3 and 6

7.3 Categories of risk

An ICT project manager is normally given the objective of installing the required application by a specified deadline and within an agreed budget. Other objectives might be set, especially with regard to quality requirements. *Project risks* are those that could prevent the achievement of the objectives given to the project manager and the project team.

As we noted in Chapter 2, there could be risks that an application after successful implementation is a business failure. Thus if an e-commerce site is established to sell a product, the site might be correctly implemented, but customers fail to use the site because of the uncompetitive prices demanded. Dealing with these *business risks* is likely to be outside the direct responsibilities of the application implementation team. However, the failure to meet any project objective could have a negative impact on the business case for the project. For example, an increase in development cost might mean that the income (or savings) generated by the delivered application no longer represents a good return on the increased investment.

See K. Lyytinen, L. Mathiassen and J. Ropponen (1996) 'A framework for risk management' *Journal of Information Technology*, 11(4).

Risks have been categorized in other ways. Kalle Lyytinen and his colleagues, for instance, have proposed a *sociotechnical model* of risk, a diagrammatic representation of which appears in Figure 7.2.

The box labelled '*Actors*' refers to all the people involved in the development of the application in question. A typical risk in this area is that high staff turnover leads to expertise of value to the project being lost.

In Figure 7.2, the box labelled '*Technology*' encompasses both the technology used to implement the application and that embedded in the delivered products. Risks here could relate to the appropriateness of the technologies and to possible faults within them, especially if they are novel.

'*Structure*' describes the management structures and systems, including those affecting planning and control. For example, the implementation might need user participation in some tasks, but the responsibility for managing the users' contribution might not be clearly allocated.

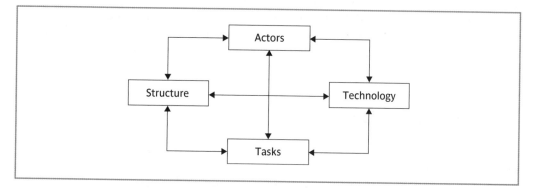

FIGURE 7.2 The Lyytinen–Mathiassen–Ropponen risk framework

'*Tasks*' relates to the work planned. For instance, the complexity of the work might lead to delays because of the additional time required integrate the large number of components.

In Figure 7.2 all boxes are interlinked. Risks often arise from the relationships between factors – for example between technology and people. If a development technology is novel then the developers might not be experienced in its use and delay results. The novelty of the new technology is really a characteristic of the developers: once they are used to the technology, it is no longer 'novel'.

EXERCISE 7.2

In the cases of the Brightmouth payroll implementation project and the IOE annual maintenance contracts development project, identify one risk for each of the four categories in Figure 7.2.

7.4 A framework for dealing with risk

Planning for risk includes these steps:

(i)   risk identification;

(ii) risk analysis and prioritization;

(iii) risk planning;

(iv) risk monitoring.

Steps (i) to (iii) above will probably be repeated. When risks that could prevent a project success are identified, plans can be made to reduce or remove their threat. The plans are then reassessed to ensure that the original risks are reduced sufficiently and no new risks inadvertently introduced. Take the risk that staff inexperience with a new technology could lead to delays in software development. To reduce this risk, consultants expert in the new technology might be recruited. However, the use of consultants might introduce the new risk that knowledge about the new technology is not transferred to the permanent staff, making subsequent software maintenance problematic. Having identified this new risk, further risk reduction activities can be planned.

7.5 Risk identification

The two main approaches to the identification of risks are the use of *checklists* and *brainstorming*.

Checklists are simply lists of the risks that have been found to occur regularly in software development projects. A specialized list of software development risks by Barry

This top ten list of software risks is based on one presented by Barry Boehm in his *Tutorial on Software Risk Management*, IEE Computer Society, 1989.

Risk	Risk reduction techniques
Personnel shortfalls	Staffing with top talent; job matching; teambuilding; training and career development; early scheduling of key personnel
Unrealistic time and cost estimates	Multiple estimation techniques; design to cost; incremental development; recording and analysis of past projects; standardization of methods
Developing the wrong software functions	Improved software evaluation; formal specification methods; user surveys; prototyping; early user manuals
Developing the wrong user interface	Prototyping; task analysis; user involvement
Gold plating	Requirements scrubbing; prototyping; cost–benefit analysis; design to cost
Late changes to requirements	Stringent change control procedures; high change threshold; incremental development (deferring changes)
Shortfalls in externally supplied components	Benchmarking; inspections; formal specifications; contractual agreements; quality assurance procedures and certification
Shortfalls in externally performed tasks	Quality assurance procedures; competitive design or prototyping; contract incentives
Real-time performance shortfalls	Simulation; benchmarking; prototyping; tuning; technical analysis
Development technically too difficult	Technical analysis; cost–benefit analysis; prototyping; staff training and development

TABLE 7.1 Software project risks and strategies for risk reduction

The 'lessons learnt' report differs from a 'post implementation review' (PIR). It is written on project completion and focuses on project issues. A PIR, produced when the application has been operational for some time, focuses on business benefits.

Boehm appears in Table 7.1 in a modified version. Ideally a group of representative project stakeholders examines a checklist identifying risks applicable to their project. Often the checklist suggests potential countermeasures for each risk.

Project management methodologies, such PRINCE2, often recommend that on completion of a project a review identifies any problems during the project and the steps that were (or should have been) taken to resolve or avoid them. These problems could in some cases be added to an organizational risk checklist for use with new projects.

Brainstorming

Ideally, representatives of the main stakeholders should be brought together once some kind of preliminary plan has been drafted. They then identify, using their individual knowledge of different parts of the project, the problems that might occur. This collaborative approach may generate a sense of ownership in the project.

'Brainstorming' is also mentioned in Chapter 13 in connection with quality circles.

Brainstorming might be used with Brigette's Brightmouth payroll implementation project as she realizes that there are aspects of college administration of which she is unaware. She therefore suggests to the main stakeholders in the project, who include staff from the finance office and the personnel office, that they meet and discuss where the risks facing the project lie.

7.6 Risk assessment

A common problem with risk identification is that a list of risks is potentially endless. A way is needed of distinguishing the damaging and likely risks. This can be done by estimating the *risk exposure* for each risk using the formula:

risk exposure = (potential damage) × (probability of occurrence)

Using the most rigorous – but not necessarily the most practical – approach, the potential damage would be assessed as a money value. Say a project depended on a data centre vulnerable to fire. It might be estimated that if a fire occurred a new computer configuration could be established for £500,000. It might also be estimated that where the computer is located there is a 1 in 1000 chance of a fire actually happening, that is a probability of 0.001.

The risk exposure in this case would be:

$$£500,000 \times 0.001 = £500$$

A crude way of understanding this value is as the minimum sum an insurance company would require as a premium. If 1000 companies, all in the same position, each contributed £500 to a fund then, when the 1 in 1000 chance of the fire actually occurred, there would be enough money to cover the cost of recovery.

EXERCISE 7.3

What conditions would have to exist for the risk pooling arrangement described above to work?

The calculation of risk exposure above assumes that the amount of damage sustained will always be the same. However, it is usually the case that there could be varying amounts of damage. For example, as software development proceeds, more software is created, and more time would be needed to re-create it if it were lost.

With some risks, there could be not only damage but also gains. The testing of a software component is scheduled to take six days, but is actually done in three days. A team leader might therefore feel justified in producing a probability chart like the one in Figure 7.3. This shows the probability of a task being completed in four days (5%), then

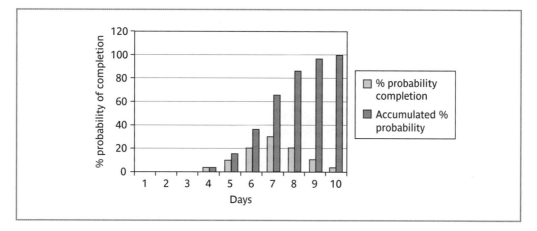

FIGURE 7.3 Probability chart

five days (10%) and so on. The accumulated probability for the seventh day (65%) means that there is a 65% chance that the task will be finished on or before the seventh day.

Clients would almost certainly insist we pick one of the days as the target. This target could be 'aggressive', for instance only five days in the above scenario, but with an 85% chance of failure according to the chart. A safer estimate would be eight days which would have a probability of failure of only 15%. We will return to this point later on in this chapter.

In Figure 7.3 the 'loss' is effectively being measured in days rather than money. In this context, days, or some other unit of personal effort, is often used as a *surrogate* for a financial loss.

Most managers resist very precise estimates of loss or of the probability of something occurring, as such figures are usually guesses. Barry Boehm has suggested that, because of this, both the risk losses and the probabilities be assessed using relative scales in the range 0 to 10. The two figures could then be multiplied together to get a notional risk exposure. Table 7.2 provides an example, based on Amanda's IOE group accounts project, of where

Ref	Hazard	Likelihood	Impact	Risk
R1	Changes to requirements specification during coding	8	8	64
R2	Specification takes longer than expected	3	7	21
R3	Significant staff sickness affecting critical path activities	5	7	35
R4	Significant staff sickness affecting non-critical activities	10	3	30
R5	Module coding takes longer than expected	4	5	20
R6	Module testing demonstrates errors or deficiencies in design	4	8	32

TABLE 7.2 Part of Amanda's risk exposure assessment

this has been done. This value could be used to prioritize the importance of risks, although more sophisticated risk calculations are not possible.

Boehm suggests that planners focus attention on the 10 risks with the highest risk exposure scores. For smaller projects – including the final-year projects of computing students – the focus could be on a smaller number of risks.

Even using indicative numbers in the range 0 to 10, rather than precise money values and probabilities, is not completely satisfactory. The values are likely to be subjective, and different analysts might pick different numbers. Another approach is to use qualitative descriptions of the possible impact and the likelihood of each risk – see Tables 7.3 and 7.4 for examples. Consistency between assessors is facilitated by associating each qualitative description with a range of values.

See P. Goodwin and G. Wright (2004) *Decision Analysis for Management Judgement*, Wiley, for further discussion of this issue.

In Table 7.4, the potential amount of damage has been categorized in terms of its impact on *project costs*. Other tables could show the impact of risks on *project duration* or on the *quality of the project deliverables*.

To some extent, the project manager, in conjunction with the project sponsor, can choose whether the damage inflicted by a risk affects cost, duration or the quality of deliverables. In Amanda's list of risks in Table 7.2, R5 refers to the coding of modules taking longer than planned. This would have an impact on both the duration of the project and the costs, as more staff time would be needed. A response might be adding software developers and splitting the remaining development work between them. This will increase costs, but could save the planned completion date. Another option is to save both duration and staff costs by reducing software testing before the

Probability level	Range
High	Greater than 50% chance of happening
Significant	30–50% chance of happening
Moderate	10–29% chance of happening
Low	Less than 10% chance of happening

TABLE 7.3 Qualitative descriptors of risk probability and associated range values

Impact level	Range
High	More than 30% above budgeted expenditure
Significant	20 to 29% above budgeted expenditure
Moderate	10 to 19% above budgeted expenditure
Low	Within 10% of budgeted expenditure.

TABLE 7.4 Qualitative descriptors of impact on cost and associated range values

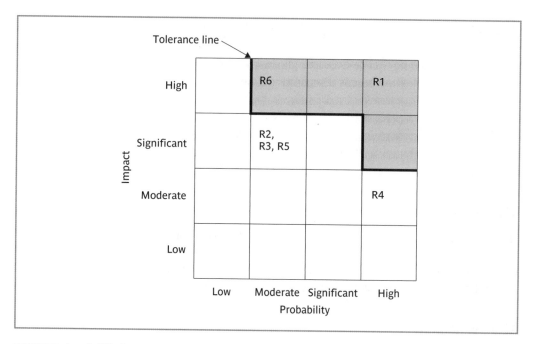

FIGURE 7.4 A probability impact matrix

software is released. This is likely to be at the price of decreased quality in the project deliverable.

Where the potential damage and likelihood of a risk are defined by qualitative descriptors, the risk exposure cannot be calculated by multiplying the two factors together. In this case, the risk exposure is indicated by the position of the risk in a matrix – see Figure 7.4. These matrices have variously been called *probability impact grids* or *summary risk profiles*.

In Figure 7.4 some of the cells in the top right of the matrix have been zoned off by a *tolerance line*. Risks that appear within this zone have a degree of seriousness that calls for particular attention.

> The term *risk proximity* is used to describe this attribute of risk.

Chapter 5 stressed the need for frequent reassessment of effort and duration estimates during a project. This applies to risk exposure as well, as some risks apply only at certain stages. A risk might be that key users are unavailable when needed to supply details of their requirements. As requirements are gathered, so this risk will diminish until it is no longer significant. In general, the element of uncertainty will lessen as a project progresses and more is learnt by the developers about user requirements and any new technology. This would be reflected in lower risk probabilities. On the other hand, the potential damage will tend to increase as the amount invested in the project grows. If you type a substantial report using a word processor and neglect to take back-ups, as each day adds more text to the report, it also adds to the number of days needed to re-key the report in the event of file loss.

7.7 Risk planning

Having identified the major risks and allocated priorities, the task is to decide how to deal with them. The choices discussed will be:

- risk acceptance;
- risk avoidance;
- risk reduction and mitigation;
- risk transfer.

Risk acceptance

This is the do-nothing option. We will already, in the risk prioritization process, have decided to ignore some risks in order to concentrate on the more likely or damaging. We could decide that the damage inflicted by some risks would be less than the costs of action that might reduce the probability of a risk happening.

Risk avoidance

Some activities may be so prone to accident that it is best to avoid them altogether. If you are worried about sharks then don't go into the water. For example, given all the problems with developing software solutions from scratch, managers might decide to retain existing clerical methods, or to buy an off-the-shelf solution.

Risk reduction

Here we decide to go ahead with a course of action despite the risks, but take precautions that reduce the probability of the risk.

> It must be appreciated that each risk reduction action is likely to involve some cost. This is discussed in the next section.

This chapter started with a scenario where two of the staff scheduled to work on Amanda's development project at IOE departed for other jobs. If this has been identified as a risk, steps might have been taken to reduce possible departures of staff. For instance, the developers might have been promised generous bonuses to be paid on successful completion of the project.

Recall that Brigette had a problem at Brightmouth College: after the purchase of the payroll package, a requirement for the payroll database to be accessed by another application was identified. Unfortunately, the application that had been bought did not allow such access. An alternative scenario might have been that Brigette identified this as a possible risk early on in the project. She might have come across Richard Fairley's four COTS (commercial off-the-shelf) software acquisition risks – see Table 7.5 – where one risk is difficulty in integrating the data formats and communication protocols of different applications. Brigette might have specified that the selected package must use a widely accepted data management system like Oracle that allows easier integration.

See R. Fairley (1994) 'Risk management for software projects' *IEEE Software* 11(3) 57–67.

Integration	Difficulties in integrating the data formats and communication protocols of different applications.
Upgrading	When the supplier upgrades the package, the package might no longer meet the users' precise requirements. Sticking with the old version could mean losing the supplier's support for the package.
No source code	If you want to enhance the system, you might not be able to do so as you do not have access to the source code.
Supplier failures or buyouts	The supplier of the application might go out of business or be bought out by a rival supplier.

TABLE 7.5 Fairley's four commercial off-the-shelf (COTS) software acquisition risks

Risk mitigation can sometimes be distinguished from risk reduction. *Risk reduction* attempts to reduce the likelihood of the risk occurring. *Risk mitigation* is action taken to ensure that the impact of the risk is lessened when it occurs. For example, taking regular back-ups of data storage would reduce the impact of data corruption but not its likelihood. Mitigation is closely associated with contingency planning which is discussed presently.

Risk transfer

Risk transfer is what effectively happens when you buy insurance.

In this case the risk is transferred to another person or organization. With software projects, an example of this would be where a software development task is outsourced to an outside agency for a fixed fee. You might expect the supplier to quote a higher figure to cover the risk that the project takes longer than the 'average' expected time. On the other hand, a well-established external organization might have productivity advantages as its developers are experienced in the type of development to be carried out. The need to compete with other software development specialists would also tend to drive prices down.

7.8 Risk management

Contingency

Risk reduction activities would appear to have only a small impact on reducing the probability of some risks, for example staff absence through illness. While some employers encourage their employees to adopt a healthy lifestyle, it remains likely that some project team members will at some point be brought down by minor illnesses such as flu. These kinds of risk need a *contingency plan*. This is a planned action to be carried out if the particular risk materializes. If a team member involved in urgent work were ill then the project manager might draft in another member of staff to cover that work.

The preventative measures that were discussed under the 'Risk reduction' heading above will usually incur some cost regardless of the risk materializing or not. The cost of a contingency measure will only be incurred if the risk actually materializes. However, there may be some things that have to be done in order for the contingency action to be feasible. An obvious example is that back-ups of a database have to be taken if the contingency action when the database is corrupted is to restore it from back-ups. There would be a cost associated with taking the backups.

EXERCISE 7.4

In the case above where staff could be absent through illness, what preconditions could facilitate contingency actions such as getting other team members to cover on urgent tasks? What factors would you consider in deciding whether these preparatory measures would be worthwhile?

Deciding on the risk actions

Five generic responses to a risk have been discussed above. For each actual risk, however, specific actions have to be planned. In many cases experts have produced lists recommending practical steps to cope with the likelihood of particular risks; see, for example, Boehm's 'top ten' software engineering risks in Table 7.1.

Whatever the countermeasures that are considered, they must be cost-effective. On those occasions where a risk exposure value can be calculated as a financial value using the (*value of damage*) × (*probability of occurrence*) formula – recall Section 7.6 – the cost-effectiveness of a risk reduction action can be assessed by calculating the *risk reduction leverage (RRL)*.

$$risk \ reduction \ leverage = (RE_{before} - RE_{after})/(cost \ of \ risk \ reduction)$$

RE_{before} is the risk exposure, as explained in Section 7.6, before risk reduction actions have been taken. RE_{after} is the risk exposure after taking the risk reduction action. An RRL above 1.00 indicates that the reduction in risk exposure achieved by a measure is greater than its cost. To take a rather unrealistic example, it might cost £200,000 to replace a hardware configuration used to develop a software application. There is a 1% chance of a fire (because of the particular location of the installation, say). The risk exposure would be 1% of £200,000, that is £2,000. Installing fire alarms at a cost of £500 would reduce the chance of fire to 0.5%. The new risk exposure would be £1,000, a reduction of £1,000 on the previous exposure. The RRL would be (2000 – 1000)/500, that is 2.0, and the action would therefore be deemed worthwhile.

Earlier in this chapter, we likened risk exposure to the amount you might pay to an insurance company to cover a risk. To continue the analogy, an insurance company in the above example might be willing to reduce the premium you pay to have cover against fire from £2,000 to £1,000 if you installed fire alarms. As the fire alarms would cost you only £500 and save £1,000, the cost would clearly be worthwhile.

Creating and maintaining the risk register

When the project planners have picked out and examined what appear to be the most threatening risks to the project, they need to record their findings in a *risk register*. The typical content of such a register is shown in Figure 7.5. After work starts on the project more risks will emerge and be added to the register. At regular intervals, probably as part of the project control life cycle described in Chapter 9, the risk register should be reviewed and amended. Many risks threaten just one or two activities, and when the project staff

RISK RECORD					
Risk id		Risk title			
Owner		Date raised		Status	
Risk description					
Impact description					
Recommended risk mitigation					
Probability/impact values					
	Probability	Impact			
		Cost	Duration	Quality	
Pre-mitigation					
Post-mitigation					
Incident/action history					
Date	Incident/action	Actor	Outcome/comment		

FIGURE 7.5 Risk register page

have completed these the risk can then be 'closed' as no longer relevant. In any case, as noted earlier, the probability and impact of a risk are likely to change during the course of the project.

7.9 Evaluating risks to the schedule

In Section 7.6 we showed a probability chart – Figure 7.3. This illustrated the point that a forecast of the time needed to do a job is most realistically presented as a graph of likelihood of a range of figures, with the most likely duration as the peak and the chances of the job taking longer or shorter shown as curves sloping down on either side of the peak. Thus we can show that a job might take five days but that there is a small chance it might need four or six days, and a smaller chance of three or seven days and so on. If a task in a project takes longer than planned, we might hope that some other task might take less and thus compensate for this delay. In the following sections we will examine PERT, a technique which takes account of the uncertainties in the durations of activities within a project. We will also touch upon Monte Carlo simulation, which is a more powerful and flexible tool that tackles the same problem.

A drawback to the application of methods like PERT is that in practice there is a tendency for developers to work to the schedule even if a task could be completed more quickly. Even if tasks are completed earlier than planned, project managers are not always quick to exploit the opportunities to start subsequent activities earlier than scheduled. Critical chain management will be explored as a way of tackling this problem.

7.10 Applying the PERT technique

Using PERT to evaluate the effects of uncertainty

PERT (Program Evaluation and Review Technique) was published in the same year as CPM. Developed for the Fleet Ballistic Missiles Program, it is said to have saved considerable time in development of the Polaris missile.

PERT was developed to take account of the uncertainty surrounding estimates of task durations. It was developed in an environment of expensive, high-risk and state-of-the-art projects – not that dissimilar to many of today's large software projects.

The method is very similar to the CPM technique (indeed many practitioners use the terms PERT and CPM interchangeably) but, instead of using a single estimate for the duration of each task, PERT requires three estimates.

- *Most likely time*: the time we would expect the task to take under normal circumstances. We shall identify this by the letter m.
- *Optimistic time*: the shortest time in which we could expect to complete the activity, barring outright miracles. We shall use the letter a for this.
- *Pessimistic time*: the worst possible time, allowing for all reasonable eventualities but excluding 'acts of God and warfare' (as they say in most insurance exclusion clauses). We shall call this b.

PERT then combines these three estimates to form a single expected duration, t_e, using the formula

$$t_e = \frac{a + 4m + b}{6}$$

EXERCISE 7.5

Table 7.6 provides additional activity duration estimates for the network shown in Figure 6.29. There are new estimates for a and b and the original activity duration estimates have been used as the most likely times, m. Calculate the expected duration, t_e, for each activity.

Activity	Optimistic (a)	Activity durations (weeks) Most likely (m)	Pessimistic (b)
A	5	6	8
B	3	4	5
C	2	3	3
D	3.5	4	5
E	1	3	4
F	8	10	15
G	2	3	4
H	2	2	2.5

TABLE 7.6 PERT activity time estimates

Using expected durations

The expected durations are used to carry out a forward pass through a network, using the same method as the CPM technique. In this case, however, the calculated event dates are not the earliest possible dates but the dates by which we expect to achieve those events.

EXERCISE 7.6

Before reading further, use your calculated expected activity durations to carry out a forward pass through the network (Figure 6.29) and verify that the project duration is 13.5 weeks. What does an expected duration of 13.5 weeks mean in terms of the completion date for the project?

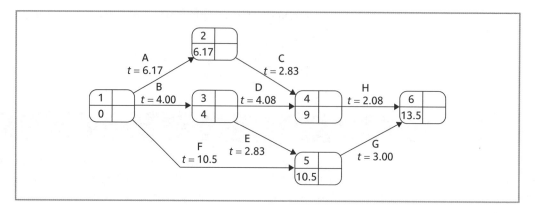

FIGURE 7.6 The PERT network after the forward pass

The PERT network illustrated in Figure 7.6 indicates that we expect the project to take 13.5 weeks. In Figure 7.6 we have used an activity-on-arrow network as this form of presentation makes it easier to separate visually the estimated activity data (expected durations and, later, their standard deviations) from the calculated data (expected completion dates and target completion dates). The method can, of course, be equally well supported by activity-on-node diagrams.

Unlike the CPM approach, the PERT method does not indicate the earliest date by which we could complete the project but the expected (or most likely) date. An advantage of this approach is that it places an emphasis on the uncertainty of the real world. Rather than being tempted to say 'the completion date for the project is . . .' we are led to say 'we expect to complete the project by . . .'.

It also focuses attention on the uncertainty of the estimation of activity durations. Requesting three estimates for each activity emphasizes the fact that we are not certain what will happen – we are forced to take into account the fact that estimates are approximate.

Even number	Target date
Expected date	Standard deviation

The PERT event labelling convention adopted here indicates event number and its target date along with the calculated values for expected time and standard deviation.

Activity standard deviations

A quantitative measure of the degree of uncertainty of an activity duration estimate may be obtained by calculating the standard deviation s of an activity time, using the formula

This standard deviation formula is based on the rationale that there are approximately six standard deviations between the extreme tails of many statistical distributions.

$$s = \frac{b - a}{6}$$

The activity standard deviation is proportional to the difference between the optimistic and pessimistic estimates, and can be used as a ranking measure of the degree of uncertainty or risk for each activity. The activity expected durations and standard deviations for our sample project are shown in Table 7.7.

Activity	Activity durations (weeks)				
	Optimistic (*a*)	Most likely (*m*)	Pessimistic (*b*)	Expected (*t_e*)	Standard deviation (*s*)
A	5	6	8	6.17	0.50
B	3	4	5	4.00	0.33
C	2	3	3	2.83	0.17
D	3.5	4	5	4.08	0.25
E	1	3	4	2.83	0.50
F	8	10	15	10.50	1.17
G	2	3	4	3.00	0.33
H	2	2	2.5	2.08	0.08

TABLE 7.7 Expected times and standard deviations

The likelihood of meeting targets

The main advantage of the PERT technique is that it provides a method for estimating the probability of meeting or missing target dates. There might be only a single target date – the project completion – but we might wish to set additional intermediate targets.

Suppose that we must complete the project within 15 weeks at the outside. We expect it will take 13.5 weeks but it could take more or, perhaps, less. In addition, suppose that activity C must be completed by week 10, as it is to be carried out by a member of staff who is scheduled to be working on another project, and that event 5 represents the delivery of intermediate products to the customer, which must take place by week 10. These three target dates are shown on the PERT network in Figure 7.7.

The PERT technique uses the following three-step method for calculating the probability of meeting or missing a target date:

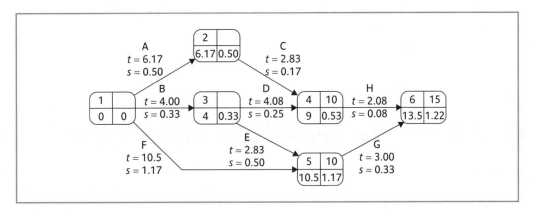

FIGURE 7.7 The PERT network with three target dates and calculated event standard deviations

- calculate the standard deviation of each project event;
- calculate the *z* value for each event that has a target date;
- convert *z* values to a probabilities.

Calculating the standard deviation of each project event

> The square of the standard deviation is known as the variance. Standard deviations may not be added together but variances may.

Standard deviations for the project events can be calculated by carrying out a forward pass using the activity standard deviations in a manner similar to that used with expected durations. There is, however, one small difference – to add two standard deviations we must add their squares and then find the square root of the sum. Exercise 7.7 illustrates the technique. One practical outcome of this is that the contingency time to be allocated to a sequence of activities as a whole would be less than the sum of the contingency allowances for each of the component activities. This has implications that can be exploited in critical chain project management, which are discussed in the next section.

EXERCISE 7.7

The standard deviation for event 3 depends solely on that of activity B. The standard deviation for event 3 is therefore 0.33.

For event 5 there are two possible paths, B + E or F. The total standard deviation for path B + E is $\sqrt{(0.33^2 + 0.50^2)} = 0.6$ and that for path F is 1.17; the standard deviation for event 5 is therefore the greater of the two, 1.17.

Verify that the standard deviations for each of the other events in the project are as shown in Figure 7.7.

Calculating the *z* values

The *z* value is calculated for each node that has a target date. It is equivalent to the number of standard deviations between the node's expected and target dates. It is calculated using the formula

$$z = \frac{T - t_e}{s}$$

where t_e is the expected date and *T* the target date.

EXERCISE 7.8

The *z* value for event 4 is $(10 - 9.00)/0.53 = 1.8867$.

Calculate the *z* values for the other events with target dates in the network shown in Figure 7.7.

Converting z values to probabilities

A z value may be converted to the probability of not meeting the target date by using the graph in Figure 7.8.

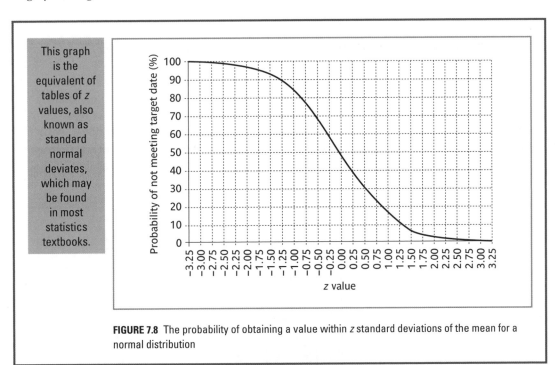

This graph is the equivalent of tables of z values, also known as standard normal deviates, which may be found in most statistics textbooks.

FIGURE 7.8 The probability of obtaining a value within z standard deviations of the mean for a normal distribution

EXERCISE 7.9

The z value for the project completion (event 6) is 1.23. Using Figure 7.8 we can see that this equates to a probability of approximately 11%, that is, there is an 11% risk of not meeting the target date of the end of week 15.

Find the probabilities of not achieving events 4 or 5 by their target dates of the end of week 10.

What is the likelihood of completing the project by week 14?

The advantages of PERT

We have seen that by requesting multi-valued activity duration estimates and calculating expected dates, PERT focuses attention on the uncertainty of forecasting. We can use the technique to calculate the standard deviation for each task and use this to rank them according to their degree of risk. Using this ranking, we can see, for example, that activity F is the one regarding which we have greatest uncertainty, whereas activity C should, in principle, give us relatively little cause for concern.

If we use the expected times and standard deviations for forward passes through the network we can, for any event or activity completion, estimate the probability of meeting any set target. In particular, by setting target dates along the critical path, we can focus on those activities posing the greatest risk to the project's schedule.

7.11 Monte Carlo simulation

As an alternative to the PERT technique, and to provide a greater degree of flexibility in specifying likely activity durations, we can use Monte Carlo simulation techniques to evaluate the risks of not achieving deadlines. The basis of this technique involves calculating activity completion times for a project network a large number of times, each time selecting estimated activity times randomly from a set of estimates for each activity. The results can then be tabulated, summarized or displayed as a graph such as that shown in Figure 7.9.

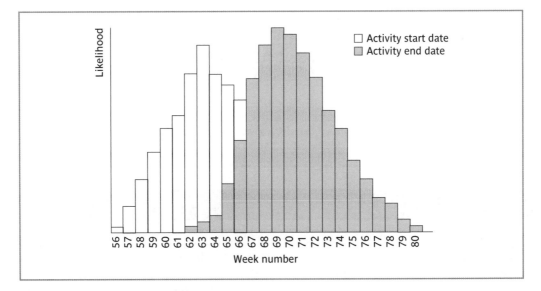

FIGURE 7.9 Risk profile for an activity generated using Monte Carlo simulation

Activity duration estimates can be specified in a variety of forms, depending upon the information available. If, for example, we have historic data available about the durations of similar activities, we might be able to specify durations as a probability distribution. With less information available we should, at least, be able to provide three time estimates as used by PERT.

The calculation required for this is clearly extensive as we may have to carry out the forward pass through the network many hundreds of times before obtaining a representative selection of possible completion times. Fortunately, there are a number of packages available for carrying out Monte Carlo simulation. Some will exchange data with project-scheduling applications and some interface to standard spreadsheet software.

The majority of these packages will apply Monte Carlo risk analysis to cost and resource as well as duration estimates.

7.12 Critical chain concepts

This chapter has stressed the idea that the forecast for the duration of an activity cannot in reality be a single number, but must be a range of durations that can be displayed on a graph such as Figure 7.3. However, we would want to pick one value in that range which would be the *target*.

The duration chosen as the target might be the one that seems to be the *most likely*. Imagine someone who cycles to work each day. It may be that on average it takes them about 45 minutes to complete the journey, but on some days it could be more and on others it could be less. These journey times could be plotted on a graph like the one in Figure 7.3. If the cyclist had a very important meeting at work, it is likely that they would give themselves more time – say an extra 15 minutes – than the average 45 minutes to make sure that they arrived in time. In the discussion above on the PERT risk technique the most likely duration was the middle value and the pessimistic estimate was the equivalent of the 45 + 15 = 60 minutes.

Of course, there will be some days when the cyclist will beat the average of 45 minutes. When a project is actually being executed, the project manager will be forced to focus on the activities where the actual durations exceed the target. Activities which are actually completed before the target date are likely to be overlooked. These early completions, properly handled, could put some time in hand that might still allow the project to meet its target completion date if the later activities are delayed.

Figure 7.10 shows the findings of Michiel van Genuchten, a researcher who analysed the reasons for delays in the completion of software development tasks. This bar chart shows that about 30% of activities were finished on time, while 9% were a week early and 17% were a week late. The big jump of 21 percentage points between being a week

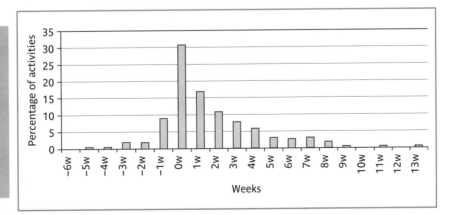

Michiel van Genuchten (1991) 'Why is software late? An empirical study of reasons for delay in software development', *IEEE Transactions in Software Engineering* 17(6) 582–90.

FIGURE 7.10 Percentage of activities early or late (after van Genuchten, 1991)

early and being on time is compatible with the 'Parkinson's Law' principle that '*work expands to fill the time available*'. This tendency should not be blamed on inherent laziness. van Genuchten found that the most common reason for delay was the time that had to be spent on non-project work. It seems that developers used spare time provided by generous estimates to get on with other urgent work.

> A good introduction is L. P. Leach (1999) 'Critical chain project management improves project performance' *Project Management Journal* 30(2) 39–51.

One approach which attempts to solve some of these problems is the application of the *critical chain* concept originally developed by Eliyahu Goldratt. In order to demonstrate the principles of this approach, the example shown in Figure 7.7 will be reworked as a Gantt chart. Figure 7.11 shows what the Gantt chart for this project might look like if a 'traditional' approach' were adopted, but we have already adopted the most likely durations.

The general steps in the Critical Chain approach are explained in the following sections.

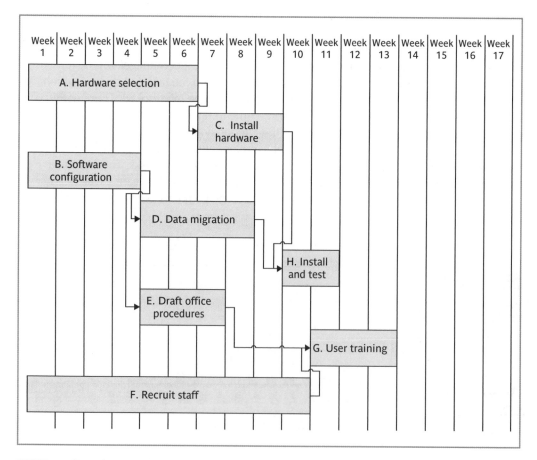

FIGURE 7.11 Gantt chart – 'traditional' planning approach

Deriving 'most likely' activity durations

The target date generated by critical chain planning is one where it is estimated that there is a 50% chance of success – this approximates to the expected time identified in the PERT risk method. In some explanations of critical chain project planning it is suggested that the most likely activity duration can be identified by halving the estimates provided. This is based on the assumption that the estimates given to the planner will be 'safe' ones based on a 95% probability of them being achieved. If you look at Figure 7.3, the 95% estimate would be 9 days and half of that (4.5 days) would not be a reasonable target as it would have a probability of only 10% of success. It also assumes that a probability profile has a bell-shaped normal distribution (like the example in Figure 7.3). If you look at the distribution which resulted from van Genuchten's research – see Figure 7.10 – you can see that it is certainly not bell-shaped. Other critical chain experts suggest deducting 33% from the safe estimate to get the target estimate – which seems less unreasonable.

However, what appear to be arbitrary managerial reductions in the estimates may not be a good way to motivate developers, especially if these staff supplied the estimates in the first place. A better approach would be to ask developers to supply two estimates. One of these would be a 'most likely' estimate and the other would include a safety margin or comfort zone. From now on we are going to assume that this is what has happened. In fact we will use the figures already presented in Table 7.6 in this new role (Table 7.8).

Activity	Most likely	Plus comfort zone	Comfort zone
A	6	8	2
B	4	5	1
C	3	3	0
D	4	5	1
E	3	4	1
F	10	15	5
G	3	4	1
H	2	2.5	0.5

TABLE 7.8 Most likely and comfort zone estimates (days)

Using latest start dates for activities

Working backwards from the target completion date, each activity is scheduled to start as late as possible. Among other things, this should reduce the chance of staff being pulled off the project on to other work. It is also argued – with some justification according to van Genuchten's research above – that most developers would tend to start work on the task at the latest start time anyway. However, it does make every activity 'critical'. If one is late the whole project is late. That is why the next steps are needed.

Inserting project and feeder buffers

To cope with activity overruns, a *project buffer* is inserted at the end of the project before the target completion date. One way of calculating this buffer is as the equivalent of 50% of the sum of lengths of the 'comfort zones' that have been removed from the *critical chain*. The critical chain is the longest chain of activities in the project, taking account of both task and resource dependencies. This is different from the *critical path* as the latter only takes account of task dependencies. A *resource dependency* is where one activity has to wait for a resource (usually a person in software development) which is being used by another activity to become available. If an activity on this critical chain is late it will push the project completion date further into the project buffer. That the buffer should be 50% of the total comfort zones for critical chain activities is based on the grounds that if the estimate for an activity was calculated as having a 50% chance of being correct, the buffer would only need to be called upon by the 50% of cases where the estimate was not correct.

An alternative proposal is to sum the squares of the comfort zones and then take the square root of the total. This is based on the idea that each comfort zone is the equivalent to the standard deviation of the activity – go back and look at the section headed *Calculating the standard deviation of each project event* in Section 7.10. This method of calculation still produces a figure which is less than simply summing all the comfort zones. This is justified on the grounds that the contingency time needed for a group of activities is less than the sum of the individual contingency allowances as the success of some activities will compensate for the shortfalls in others.

Buffers are also inserted into the project schedule where a subsidiary chain of activities feeds into the critical chain. These *feeding buffers* could once again be set at 50% of the length of the 'comfort zone' removed from the subsidiary or *feeding chain*.

A worked example

Figure 7.12 shows the results of this process. The critical chain in this example happens to be the same as the critical path, that is activities F and G which have comfort zones of 5 weeks and 1 week respectively, making a total of 6 weeks. The project buffer is therefore 3 weeks.

Subsidiary chains feed into the critical chain where activity H links into the project buffer and where activity E links into G which is part of the critical chain. Feeding buffers are inserted at these points. For the first buffer the duration would be 50% of the saved comfort zones of A, C and H, that is (2 + 0 + 0.5)/2 = 1.25 weeks. It could be argued that B, D and H could form a feeder chain which also has a combined comfort zone of (1 + 1 + 0.5)/2 = 1.25 weeks. In the situations where there are parallel alternative paths on a feeder chain, the practice is to base the feeding buffer on whichever comfort zone total is greater. This because if one or other or both parallel paths were late they could still use the same buffer. (Imagine that in the example above there are two cyclists who live 45 minutes away from work and they both have the same important meeting – they might each add a 15-minute comfort zone to the ride on that day but that 15 minutes could effectively be the same 15 minutes between 7.45 and 8.00 am in the morning). It could be argued that

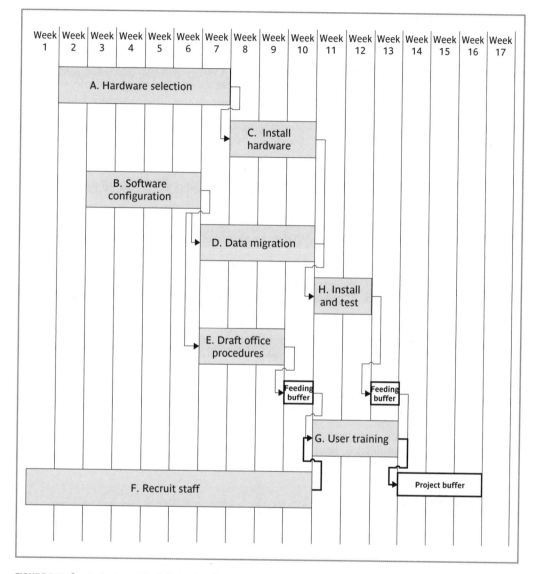

FIGURE 7.12 Gantt chart – critical chain planning approach

the feeding buffer and the final project buffer could also be merged, but explanations of critical chain planning, such as that of Larry Leach (see above), make clear that this is not to be done. This could be because a delay penetrating the feeding buffer time does not affect the completion date of the project, while penetrating the project buffer does.

In the second place, where a feeder chain of activities joins the critical chain, the feeder buffer would be 50% of the comfort zones of activities B and E, that is 1 week.

Project execution

When the project is executed, the following principles are followed:

■ No chain of tasks should be started earlier than scheduled, but once it has been started it should be finished as soon as possible – this invokes the *relay race principle*, where developers should be ready to start their tasks as soon as the previous, dependent, tasks are completed.

■ Buffers are divided into three zones: green, amber and red, each of an even (33%) size:
  ● *green*, where no action is required if the project completion date creeps into this zone;
  ● *amber*, where an action plan is formulated if the project completion dates moves into this zone;
  ● *red*, where the action plan above is executed if the project penetrates this zone.

See, for example, D. Trietsch (2005) 'Why a critical path by any other name would smell less sweet' *Project Management Journal* 36(1) 27–36 and T. Raz et al. (2003) 'A critical look at critical chain project management' *Project Management Journal* 34(4) 24–32.

Critical chain planning concepts have the support of a dedicated group of enthusiasts. However, the full application of the model has attracted controversy on various grounds. Our personal view is that the ideas of:

■ requiring two estimates: the most likely duration/effort and the safety estimate which includes additional time to deal with problems that could arise with the task, and

■ placing the contingency time, based on the 'comfort zone' which is the difference between the most likely and safety estimates, in common buffers rather than associating it with individual activities

are sound ones that could usefully be absorbed into software project management practice.

7.13 Conclusion

In this chapter, we have seen how to identify and manage the risks that might affect the success of a project. Risk management is concerned with assessing and prioritizing risks and drawing up plans for addressing those risks before they become problems.

This chapter has also described techniques for estimating the effect of risk on the project's activity network and schedule.

Many of the risks affecting software projects can be reduced by allocating more experienced staff to those activities that are affected. In the next chapter we consider the allocation of staff to activities in more detail.

7.14 Further exercises

1   Fiona is a final-year computing undergraduate student who in her third year undertook a placement with the ICT department of an insurance company as a support analyst

and then a network manager. The placement year was very busy and rewarding as the company saw ICT as providing business advantage in a what was a very dynamic and aggressively competitive sector. The project that Fiona proposes to do in her final year will use the insurance company as a client. The proposed project involves gathering requirements for an application that records details of change requests for operational systems made by users and then tracks the subsequent progress of the change. Having gathered the requirements she is to design the application, then build and implement it. Identify possible risks in the proposed project of which Fiona should take account.

2 Mo is a systems analyst who is gathering requirements for an application which will record details of the training undertaken by fire-fighters in the client fire brigade. Details of the training units successfully completed by fire-fighters are to be input to the application by trainers who are themselves senior and active fire-fighters. Mo needs to interview a trainer to obtain his/her requirements. Because of the senior fire-fighters' other duties the interview has to be arranged two weeks in advance. There is then a 20% chance of the fire-fighter being unable to attend the interview because of an emergency call-out. Each week that the project is delayed costs the fire brigade approximately £1,000.

(a) Provide an estimate of the risk exposure (as a financial value) for the risk that the senior fire-fighter might not be able to attend at the times needed.

(b) Suggest possible risk mitigation actions.

3 In Exercise 7.2 you were asked to identify risks under the four headings of Actors, Technology, Structure and Tasks for the IOE annual maintenance contracts and the Brightmouth College payroll scenarios. Now identify risks for each scenario that relate to pairs of domains, for example Actors–Technology, Actors–Tasks and so on.

4 The Wet Holiday Company specializes in the provision of holidays which involve water sports of various types. There are three major divisions with the following lines of business:

■ boat holidays on canals;
■ villa holidays in various parts of the Mediterranean which involve sailing in some way;
■ canoeing holidays in France.

Wet Holiday feel that they are particularly appealing to a young active market and that having the facility for customers to book via the web is essential. They call in ICT consultants to advise them on their IT strategy. The consultants advise them that before they can have a web presence, they need to have a conventional ICT-based booking system to support their telesales operation first. Because of the specialized nature of their business, an off-the-shelf application would not be suitable and they would need to have a specially written software application, based on a client–server architecture. The top priority needs to be given to a system to support villa holiday bookings because this has the largest number of customers and generates the most revenue.

Wet Holiday have some in-house IT development staff, but these are inexperienced in client–server technology. To meet this shortfall, contractors are employed.

It turns out that development takes much longer than planned. Much of this delay occurs at acceptance testing when the users find many errors and performance shortcomings, which require extensive rework. Part of the problem relates to getting the best performance out of the new architecture; this has a particular impact on response times which are initially unacceptable to staff who are dealing with customers over the phone. The contractors are not closely monitored and some of the code that they produce is found to have many careless mistakes and to be poorly structured and documented. This makes it difficult to make changes to the software after the contractors have left on the expiry of their contracts.

The villa booking system can only be implemented at the beginning of a holiday season and the deadline for the beginning of the 2002 to 2003 season is missed, leading to a 12-month delay in the implementation. The delay in implementation seems to encourage the users to ask for further modifications to the original requirements, which adds even more to development costs.

The delays in implementing this application mean that the other scheduled IT development, for other lines of business, have to be put back. Managers of customer-facing business functions at Wet Holiday are suggesting that the whole IT function should be completely outsourced.

(a) Identify the problems that were faced by Wet Holiday, and describe actions that could have been taken to avoid or reduce them.

(b) Use your findings in (a) to create a risk checklist for future projects.

5 Below are details of a project. All times are in days.

Activity	Depends on	Optimistic time	Most likely	Pessimistic
A	–	8	10	12
B	A	10	15	20
C	B	5	7	9
D	–	8	10	12
E	D,C	3	6	9

Using the activity times above:

■ Calculate the expected duration and standard deviation for each activity.

■ Identify the critical path.

■ Draw up an activity diagram applying critical chain principles for this project:

● Locate the places where buffers will need to be located.
● Assess the size of the buffers.
● Start all activities as late as possible.

6 Below are details of a project. All times are in days.

Activity	Depends on	Most likely	Plus safety
A		10	14
B	A	5	7
C	B	15	21
D	A	3	5
E	A	8	12
F	E	20	22
G	D	6	8
H	C,F,G	10	14

(a) Using (i) the most likely and then (ii) the safety estimates:
  - Calculate the earliest and latest start and end days and float for each activity.
  - Identify the critical path.

(b) Draw up an activity diagram applying critical chain principles for this project:
  - Locate the places where buffers will need to be located.
  - Assess the size of the buffers.
  - Start all activities as late as possible.

7 In this chapter the application of risk management to software development projects has been strongly advocated. In practice, however, managers are often reluctant to apply the techniques. What do you think might be the reasons for this?

Resource allocation

❖ OBJECTIVES

When you have completed this chapter you will be able to:

- ❖ identify the resources required for a project;

- ❖ make the demand for resources more even throughout the life of a project;

- ❖ produce a work plan and resource schedule.

8.1 Introduction

In Chapter 6, we saw how to use activity network analysis techniques to plan *when* activities should take place. This was calculated as a time span during which an activity should take place – bounded by the earliest start and latest finish dates. In Chapter 7 we used the PERT technique to forecast a range of expected dates by which activities would be completed. In both cases these plans took no account of the availability of resources.

In this chapter we shall see how to match the activity plan to available resources and, where necessary, assess the efficacy of changing the plan to fit the resources. Figure 8.1 shows where resource allocation is applied in Step Wise.

In general, the allocation of resources to activities will lead us to review and modify the ideal activity plan. It may cause us to revise stage or project completion dates. In any event, it is likely to lead to a narrowing of the time spans within which activities may be scheduled.

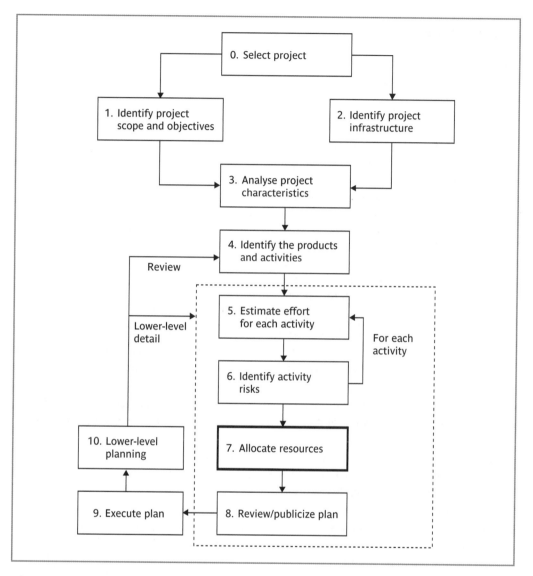

FIGURE 8.1 Resource allocation is carried out as Step 7

These schedules will provide the basis for the day-to-day control and management of the project. These are described in Chapter 9.

The final result of resource allocation will normally be a number of schedules, including:

- an *activity schedule* indicating the planned start and completion dates for each activity;

- a *resource schedule* showing the dates on which each resource will be required and the level of that requirement;

- a *cost schedule* showing the planned cumulative expenditure incurred by the use of resources over time.

8.2 The nature of resources

A resource is any item or person required for the execution of the project. This covers many things – from paper clips to key personnel – and it is unlikely that we would wish to itemize every resource required, let alone draw up a schedule for their use. Stationery and other standard office supplies, for example, need not normally be the concern of the project manager – ensuring an adequate supply is the role of the office manager. The project manager must concentrate on those resources which, without planning, might not be available when required.

Some resources, such as a project manager, will be required for the duration of the project whereas others, such as a specific software developer, might be required for a single activity. The former, while vital to the success of the project, does not require the same level of scheduling as the latter. As we saw in Chapter 2, a project manager may not have unrestricted control over a developer who may be needed to work on a range of projects. The manager may have to request the use of a developer who belongs to a pool of resources controlled at programme level.

In general, resources will fall into one of seven categories.

- *Labour* The main items in this category will be members of the development project team such as the project manager, systems analysts and software developers. Equally important will be the quality assurance team and other support staff and any employees of the client organization who might be required to undertake or participate in specific activities.

- *Equipment* Obvious items will include workstations and other computing and office equipment. We must not forget that staff also need basic equipment such as desks and chairs.

- *Materials* Materials are items that are consumed, rather than equipment that is used. They are of little consequence in most software projects but can be important for some – software that is to be widely distributed might, for example, require supplies of disks to be specially obtained.

- *Space* For projects that are undertaken with existing staff, space is normally readily available. If any additional staff (recruited or contracted) should be needed then office space will need to be found.

- *Services* Some projects will require procurement of specialist services – development of a wide area distributed system, for example, requires scheduling of telecommunications services.

- *Time* Time is the resource that is being offset against the other primary resources – project timescales can sometimes be reduced by increasing other resources and will almost certainly be extended if they are unexpectedly reduced.

The cost of money as a resource is a factor taken into account in DCF evaluation.

- *Money* Money is a secondary resource – it is used to buy other resources and will be consumed as other resources are used. It is similar to other resources in that it is available at a cost – in this case interest charges.

8.3 Identifying resource requirements

The first step in producing a resource allocation plan is to list the resources that will be required along with the expected level of demand. This will normally be done by considering each activity in turn and identifying the resources required. It is likely, however, that there will also be resources required that are not activity specific but are part of the project's infrastructure (such as the project manager) or required to support other resources (office space, for example, might be required to house contract software developers).

CASE STUDY EXAMPLES

Amanda has produced a precedence network for the IOE project (Figure 8.2) and used this as a basis for a resource requirements list, part of which is shown in Table 8.1. Notice that, at this stage, she has not allocated individuals to tasks but has decided on the type of staff that will be required. The activity durations assume that they will be carried out by 'standard' analysts or software developers.

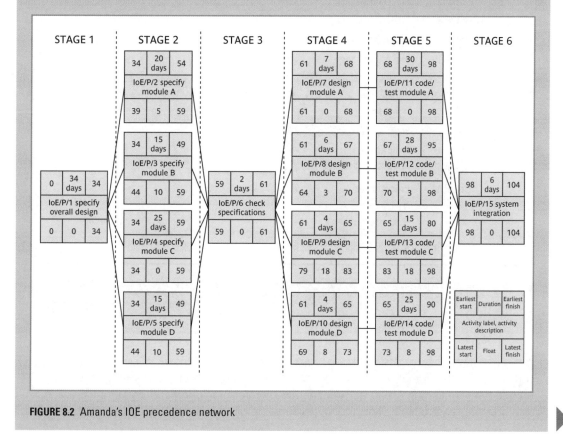

FIGURE 8.2 Amanda's IOE precedence network

Stage	Activity	Resource	Days	Quantity	Notes
ALL		Project manager	104 F/T		
1	All	Workstation	–	34	Check software availability
	IoE/P/1	Senior analyst	34 F/T		
2	All	Workstation	–	3	One per person essential
	IoE/P/2	Analyst/designer	20 F/T		
	IoE/P/3	Analyst/designer	15 F/T		
	IoE/P/4	Analyst/designer	25 F/T		
	IoE/P/5	Analyst/designer	15 F/T		Could use analyst/programmer
3	All	Workstation	–	2	
	IoE/P/6	Senior analyst*	2 F/T		
4	All	Workstation	–	3	As stage 2
	IoE/P/7	Analyst/designer	7 F/T		
	IoE/P/8	Analyst/designer	6 F/T		
	IoE/P/9	Analyst/designer	4 F/T		
	IoE/P/10	Analyst/designer	4 F/T		
5	All	Workstation	–	4	One per programmer
	All	Office space	–		If contract programmers used
	IoE/P/11	Programmer	30 F/T		
	IoE/P/12	Programmer	28 F/T		
	IoE/P/13	Programmer	15 F/T		
	IoE/P/14	Programmer	25 F/T		
6	All	Full system access	–		Approx. 16 hours for full system test
	IoE/P/15	Analyst/designer	6 F/T		

TABLE 8.1 Part of Amanda's resource requirements list
* In reality, this would normally be done by a review involving all the analysts working on stage 2.

At this stage, it is necessary that the resource requirements list be as comprehensive as possible – it is better that something is included that may later be deleted as unnecessary than to omit something essential. Amanda has therefore included additional office space as a possible requirement, should contract software development staff be recruited.

8.4 Scheduling resources

Note that in Section 7.12 an argument for starting activities as late as possible was presented. The resource allocation process is similar regardless of the policy adopted in this respect.

Having produced the resource requirements list, the next stage is to map this on to the activity plan to assess the distribution of resources required over the duration of the project. This is best done by representing the activity plan as a bar chart and using this to produce a resource histogram for each resource.

Figure 8.3 illustrates Amanda's activity plan as a bar chart and a resource histogram for analyst/designers. Each activity has been scheduled to start at its earliest start date – a sensible initial strategy, since we would, other things being equal, wish to save any float to allow for contingencies. Earliest start date scheduling, as is the case with Amanda's project, frequently creates resource histograms that start with a peak and then tail off.

White rectangles indicate when an activity is scheduled and shaded rectangles the total float.

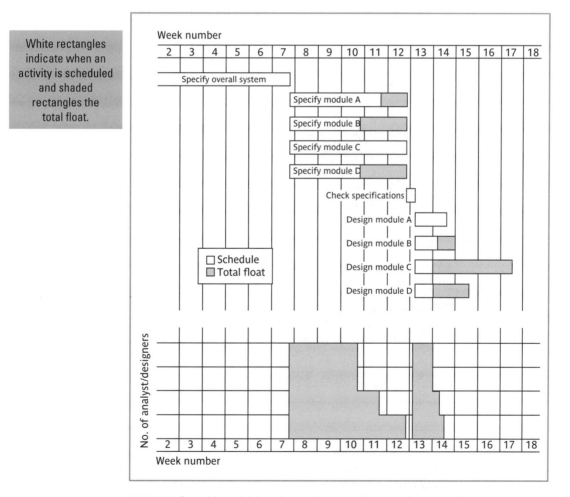

FIGURE 8.3 Part of Amanda's bar chart and resource histogram for analyst/designers

Changing the level of resources on a project over time, particularly personnel, generally adds to the cost of a project. Recruiting staff has costs and, even where staff are transferred internally, time will be needed for familiarization with the new project environment.

The resource histogram in Figure 8.3 poses particular problems in that it calls for two analyst/designers to be idle for twelve days, one for seven days and one for two days between the specification and design stage. It is unlikely that IOE would have another project requiring their skills for exactly those periods of time. This raises the question whether this idle time should be charged to Amanda's project. The ideal resource histogram will be smooth with, perhaps, an initial build-up and a staged run-down.

An additional problem with an uneven resource histogram is that it is more likely to call for levels of resource beyond those available. Figure 8.4 illustrates how, by adjusting the start date of some activities and splitting others, a resource histogram can, subject to constraints such as precedence requirements, be smoothed to contain resource demand at available levels. The different letters represent staff working on a series of module testing tasks, that is, one person working on task A, two on tasks B and C etc.

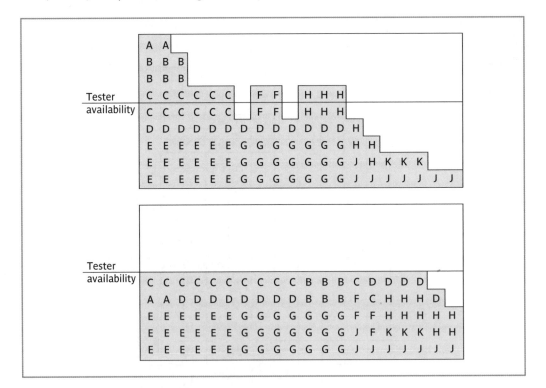

FIGURE 8.4 A resource histogram showing demand for staff before and after smoothing

In Figure 8.4, the original histogram was created by scheduling the activities at their earliest start dates. The resource histogram shows the typical peaked shape caused by earliest start date scheduling and calls for a total of nine staff where only five are available for the project.

By delaying the start of some of the activities, it has been possible to smooth the histogram and reduce the maximum level of demand for the resource. Notice that some activities, such as C and D, have been split. Where non-critical activities can be split they can provide a useful way of filling troughs in the demand for a resource, but in software projects it is difficult to split tasks without increasing the time they take.

Some of the activities call for more than one unit of the resource at a time – activity F, for example, requires two programmers, each working for two weeks. It might be possible to reschedule this activity to use one programmer over four weeks, although that has not been considered in this case.

Some project planning software tools will carry out resource smoothing automatically, although they are unlikely to take into account all the factors that could be used by a project manager. The majority of project planning software tools will produce resource histograms based on earliest activity start dates.

EXERCISE 8.1

Amanda has already decided to use only three analyst/designers on the project in order to reduce costs. Her current resource histogram, however, calls for four during both stage 2 and stage 4. Suggest what she might do to smooth the histogram and reduce the number of analyst/designers required to three.

In practice, resources have to be allocated to a project on an activity-by-activity basis and finding the 'best' allocation can be time consuming and difficult. As soon as a member of the project team is allocated to an activity, that activity acquires a scheduled start and finish date and the team member becomes unavailable for other activities for that period. Thus, allocating a resource to one activity limits the flexibility for resource allocation and scheduling of other activities.

It is therefore helpful to prioritize activities so that resources can be allocated to competing activities in some rational order. The priority must almost always be to allocate resources to critical path activities and then to those activities that are most likely to affect others. In that way, lower-priority activities are made to fit around the more critical, already scheduled activities.

There are some exceptional cases where it is better to favour a small non-critical activity if a number of large activities are dependent upon it.

Of the various ways of prioritizing activities, two are described below.

■ *Total float priority* Activities are ordered according to their total float, those with the smallest total float having the highest priority. In the simplest application of this method, activities are allocated resources in ascending order of total float. However, as scheduling proceeds, activities will be delayed (if resources are not available at their earliest start dates) and total floats will be reduced. It is therefore desirable to recalculate floats (and hence reorder the list) each time an activity is delayed.

EXERCISE 8.2

Amanda considers whether, with only three analyst/designers, the specification of module D (see Figure 8.3) will have to be deferred until after the specification of module B. This will add five days to the overall project duration (making 109 in total). She had hoped to have the project completed within 100 days and this is a further disappointment. She therefore decides to have another look at her activity plan.

You will remember that early on she decided that she should check all of the specifications together (activity IoE/P/6) before allowing design to start. It is now apparent that this is causing a significant bottleneck and delaying module D will only exacerbate the problem. She therefore decides on a compromise – she will check the specifications for modules A, B and D together but will then go ahead with their design without waiting for the module C specification. This will be checked against the others when it is complete.

She redraws her precedence network to reflect this, inserting the new activity of checking the module C specification against the others (activity IoE/P/6a). This is shown in Figure 8.5. Draw a new resource histogram to reflect this change.

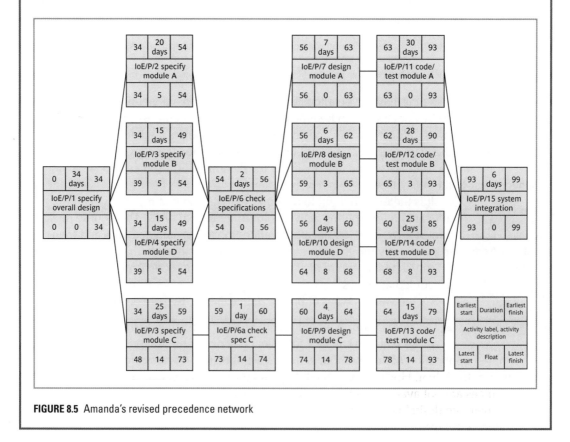

FIGURE 8.5 Amanda's revised precedence network

P. J. Burman (1972)
*Precedence
Networks for
Planning and
Control*, McGraw-
Hill.

■ *Ordered list priority* With this method, activities that can proceed at the same time are ordered according to a set of simple criteria. An example of this is Burman's priority list, which takes into account activity duration as well as total float:

1 shortest critical activity;

2 critical activities;

3 shortest non-critical activity;

4 non-critical activity with least float;

5 non-critical activities.

Unfortunately, resource smoothing, or even containment of resource demand to available levels, is not always possible within planned timescales – deferring activities to smooth out resource peaks often puts back project completion. Where that is the case, we need to consider ways of increasing the available resource levels or altering working methods.

8.5 Creating critical paths

Scheduling resources can create new critical paths. Delaying the start of an activity because of lack of resources will cause that activity to become critical if this uses up its float. Furthermore, a delay in completing one activity can delay the availability of a resource required for a later activity. If the later one is already critical then the earlier one might now have been made critical by linking their resources.

Amanda's revised schedule, which still calls for four analyst/designers but only for a single day, is illustrated in the solution to Exercise 8.2 (check it in the back of the book if you have not done so already). Notice that in rescheduling some of the activities she has introduced additional critical activities. Delaying the specification of module C has used up all of its float – and that of the subsequent activities along that path! Amanda now has two critical paths – the one shown on the precedence network and the new one.

In a large project, resource-linked criticalities can be quite complex – a hint of the potential problems may be appreciated by looking at the next exercise.

EXERCISE 8.3

Amanda decides to delay the specification of module C for a further day to ensure that only three analyst/designers will be required. The relevant part of her revised bar chart and resource histogram are shown in Figure 8.6.

Which activities will now be critical?

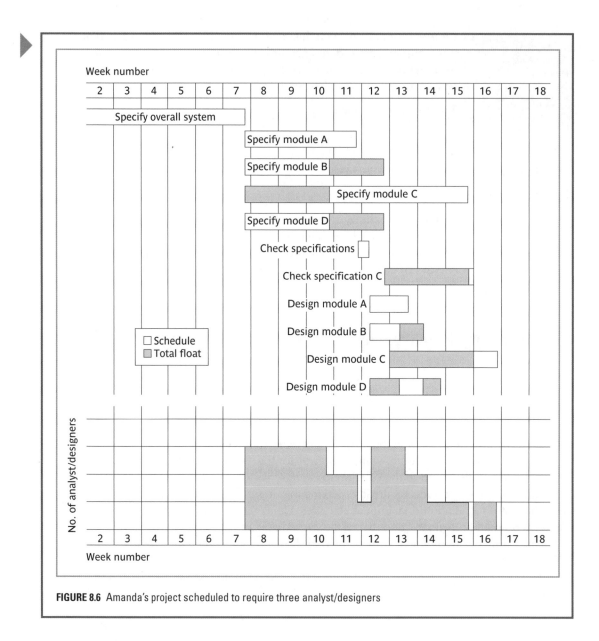

FIGURE 8.6 Amanda's project scheduled to require three analyst/designers

8.6 Counting the cost

The discussion so far has concentrated on trying to complete the project by the earliest completion date with the minimum number of staff. We have seen that doing this places constraints on when activities can be carried out and increases the risk of not meeting target dates.

Alternatively, Amanda could have considered using additional staff or lengthening the overall duration of the project. The additional costs of employing extra staff would need to be compared to the costs of delayed delivery and the increased risk of not meeting the scheduled date. The relationship between these factors is discussed later in this chapter.

8.7 Being specific

Allocating resources and smoothing resource histograms is relatively straightforward where all resources of a given type can be considered more or less equivalent. When allocating labourers to activities in a large building project we need not distinguish among individuals – there are likely to be many labourers and they may be treated as equals so far as skills and productivity are concerned.

This is seldom the case with software projects. We saw in Chapter 5 that, because of the nature of software development, skill and experience play a significant part in determining the time taken and, potentially, the quality of the final product. With the exception of extremely large projects, it makes sense to allocate individual members of staff to activities as early as possible, as this can lead us to revise our estimate of their duration.

In allocating individuals to tasks, a number of factors need to be taken into account.

- *Availability* We need to know whether a particular individual will be available when required. Reference to the departmental work plan determines this but the wise project manager will always investigate the risks that might be involved – earlier projects might, for example, overrun and affect the availability of an individual.

- *Criticality* Allocation of more experienced personnel to activities on the critical path often helps in shortening project durations or at least reduces the risk of overrun.

> Reappraisal of the critical path and PERT or Monte Carlo risk analysis might need to be carried out in parallel with staff allocation.

- *Risk* We saw how to undertake activity risk assessment in the previous chapter. Identifying those activities posing the greatest risk, and knowing the factors influencing them, helps to allocate staff. Allocating the most experienced staff to the highest-risk activities is likely to have the greatest effect in reducing overall project uncertainties. More experienced staff are, however, usually more expensive.

- *Training* It will benefit the organization if positive steps are taken to allocate junior staff to appropriate non-critical activities where there will be sufficient slack for them to train and develop skills. There can even be direct benefits to the particular project since some costs may be allocated to the training budget.

- *Team building* The selection of individuals must also take account of the final shape of the project team and the way they will work together. This and additional aspects of team management are discussed in Chapter 12.

EXERCISE 8.4

Amanda has decided that, where possible, whoever writes the specification for a module should also produce the design, as she believes this will improve the commitment and motivation of the three analyst/designers, Belinda, Tom and Daisy.

▶

> She has decided that she will use Tom, a trainee analyst/designer, for the specification and design of module D as both of these activities have a large float compared to their
>
> | **'Span' in this context is the period of time between the earliest start for an activity and its latest finish.** | activity span (6/21 and 9/13 of their span respectively). Since the specification and design of module C are on the critical path, she decides to allocate both of these tasks to Belinda, a particularly experienced and capable member of staff. |
> | --- | --- |
>
> Having made these decisions, she has almost no flexibility in how she assigns the other specification and design activities. Work out from the activity bar chart produced as part of the solution to Exercise 8.2 (shown in Figure 8.6) whom she assigns to which of the remaining specification and design activities.

8.8 Publishing the resource schedule

In allocating and scheduling resources we have used the activity plan (a precedence network in the case of the examples in this chapter), activity bar charts and resource histograms. Although good as planning tools, they are not the best way of publishing and communicating project schedules. For this we need some form of work plan. Work plans are commonly published as either lists or charts such as that illustrated in Figure 8.7. In this case Amanda has chosen not to include activity floats (which could be indicated by shaded bars) as she fears that one or two members of the team might work with less urgency if they are aware that their activities are not critical.

Notice that, somewhat unusually, it is assumed that there are no public holidays or other non-productive periods during the 100 days of the project and that none of the team has holidays for the periods they are shown as working.

Amanda has also made no explicit allowance for staff taking sick leave.

Amanda now transfers some of the information from the work schedule to her precedence network. In particular, she amends the earliest start dates for activities and any other constraints (such as revised latest finish dates where resources need to be made available) that have been introduced. A copy of her revised precedence network is shown in Figure 8.8 – notice that she has highlighted all critical activities and paths.

8.9 Cost schedules

It is now time to produce a detailed cost schedule showing weekly or monthly costs over the life of the project. This will provide a more detailed and accurate estimate of costs and will serve as a plan against which project progress can be monitored.

Calculating cost is straightforward where the organization has standard cost figures for staff and other resources. Where this is not the case, then the project manager will have to calculate the costs.

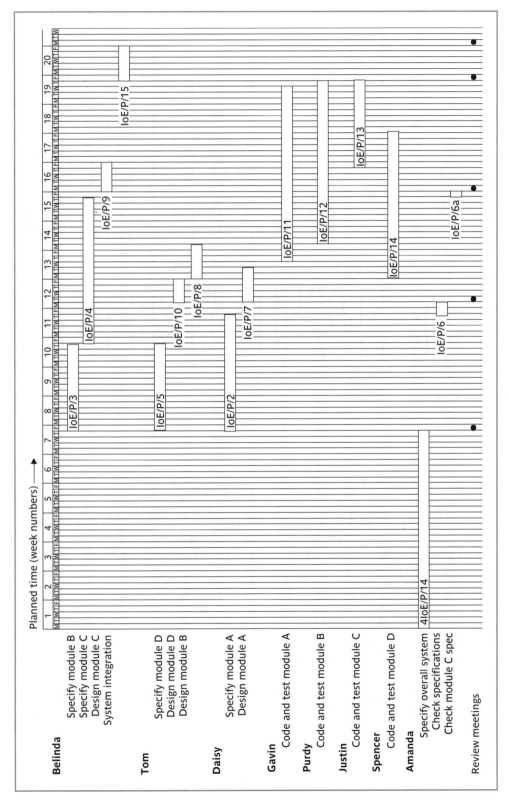

FIGURE 8.7 Amanda's work schedule

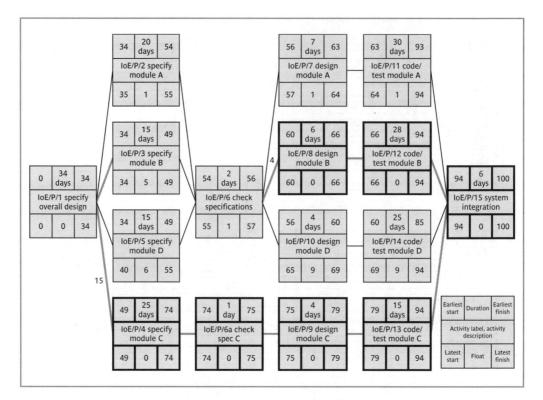

FIGURE 8.8 Amanda's revised precedence network showing scheduled start and completion dates

In general, costs are categorized as follows.

- *Staff costs* These will include staff salaries as well as the other direct costs of employment such as the employer's contribution to social security funds, pension scheme contributions, holiday pay and sickness benefit. These are commonly charged to projects at hourly rates based on weekly work records completed by staff. Note that contract staff are usually charged by the week or month – even when they are idle.

- *Overheads* Overheads represent expenditure that an organization incurs, which cannot be directly related to individual projects or jobs, including space rental, interest charges and the costs of service departments (such as human resources). Overhead costs can be recovered by making a fixed charge on development departments (in which case they usually appear as a weekly or monthly charge for a project), or by an additional percentage charge on direct staff employment costs. These additional charges or on-costs can easily equal or exceed the direct employment costs.

- *Usage charges* In some organizations, projects are charged directly for use of resources such as computer time (rather than their cost being recovered as an overhead). This will normally be on an 'as used' basis.

EXERCISE 8.5

Amanda finds that IOE recovers some overheads as on-costs on direct staff costs, although others are recovered by charging a fixed £200 per day against projects. Staff costs (including overheads) are as shown in Table 8.2. Amanda has been working as project leader on the project for its duration. She also estimates that, in total, she will have spent an additional 10 days planning the project and carrying out the post-project review.

Calculate the total cost for Amanda's project on this basis. How is the expenditure spread over the life of the project?

Staff member	Daily cost (£)
Amanda	300
Belinda	250
Tom	175
Daisy	225
Gavin	150
Purdy	150
Justin	150
Spencer	150

TABLE 8.2 Staff costs (including on-costs) for Amanda's project team

Figure 8.9 shows the weekly costs over the 20 weeks that Amanda expects the project to take. This is a typical cost profile – building up slowly to a peak and then tailing off quite rapidly at the end of the project. Figure 8.10 illustrates the cumulative cost of the project and it is generally this that would be used for cost control purposes.

8.10 The scheduling sequence

Going from an ideal activity plan to a cost schedule can be represented as a sequence of steps, rather like the classic waterfall life-cycle model. In the ideal world, we would start with the activity plan and use this as the basis for our risk assessment. The activity plan and risk assessment would provide the basis for our resource allocation and schedule from which we would produce cost schedules.

In practice, as we have seen by looking at Amanda's project, successful resource allocation often necessitates revisions to the activity plan, which, in turn, will affect our risk assessment. Similarly, the cost schedule might indicate the need or desirability to

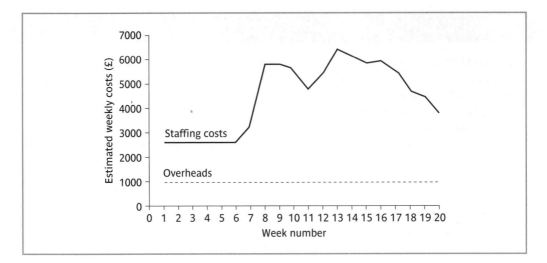

FIGURE 8.9 Weekly project costs for the IOE project

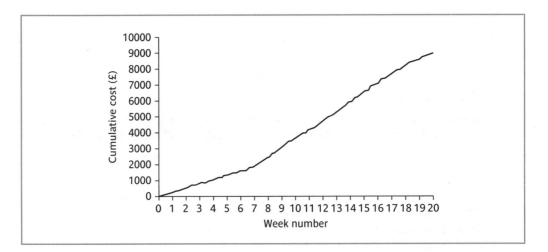

FIGURE 8.10 Cumulative project costs for the IOE project

reallocate resources or revise activity plans – particularly where that schedule indicates a higher overall project cost than originally anticipated.

The interplay between the plans and schedules is complex – any change to any one will affect each of the others. Some factors can be directly compared in terms of money – the cost of hiring additional staff can be balanced against the costs of delaying the project's end date. Some factors, however, are difficult to express in money terms (the cost of an increased risk, for example) and will include an element of subjectivity.

While good project planning software will assist greatly in demonstrating the consequences of change and keeping the planning synchronized, successful project scheduling is largely dependent upon the skill and experience of the project manager in juggling the many factors involved (Figure 8.11).

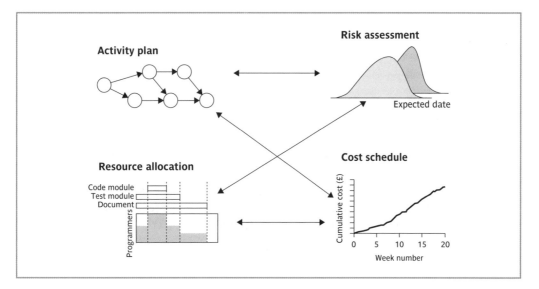

FIGURE 8.11 Successful project scheduling is not a simple sequence

8.11 Conclusion

In this chapter we have discussed the problems of allocating resources to project activities and the conversion of an activity plan to a work schedule. In particular, we have seen the importance of the following:

■ identifying all the resources needed;

■ arranging activity starts to minimize variations in resource levels over the duration of the project;

■ allocating resources to competing activities in a rational order of priority;

■ taking care in allocating the right staff to critical activities.

8.12 Further exercises

1   Burman's priority ordering for allocating resources to activities takes into account the activity duration as well as its total float. Why do you think this is advantageous?

2   If you have access to project planning software, use it to produce an activity plan for Amanda's project and include the staff resource requirements for each activity.

Explore the facilities of your software and answer the following questions.

● Can you set up resource types and ask the application to allocate individuals to tasks?

- Will your software allow you to specify productivity factors for individual members of staff so that the duration of an activity depends upon who is carrying it out?
- Will your software carry out resource smoothing or provide a minimum cost solution?
- Can you replicate Amanda's work schedule (see Figure 8.7) – or produce a better one?

3   On a large project it is often the responsibility of a team leader to allocate tasks to individuals. Why might it be unsatisfactory to leave such allocations entirely to the discretion of the team leader?

4   In scheduling her project, Amanda ignored the risks of absence due to staff sickness. What might she have done to estimate the likelihood of this occurring and how might she have taken account of the risk when scheduling the project?

5   (a) Draw up an activity network and calculate the earliest finish for the following project:

Activity	Duration	Depends on	Resource type
A	3 days		SA
B	1 day	A	SD
C	2 days	A	SD
D	4 days	A	SD
E	3 days	B	SC
F	3 days	C	SC
G	6 days	D	SC
H	3 days	E,F,G	SA

SA = systems analyst; SD = systems designer; SC = software coder

(b) Produce a table showing the number of specialists of each type needed on each day of the project if every activity was started as soon as possible. How many of each type of resource will need to be recruited for the project as a whole if the earliest finish date is to be preserved?

(c) What impact would there be on the project if there were only two systems designers?

(d) What impact would there be on the project if there was only one systems designer, but you had three software coders?

(e) Assuming that the systems designers were employed for the duration of the project, what would be the percentage utilization of the systems designers in the case of both (c) and (d) above?

6 (a) Draw up an activity network for the activities below, identifying the critical path.

Activity	Duration	Depends on	Resource type
A	2 days		SA
B	10 days	A	SD
C	2 days	A	SD
D	2 days	C	SC
E	3 days	C	SC
F	2 days	C	SC
G	4 days	B,D,E,F	SA

SA = systems analyst; SD = systems designer; SC = software coder

(b) Draw up a resource table showing the number of each type of resource needed on each day of the project and assuming that there is only one systems designer.

(c) Identify the best way of revising the plan to remove resource clashes.

CHAPTER
9
Monitoring and control

❖ **OBJECTIVES**

When you have completed this chapter you will be able to:

❖ monitor the progress of projects;

❖ assess the risk of slippage;

❖ visualize and assess the state of a project;

❖ revise targets to correct or counteract drift;

❖ control changes to a project's requirements.

9.1 Introduction

Once work schedules have been published and the project is started, attention must be focused on progress. This requires monitoring of what is happening, comparison of actual achievement against the schedule and, where necessary, revision of plans and schedules to bring the project as far as possible back on target.

In earlier chapters we have stressed the importance of producing plans that can be monitored – for example, ensuring that activities have clearly defined and visible completion points. We will discuss how information about project progress is gathered and what actions must be taken to ensure that a project meets its targets.

The final part of this chapter discusses how we can deal with changes that are imposed from outside – in particular, changes in requirements.

9.2 Creating the framework

Exercising control over a project and ensuring that targets are met is a matter of regular monitoring – finding out what is happening and comparing it with targets. There may be a mismatch between the planned outcomes and the actual ones. Replanning may then be needed to bring the project back on target. Alternatively, the target could have to be revised. Figure 9.1 illustrates a model of the project control cycle and shows how, once the initial project plan has been published, project control is a continual process of monitoring progress against that plan and, where necessary, revising the plan to take account of deviations. It also illustrates the important steps that must be

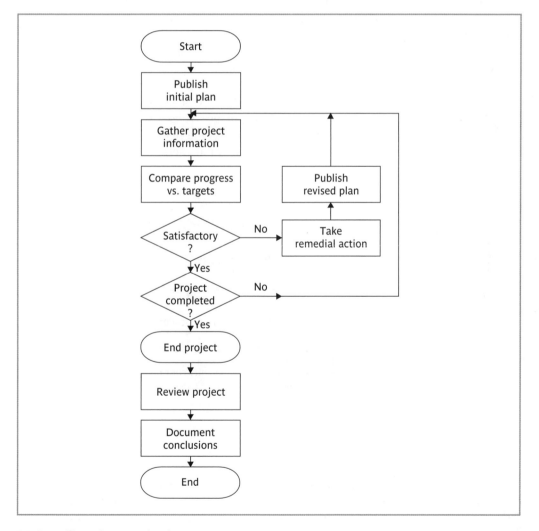

FIGURE 9.1 The project control cycle

taken after completion of the project so that the experience gained in any one project can feed into the planning stages of future projects, thus allowing us to learn from past mistakes.

See Chapter 13 for a discussion of software quality.

In practice we are normally concerned with four types of shortfall – delays in meeting target dates, shortfalls in quality, inadequate functionality, and costs going over target. In this chapter we are mainly concerned with the first and last of these.

Responsibility

The overall responsibility for ensuring satisfactory progress on a project is often the role of the *project steering committee, project management board* or, in PRINCE2, *Project Board*. Day-to-day responsibility will rest with the project manager and, in all but the smallest of projects, aspects of this can be delegated to team leaders.

Figure 9.2 illustrates the typical reporting structure found with medium and large projects. With small projects (employing around half a dozen or fewer staff) individual

The concept of a reporting hierarchy was introduced in Chapter 1.

team members usually report directly to the project manager, but in most cases team leaders will collate reports on their section's progress and forward summaries to the project manager. These, in turn, will be incorporated into project-level reports for the steering committee and, via them or directly, progress reports for the client.

In a PRINCE2 environment, there may be a Project Assurance function reporting to the Project Board and independent of the Project Manager.

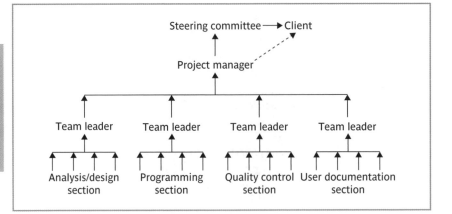

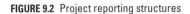

FIGURE 9.2 Project reporting structures

Chapter 12 will explore communication in a more general project context.

Reporting may be oral or written, formal or informal, and regular or ad hoc – see Table 9.1. Informal communication is necessary and important, but any such informal reporting of project progress must be complemented by formal reporting procedures – and it is those we are concerned with in this chapter.

Report type	Examples	Comment
Oral formal regular	Weekly or monthly progress meetings	While reports may be oral, formal written minutes should be kept
Oral formal ad hoc	End-of-stage review meetings	While largely oral, likely to receive and generate written reports
Written formal regular	Job sheets, progress reports	Normally weekly using forms
Written formal ad hoc	Exception reports, change reports	
Oral informal ad hoc	Canteen discussion, social interaction	Often provides early warning; must be backed up by formal reporting

TABLE 9.1 Categories of reporting

Assessing progress

Some information used to assess project progress will be collected routinely, while other information will be triggered by specific events. Wherever possible, this information should be objective and tangible – whether or not a particular report has been delivered, for example. Sometimes, however, assessment will have to depend on estimates of the proportion of the current activity that has been completed.

Setting checkpoints

The PRINCE2 standard described in Appendix A has its own terminology.

It is essential to set a series of checkpoints in the initial activity plan. Checkpoints may be:

- regular (monthly, for example);
- tied to specific events such as the production of a report or other deliverable.

Taking snapshots

The frequency of progress reports will depend upon the size and degree of risk of the project. Team leaders, for example, may want to assess progress daily (particularly when employing inexperienced staff) whereas project managers may find weekly or monthly reporting appropriate. In general, the higher the level, the less frequent and less detailed the reporting needs to be.

Recall that in Chapter 4, Beck recommended weekly work cycles in an XP environment.

At the level of individual developers, however, strong arguments exist for the formal weekly collection of information. This ensures that information is provided while memories are still relatively fresh and provides a mechanism for individuals to review and reflect upon their progress. If reporting is to be weekly then it makes sense to have basic units of work that last about a week.

Major, or project-level, progress reviews will generally take place at particular points during the life of a project – commonly known as *review points* or *control points*. PRINCE2, for example, designates a series of checkpoints where the status of work in a project or for a team is reviewed. At the end of each project Stage, PRINCE2 provides for an End Stage Assessment where an assessment of the project and consideration of its future are undertaken.

9.3 Collecting the data

As a rule, managers will try to break down long activities into more controllable tasks of one or two weeks' duration. However, it will still be necessary to gather information about partially completed activities and, in particular, forecasts of how much work is left to be completed. It can be difficult to make such forecasts accurately.

EXERCISE 9.1

A software developer working on Amanda's project has written the first 250 lines of a Java program that is estimated to require 500 lines of code. Explain why it would be unreasonable to assume that the programming task is 50% complete.

How might you make a reasonable estimate of how near completion it might be?

Where there is a series of products, partial completion of activities is easier to estimate. Counting the number of record specifications or screen layouts produced, for example, can provide a reasonable measure of progress.

In some cases, intermediate products can be used as in-activity milestones. The first successful compilation of a program, for example, might be considered a milestone even though it is not a final product.

Partial completion reporting

Weekly timesheets are a valuable source of information about resources used. They are often used to provide information about what has been achieved. However, requesting partial completion estimates where they cannot be obtained from objective measures encourages the 99%

Many organizations use standard accounting systems with weekly timesheets to charge staff time to individual jobs. The staff time booked to a project indicates the work carried out and the charges to the project. It does not, however, tell the project manager what has been produced or whether tasks are on schedule.

It is therefore common to adapt or enhance existing accounting data collection systems to meet the needs of project control. Weekly timesheets, for example, are frequently adapted by breaking jobs down to activity level and requiring information about work done in addition to time spent. Figure 9.3 shows an example of a report form, in this case requesting information about likely slippage of completion dates as well as estimates of completeness. Other reporting templates are possible. For example, rather than ask for estimates of percentage complete, some managers would prefer to ask for the number of hours already worked on the task and an estimate of the number of hours needed to finish the task off.

Time Sheet

Staff_____John Smith_____   Week ending _____30/3/07_____

Rechargeable hours

Project	Activity code	Description	Hours this week	% complete	Scheduled completion	Estimated completion
P21	A243	Code mod A3	12	30	24/4/07	24/4/07
P34	B771	Document take-on	20	90	6/4/07	4/4/07

Total recharged hours	32

Non-rechargeable hours

Code	Description	Hours this week	Comment and authorization
Z99	Day in lieu	8	Authorized by RB

Total non-rechargeable hours	8

FIGURE 9.3 A weekly timesheet and progress review form

complete syndrome – tasks are reported as on time until 99% complete, and then stay at 99% complete until finished.

There are a number of variations on the traffic-light technique. The version described here is in use in IBM and is described in A. Down,

Red/amber/green (RAG) reporting

One popular way of overcoming the objections to partial completion reporting is to avoid asking for estimated completion dates, but to ask instead for the team members' estimates of the likelihood of meeting the planned target date.

One way of doing this is the traffic-light method. This consists of the following steps:

- identify the key (first level) elements for assessment in a piece of work;
- break these key elements into constituent elements (second level);
- assess each of the second-level elements on the scale *green* for 'on target', *amber* for 'not on target but recoverable', and *red* for 'not on target and recoverable only with difficulty';
- review all the second-level assessments to arrive at first-level assessments;

M. Coleman and
P. Absolon (1994)
*Risk Management for
Software Projects*,
McGraw-Hill.

■ review first- and second-level assessments to produce an overall assessment.

For example, Amanda decides to use a version of the traffic-light method for reviewing activities on the IOE project. She breaks each activity into a number of component parts (deciding, in this case, that a further breakdown is unnecessary) and gets the team members to complete a return at the end of each week. Figure 9.4 illustrates Justin's completed assessment at the end of week 16.

Traffic-light assessment highlights only risk of non-achievement; it is not an attempt to estimate work done or to quantify expected delays.

Following completion of assessment forms for all activities, the project manager uses these as a basis for evaluating the overall status of the project. Any critical activity classified as amber or red will require further consideration and often leads to a revision of the project schedule. Non-critical activities are likely to be considered as a problem if they are classified as red, especially if all their float is likely to be consumed.

Note that this form refers only to uncompleted activities. Justin would still need to report activity completions and the time spent on activities.

Activity Assessment Sheet

Staff _____Justin_____

Ref: IoE/P/13   Activity: Code and test module C

Week number	13	14	15	16	17	18	
Activity summary	G	A	A	R			

Component							Comments
Screen handling procedures	G	A	A	G			
File update procedures	G	G	R	A			
Housekeeping procedures	G	G	G	A			
Compilation	G	G	G	R			
Test data runs	G	G	G	A			
Program documentation	G	G	A	R			

FIGURE 9.4 A traffic-light assessment of IoE/P/13

9.4 Visualizing progress

Having collected data about project progress, a manager needs some way of presenting that data to greatest effect. In this section, we look at some methods of presenting a picture of the project and its future. Some of these methods (such as Gantt charts) provide a static picture, a single snapshot, whereas others (such as timeline charts) try to show how the project has progressed and changed through time.

The Gantt chart

Henry Gantt (1861–1919) was an industrial engineer interested in the efficient organization of work.

One of the simplest and oldest techniques for tracking project progress is the Gantt chart. This is essentially an activity bar chart indicating scheduled activity dates and durations, frequently augmented with activity floats. Reported progress is recorded on the chart (normally by shading activity bars) and a 'today cursor' provides an immediate visual indication of which activities are ahead or behind schedule. Figure 9.5 shows part of Amanda's Gantt chart as at the end of Tuesday of week 17. 'Code and test module D' has been completed ahead of schedule and 'Code and test module A' appears also to be ahead of schedule. The coding and testing of the other two modules are behind schedule.

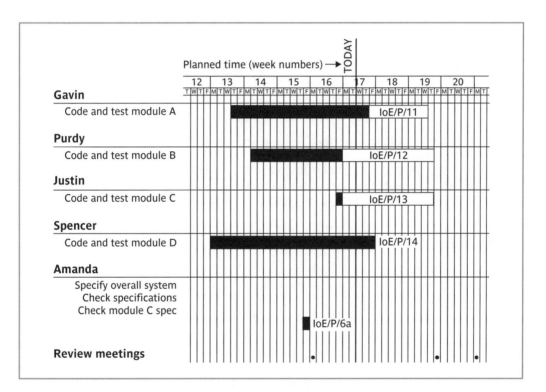

FIGURE 9.5 Part of Amanda's Gantt chart with the 'today cursor' in week 17

The slip chart

A slip chart (Figure 9.6) is a very similar alternative favoured by some project managers who believe it provides a more striking visual indication of those activities that are not progressing to schedule – the more the slip line bends, the greater the variation from the

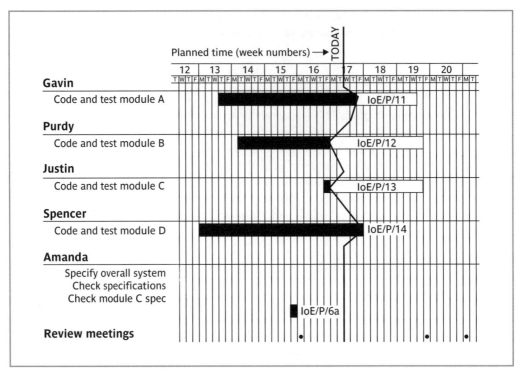

FIGURE 9.6 The slip chart emphasizes the relative position of each activity

plan. Additional slip lines are added at intervals and, as they build up, the project manager will gain an idea as to whether the project is improving (subsequent slip lines bend less) or not. A very jagged slip line indicates a need for rescheduling.

The timeline

One disadvantage of the charts described so far is that they do not show clearly the slippage of the project completion date through the life of the project. Analysing and understanding trends in the project so far allows us to predict the future progress of the project. For example, if a project is behind schedule because so far productivity has not been as high as assumed at the planning stage, it is likely that the scheduled completion date will be pushed back even further unless action is taken to compensate for or improve productivity.

The timeline chart is a method of recording and displaying the way in which targets have changed throughout the duration of the project.

Figure 9.7 shows a timeline chart for Brigette's project at the end of the sixth week. Planned time is plotted along the horizontal axis and elapsed time down the vertical axis. The lines meandering down the chart represent scheduled activity completion dates – at the start of the project 'analyse existing system' is scheduled to be completed by the Tuesday of week 3, 'obtain user requirements' by Thursday of week 5, 'issue tender', the final activity, by Tuesday of week 9, and so on.

Brigette's timeline chart contains only the critical activities for her project; ● indicates actual completion of an activity.

For the sake of clarity, the number of activities on a timeline chart must be limited. Using colour helps to distinguish activities, particularly where lines cross.

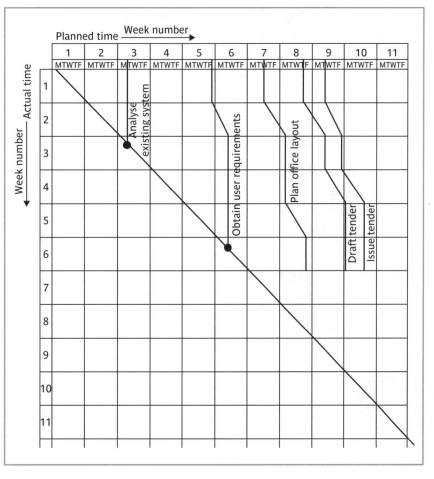

FIGURE 9.7 Brigette's timeline chart at the end of week six

At the end of the first week Brigette reviews these target dates and leaves them as they are – lines are therefore drawn vertically downwards from the target dates to the end of week 1 on the actual time axis.

At the end of week 2, Brigette decides that 'obtain user requirements' will not be completed until Tuesday of week 6 – she therefore extends that activity line diagonally to reflect this. The other activity completion targets are also delayed correspondingly.

By the Tuesday of week 3, 'analyse existing system' is completed and Brigette puts a blob on the diagonal timeline to indicate that this has happened. At the end of week 3 she decides to keep to the existing targets.

At the end of week 4 she adds another three days to 'draft tender' and 'issue tender'.

Note that, by the end of week 6, two activities have been completed and three are still unfinished. Up to this point she has revised target dates on three occasions and the project as a whole is running seven days late.

EXERCISE 9.2

By the end of week 8 Brigette has completed planning the office layout but finds that drafting the tender is going to take one week longer that originally anticipated.

What will Brigette's timeline chart look like at the end of week 8?

If the rest of the project goes according to plan, what will Brigette's timeline chart look like when the project is completed?

The timeline chart is useful both during the execution of a project and as part of the post-implementation review. Analysis of the timeline chart, and the reasons for the changes, can indicate failures in the estimation process or other errors that might, with that knowledge, be avoided in future.

9.5 Cost monitoring

Project costs may be monitored by a company's accounting system. By themselves, they provide little information about project status.

Expenditure monitoring is an important component of project control, not only in itself, but also because it provides an indication of the effort that has gone into (or at least been charged to) a project. A project might be on time but only because more money has been spent on activities than originally budgeted. A cumulative expenditure chart such as that shown in Figure 9.8 provides a simple method of comparing actual and planned expenditure. By itself it is not particularly meaningful – Figure 9.8 could, for example, illustrate a project that is running late or one that is on time but has shown substantial costs savings. We need to take account of the current status of the project activities before attempting to interpret the meaning of recorded expenditure.

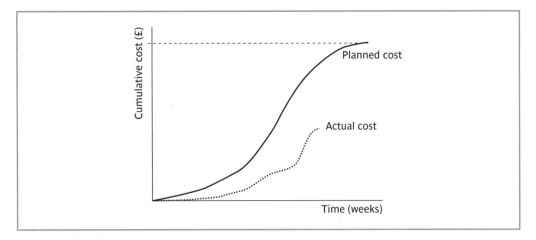

FIGURE 9.8 Tracking cumulative expenditure

Cost charts become much more useful if we add projected future costs calculated by adding the estimated costs of uncompleted work to the costs already incurred. Where a computer-based planning tool is used, revision of cost schedules is generally provided automatically once actual expenditure has been recorded. Figure 9.9 illustrates the additional information available once the revised cost schedule is included – in this case it is apparent that the project is behind schedule and over budget.

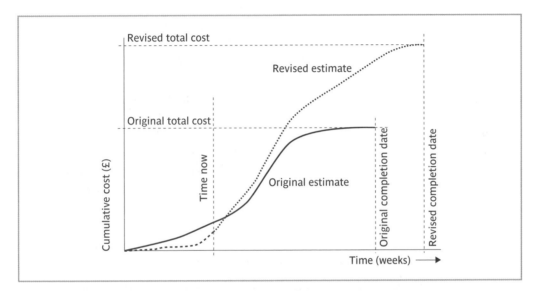

FIGURE 9.9 The cumulative expenditure chart can also show revised estimates of cost and completion date

9.6 Earned value analysis

Earned value analysis has gained in popularity in recent years and may be seen as a refinement of the cost monitoring discussed in the previous section. It originated in the USA's Department of Defense (DOD) as a part of a set of measures to control projects being carried out by contractors for the DOD. Earned value analysis is based on assigning a 'value' to each task or work package (as identified in the WBS) based on the original expenditure forecasts. One way of looking at this is as the equivalent of the price that might be agreed by a contractor to do the unit of work. The assigned value is the original budgeted cost for the item and is known as the *planned value* (PV) or *budgeted cost of work scheduled* (BCWS). A task that has not started is assigned an earned value of zero and when it has been completed, it, and hence the project, is credited with the original planned value of the task. The total value credited to a project at any point is known as the *earned value* (EV) or budgeted cost of work performed (BCWP) and this can be represented as a money value, an amount of staff time or as a percentage of the PV. EV is thus analogous to the agreed price to be paid to the contractor once the work is completed.

Where tasks have been started but are not yet complete, some consistent method of assigning an earned value must be applied. Common methods in software projects are:

- *the 0/100 technique:* where a task is assigned a value of zero until such time that it is completed when it is given a value of 100% of the budgeted value;

- *the 50/50 technique:* where a task is assigned a value of 50% of its value as soon as it is started and then given a value of 100% once it is complete – this matches some contractual arrangements where a contractor is given half the agreed price when starting the work, perhaps to help pay for raw materials, and the remainder on successful completion;

- *the 75/25 technique:* where the task is assigned 75% on starting and 25% on completion – this is often used when a large item of equipment is being bought: 75% is paid when the equipment is actually delivered and the remainder when installation and testing has been satisfactorily completed;

- *the milestone technique:* where a task is given a value based on the achievement of milestones that have been assigned values as part of the original budget plan;

- *percentage complete:* in some cases there may be a way of objectively measuring the amount of work completed – for example, as part of the implementation of an information system, a number of data records have to be manually typed into a database and the actual number so far completed can be objectively counted.

Of these, we prefer the 0/100 technique for software development. The 50/50 technique can give a false sense of security by over-valuing the reporting of activity starts. The milestone technique might be appropriate for activities with a long duration estimate but, in such cases, it is better to break that activity into a number of smaller ones.

The baseline budget

The first stage in setting up an earned value analysis is to create the *baseline budget*. The baseline budget is based on the project plan and shows the forecast growth in earned value through time. Earned value may be measured in monetary values but, in the case of staff-intensive projects such as software development, it is common to measure earned value in person-hours or workdays. Amanda's baseline budget, based on the schedule shown in Figure 8.7, is shown in Table 9.2 and diagrammatically in Figure 9.10. Notice that she has based her baseline budget on workdays and is using the 0/100 technique for crediting earned value to the project.

Amanda's project is not expected to be credited with any earned value until day 34, when the activity 'specify overall system' is to be completed. This activity was forecast to consume 34 person-days and it will therefore be credited with 34 person-days of earned value when it has been completed. The other steps in the baseline budget chart coincide with the scheduled completion dates of other activities.

Task	Budgeted workdays	Scheduled completion	Cumulative workdays	% cumulative earned value
Specify overall system	34	34	34	14.35
Specify module B	15	49	64	27.00
Specify module D	15	49		
Specify module A	20	54	84	35.44
Check specifications	2	56	86	36.28
Design module D	4	60	90	37.97
Design module A	7	63	97	40.93
Design module B	6	66	103	43.46
Specify module C	25	74	128	54.01
Check module C spec	1	75	129	54.43
Design module C	4	79	133	56.12
Code and test module D	25	85	158	66.67
Code and test module A	30	93	188	79.32
Code and test module B	28	94	231	97.47
Code and test module C	15	94		
System integration	6	100	237	100.00

TABLE 9.2 Amanda's baseline budget calculation

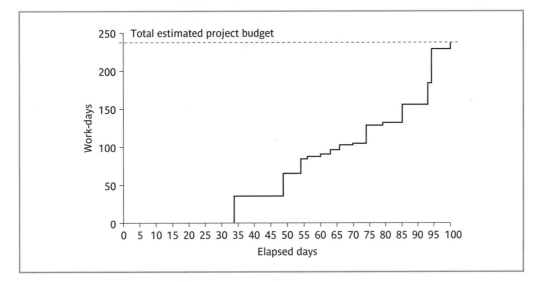

FIGURE 9.10 Amanda's baseline budget

Monitoring earned value

Having created the baseline budget, the next task is to monitor earned value as the project progresses. This is done by monitoring the completion of tasks (or activity starts and milestone achievements in the case of the other crediting techniques).

EXERCISE 9.3

Figure 9.11 shows Amanda's earned value analysis at the start of week 12 of the project. Note that here both PV and EV are measured in 'work-days' and that the 0/100 rule is being applied. The earned value (EV) is clearly lagging behind the baseline budget, indicating that the project is behind schedule.

By studying Figure 9.12, can you tell exactly what has gone wrong with her project and what the consequences might be?

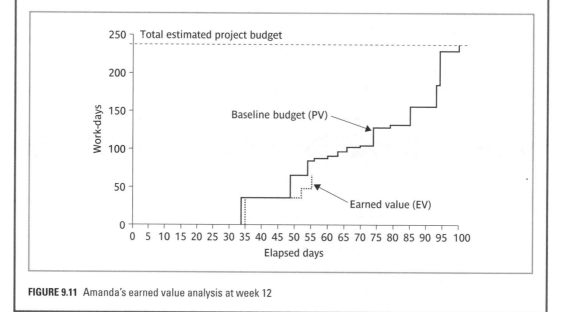

FIGURE 9.11 Amanda's earned value analysis at week 12

As well as recording EV, the actual cost of each task can be collected as *actual cost* (AC). This is also known as the *actual cost of work performed* (ACWP). This is shown in Figure 9.12, which, in this case, records the values as percentages of the total budgeted cost.

Figure 9.12 also illustrates the following performance statistics, which can be shown directly or derived from the earned value chart.

Schedule variance (SV)

The schedule variance is measured in cost terms as EV – PV and indicates the degree to which the value of completed work differs from that planned. Say, for example, that

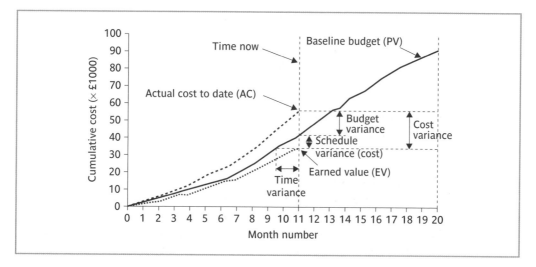

FIGURE 9.12 An earned value tracking chart

work with a PV of £40,000 should have been completed by now. In fact, some of that work has not been done so that the EV is only £35,000. The SV would therefore be £35,000 – £40,000, that is –£5,000. A negative SV means the project is behind schedule.

Time variance (TV)

Figure 9.12 also indicates the *time variance* (TV). This is the difference between the time when the achievement of the current earned value was planned to occur and the time now. In this case, the current EV should have been achieved in the early part of month 9 and as the time now is the end of month 11, the TV is about –1.75 months.

Cost variance (CV)

This is calculated as EV – AC and indicates the difference between the earned value or budgeted cost and the actual cost of completed work. Say that when the SV above was calculated as –5,000, £55,000 had actually been spent to get the EV. The CV in this case would have been £35,000 – £55,000 or –£20,000. It can also be an indicator of the accuracy of the original cost estimates. A negative CV means that the project is over cost.

Performance ratios

Two ratios are commonly tracked: the cost performance index (CPI = EV/AC) and the schedule performance index (SPI = EV/PV). Using the examples above, CPI would be £35,000/£55,000, that is, 0.64, and SPI would be £35,000/£40,000, that is, 0.88. The two ratios can be thought of as a 'value-for-money' indices. A value greater than one indicates that work is being completed better than planned, whereas a value of less than one means that work is costing more than and/or proceeding more slowly than planned.

CPI can be used to produce a revised cost estimate for the project (or *estimate at completion* – EAC). EAC is calculated as BAC/CPI where BAC (budget at completion) is the current projected budget for the project. If the BAC was £100,000 then a revised estimate at completion (EAC) would be £100,000/0.64 or £156,250. Similarly, the current SPI can be used to project the possible duration of the project given the current rate of progress. Say the planned total duration for the project is 23 months – in earned value terminology this is the *schedule at completion* (SAC). A time estimate at completion (TEAC) can be calculated as SAC/SPI. In this case it would be 23/0.88, that is, 26.14 months. This is only an approximate guide: where there are several parallel chains of activities being carried out concurrently – as we saw in Chapter 6 – the project duration will depend on the degree to which the activities that have been delayed are on the critical path.

In the same way that the expenditure analysis in Figure 9.8 was augmented to show revised expenditure forecasts, we can augment the simple earned value tracking chart with forecasts as illustrated in Figure 9.13.

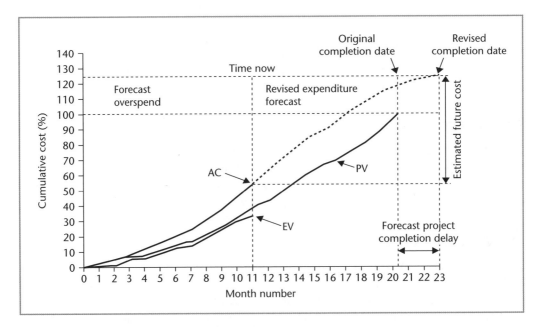

FIGURE 9.13 An earned value chart with revised forecasts

Earned value analysis has not yet gained universal acceptance for use with software development projects, perhaps largely because of the attitude that, whereas a half-built house has a value reflected by the labour and materials that have been used, a half-completed software project has virtually no value at all. This is to misunderstand the purpose of earned value analysis, which, as we have seen, is a method for tracking what has been achieved on a project – measured in terms of the budgeted costs of completed tasks or products.

9.7 Prioritizing monitoring

So far we have assumed that all aspects of a project will receive equal treatment in terms of the degree of monitoring applied. We must not forget, however, that monitoring takes time and uses resources that might sometimes be put to better use!

In this section we list the priorities we might apply in deciding levels of monitoring.

- *Critical path activities* Any delay in an activity on the critical path will cause a delay in the completion date for the project. Critical path activities are therefore likely to have a very high priority for close monitoring.

> Free float is the amount of time an activity may be delayed without affecting any subsequent activity.

- *Activities with no free float* A delay in any activity with no free float will delay at least some subsequent activities even though, if the delay is less than the total float, it might not delay the project completion date. These subsequent delays can have serious effects on our resource schedule as a delay in a subsequent activity could mean that the resources for that activity will become unavailable before that activity is completed because they are committed elsewhere.

- *Activities with less than a specified float* If any activity has very little float it might use up this float before the regular activity monitoring brings the problem to the project manager's attention. It is common practice to monitor closely those activities with less than, say, one week free float.

> PERT and the significance of activity duration variance was described in Chapter 7.

- *High-risk activities* A set of high-risk activities should have been identified as part of the initial risk profiling exercise. If we are using the PERT three-estimate approach we will designate as high risk those activities that have a high estimated duration variance. These activities will be given close attention because they are most likely to overrun or overspend.

- *Activities using critical resources* Activities can be critical because they are very expensive (as in the case of specialized contract programmers). Staff or other resources might be available only for a limited period, especially if they are controlled outside the project team. In any event, an activity that demands a critical resource requires a high level of monitoring.

9.8 Getting the project back to target

> A contingency plan should, of course, already exist as a result of the risk analysis methods described in Chapter 7.

Almost any project will, at one time or another, be subject to delays and unexpected events. One of the tasks of the project manager is to recognize when this is happening (or, if possible, about to happen) and, with the minimum delay and disruption to the project team, attempt to mitigate the effects of the problem. In most cases, the project manager, at least initially, tries to ensure that the scheduled project end date remains unaffected. This can be done by shortening remaining activity durations or shortening the overall duration of the remaining project in the ways described in the next section.

> The schedule is not sacrosanct – it is a plan that should be adhered to so long as it is relevant and cost-effective.

It should be remembered, however, that this might not always be the most appropriate response to disruptions to a plan. There is little point in spending considerable sums in overtime payments in order to speed up a project if the customer is not overly concerned with the delivery date and there is no other valuable work for the team members once this project is completed.

There are two main strategies to consider when drawing up plans to bring a project back on target – shortening the critical path or altering the activity precedence requirements.

Shorten the critical path

The overall duration of a project is determined by the current critical path, so speeding up non-critical path activities will not bring forward a project completion date. However, there are several ways in which this might be done.

> Time/cost trade-off: there is a general rule that timescales can be shortened by buying more (or more expensive) resources; sometimes this is true.

- *Adding resources – especially staff* Exhorting staff to 'work harder' might have some effect, although frequently a more positive form of action is required, such as increasing the resources available for some critical activity. Fact-finding, for example, might be speeded up by allocating an additional analyst to interviewing users. It is unlikely, however, that the coding of a small module would be shortened by allocating an additional programmer – indeed, it might be counterproductive because of the additional time needed for organizing and allocating tasks and communicating. While adding more staff may be able to speed up progress, this would be at an additional cost. In EV terms, negative schedule variance (SV) may be reduced, but at the price of increasing a negative cost variance (CV).

- *Increase use of current resources* Resource levels can be increased by making them available for longer. Thus, staff might be asked to work overtime for the duration of an activity and computing resources might be made available at times (such as evenings and weekends) when they might otherwise be inaccessible.

- *Reallocate staff to critical activities* The project manager might consider allocating more efficient staff to activities on the critical path or swapping resources between critical and non-critical activities. When a project is actually executed, the critical path may change as the actual durations of activities will vary from the original estimates and staff allocations may be adjusted to reflect this.

- *Reduce scope* The amount of work to be done could be reduced by reducing the scope of the functionality to be delivered. The client may prefer to have a subset of the promised features on time – especially if they are the most useful ones – rather than have the delivery of the whole application delayed.

- *Reduce quality* Some quality-related activities such as system testing could be curtailed. This would probably lead to more corrective work having to be done to the 'live' system once it has been implemented.

By such means we can attempt to shorten the timescale for critical activities until such time as either we have brought the project back to schedule or further efforts prove unproductive or not cost-effective. Remember, however, that shortening a critical path often causes some other path, or paths, to become critical (see Section 6.14).

Reconsider the precedence requirements

If attempting to shorten critical activities proves insufficient, the next step is to consider the constraints by which some activities have to be deferred pending completion of others. The original project network would most probably have been drawn up assuming 'ideal' conditions and 'normal' working practices. It might be that, to avoid the project delivering late, it is now worth questioning whether as yet unstarted activities really do have to await the completion of others. It might, in a particular organization, be 'normal' to complete system testing before commencing user training. In order to avoid late completion of a project it might, however, be considered acceptable to alter 'normal' practice and start training earlier.

One way to overcome precedence constraints is to subdivide an activity into a component that can start immediately and one that is still constrained as before. For example, a user handbook can be drawn up in a draft form from the system specification and then be revised later to take account of subsequent changes.

If we do decide to alter the precedence requirements in such a way, it is clearly important to be aware that quality might be compromised and to make a considered decision to compromise quality where needed. It is equally important to assess the degree to which changes in work practices increase risk. It is possible, for example, to start coding a module before its design has been completed. It would normally, however, be considered foolhardy to do so since, as well as compromising quality, it would increase the risk of having to redo some of the coding once the final design had been completed and thus delay the project even further.

Maintaining the business case

In making decisions about the management of the project, the main concern of the project sponsor, that is, the stakeholder who is putting up the money for the project, is whether the business case for the project has been preserved. You may recall from Chapter 2 that the value of the benefits of a project must be greater than its cost for the project to be viable. If costs increase, then this reduces the value of the benefits at the end of the project. If the project is delayed or the amount of functionality in the deliverables is curtailed, it means that the benefits that the project will generate will be reduced. At some point the costs may exceed the benefits and the project then loses its viability. A decision could then be made to cancel the project.

Exception planning

The project manager will normally be allowed to change the detail of a plan as long as the agreed project outcomes are produced on time and within budget.

In some cases, an operational change may affect other stakeholders. One such case would be where the timing of acceptance testing by users had to be changed. In such a case the project manager would need to gain the acceptance of these stakeholders for the change.

Some changes to the plan might have an impact on the delivery date, project scope or costs. These in turn could affect the business case for the project. Here the project manager would need to gain the approval of the business sponsors of the project. We saw above that the interests of the sponsors could be represented through a group variously known as a Project Board (in PRINCE2), project management board or steering committee.

One approach, adopted by PRINCE2, is to require the project manager to write an *exception report* that explains the reasons for the deviation from the existing plan. The consequences of the deviation should be detailed, and if possible a number of options for dealing with the problem. The probable impact of each option on the business case is projected, and a recommendation on a course of action is presented. The Project Board, or equivalent, having considered the report and having approved one of the options, may then task the project manager with producing a more detailed *exception plan*. If this is then approved it replaces the existing plan.

9.9 Change control

So far in this chapter, we have assumed that the nature of the deliverables has not changed. A project leader like Amanda or Brigette might find, however, that requirements are modified because of changing circumstances or because the users get a clearer idea of what is really needed. The payroll system that Brigette is implementing might, for instance, need to be adjusted if the staffing structure at the college is reorganized.

Other, internal, changes will crop up. Amanda might find that there are inconsistencies in the program specifications that become apparent only when the programs are coded, and these would result in amendments to those specifications.

When a document such as the user requirements is being developed there may be many different versions of the document as it undergoes cycles of development and review. Any change control process at this point would be very informal and flexible. At some point what is assumed to be the final version will be created. This is *baselined*, effectively frozen. Baselined products are the foundation for the development of further products – for instance interface design documents may be developed from baselined user requirements. Thus any changes to the baselined document could have knock-on effects on other parts of the project. The Product Flow Diagrams (explained in Chapter 3) indicate relationships between the products of a project where this is the case. For this reason subsequent changes to baselined documents need to be stringently controlled.

EXERCISE 9.4

A change in a program specification will normally be carried through into changes to the program design and then changed code. What other products might need to be modified?

Change control procedures

A simple change control procedure for operational systems might have the following steps:

1 One or more users might perceive a need for a modification to a system and ask for a change request to be passed to the development staff.

2 The user management would consider the change request and, if they approve it, pass it to the development management. It important that there is a single authorized channel for *requests for change (RFCs)* between the client community and the management of the developers. There would be some filtering within the client community to ensure that the proposed change does genuinely provide a benefit before the RFC is generated.

3 There would be one person within the development area who would receive and process RFCs. They would delegate a member of staff to look at the request and to report on the practicality and cost of carrying out the change. The developer would, as part of this, assess the products that would be affected by the change.

4 The development representative would report back to the user management on the findings and the user management would decide whether, in view of the cost quoted, they wish to go ahead.

5 There would be some individual or group who represented the major stakeholders, both users and developers and also the project sponsor, who would have the authority to prioritize the RFCs for action. Ultimately this should be the Project Board or equivalent. However, the large proportion of RFCs would be relatively small in scope. This could cause a bureaucratic bottleneck if all these changes had to considered at the highest level. A smaller group of active stakeholder representatives might therefore be delegated the responsibility for considering and approving changes up to a certain level of expenditure. This group would adopt the role of a *change control board*, although they might not actually be called that. A further step is to give the project managers allowances that would allow them accept minor changes (as long as they are documented with an RFC etc.) as long as they do not exceed planned cost and delivery targets. There is thus a general principle that the larger the amendment the higher in the control hierarchy it would have to be reported. However, this is not simply a matter of size. A very large number of seemingly small changes could have a serious accumulative effect on project progress which may call for the attention of higher management. A very large set of changes might trigger the project manager to produce an exception report – see above.

6 Once an RFC has been approved for action, one or more developers are authorized to take copies of the master products that are to be modified. This would need to be done through the configuration librarian – see below.

7 The copies are modified. In the case of software components this would involve modifying the code and recompiling and testing it.

8 When the development of new versions of the product has been completed the user management will be notified and copies of the software will be released for user acceptance testing.

9   When the user is satisfied that the products are adequate they will authorize their operational release. The master copies of configuration items will be replaced.

EXERCISE 9.5

The above steps relate to changes to operational systems. How could they be modified to deal with systems under development?

Changes in scope of a system

This is sometimes called scope creep.

A common occurrence with IS development projects is for the size of the system gradually to increase. One cause of this is changes to requirements that are requested by users.

EXERCISE 9.6

Think of other reasons why there is a tendency for scope creep.

The scope of a project needs to be carefully monitored and controlled. One way is to re-estimate the system size in terms of SLOC or function points at key milestones.

Configuration librarian's role

Control of changes and documentation ought to be the responsibility of someone who may variously be named the configuration librarian, the configuration manager or the project librarian. Among this person's duties would be:

BS EN ISO 9001:1994 (formerly BS 5750) requires that a formal change control procedure be in place.

- the identification of all items that are subject to change control;
- the establishment and maintenance of a central repository of the master copies of all project documentation and software products;
- the setting up and running of a formal set of procedures to deal with changes;
- the maintenance of records of who has access to which library items and the status of each library item (e.g. whether under development, under test or released).

It will be recalled that it was suggested that the setting up of change control procedures might be one of the first things the Brigette would want to do at Brightmouth College.

9.10 Conclusion

In this chapter we have discussed the requirements for the continual monitoring of projects and the need for making progress visible. Among the important points to emerge were:

- planning is pointless unless the execution of the plan is monitored;
- activities that are too long need to be subdivided to make them more controllable;
- ideally, progress should be measured through the delivery of project products;
- progress needs to be shown in a visually striking way, such as through bar charts, in order to communicate information effectively;
- costs need to be monitored as well as elapsed time;
- delayed projects can often be brought back on track by shortening activity times on the critical path or by relaxing some of the precedence constraints.

9.11 Further exercises

1 Take a look at Amanda's project schedule shown in Figure 8.7. Identify those activities scheduled to last more than three weeks and describe how she might monitor progress on each of them on a fortnightly or weekly basis.

2 Amanda's Gantt chart at the end of week 17 (Figure 9.5) indicates that two activities are running late. What effect might this have on the rest of the project? How might Amanda mitigate the effects of this delay?

3 Table 9.2 illustrates Amanda's earned value calculations based on work-days. Revise the table using monetary values based on the cost figures that you used in Exercise 8.5. Think carefully about how to handle the costs of Amanda as project manager and the recovered overheads and justify your decisions about how you treat them.

4 If you have access to project planning software, investigate the extent to which it offers support for earned value analysis. If it does not do so directly, investigate ways in which it would help you to generate a baseline budget (PV) and track the earned value (EV).

5 Describe a set of change control procedures that would be appropriate for Brigette to implement at Brightmouth College.

CHAPTER 10

Managing contracts

❖ OBJECTIVES

When you have completed this chapter you will be able to:

❖ distinguish between the different types of contract;

❖ outline the contents of a contract for goods and services;

❖ plan the evaluation of a proposal or product;

❖ administer a contract from its signing until the final acceptance of project completion.

10.1 Introduction

In the Brightmouth College scenario, the college management have decided to obtain their software externally. Given their limited capability for developing new and reliable software, this seems sensible. At IOE, Amanda has a team of software developers employed by IOE. However, the demand for development effort fluctuates as projects come and go. The IOE management might therefore decide that it is more cost-effective to employ outside software developers for new development while a reduced group of in-house software development staff maintain and support existing systems.

> It is not unusual for a major organization to spend 6 to 12 months and 40% of the total acquisition and implementation budget on package evaluation

The buying of goods and services, rather than 'doing it yourself', is attractive when is money is available but other, less flexible, types of resource, especially staff time, are in short supply. However, there are risks arising from the considerable staff time and attention still needed with major customer service and support applications (Demian Martinez, Decision Drivers Inc., *Computing*, 23 July, 1998).

It was, for example, reported that two consortia led by Sema and EDS, respectively, had spent £4 million over 2 years bidding for a UK government project to renew the ICT infrastructure in the prison service – the final job was estimated as being worth £350 million (*Computing*, 13 August, 1998).

to manage a contracted-out project successfully. It is essential that customer organizations such as Brightmouth College and IOE find time to clarify their exact requirements at the beginning, and to ensure that the goods and services delivered are satisfactory.

Potential suppliers are likely to be more accommodating before any contract is signed than afterwards – especially if the contract is for a fixed price. Thus, as much forethought and planning is needed with an acquisition project as with internal development.

In the remainder of this chapter, the different types of contract that can be used will be explored. This is followed by the general steps to be followed when placing a contract. The issues to be considered when drafting a contract are then examined. We conclude by describing some of the things done while the contract is executed.

The bargaining position of the customer will stronger if their business is going to be valuable. If you are buying a cut-price computer game, you are unlikely to be able to negotiate variations on the supplier's standard contract of sale. (In fact, because of the inequality of the parties, such sales are subject to special consumer protection laws.) Potential suppliers will carefully assess the time and money to be spent responding to a customer's requests as there is no guarantee of the final contract.

10.2 Types of contract

The external resources required could be in the form of *services,* for example staff on short-term contracts carrying out some project tasks. At Brightmouth College, Brigette could use temporary staff to input employee details needed for the new payroll system. IOE might carry out application-building in-house but augment the permanent staff with contract developers. The contractor might not only supply the new system but also operate it on the customer's behalf. For example, Brightmouth College might abandon buying a package and instead get a payroll services agency to carry out the payroll work.

On the other hand, a contract for a *completed software package* could be placed. This could be:

- a *bespoke* system created specifically for one customer;
- an *off-the-shelf* package bought 'as is' – this is sometimes referred to as *shrink-wrapped* software;

David Bainbridge (2007) *Introduction to Computer Law*, Longman, 6th edition, is highly recommended as a guide to the legal aspects of IT contracts.

- *customized off-the-shelf* (COTS) software – where a core system is modified to meet the needs of the client.

Where equipment is purchased, in English law, this is normally a contract for the supply of *goods*. With the supply of software this may be regarded as supplying a service (i.e. to write the software) or the granting of a *licence* (i.e. permission) to use the software which remains in the ownership of the supplier. These distinctions will have legal implications.

EXERCISE 10.1

Which of the three system options (i.e. bespoke, off-the-shelf or COTS) might Amanda consider with regard to the IOE maintenance group accounts system? What factors would she need to take into account?

The section on ways of assessing supplier payments draws heavily on material from Paul Radford and Robyn Lawrie of Charismatek Software Metrics, Melbourne, Australia.

Another way of classifying contracts is by the way that the payment to suppliers is calculated. We will look at:

- fixed price contracts;
- time and materials contracts;
- fixed price per delivered unit contracts.

Fixed price contracts

In this situation a price is fixed when the contract is signed. The customer knows that, if there are no changes in the contract terms, this is the price they pay on completion. For this to be effective, the customer's requirement has to be fixed at the outset. In other words, when the contract is to construct a software system, the detailed requirements analysis must already have been carried out. Once the development is under way the customer cannot change their requirements without renegotiating the price of the contract.

The advantages of this method are:

- *Known customer expenditure* As long as the requirements are precise and not changed, the customer has a known cost.
- *Supplier motivation* The supplier has a motivation to work in a cost-effective manner.

The disadvantages include:

The cost could still be lower than in-house development because the supplier may be able to exploit economies of scale and also expertise acquired doing similar jobs in the past.

- *Higher prices to allow for contingency* The supplier absorbs the risk for any errors in the estimates. To reduce the impact of this risk, the supplier will add a margin to the price quoted.
- *Difficulties in modifying requirements* The need to change the scope of the requirements may become apparent during development – this may cause friction between the supplier and customer.
- *Upward pressure on the cost of changes* When competing against other potential suppliers, the supplier will try to quote as low a price as possible. Once the contract is signed, if further requirements are put forward, the supplier is in a strong position to demand a high price for these changes.
- *Threat to system quality* The need to meet a fixed price could mean that the quality of the software suffers.

Time and materials contracts

With this type of contract, the customer is charged at a fixed rate per unit of effort, for example per staff-hour. The supplier may provide an initial estimate of the cost based on their current understanding of the customer's requirements, but this is not the basis for the final payment. The supplier usually invoices the customer for work done at regular intervals, say each month.

The advantages of this approach are:

■ *Ease of changing requirements* Where a project has a research orientation and the direction of the project may change as options are explored, then this may be an appropriate method of payment.

■ *Lack of price pressure* The lack of price pressure may promote better quality deliverables.

The disadvantages of this approach are:

■ *Customer liability* The customer absorbs the risks associated with poorly defined or changing requirements.

■ *Lack of incentives for supplier* The supplier has no incentive to work in a cost-effective manner or to control the scope of the deliverables.

Because the supplier appears to be given a blank cheque, this approach does not find favour with customers. However, the employment of contract development staff may in effect involve this type of contract.

Fixed price per unit delivered contracts

Function point counting was discussed in Chapter 5.

This is often associated with function point (FP) counting. The size of the system to be delivered is calculated or estimated at the outset of the project. The size could be estimated in lines of code, but FPs can be more easily derived from requirements documents. A price per unit is also quoted. The final price is then the unit price multiplied by the number of units. Table 10.1 shows a typical schedule of prices.

This table comes from David Garmus and David Herron (1996) *Measuring the software process*, Prentice Hall.

Function point count	Function design cost per FP	Implementation cost per FP	Total cost per FP
Up to 2,000	$242	$725	$967
2,001–2,500	$255	$764	$1,019
2,501–3,000	$265	$793	$1,058
3,001–3,500	$274	$820	$1,094
3,501–4,000	$284	$850	$1,134

TABLE 10.1 A schedule of charges per function point

The company in question was RDI Technologies in the USA. These figures are now several years old.

The company that produced this table in fact charge a higher fee per FP for larger systems. For example, a system to be implemented contains 2600 FPs. The overall charge would be 2000 × $967, plus 500 × $1,019, plus 100 × $1,058.

We have already noted that the scope of the application can grow during development. It would be unrealistic for a contractor to be asked to quote a single price for all the stages of a development project: how can they estimate the construction effort needed when the requirements are not yet established? One approach would be to negotiate a series of contracts, each covering a different stage of system development.

Alternatively, the software supplier might first carry out the system design. A charge could then be made for design work based on the figures in the 'Function design cost per FP' column. This, if the designed system was counted at 1000 FPs, would be 1000 × $242 i.e. $242,000. If the design was then implemented, and the actual software delivered, then the additional 1000 × $725 would be charged i.e. $725,000. If the scope of the system grows because the users find new requirements, these new requirements would be charged at the combined rate for design and implementation, e.g. if new requirements amounting to 100 extra FPs were found, then the charge for this extra work would be $967 × 100 i.e. $96,700.

EXERCISE 10.2

A system to be designed and implemented is counted as comprising 3200 FPs. What would be the total charge according to the schedule in Table 10.1?

The advantages of this approach are:

- *Customer understanding* The customer can see how the price is calculated and how it will vary with changed requirements.
- *Comparability* Pricing schedules can be compared.
- *Emerging functionality* The supplier does not bear the risk of increasing functionality.
- *Supplier efficiency* The supplier still has an incentive to deliver the required functionality in a cost-effective manner (unlike with time and materials contracts).
- *Life-cycle range* The requirements do not have to be definitively specified at the outset. Thus the development contract can cover both the analysis and design stages of the project.

The disadvantages of this approach are:

- *Difficulties with software size measurement* Lines of code can easily be inflated by adopting a verbose coding style. With FPs, there may be disagreements about what the FP count should really be: in some cases, FP counting rules may be seen as unfairly favouring either the supplier or customer. Users, in particular, will almost certainly not be familiar with the concept of FPs and special training may be needed for them. The solution to these problems may be to employ an independent FP counter.

> The impact of late changes will be further discussed in Chapter 13 on software quality.

- *Changing requirements* Some requested changes may affect existing code drastically but not increase the overall FP count. A change made late in the development cycle will usually require more effort to implement than one made earlier.

To reduce the last difficulty, one suggestion from Australia has been to vary the charge depending on the point at which they have been requested – see Table 10.2.

> This table comes from the draft *Acquisition of Customised Software Policy* document, published by the Department of State Development, Victoria, 1996.

	Pre-acceptance testing handover	Post-acceptance testing handover
Additional FPs	100%	100%
Changed FPs	130%	150%
Deleted FPs	25%	50%

TABLE 10.2 Examples of additional charges for changed functionality

---

EXERCISE 10.3

A contract stipulates that a computer application is to be designed, constructed and delivered at a cost of $600 per FP. After acceptance testing, the customer asks for changes to some of the functions in the system amounting to 500 FPs and some new functions which amount to 200 additional FPs. Using Table 10.2, calculate the additional charge.

There are other options and permutations of options for payments. The implementation of a specification could be at a fixed price, with any additions or changes to the requirements to be charged per FP. Where the contractor has buy in equipment, the price of which may fluctuate, it is possible to negotiate a contract where the final price contains a fixed portion for labour plus an amount that depends on the actual cost of purchased components.

EXERCISE 10.4

It is easy to see why passing on fluctuations in equipment costs may be advantageous to the contractor. However, is there any advantage to the customer in such an arrangement?

Another way of categorizing contracts, at least initially, is according to the approach that is used in contractor selection, namely

> This categorization is based on European Union regulations.

- open
- restricted
- negotiated.

Open tendering process

> Invitation to tender (ITT) and request for proposal (RFP) are interchangeable terms.

In this case, any supplier can bid to supply the goods and services. All bids compliant with the original conditions in the *invitation to tender* must be considered and evaluated in the same way. With a major project this evaluation process can be time consuming and expensive.

There has been a global movement towards removing barriers to businesses in one country supplying goods and services in another. Examples of this are efforts by the World Trade Organization (WTO) and the European Union to ensure that public bodies do not unfairly favour local businesses. Among the agreements overseen by the WTO is one on government procurement which lays down rules on tendering processes. Where the client is a public body, an open tendering process may be compulsory.

Restricted tendering process

In this case, there are bids only from suppliers who have been invited by the customer. Unlike the open tendering process, the customer may at any point reduce the number of potential suppliers being considered. This is usually the best approach to adopt.

Negotiated procedure

There may, however, be some good reasons why the restricted tendering process may not be the most suitable in some particular sets of circumstances. Say, for example, that there is a fire that destroys some ICT equipment. The key concern here may be to get replacement equipment up and running as quickly as possible and there may simply not be the time to embark on a lengthy tendering process. Another situation might be where a new software application had been successfully built by an outside supplier, but some extensions are required to the system. As the original supplier has staff familiar with the existing system, it might be inconvenient to approach other potential suppliers via a full tendering process. In these cases, an approach to a single supplier may be justified. However, approaching a single supplier could expose the customer to charges of favouritism and should only be done with a clear justification.

10.3 Stages in contract placement

Requirements analysis

This discussion assumes that a feasibility study has already provisionally identified the need for the intended software.

Before potential suppliers can be approached, you need to have a clear set of requirements. It is easy for this step to be skimped where the user management have day-to-day pressures and little time to think about future developments. In this situation, an external consultant could draw up a requirements document. Even here, users and their managers need to look carefully at the resulting requirements document to ensure that it accurately reflects their needs. As David Bainbridge has pointed out: *'the lack of, or defects in, the specification are probably the heart of most disputes resulting from the acquisition of computer equipment and software'.*

The requirements document might typically have sections with the headings shown in Table 10.3.

This requirements document is sometimes called an *operational requirement* or OR.

1   Introduction

2   A description of any existing systems and the current environment

3   The customer's future strategy or plans

4   System requirements
    – mandatory
    – desirable

5   Deadlines

6   Additional information required from potential suppliers

TABLE 10.3 Main sections in a requirements document

Chapter 13 on software quality discusses how aspects of quality can be measured.

The requirements define carefully the *functions* of the new application and all the necessary *inputs* and *outputs* for these functions. They also state any *standards* that apply, and the existing systems with which the new system should be compatible. There will also need to be operational and quality requirements, concerning such matters as the required response times, reliability, usability and maintainability of the new system.

In general, the requirements document should state *needs* as accurately as possible and avoid technical specifications of possible solutions. The onus should be placed on the potential suppliers to identify the technical solutions judged to meet the customer's needs as they should be technical experts with access to the most up-to-date information about current technology.

Each requirement needs to be identified as being either *mandatory* or *desirable*.

- *Mandatory* If a proposal does not meet this requirement then the proposal is to be immediately rejected.

- *Desirable* A proposal may be deficient in this respect, but other features of the proposal could compensate for this.

One suggestion is that the weighting between product criteria and supplier criteria when selecting software ought to be 50:50 (Demian Martinez, Decision Drivers Inc., *Computing*, 23 July, 1998).

For example, in the case of the Brightmouth College payroll package acquisition project, Brigette might identify a mandatory requirement that any new system carry out all the processes carried out by the old system. However, a desirable feature might be that the new payroll package should be able to produce staff costing details in a format accessible to the college's accounting computer system.

The requirements document issued to potential suppliers would also contain requests for information needed to judge the standing of the organization itself. This could include financial reports, references from past customers and the CVs of key development staff.

Evaluation plan

Having drawn up a list of requirements, we now need a plan of how the proposals are to be evaluated. The situation will be different if the contract is for a system that is to be specially written rather than an off-the-shelf package. In the latter case, it is the *application* itself that is being evaluated while in the former situation it is a *proposal* for an application.

Ways of checking that the mandatory requirements are met need to be identified. The next consideration is how the desirable requirements can be evaluated. The problem here is weighing the value of one quality against another. The ISO 9126 standard, which is discussed in Chapter 13 on software quality, can assist in deciding whether one system has more of some quality than another, but if there is a difference in price between the two, we need to estimate if the increase in quality is worth the additional price. Hence 'value for money' is often the key criterion. For example, a financial value could be placed on a link between the payroll and accounting applications. If we were to cost clerical effort at £20 an hour and knew that four hours of clerical effort a month went into inputting staffing costs into the accounting computer system, we could conclude that over a four-year period (£20 an hour × 4 hours a month × 48 months), or £3,840, would be saved. If system A has this feature and costs only £1,000 more than system B which does not, this would give system A an advantage.

The costs to be taken into account are those for the whole of the lifetime of the proposed system, not just the costs of acquiring the system. Also, where the relationship with the supplier is likely to be ongoing, the supplier organization needs to be assessed as well as its products.

EXERCISE 10.5

One desirable feature sought in the Brightmouth College payroll is the ability to raise staff automatically to the next point in their salary scale at the beginning of each payroll year. At present, the new scale points are entered clerically and then checked. This

▶

takes about 20 hours of staff effort each year, which costs £20 an hour. System X has this feature, but system Y does not. System X also has a feature which can automatically produce bar charts showing payroll expenditure per department. Such a report currently is produced twice a year by hand and on each occasion takes about 12 hours' effort. With system Y, changes to department names can be carried out without any coding effort whereas in the case of system X, the supplier would charge a minimum of £300 to do this. The college authorities estimate there is a 50% chance that this could occur during the expected four-year lifetime of the system. System X costs £500 more than system Y. Given this information, which system appears to give better value for money?

Invitation to tender

Having produced the requirements and the evaluation plan, it is now possible to issue the invitation to tender to prospective suppliers. Essentially, this will be the requirement document with a supporting letter containing information about how responses to the invitation are to be lodged. A deadline will be specified and it is hoped that by then a number of proposals with price quotations will have been received.

In English law, for a contract to exist there must be an offer on one side

In English law, with certain exceptions, a contract does not have to be in writing. Clearly it is desirable that it should be.

which is accepted by the other. The invitation to tender is not an offer itself, but an invitation for prospective suppliers to make an offer.

Certain problems might now emerge. The requirements specified could be satisfied in a various ways. The customer not only needs to know a potential supplier's price but also how they intend to satisfy the requirements – this will be particularly important where the contract is to build a completely new system.

In relatively straightforward cases, it would be enough to have post-tender clarification and negotiation to resolve issues in the supplier's proposal. With more complex projects a more sophisticated approach may be needed. One way of getting the detail of the suppliers' proposals elaborated is to have a two-stage tendering process.

In the first stage, technical proposals are requested from potential suppliers who do not necessarily quote any prices. Some of these proposals can be dismissed as not meeting mandatory requirements. The remaining ones could be discussed with representatives of the suppliers in order to clarify and validate the technical proposals. The suppliers might be asked to demonstrate certain aspects of their proposals. Where shortcomings in the proposal are detected, the supplier could be given the opportunity to remedy these.

These discussions could result in a *Memorandum of Agreement* (MoA)

This approach has been recommended for government ICT contracts in the United Kingdom.

with each prospective supplier. This is an acceptance by the customer that the proposed solution (which might have been modified during discussions) offered by the supplier satisfactorily meets the customer's requirement.

Tenders are then invited from the suppliers who have signed individual Memoranda of Agreement. The tender would incorporate the MoA and would be concerned with the financial terms of a potential contract.

If a design has to be produced as part of the proposal made by a supplier in response to an invitation to tender then the supplier would have to do a considerable amount of work with only a limited prospect of being paid for it. One way of reducing this burden is for the customer to choose a small number of likely candidates who will be paid a fee to produce design proposals. These can then be compared and the final contract for construction awarded to the most attractive proposal.

Evaluation of proposals

We have already mentioned the need to produce an evaluation plan describing how each proposal will be checked against the selection criteria. This reduces risks of requirements being missed and ensures that all proposals are treated consistently. It would be unfair to favour a proposal because of the presence of a feature not requested in the original requirement.

We noted earlier that an application could be bespoke, off-the-shelf, or customized. In the case of off-the-shelf packages the software itself could be evaluated and it might be possible to combine some of the evaluation with acceptance testing. With bespoke development it would be a proposal that is evaluated, while COTS may involve elements of both. Thus different approaches would be needed.

The process of evaluation may include:

- scrutiny of the proposal documents;
- interviewing suppliers' representatives;
- demonstrations;
- site visits;
- practical tests.

The proposal documents provided by the suppliers can be scrutinized to see if they contain features satisfying all the original requirements. Clarification might be sought over certain points. Factual statements made by a supplier have a legal commitment if they influence the customer to offer the contract to that supplier. It is therefore important to get a written, agreed, record of these clarifications. The customer might take the initiative here by taking minutes of meetings and then writing afterwards to the suppliers to get them to confirm their accuracy. A supplier could, in the final contract document, attempt to exclude any commitment to any representations made in pre-contract negotiations – the terms of the contract need to be scrutinized for this.

Where there is an existing product there could be a demonstration. A danger is that demonstrations can be controlled by the supplier and as a passive observer it may be difficult to maintain full attention for more than, say, half an hour. Because of this, the customer organization should have their own schedule of what needs to be demonstrated, ensuring that all the important features are seen in operation.

With off-the-shelf software, the customer could actually try out the package. For example, a demonstration version could be made available which closes itself down after 30 days. Once again a test plan is needed to ensure that all the important features are evaluated in a complete and consistent manner. Once a package is identified as the most likely candidate, it needs to be examined for any previously unforeseen factors that might invalidate this choice.

A frequent problem is that while an existing application works well on one platform with a certain level of transactions, it does not work satisfactorily with the customer's ICT configuration or level of throughput. Demonstrations might not reveal this problem. Visits to operational sites already using the system could be more informative. In the last resort a special volume test could be conducted.

EXERCISE 10.6

How would you evaluate the following aspects of a proposal?

(i)   The usability of an existing software application.

(ii) The usability of a software application which is yet to be designed and constructed.

(iii) The maintenance costs of hardware to be supplied.

(iv) The time taken to respond to requests for software support.

(v)   Training.

Where substantial sums of money are involved, legal advice on the terms of the contract is essential.

A decision is made to award the contract to a supplier. One reason for a structured and, as far as possible, objective approach to evaluation is to demonstrate that the decision has been made impartially. In most large organizations, placing a contract involves the participation of a second party within the organization, such as a contracts department, who can check that the correct procedures have been carried out. Also, the final legal format of a contract will almost certainly require some legal expertise. Not only should the successful candidate be notified but the unsuccessful candidates should also be told of the decision. This might not be simply a matter of courtesy: under WTO or EU rules, there is a legal requirement to do this in certain circumstances. It makes dealing with unsuccessful bidders easier if they can be given clear and objective reasons why their proposals did not find favour.

10.4 Typical terms of a contract

In a textbook such as this, it is not possible to describe the all necessary content of contracts for ICT goods or services. It is possible, however, to outline some of the major areas of concern.

Definitions

The terminology used in the contract document may need to be defined, e.g. who is meant by the words 'client' and 'supplier'.

Form of agreement

For example, is it a contact of sale, a lease, or a licence? Also, can the subject of the contract, such as a licence to use a software package, be transferred to another party?

Goods and services to be supplied

Equipment and software to be supplied This should include an actual list of the individual pieces of equipment to be delivered, complete with the specific model numbers.

Services to be provided This would cover such things as:

- training;
- documentation;
- installation;
- conversion of existing files;
- maintenance agreements;
- transitional insurance arrangements.

Ownership of the software

Who has ownership of the software? There may be two key issues here: first, whether the customer can sell the software to others and, second, whether the supplier can sell the software to others. Where an off-the-shelf package is concerned, the supplier often simply grants a licence for the customer to use the software. Where the software is written for a specific customer then that customer may want exclusive use of the software – they might object to software which they hoped would provide a competitive edge being sold to rivals. They could ensure this by acquiring the copyright to the software outright or by specifying in a contract that they should have *exclusive use* of the software. Where a core system has been customized by a supplier then there is less scope for the customer to insist on exclusive use.

Where software is written by an employee as part of their normal job, it is assumed that the copyright belongs to the employer. Where the customer organization has contracted an external supplier to write software for them, the contract needs to make clear who is going to retain the copyright – it cannot, in this case, be automatically assumed that it is the customer. The customer may decide to take responsibility for maintenance and development once the software is delivered and would need the source code. In other cases, where the customer does not have an adequate in-house maintenance function, the supplier may retain the source code, and the customer may have to approach the supplier for any further changes. There are dangers with this, for example that the supplier could go out of business. An *escrow* agreement can be included in the contract so that up-to-date copies of the source code are deposited with a third party. In the United Kingdom, the NCC Group provides an escrow service.

> Any assignment of copyright would need to be in writing.

Environment

Where physical equipment is to be installed, the demarcation line between the supplier's and customer's responsibilities with regard to such matters as accommodation and electrical supply needs to be specified. Where software is being supplied, the compatibility of the software with the existing hardware and operating system platforms would need to be confirmed.

Customer commitments

Even when work is carried out by external contractors, a development project still needs the participation of the customer. The customer may have to provide accommodation for the suppliers and perhaps other facilities such as telephone lines.

Acceptance procedures

Some customers find that specially written or modified software is not thoroughly tested by the supplier before delivery. Some suppliers seem to think that it is cheaper to get the customer to do the testing for them!

Good practice is to accept a delivered system only after user acceptance tests. Part of the contract would specify such details as the time that the customer will have to conduct the tests, deliverables upon which the acceptance tests depend and the procedure for signing off the testing as completed.

Standards

This covers the standards with which the goods and services should comply. For example, a customer could require the supplier to conform to the ISO 12207 standard relating to the software life cycle and its documentation (or, more likely, a customized sub-set of the standard). Within the European Union, government customers with contracts for projects above a certain threshold value must, by law, ensure that the work conforms to certain standards.

Project and quality management

The arrangements for the management of the project must be agreed. These include the frequency and nature of progress meetings and the progress information to be supplied to the customer. The contract could require that appropriate ISO 9001 standards are followed.

Timetable

This provides a schedule of when the key parts of the project should be completed. This timetable will commit both the supplier and the customer. For example, the supplier may only be able to install the software on the agreed date if the customer makes the hardware platform available at that time.

Price and payment method

Obviously the price is very important. What also needs to be agreed is when the payments are to be made. The supplier's desire to be able to meet costs as they are incurred needs to be balanced by the customer's requirement to ensure that goods and services are satisfactory before parting with their money.

Miscellaneous legal requirements

This is the legal small print. A contract may require clauses which deal with such matters as the definition of terms used in the contract, the legal jurisdiction that will apply to the contract, what conditions would apply to the subcontracting of the work, liability for damage to third parties, and liquidated damages. *Liquidated damages* are estimates of the financial losses that the customer would suffer if the supplier were to fall short of their obligations. It is worth noting that under English law, the penalties laid down in penalty clauses must reflect the actual losses the customer would suffer and cannot be unrealistic and merely punitive. Even this limitation may not be enough in some cases as far as the supplier is concerned. As computer systems assume increasingly critical roles and in safety-critical applications can even be life-threatening in the case of malfunction, consequential damage could be astronomical. Suppliers will try to limit this liability. The courts (in England and Wales) have tended to look critically at such attempts at limiting liability, so that suppliers may, in the case of major contracts, take out insurance to cover such liabilities.

If there is a dispute, resorting to litigation, while being lucrative for the lawyers involved, is likely to be time-consuming and expensive. An alternative is to agree that disputes be settled by *arbitration*. This requires disputes to be referred to an expert third party whose decision on the facts of the case is binding. Even this procedure might not be quick and inexpensive and another option is *alternative dispute resolution* where a mediator acts in an advisory capacity only and attempts to broker an agreement between the two sides.

10.5 Contract management

ISPL Euromethod offers guidance about how decision points may be planned.

We have already noted that forms of communication between the supplier and customer during the project could be specified in the contract. It would probably suit all concerned if the contractor is left to get on with the work. However, at certain *decision points* (or *milestones*) the customer might wish to examine work already done and make decisions about the future direction of the project. The project could require representatives of the supplier and customer to interact at key points in the development cycle – for example, users may need to provide information to assist interface design.

Chapter 4 discusses incremental delivery.

One way of identifying the decision points is to divide a large project into increments. For each increment there could be an interface design phase, and the customer might need to approve the designs before the increment is built. There could also be decision points between increments.

For each decision point, the deliverables from the suppliers, the decisions to be made by the customer and the possible outcomes need to be defined. These decision points have added significance if they are the basis for payment to the contractor. The customer also has responsibilities at these decision points – for example, the contractor should not be delayed unnecessarily awaiting customer approval of interim deliverables.

There will be concerns about the quality of contracted work. The ISO 12207 standard envisages the possibility of there being agents, independent of both the supplier and customer, who will carry out verification, validation and quality assurance. It also allows for joint reviews of project processes and products to be agreed when the contract is negotiated.

We saw earlier that changes to requirements will vary the contract terms. Oral evidence is not normally admissible to contradict, add to, or vary the terms of a written contract, so that agreed changes need to be documented. A change control procedure must record requests for changes, the supplier's agreement to them and the cost for additional work.

The supplier might not meet a legal obligation. This might not be their fault, if, for example, the customer causes the delay by lateness in giving the necessary approvals for intermediate products. If no action is taken when the default occurs, this might imply that the customer in fact condones the failure and could lead to the loss of legal rights. The customer should protect their legal rights by officially notifying the supplier that the failure has been recognized. It will be recalled that under English law any claim for liquidated damages should be based on actual losses, so the customer needs to keep an accurate record of the actual losses incurred as a result of the default.

10.6 Acceptance

When the work has been completed, the customer needs to arrange acceptance testing. The contract may limit how long acceptance testing can take, so the customer must be organized to carry out this testing before the time limit for requesting corrections expires.

We have already noted that some software suppliers are rather cursory with their pre-acceptance testing. It seems that they would rather the users spent their time on testing than them. This imposition can be reduced by asking to approve the supplier's internal test plans. An associated pitfall is that once the main development work is completed, the supplier not unnaturally wants to reallocate their most productive staff to other projects. The customer could find that all their problem reports are being dealt with by relatively junior members of the supplier's staff, who may not be familiar with all aspects of the delivered system.

Part or all of the payment to the supplier should depend on this acceptance testing. Sometimes part of the final payment is retained for a period of operational running and is paid if the levels of performance are as contracted for. There may also be a period of warranty during which the supplier should fix any errors found for no charge. The supplier might suggest a very short warranty period of, say, 30 days. It may be in the customer's interests to negotiate a more realistic period of, say, at least 120 days.

10.7 Conclusion

Some of the key points in this chapter have been:

- the successful contracting out of work requires considerable amounts of management time;
- it is easier to gain concessions from a supplier before a contract is signed rather than afterwards;
- alternative proposals need to be evaluated as far as possible by comparing costs over the whole lifetime of the system rather than just the acquisition costs;
- a contract will place obligations on the customer as well as the supplier;
- contract negotiation should include reaching agreement on the management of the supplier–customer relationship during the execution of the project.

10.8 Further exercises

1. At IOE, the management are considering 'outsourcing' the maintenance accounting system, i.e. getting an outside specialist organization to take over the operation, maintenance and support activities associated with the system. Write a short memorandum to management outlining the advantages and disadvantages of such a reorganization.

2. Further exercise 4 at the end of Chapter 1 concerned a software house that needed a training course developed to introduce new users to an order processing application that they had developed. Assume that you are an independent training consultant who has been approached by the software house to develop the training package. You have agreed in principle and now a contract is being negotiated for the work.
   (a) List the points that you would want clarified and included in the contract.
   (b) Having produced the list of points requiring clarification, examine it from the point of view of the software house. Are there any additional points that they would want clarified?

3. In each of the following cases, discuss whether the type of application package to be adopted would be most likely to be bespoke, off-the-shelf or COTS.
   (a) A college requires a student fees application. It is suggested that the processes required in the application are similar to those of any billing system, with some requirements that are peculiar to the administration of higher education.
   (b) A computer-based application is needed at IOE to hold personnel details of staff employed.
   (c) A system is required by a national government that calculates, records and notifies individual taxpayers about income tax charges.
   (d) An expert system for use in a hospital to diagnose the causes of eye complaints.

4 The schedule of charges per function point shown in Table 10.1 has higher rates for larger systems. Give arguments explaining why this might be justified and also arguments against.

5 Table 10.2 has a charge of 25% and 50% of the normal rate for deleting transactions from an application. This may seem to be rather high for simply removing code. What work would be involved in deleting functionality that could justify this cost?

6 Assume that IOE has decided on a COTS solution that will replace the whole of the existing maintenance accounting system rather than simply plugging in additional modules to deal with annual contracts. Write a memorandum that Amanda could send to IOE's legal department outlining the important provisions that a contract to supply this system should have.

CHAPTER

11

Managing people in software environments

11.1 Introduction

We are going to examine some of the problems that Amanda and Brigette could meet when dealing with members of their teams. Where possible, we want to base any advice on the findings of writers on organizational behaviour (OB). We will pay special attention where the sources refer to software development environments. Some of these human considerations affect staff as individuals. These will be the subject of this chapter. Others arise from the need for people involved in ICT system development and implementation to work in cooperation with others. These team and organizational issues are the topics of the following chapter. A group is, of course, made up of individuals so despite this division of concerns, the two chapters will have some overlaps.

There will be four main concerns in the current chapter: staff selection, staff development, staff motivation and the continued well-being of staff during the course of a project.

The issues raised in this chapter have impacts at all stages of project planning and execution but in particular at the following points (see also Figure 11.1).

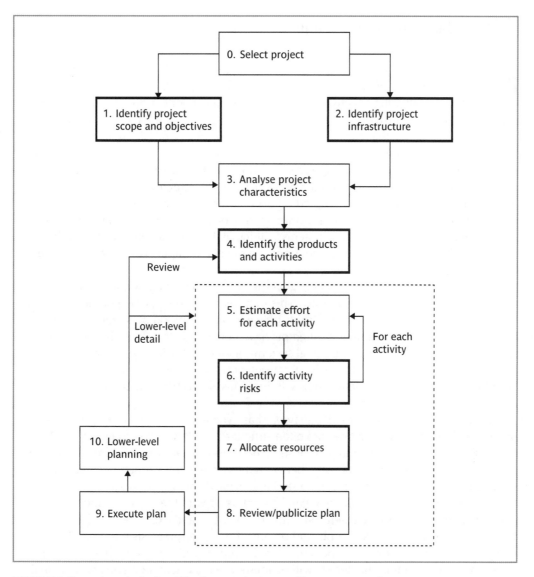

FIGURE 11.1 Some places in the Step Wise framework where staffing concerns are important

- Some objectives can address health and safety during the project (Step 1).
- Although project leaders might have little control over organizational structure, they need to be aware of its implications (Step 2).
- The scope and nature of activities can be set in a way that will enhance staff motivation (Step 4).
- Many risks to project success relate to staffing (Step 6).
- The qualities of individual members of staff should be taken into account when allocating staff to activities (Step 7).

11.2 Understanding behaviour

People with practical experience of projects invariably identify the handling of people as an important aspect of project management. People like Amanda and Brigette would want to know whether the effective and sensitive management of staff comes only from experience or whether expert advice can help. Such advice may be more convincing if it is based on evidence that has been gathered through some kind of research.

This research into individual and group behaviour in software and ICT development environments needs to adopt social science research methods. This type of research requires a different mindset to that usually needed by software developers. Although the development of systems is usually based on user requirements that can be interpreted in more than one way, the end result is a system that works in a perfectly consistent way. The developers who produce such systems will inevitably have a tendency to see things in terms of deterministic systems where once a sequence of inputs is known, the outputs can be forecast with some certainty.

Such systems are perceived as being governed by mechanistic laws, just as there are in the physical sciences such as chemistry. This mindset tends to favour experimentation as the means of establishing the relationships between inputs and outputs and is sometimes referred to as a *positivist* approach. Attempts have been made to extend this model to social systems. However, because social systems, including business organizations, are so complex, it is not possible to predict their outcomes with any certainty. What can be done is to detect statistical relationships within such systems that can be expressed as generalized models or theories.

The discipline of *organizational behaviour* has evolved theories that try to explain people's behaviour. These theories are often structured as *'If A is the situation then B is likely to result'*. Attempts are made to observe behaviour where variables for A and B are measured and a statistical relationship between the two variables sought. Unlike physical science it is rarely, if ever, that it can be said that B *must* always follow A.

An *interpretivist* school of thought can be contrasted with the positivist one, particularly in relation to the extension of the quantitative and experimental methods from the physical sciences to people and organizations. Interpretivists point out that many concepts are not objective but are inter-subjective ones created by human beings. For example, later in this chapter we will examine whether there are particular personal characteristics that are associated with successful software developers. Some studies have found personal characteristics that seem to be strongly associated with 'software engineers' while other studies have found none. One question here would be how 'software engineer' is defined. Would someone who customizes and installs off-the-shelf packaged software count as a 'software engineer'? Would the description 'software engineer' cover the role of the ICT business analyst? Furthermore, how would you define 'successful'? Is it someone who can write lots of code very quickly? Or someone who knows where to find the right existing software to do a job? One way of resolving such questions would be to look closely at specific ICT environments and observe the different types of role that people undertake and the tasks and skills associated with such roles. The typical way of doing this is an in-depth study of a small number (perhaps only one) of instances of a particular type of organization which produces a description of how things are done in that context.

The two viewpoints labeled positivist and interpretivist can both be valid and useful. In the types of research that underpin the material in the current chapter on individuals in work environments the quantitative (or 'positivist') type predominates. In the following chapter on working in teams the research drawn upon tends to be more qualitative and based on case studies in the interpretivist tradition.

In the real world there will be a wide range of influences on a situation, many invisible to the observer. It is therefore difficult to decide which set of research findings is relevant. A danger is that we end up with a set of maxims which are little better than superstitions. However, by examining these issues people can at least become more sensitive and thoughtful about them.

> *Work Psychology* by J. Arnold, C. L. Cooper and I. T. Robertson (2004) 4th edition, FT Prentice Hall, is a good general text on these topics.

In what follows we will be making references to workers in the OB field such as Taylor, McGregor and Herzberg. Rather than overwhelming the reader with references, we recommend the reader who is interested in exploring this topic further to look at some of the books in the Further Reading section at the back of the book. Where we have given references these tend to be for works related specifically to an ICT environment.

11.3 Organizational behaviour: a background

> Frederick Winslow Taylor, 1856–1915, is regarded as the father of 'scientific management' of which OB is a part.

The roots of studies in OB can be traced back to work done in the late 19th and early 20th centuries by Frederick Taylor. Taylor attempted to analyse the most productive way of doing manual tasks. The workers were then trained to do the work in this way.

Taylor had three basic objectives:

- to select the best people for the job;
- to instruct them in the best methods;
- to give incentives in the form of higher wages to the best workers.

'Taylorism' is often represented as crude and mechanistic. However, a concern for identifying best practice is valid. In the more mundane world of software development, the growth of both structured and agile methods is an example of an emphasis on best practice. Both Amanda and Brigette will be concerned that tasks are carried out in the proper way. More contentious is Taylor's emphasis on the exclusively financial basis of staff motivation, although Amanda and Brigette will find many colleagues who hold Taylor's view on the importance of 'performance-related pay'. Unfortunately, Amanda and Brigette are likely to have very little control over the financial rewards of their staff. However, they should be encouraged by findings that motivation rests not just on such rewards.

> The research that obtained these findings was done at

During the 1920s, OB researchers discovered, while carrying out a now famous set of tests on the conditions under which staff worked best, that not only did a group of workers for whom conditions were improved

the Hawthorne
Works of Western
Electric in Chicago,
hence the
'Hawthorne Effect'.

increase their work-rates, but also a control group for whom conditions were unchanged. Simply showing a concern for what workers did increased productivity. This illustrated how the state of mind of workers influenced their productivity.

The cash-oriented, or *instrumental*, view of work of some managers can thus be contrasted with a more rounded vision of people in their place of work. The two attitudes were labelled Theory X and Theory Y by Donald McGregor. *Theory X* holds that:

- the average human has an innate dislike of work;
- there is a need therefore for coercion, direction and control;
- people tend to avoid responsibility.

Theory Y, on the other hand, holds that:

- work is as natural as rest or play;
- external control and coercion are not the only ways of bringing about effort directed towards an organization's ends;

A 'reward' does not
have to be a
financial reward – it
could be something
like a sense of
achievement.

- commitment to objectives is a function of the rewards associated with their achievement;
- the average human can learn to accept and further seek responsibility;
- the capacity to exercise imagination and other creative qualities is widely distributed.

One way of judging whether a manager espouses Theory X or Theory Y is to observe how staff react when the boss is absent: if there is no discernible change then this is a Theory Y environment; if everyone visibly relaxes, it is a Theory X environment. McGregor's distinction between the two theories also draws attention to the way that expectations influence behaviour. If a manager (or teacher) assumes that you are going to work diligently and create products of good quality then you are likely to try to meet their expectations.

11.4 Selecting the right person for the job

B. W. Boehm
considered the
quality of staff the
most important
influence on
productivity when
constructing the
COCOMO software
cost model
(Chapter 5).

Taylor stressed the need for the right person for the job. Many factors, such as the use of software tools and methodologies, affect programming productivity. However, one of the biggest differences in software development performance is between individuals. As early as 1968 a comparison of experienced professional programmers working on the same programming task found a ratio, in one case, of 1:25 between the shortest and longest time to code the program and, more significantly perhaps, of 1:28 for the time taken to debug it. Amanda and Brigette would therefore be rightly concerned to get the best possible people working for them.

P. M. Cheney (1984) 'Effects of individual characteristics, organizational factors and task characteristics on computer programmer productivity and job satisfaction' *Information and Management*, 7.

What sort of characteristics should they be looking for? Is an experienced programmer better than a new graduate with a first-class mathematics degree? It is dangerous to generalize but, looking at behavioural characteristics, the American researcher Cheney found that the most important influence on programmer productivity seemed to be experience. This is not surprising as the impact of experience is the most important factor in software productivity in Boehm's COCOMO models – see Chapter 5. Cheney found that mathematical aptitude had quite a weak influence in comparison.

Amanda and Brigette will want staff who can communicate well with each other and with users. Unfortunately, the American researchers Couger and Zawacki found that information systems (IS) professionals seemed to have much weaker 'social needs' than people in other professions. They quote Gerald Weinberg: '*If asked, most programmers probably say they prefer to work alone where they wouldn't be disturbed by other people.*' We see many who are attracted to writing software, and are good at it, but do not make good managers later in their careers.

J. D. Couger and R. A. Zawacki (1978) 'What motivates DP Professionals?' *Datamation*, 24.

Later surveys, however, have *not* found significant differences between IS and other staff. An explanation of this could be that IS has become broader and less purely technical in recent years.

The recruitment process

It must be stressed that often project leaders have little choice about the people who will make up their team – they have to make do with the 'materials that are to hand'. Recruitment is often an organizational responsibility: the person recruited might, over a period of time, work in many different parts of the organization.

R. Meredith Belbin (1996) *Team Roles at Work*, 2nd edition, Butterworth-Heinemann.

Meredith Belbin usefully distinguishes between *eligible* and *suitable* candidates. *Eligible* candidates have a curriculum vitae (CV) which shows, for example, the 'right' number of years in some previous post and the 'right' paper qualifications. *Suitable* candidates can actually do the job well. A mistake is to select an eligible candidate who is not in fact suitable. Suitable candidates who are not officially eligible can, on the other hand, be ideal candidates as once in post they are more likely to remain loyal. Belbin suggests we should try to assess actual skills rather than past experience and provide training to make good minor gaps in expertise. It seems to us to show that policies that avoid discrimination on the grounds of race, gender, age or irrelevant disabilities can be not just socially responsible but also a shrewd recruitment policy.

A general approach might be the following.

- *Create a job specification* Advice is often needed as there could be legal implications in an official document. However, formally or informally, the requirements of the job, including the types of task to be carried out, should be documented and agreed.

- *Create a job holder profile* The job specification is used to construct a profile of the person needed to carry out the job. The qualities, qualifications, education and experience required would be listed.

- *Obtain applicants* Typically, an advertisement would be placed, either within the organization or outside in the trade or local press. The job holder profile would be examined carefully to identify the medium most likely to reach the largest number of potential applicants at least cost. For example, if a specialist is needed it would make sense to advertise in the relevant specialist journal. The other principle is to give enough information in the advertisement to allow an element of self-elimination. By giving the salary, location, job scope and any essential qualifications, the applicants will be limited to the more realistic candidates.

> A standard form which lists each selection criterion and the degree to which the candidate meets it should be used to ensure a consistent and fair approach.

- *Examine CVs* These should be read carefully and compared to the job holder profile – nothing is more annoying for all concerned than when people have CVs which indicate clearly that they are not eligible for the job and yet are called for interview.

- *Interviews etc.* Selection techniques include aptitude tests, personality tests and the examination of samples of previous work. Any method must test specific qualities detailed in the job holder profile. Interviews are the most commonly used method. It is better if there is more than one interview session with an applicant and within each session there should not be more than two interviewers as a greater number reduces the possibility of follow-up questions and discussion. Some formal scoring system for the qualities being judged should be devised and interviewers should then individually decide scores which are then compared. An interview might be of a technical nature where the practical expertise of the candidate is assessed, or of a more general nature. In the latter case, a major part of the interview could be evaluating and confirming statements in the CV – for example, time gaps in the education and employment history would be investigated, and the precise nature of previous jobs would need to be explored.

- *Other procedures* References will need to be taken up where necessary, and a medical examination might be needed.

EXERCISE 11.1

A new analyst/programmer is to be recruited to work in Amanda's team at IOE. The intention is to recruit someone who already has some experience. Make a list of the types of activities that the analyst/programmer should be capable of carrying out that can be used as the basis for a job specification.

11.5 Instruction in the best methods

> Decisions will need to be made about whether a newcomer can more effectively pick up technical expertise on the job or on formal training courses.

This is the second concern that we have taken from Taylor. When new members of the team are recruited, the team leader will need to plan their induction into the team very carefully. Where a project is already well under way, this might not be easy. However, the effort should be made – it should pay off as the new recruit will become a fully effective member of the team more quickly.

The team leader should be aware of the need to assess continually the training needs of their team members. Just as you formulate a user requirement before considering a new system, and a job holder profile before recruiting a member of staff, so a training needs profile ought to be drawn up for each staff member when considering specific courses. Some training might be provided by commercial training companies. Where money is tight, alternative sources of training should be considered but training should not be abandoned. It could just be a team member finding out about a new software tool and then demonstrating it to colleagues. Of course, the nice thing about external courses is talking to colleagues from other organizations – but attending meetings of your local branch of a computer-related professional association, such as the British Computer Society (BCS) in the United Kingdom, can serve the same purpose.

The methods learnt need, of course, to be actually applied. Reviews and inspections help to ensure this.

In the next chapter we will return to this topic from the point of view of integrating outsiders into a new group environment.

11.6 Motivation

The third of Taylor's concerns was that of motivating people to work. We are going to look at some models of motivation.

The Taylorist model

> Piece-rates are where workers are paid a fixed sum for each item they produce. Day-rates refer to payment for time worked.

Taylor's viewpoint is reflected in the use of piece-rates in manufacturing industries and sales bonuses amongst sales forces. Piece-rates can cause difficulties if a new system will change work practices. If new technology improves productivity, adjusting piece-rates to reflect this will be a sensitive issue. Usually, radical changes in work practices have to be preceded by a move from piece-rates to day-rates. As will be seen later, the tendency towards dispersed or 'virtual projects' where staff work on their own premises at some distance from the sponsoring organization's site has seen a movement away from payment based on time worked.

Even where work practices are stable and output can be easily related to reward, people paid by the amount they produce will not automatically maximize their output in order to maximize their income. The amount of output will often by constrained by 'group

Group norms are discussed further under group decision making.

Quoted by Wanda J. Orlikowski in *Groupware & Teamwork*, edited by Claudio U. Ciborra, Wiley and Sons, 1996.

norms': informal, even unspoken, agreements among colleagues about the amount to be produced.

Rewards based on piece-rates need to relate directly to work produced. Where a computer application is being developed, it is difficult to isolate and quantify work done by an individual, as system development and support is usually a team effort. As one member of staff in a study of software support work said: '*This support department does well because we're a team, not because we're all individuals. I think it's the only way the support team can work successfully.*'

In this kind of environment, a reward system that makes excessive distinctions between co-workers could damage morale and productivity. Organizations sometimes get around this problem by giving bonuses to project team members at the end of a successful project, especially if staff have 'volunteered' considerable unpaid overtime to get the project completed.

EXERCISE 11.2

A software development department want to improve productivity by encouraging the reuse of existing software components. It has been suggested that this could be encouraged through financial rewards. To what extent do you think this could be done?

Maslow's hierarchy of needs

The motivation of individuals varies. Money is a strong motivator when you are broke. However, as the basic need for cash is satisfied, other motivators are likely to emerge. Abraham Maslow, an American psychologist, suggested a hierarchy of needs. As a lower level of needs is satisfied then gradually a higher level of needs emerges. If these are then satisfied then another level will emerge. Basic needs include food, shelter and personal safety. The highest-level need, according to Maslow, is the need for 'self-actualization', the feeling that you are completely fulfilling your potential.

However, salary level can be important to staff approaching retirement because the amount of pension paid can depend on it.

In practice, people are likely to be motivated by different things at different stages of their life. For example, salary increases, while always welcome, probably have less impact on the more mature employee who is already relatively well paid than on a lowly paid trainee. Older team-members might place more value on qualities of the job, such as being given autonomy, which show respect for their judgement and sense of responsibility.

Some individual differences in motivation relate simply to personality differences. Some staff have 'growth needs' – they are interested in their work and want to develop their work roles – while others simply see the job as a way of earning a living.

EXERCISE 11.3

Newspapers often report on the vast sums of money that are paid to the top executives of many companies. Does this mean that these people are at a low level in the Maslow hierarchy of motivation? Do they really need all this money to be motivated? What do you think the significance of these salaries really is?

Herzberg's two-factor theory

Some things about a job can make you dissatisfied. If the causes of this dissatisfaction are removed, this does not necessarily make the job more exciting. Research into job satisfaction by Herzberg and his associates found two sets of factors about a job:

■ *hygiene or maintenance factors*, which can make you dissatisfied if they are not right, for example the level of pay or the working conditions;

■ *motivators*, which make you feel that the job is worthwhile, like a sense of achievement or the challenge of the work itself.

Brigette, at Brightmouth College, might be in an environment where it is difficult to compete with the high level of maintenance factors that can be provided by a large organization like IOE, but the smaller organization with its closer contact with the users might be able to provide better motivators.

EXERCISE 11.4

Identify three incidents or times when you felt particularly pleased or happy about something to do with your work or study. Identify three occasions when you were particularly dissatisfied with your work or study. Compare your findings with those of your colleagues and try to identify any patterns.

The expectancy theory of motivation

Amanda and Brigette need to be aware of how the day-to-day ups and downs of system development affect motivation. A model of motivation developed by Vroom and his colleagues illustrates this. It identifies three influences on motivation:

■ *expectancy:* the belief that working harder will lead to a better performance;

■ *instrumentality:* the belief that better performance will be rewarded;

■ *perceived value:* of the resulting reward.

Motivation will be high when all three factors are high. A zero level for any one of the factors can remove motivation.

Imagine trying to get a software package supplied by a third party to work. You realize that you will never get it to work because of a bug, and you give up. No matter how hard you work you will not be able to succeed (*zero expectancy*).

You are working on a package for a user and, although you think you can get it to work, you discover that the user has started employing an alternative package and no longer needs this one. You will probably feel you are wasting your time and give up (*zero instrumentality*).

Given that the users really do want the package, your reward might simply be the warm feeling of helping your colleagues and their gratitude. If in fact, when the users employ the package, all they do is complain and hold you responsible for shortcomings, then you might avoid getting involved if they later ask for help implementing a different package (*low perceived value of reward*).

11.7 The Oldham–Hackman job characteristics model

Managers should group together the elements of tasks to be carried out so that they form meaningful and satisfying assignments. Oldham and Hackman suggest that the satisfaction that a job gives is based on five factors. The first three factors make the job 'meaningful' to the person who is doing it:

- *skill variety:* the number of different skills that the job holder has the opportunity to exercise;
- *task identity:* the degree to which your work and its results are identifiable as belonging to you;
- *task significance:* the degree to which your job has an influence on others.

The other two factors are:

- *autonomy:* the discretion you have about the way that you do the job;
- *feedback:* the information you get back about the results of your work.

Oldham and Hackman also noted that both the job holders' personal growth needs and their working environment influenced their perception of the job. Some writers have pointed out that if people are happy with their work for other reasons, they are likely to rate it higher on the Oldham–Hackman dimensions anyway. Thus it might be that cause and effect are reversed.

In practical terms, activities should be designed so that, where possible, staff follow the progress of a particular product and feel personally associated with it.

Methods of improving motivation

To improve motivation the manager might therefore do the following.

- *Set specific goals* These goals need to be demanding and yet acceptable to staff. Involving staff in the setting of goals helps to gain acceptance for them.

■ *Provide feedback* Not only do goals have to be set but staff need regular feedback about how they are progressing.

■ *Consider job design* Jobs can be altered to make them more interesting and give staff more feeling of responsibility.

Two measures are often used to enhance job design – job enlargement and job enrichment.

Job enlargement and job enrichment are based on the work of F. Herzberg.

■ *Job enlargement* The person doing the job carries out a wider variety of activities. It is the opposite of increasing specialization. For example, a software developer in a maintenance group might be given responsibility for specifying minor amendments as well as carrying out the actual code changes. Couger and Zawacki found that programmer/analysts had higher job satisfaction than programmers.

Sarah Beecham et al. (2008) 'Motivation in software engineering' *Information and software technology* 50 860–78.

■ *Job enrichment* The job holder carries out tasks that are normally done at a managerial or supervisory level. With programmers in a maintenance team, they might be given authority to accept requests for changes that involve less than five days' work without the need for their manager's approval.

A comprehensive survey of research into the motivation of software developers can be found in paper published by Sarah Beecham and colleagues in 2008.

11.8 Stress

Quoted in *Death March* by Edward Yourdon, 2nd edition, Prentice-Hall, 2003.

Projects are about overcoming obstacles and achieving objectives. Almost by definition, both the project manager and team members will be under pressure. An American project manager is quoted as saying: '*Once a project gets rolling, you should expect members to be putting in at least 60 hours a week. . . . The project leader must expect to put in as many hours as possible. . . .*'

Kent Beck advocates a maximum 40-hour working week as an extreme programming practice – see Chapter 4.

Some pressure is actually healthy. Boredom can make many jobs soul-destroying. Beyond a certain level of pressure, however, the quality of work decreases and health can be affected. There is good evidence that productivity and the quality of output go down when more than about 40 hours a week are worked. As long ago as 1960 it was found in a US study that people under 45 years of age who worked more than 48 hours a week had twice the risk of death from coronary heart disease.

Many software developers are expected to work overtime on projects for no additional payment. In these cases, a fall in productivity is more than compensated for by the fact that the work is effectively free to the employer.

Clearly, it is sometimes necessary to put in extra effort to overcome some temporary obstacle or to deal with an emergency, but if overtime working becomes a way of life then there will be longer-term problems.

Good project management can reduce the reliance on overtime by the more realistic assessment of effort and elapsed time needed, based on careful recording and analysis of the performance of previous projects. Good planning and control will also help to reduce 'unexpected' problems generating unnecessary crises.

Stress can be caused by *role ambiguity* when staff do not have a clear idea of the objectives that their work is supposed to be fulfilling, what is expected of them by others and the precise scope of their responsibilities. The project manager could clearly be at fault in these instances.

Role conflict can also heighten stress. This is where the person is torn between the demands of two different roles. The parent of young children might be torn between the need to look after a sick child and the need to attend an important meeting to win new business.

Some managers claim to be successful through the use of essentially bullying tactics to push projects through. They need to create crises in order to justify the use of such tactics. This, however, is the antithesis of professional project management which aims at a rational, orderly and careful approach to the creation of complex products.

11.9 Health and safety

Health and safety issues are more prominent in construction and other heavy engineering projects than in ICT development. Sometimes, however, the implementation of office systems requires the creation of physical infrastructure which can have inherent physical dangers. ICT infrastructure could, for example, be installed in a building where construction work is still going on.

In this section we are not addressing general concerns relating to the safety of ICT equipment of which any organization using such equipment would need to be aware. Nor are we discussing the safety of products created by the software development process. We are focusing briefly on the health and safety issues that relate to the conduct of a project.

Various pieces of legislation govern safety policy and the details of these can be consulted in the appropriate literature. In the United Kingdom, legislation requires organizations employing more than five employees to have a written *safety policy* document. A project manager should be aware of the contents of the document that applies to the environment in which the project is to be undertaken.

Professional Issues in Software Engineering (3rd edition) by M. F. Bott et al., Taylor and Francis, 2001, explores these issues in greater depth.

As far as the project manager is concerned, safety objectives, where appropriate, should be treated like any other project objectives, such as the level of reliability of the completed application or the overall cost of the project. The management of safety should therefore be embedded in the general management of the project.

Responsibility for safety must be clearly defined at all levels. Some points that will need to be considered include:

- top management must be committed to the safety policy;
- the delegation of responsibilities for safety must be clear;
- job descriptions should include definitions of duties related to safety;

- those to whom responsibilities are delegated must understand the responsibilities and agree to them;
- deployment of a safety officer and the support of experts in particular technical areas;
- consultation on safety;
- an adequate budgeting for safety costs.

Safety procedures must be brought to the attention of employees and appropriate training be given where needed.

This is a very cursory glimpse at some of the issues in this area. For a fuller treatment, the specialized literature should be consulted.

11.10 Some ethical and professional concerns

As we saw above, there is now a legal requirement to act to reduce the threats to the health and safety of employees at work. Yet even if there were no such law, there would be very few who would not at least pay lip service to the moral obligation to prevent foreseeable injury to those at work. This would be an *ethical* judgement. There are bound to be cases where we would agree that people are, unethically, acting in a way potentially harmful to others even though laws have not – yet – been passed to prohibit that precise behaviour.

Some ethical responsibilities are shared by all members of the community, regardless of their position – for example, to alert the emergency services when a serious motor accident has taken place. Other ethical responsibilities affect particular organizations and the people who belong to them. Further responsibilities relate to a person's professional expertise, such as that of the software engineer or IT practitioner.

See Milton Friedman (1970) 'The social responsibility of business is to increase profits' *The New York Times Magazine* 13 September. Available at: www.umich.edu/ ~thecore/doc/ Friedman.doc

It might be thought that organizations have greater ethical responsibilities given their greater power to inflict damage than individuals, particular when they implement large development projects of various kinds. However, there is an argument – associated particularly with the economist Milton Friedman – that those working for commercial organizations have a contract to safeguard and enhance the assets of the stockholders of the company. These stockholders are those who have invested money in the company and are legally its owners – they could include ordinary people who have invested their retirement savings in the company. It was argued that pursuing other goals that might benefit the community as a whole at the expense of the stockholders would be dishonest behaviour by the company's employees.

EXERCISE 11.5

Identify some of the possible objections and criticisms that can be made of the stockholder business ethics model described above.

A rather extreme argument that normal ethical rules do not apply in business can be found in Alfred Carr (1968) 'Is business bluffing ethical?' *Harvard Business Review* 46(1) 143–53.

Another argument for the reduced – or at least peculiar – ethical responsibilities of commercial organizations is that they are competing with other businesses. If my business wins some aspect of this game, then my competitors must lose: investors might lose money and employees their jobs. But, it is argued, that is the way the market works, and as a result consumers benefit from reduced prices. However, in the longer term competition which destroys competitors leads to the domination of monopolies and increased prices.

Most organizations will, however, recognize that they do have ethical responsibilities. This could be purely out of self-interest. You may, as a potential customer, be wary of entrusting your custom to organizations which are transparently motivated by pure greed. Organizations often express their objectives and aspirations – perhaps in the form of a mission statement – and these tend to include some objectives that relate to matters of the general public good such as concern for the environment.

Despite removing levels of management (delayering) and creating flatter reporting structures, large organizations will always have some sort of hierarchy. As we saw in Chapter 1, the people at the top will specify a general strategy, hopefully consistent with the aspirations of the mission statement. Managers at the next level will take the strategy and devise programmes of work to achieve the strategic goals in their areas of responsibility. When doing this they are making decisions within their designated areas of responsibility. This process will be repeated at successively lower levels in the company until we get to the people who actually implement the decisions.

An excellent detailed exploration on these issues is Rosa Lynn B. Pinkus et al. (1997) *Engineering Ethics*, Cambridge University Press, which uses the Challenger space shuttle disaster as a case study.

Any decision that is made will have to satisfy a number of organizational requirements which could appear to conflict. For example, a new ICT application may be needed to meet a legal requirement with a fixed deadline. A high-quality system where reliability and correctness can be guaranteed would require a large team to develop it. This would be very costly and require the normal service to customers to be degraded. Some kind of balance would need to be struck between the need for reliability in the new system and the current quality of customer service. Whatever the final decision, there would some risk about the final outcomes.

Among the decisions involving risks will be those allocated to technical experts such as engineers and ICT practitioners. These will have special ethical responsibilities as they have knowledge and expertise that others may not fully understand but upon which they depend. These experts are likely to be entrusted with decisions about the deployment of new technologies.

ICT practitioners are unlikely to be expert in all areas of ICT and its development, so identifying a person's area of expertise is crucial. It would clearly be unethical for an ICT practitioner to pretend to be knowledgeable about some area where they are not. It also follows that if an ICT practitioner has expertise that would prevent a colleague from doing something harmful, it would be unethical for them to remain silent.

The decisions entrusted to these specialists would not only have to be technically justifiable but be unbiased. Accepting what amounts to bribes is clearly an example of unacceptable behaviour. However, recommending a particular technology because it happens to be one that the practitioner is expert in and its adoption would enhance his or her career might not immediately appear to be unethical to an individual.

As noted above, all decisions involve risks and true professionals would need to identify and warn about these risks. We also saw above that organizational actions tend to be implemented in a top-down manner, with the big decisions about strategy being decided first, and then the different elements of the overall plan being examined and more detailed decisions being made. Sometimes these high-level decisions have technical flaws and it would be the responsibility of the software engineer or ICT practitioner to point out such deficiencies.

This responsibility for emerging technical risks is not a matter solely for the practitioner. The organization must have a mechanism whereby such concerns can be communicated to a responsible manager who is competent to evaluate the issue and to take necessary actions. This might include escalating the issue to a higher level of management.

Long-established professions, such as medicine, have ways of certifying the competence of practitioners and enforcing ethical codes of conduct. In the United Kingdom, the British Computer Society (BCS) is a body which has produced *Codes of Conduct* and *Good Practice* (www.bcs.org/upload/pdf/conduct.pdf and www.bcs.org/upload/pdf/cop.pdf) – as has the IEEE (www.ieee.org/web/aboutus/ethics) and ACM (www.acm.org/about/se_code) in the United States – and various schemes for certifying the competence of different ICT specialists. However, BCS membership is still held by only a small minority of ICT practitioners so there is a long way to go in establishing ICT as a true profession.

11.11 Conclusion

Some of the important points that have been made in this chapter are:

- people may be motivated by money, but they are motivated by other things as well;
- both staff selection and the identification of training needs should be done in an orderly, structured, way where requirements are clearly defined first;
- thoughtful job design can increase staff motivation;
- undue pressure on staff can have short-term gains, but is harmful to both productivity and personal health in the longer term;
- project objectives should include, where appropriate, those relating health and safety.

11.12 Further exercises

1 An organization has detected low job satisfaction in the following departments:
   - the system testing group;
   - the computer applications help desk;
   - computer batch input.

   How could these jobs be redesigned to give more job satisfaction?

2 In Exercise 11.1, a job specification was requested.
   (a) Write a job holder profile of the sort of person who would be able to fulfil the specification in terms of qualities, qualifications, previous education and experience.
   (b) For each element in the job holder profile that you have produced in (a) above, describe ways of finding out whether an applicant has met the requirement.

3 Section 11.8 focuses on the responsibilities of management in relation to staff stress. Evaluate an alternative view that individual staff members need themselves to be responsible for reducing their own stress levels, perhaps through changes in personal working practices.

4 Job enlargement sounds like a good thing. Explore what the possible disadvantages of job enlargement might be for both employers and staff.

Working in teams

12

❖ OBJECTIVES

When you have completed this chapter you will be able to:

- ❖ improve group working;
- ❖ analyse the coordination needs of a project;
- ❖ select the best communication genres to support the coordination needs of a project;

- ❖ draw up a communication plan;
- ❖ evaluate the characteristics of the various team structures;
- ❖ use the most appropriate leadership styles.

12.1 Introduction

We associate software development with advanced technologies yet it is a task requiring intense human mental activity. Software-based systems can be huge – the software to control a telephone switching system can contain five million lines of code – so that this human effort has to be shared between individual software developers within teams and between groups of developers. Amanda at IOE wants to get the best out of her team, but also needs to coordinate the work of her group with other parts of IOE, including the users. At Brightmouth College, Brigette does not have a big team to manage, but the need to coordinate her efforts with those of other project stakeholders is probably greater.

This chapter will look enhancing communication between individual developers within teams and across teams. It will also look at how the efforts of individuals and teams can be coordinated through communication.

By 'teams' we usually mean groups of people who working together. Typically the individuals work in the same office, that is, are *co-located* – although we will see that this is not always so. However, the term 'project team' is sometimes used to refer to *all* the people working on a project. These people may sit in different work groups at some distance from each other. These groups can also change over time. Thus individual software developers are likely to transfer between teams as projects start and finish.

We will start by looking at the small group environment where the term 'team' is perhaps most justified. We will look at how true teams come to be formed. We will see how, apart from their technical roles, team members take on social roles that help team effectiveness.

A team is created to carry out a joint assignment. We will see how some tasks contributing to project objectives are best done by an individual. Other tasks, usually those that involve judgement or decision-making, may be better done by groups.

We will look at how teams can be coordinated. An organization needs to control the allocation of staff to work assignments. This is one form of coordination needed between groups and individuals within a project and other types will be outlined.

Communication genres refer to methods of communication. This goes beyond technologies used and includes the organizational conventions involved in the communication. Communication genres can be selected and developed to deal with particular need for project coordination. We will see how arrangements for communication between project stakeholders can be documented in a *communication plan*.

As well as coordination which reacts to day-to-day problems, but there needs to be proactive central direction. This introduces issues related to leadership.

The collaborative nature of project work will have an influence on nearly all stages of the Step Wise project planning framework (Figure 12.1).

1 *Identify project scope and objectives.* Here stakeholders in the project are identified and communications channels are established.

2 *Identify project infrastructure.* The organization structure within which the project team will exist is identified.

3 *Analyse project characteristics.* Decisions made about how the project is to be executed – for example buying versus building software functionality – will affect the team structure needed.

5 *Estimate effort for each activity.* Individual and group experience will have a key influence on developer productivity.

6 *Identify activity risks.* Risks will include those that relate to staff such as continued availability.

7 *Allocate resources.*

8 *Review/publicize plan.* A communication plan could be produced at this point.

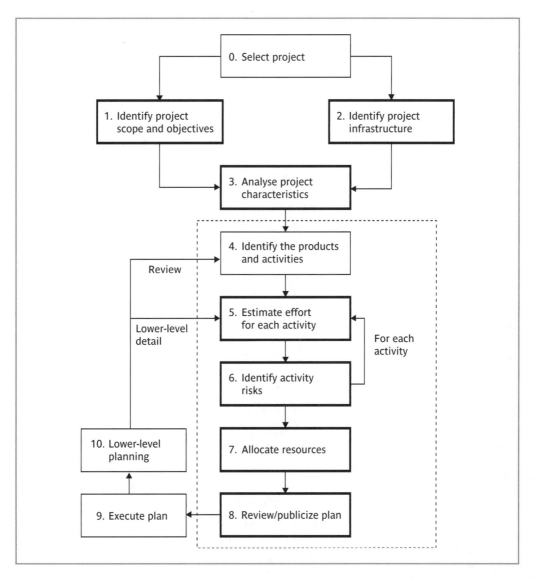

FIGURE 12.1 Some places in the Step Wise framework influenced by collaborative working

12.2 Becoming a team

First we look at how small work groups – where the description 'team' is perhaps most apt – are formed. Simply throwing people together will not immediately enable them to work together as a team. It is suggested that teams go through five basic stages of development:

■ *Forming* The members of the group get to know each other and try to set up some ground rules about behaviour.

This classification is associated with B. W. Tuckman and M. A. Jensen.

- *Storming* Conflicts arise as various members of the group try to exert leadership and the group's methods of operation are being established.

- *Norming* Conflicts are largely settled and a feeling of group identity emerges.

- *Performing* The emphasis is now on the tasks at hand.

- *Adjourning* The group disbands.

Sometimes specific team-building exercises can be undertaken. Some organizations, for example, send their management teams off on outdoor activities. Without going to these lengths, Amanda and Brigette might devise some training activities which promote team building.

R. Meredith Belbin (2003) *Management Teams: Why They Succeed or Fail*, 2nd edition, Elsevier, contains a self-assessment questionnaire which identifies the role a person is best suited to.

Valuable research has examined the best mix of personalities in a project team. Belbin studied teams working together on management games. He initially tried putting the most able people into one group. Surprisingly, these élite teams tended to do very badly – they argued a lot and as a result important tasks were often neglected.

Belbin came to the conclusion that teams needed a balance of different types of people.

In *Team roles at work*, 1996, Belbin suggests that 'co-ordinator' and 'implementer' are better descriptions than 'chair' and 'team worker'. A new role is added: the 'specialist', the 'techie' who likes to acquire knowledge for its own sake.

- *The chair:* not necessarily brilliant leaders but they must be good at running meetings, being calm, strong but tolerant.

- *The plant:* someone who is essentially very good at generating ideas and potential solutions to problems.

- *The monitor–evaluator:* good at evaluating ideas and potential solutions and helping to select the best one.

- *The shaper:* rather a worrier, who helps to direct the team's attention to the important issues.

- *The team worker:* skilled at creating a good working environment, for example, by 'jollying people along'.

- *The resource investigator:* adept at finding resources in terms of both physical resources and information.

- *The completer–finisher:* concerned with completing tasks.

- *The company worker:* a good team player who is willing to undertake less attractive tasks if they are needed for team success.

A person can have elements of more than one type. On the other hand, about 30% of the people examined by Belbin could not be classified at all.

Problems can occur when there is an imbalance between the role types of people in a group. For example, if there are two or more shapers within a group and nobody who takes a chair role to moderate conflicting views, there is likely to be a stormy atmosphere. On the other hand, if a group mainly consists of plants and specialists with no shapers or completer–finishers, the team is likely to have interesting discussions but may not get around to actually implementing anything. When putting together a team Belbin recommends selecting the essential technical specialists first. The group roles of these individuals can then be assessed and any remaining team members can then be allocated with an eye on making the group roles more balanced.

Group performance

The IBM manager was quoted by Angelo Failla in 'Technologies for co-ordination in a software factory' in *Groupware & Teamwork*, edited by C. U. Ciborra, Wiley & Sons, 1996.

Are groups more effective than individuals working alone? Given the preference of many people attracted to software development for working on their own, this is an important question. In many projects, judgements are needed about which tasks are best carried out collectively and which are best delegated to individuals. As one manager at IBM said: '*Some work yields better results if carried out as a team while some things are slowed down if the work is not compartmentalized on an individual basis.*' Part of the answer lies in the type of task being undertaken.

One way of categorizing group tasks is into:

- additive tasks;
- compensatory tasks;
- disjunctive tasks;
- conjunctive tasks.

Additive tasks mean that the efforts of each participant are added to get the final result, e.g. a gang clearing snow. The people involved are interchangeable.

Code reviews could be seen as an example of a compensatory task.

With *compensatory tasks* the judgements of individual group members are pooled so that the errors of some are compensated for by the inputs from others. For example, individual members of a group are asked to provide estimates of the effort needed to produce a piece of software and the results are then averaged. In these circumstances group work is generally more effective than the efforts of individuals.

With *disjunctive tasks* there is only one correct answer. The effectiveness of the group depends on:

- someone coming up with the right answer;
- the others recognizing it as being correct.

Here the group can only be as good as its best member – and could be worse!

Conjunctive tasks are where progress is governed by the rate of the slowest performer. Software production where different staff are responsible for different modules is a good example of this. The overall task is not completed until all participants have completed their part of the work. In this case cooperative attitudes are productive: the team members who are ahead can help the meeting of group objectives by assisting those who are behind. As we will see in a moment, this is an example of *group heedfulness*.

The source of the quotation is the paper by Failla that is cited above.

With all types of collective task, but particularly with additive ones, there is a danger of *social loafing*, where some individuals do not make their proper contribution. This can certainly occur with student group activities, but is not unknown in 'real' work environments. As one software developer has commented: '*[The contribution made to others] is not always recognized. Nor is the lack of any contributions . . . nobody points out those who fail to make any contributions. Like when there's somebody with vital skills and you ask him for help, but he doesn't provide it.'*

EXERCISE 12.1

Social loafing is a problem that students often encounter when carrying out group assignments. What steps can participants in a group take to encourage team members to 'pull their weight' properly?

12.3 Decision making

> Many of the evaluation techniques in Chapter 2 are attempts to make decision making more structured.

Before we can look more closely at the effectiveness with which groups can make decisions, we need to look in general terms at the decision-making process.

Decisions can be categorized as being:

- *structured:* generally relatively simple, routine decisions where rules can be applied in a fairly straightforward way, or

- *unstructured:* more complex and often requiring a degree of creativity.

Another way of categorizing decisions is by the amount of *risk* and *uncertainty* that is involved.

Some mental obstacles to good decision making

> Many of the techniques in Chapter 2 on project selection are based on the rational-economic model.

So far we have rightly stressed a structured, rational, approach to decision making. Many management decisions in the real world, however, are made under pressure and based on incomplete information. We have to accept the role of intuition in such cases, but be aware of some mental obstacles to effective intuitive thinking, for example:

- *Faulty heuristics* Heuristics or 'rules of thumb' can be useful but there are dangers:
  - they are based only on information that is to hand, which might be misleading;
  - they are based on stereotypes, such as accepting a Welshman into a male voice choir without an audition because of the 'well-known' fact that the Welsh are a great singing nation.

- *Escalation of commitment* This refers to the way that once you have made a decision it is increasingly difficult to alter it even in the face of evidence that it is wrong.

- *Information overload* It is possible to have too much information so that you 'cannot see the wood for the trees'.

Group decision making

A different type of participatory decision making might occur when end-users are consulted about the way a projected computer system is to operate.

There might be occasions where Amanda at IOE, for instance, might want to consult with her whole project team. With a project team different specialists and points of view can be brought together. Decisions made by the team as a whole are more likely to be accepted than those that are imposed.

Assuming that the meetings are genuinely collectively responsible and have been properly briefed, research would seem to show that groups are better at solving complex problems when the members of the group have complementary skills and expertise. The meeting allows them to communicate freely and to get ideas accepted.

Joint Application Development (JAD) was discussed in Chapter 4.

Groups deal less effectively with poorly structured problems needing creative solutions. Brainstorming techniques can help groups in this situation but research shows that people often come up with more ideas individually than in a group. Where the aim is to get the involvement of end-users of a computer system, then prototyping and participatory approaches such as JAD might be adopted.

Obstacles to good group decision making

Amanda could find that group decision making has disadvantages: it is time-consuming; it can stir up conflicts within the group; and decisions can be unduly influenced by dominant personalities.

Once established, group norms can survive many changes of membership in the group.

Conflict can, in fact, be less than might be expected. Experiments have shown that people will modify their personal judgements to conform to *group norms*, common attitudes developed by a group over time.

You might think that this would moderate the more extreme views that some in the group might hold. In fact, people in groups sometimes make decisions that carry more risk than where they make the decision on their own. This is known as the *risky shift*.

Measures to reduce the disadvantages of group decision making

One method of making group decision making more efficient and effective is by training members to follow a set procedure. The *Delphi technique* endeavours to collate the judgements of a number of experts without actually bringing them face to face. Given a problem, the following procedure is carried out:

- the cooperation of a number of experts is enlisted;
- the problem is presented to the experts;
- the experts record their recommendations;
- these recommendations are collated and reproduced;
- the collected responses are recirculated;

- the experts comment on the ideas of others and modify their recommendations if so moved;
- if the leader detects a consensus then the process is stopped, otherwise the comments are recirculated to the experts.

An advantage of this approach is that the experts could be geographically dispersed. However, this means that the process can be time-consuming.

EXERCISE 12.2

What developments in information technology would be of particular assistance to use of the Delphi technique?

Team heedfulness

These ideas are explored further in K. Crowston and E. E. Kammerer (1998) 'Coordination and collective mind in software requirements development' *IBM Systems Journal* 37(2) 227–45.

Sometimes, despite all these problems, teams work well together. To use the inevitable sporting analogy, a football team does not play at its best when individual players simply display their skills as individuals but do not support one another. A successful move can be triggered where one players sees that another is in a position to score a goal if provided with a ball. This is an example of team heedfulness, where group members are aware of the activities of others that contribute to overall group success and can identify ways of supporting that contribution. In these cases there almost seems to be a 'collective mind'. Clearly there is no such physical entity in reality, and the appearance of a 'collective mind' comes from shared understanding, familiarity and good communications. Some attempts have been made actively to promote this in a software development environment, such as the concept of egoless programming, chief programmer teams and Scrum.

Egoless programming

G. M. Weinberg (1998) *The Psychology of Computer Programming*, Silver Anniversary Edition, Dorset House.

In the early days of computer development managers tended to think of the software developer as communing mysteriously with the machine. The tendency was for programmers to see programs as being an extension of themselves and to feel over-protective towards them. The effects of this on the maintainability of programs can be imagined. Gerald Weinberg made the then revolutionary suggestion that programmers and programming team leaders should read each others' programs. Programs would become in effect the common property of the programming group and programming would become 'egoless'. Peer code reviews are based on this idea where items produced by individual team members are checked by selected colleagues – see Chapter 13.

Chief programmer teams

Brooks' *Mythical Man-Month* has already been referred to. He was in charge of the huge team that created the operating system for the IBM 360 range.

The larger the development group the slower it becomes because of the increased communication. Thus large time-critical projects tend to have a more formalized, centralized structure. Brooks stressed the need for design consistency when producing a large complex system and how this is difficult where large numbers of people are involved in development. He suggested reducing this number but making the remaining programmers as productive as possible by giving them more support.

The result was the *chief programmer team*. The chief programmer defines the specification, and designs, codes, tests and documents the software. He or she is assisted by a *co-pilot*, with whom the chief programmer can discuss problems and who writes some code. They are supported by an *editor* to write up the documentation drafted by the chief programmer, a *program clerk* to maintain the actual code, and a *tester*. The general idea is that this team is under the control of a single unifying intellect.

The chief programmer concept was used on the influential *New York Times* data bank project where many aspects of structured programming were tried out. In this case each chief programmer managed a senior-level programmer and a program librarian. Additional members could be added to the team on a temporary basis to deal with particular problems or tasks.

The problem with this kind of organization is getting hold of really outstanding programmers to carry out the chief programmer role. There is also the danger of information overload on the chief programmer. There is in addition the potential for staff dissatisfaction among those who are there simply to minister to the needs of the superstar chief programmers.

Extreme programming (XP)

Extreme programming was discussed in Chapter 4.

The new *extreme programming* (XP) concepts have inherited some of these ideas. Most XP practices can be seen as ways of promoting a 'collective mind'. In conventional software development projects, a typical approach to improving communication and coordination is to introduce more documentation. The advocates of XP argue that this is self-defeating. They suggest other, less formal, methods of communication and coordination. Rather than creating separate documents, the key software products, software code and test data, are enhanced. For example, coding is constantly *refactored* (that is, rewritten) and coding standards are followed to make the code clearly convey how the system works. Test cases and expected results are produced before the code, and act effectively as a form of specification. A user representative should be on hand to clarify user needs. The fit between software components is ensured by continual integration testing. Software development by pairs of developers is advocated – this seems to be a new version of the chief programmer/co-pilot relationship.

We will see that while internal group coordination is enhanced, the problem of coordination between teams remains.

Scrum

Linda Rising and Norman S. Janoff (2000) 'The Scrum software development process for small teams' *IEEE Software* July/August 26–32 provides a good overview of Scrum in practice.

It would be self-defeating if the practices advocated by agile approaches should themselves become codified, structured and rigid in application. Promoters of agile methods, such as Kent Beck, are the first to stress that different types of project will need different approaches.

The *Scrum* software development process illustrates some of these points as it has many elements found in agile methods but also has an element of the chief programmer philosophy. The name 'Scrum' comes from rugby scrums and the image of everyone pushing together in a common undertaking. The process was originally designed for new software product development for a competitive market rather than as a commission for a single client. Here, getting something to market before your competitors may be more important than having a comprehensive range of non-essential features. There is no precise specification of the requirements of a particular client, while having a product that is attractive to a number of customers is important. Proposals for features are likely to evolve as ideas are tried out during development.

The Scrum process starts with a systems architecture and planning phase. This has something of the chief programmer approach as a chief architect defines the overall architecture of the product. The required release date for the product and a set of the desired features of the product, each with a priority, would be defined at this stage.

This phase is now followed by a number of *sprints*, each of which typically lasts between one and four weeks. The features that it is hoped can be developed during a sprint are selected. The tasks needed to implement the features are lised. Sprints are carried out by groups, ideally with about seven developers and at a maximum ten. It is possible for Scrum teams to work in parallel on different sprints, but all teams must finish their sprint on the same day.

The progress of a sprint is marked by short (typically 15 minute) meetings each day. During the meeting, team members report on progress with their current task, describing any obstacles they are experiencing. The meeting allows any colleagues who can assist with a problem to come forward. This might be because the co-worker had a similar problem in the past for which they found a solution. Any resulting problem-solving discussions take place after the meeting. These Scrum meetings should promote shared understanding in the group but also help motivate the team as each person's progress is visible to the whole group.

Sprints are time-boxed and at the end of the sprint period some uncompleted, lower-priority features may be held over. Unlike XP, external requirements are frozen during the sprint – it will be recalled that with XP, changes can be requested at any point. However, at the end of the sprint, all sprint teams meet with the other project stakeholders to review the products created. It is at this point that new features could be added, and previous ones deleted or modified. The priority of desired features could be modified. The features to be built in the next sprint are then chosen, and the tasks needed to deliver those features are planned. The sprint process described above is then repeated.

When all the sprints have been completed, there is a final closure phase where tasks like regression and integration testing and the writing of user and training guides take place to create a final package for delivery to market.

Linda Rising and Norman S. Janoff (2000) have described the implementation of Scrum at AG Communications in the USA. Of interest in their account is the evidence of flexibility in implementing the process. One team, for example, decided to have Scrum meetings three times a week, rather than each day. In another case, a team decided to break the rule that externally imposed changes should be ignored during a sprint, when an unusually severe externally imposed change was clearly unavoidable.

12.4 Organizational structures

Organizational structures and projects

On a large project there could be several groups contributing to different aspects of the project. Some organizational structure is needed to form and manage these groups. This organizational structure would take account of the totality of projects and other, non-project, activities being undertaken by the organization. Project leaders such as Amanda at IOE need to be aware of these organizational issues, which can have an enormous impact on their projects.

Formal versus informal structures

The *formal* structure is expressed in the staff hierarchy chart. It focuses on *authority*, about who has which boss. However, an *informal* structure of contacts and communication emerges spontaneously between members of staff while working. This system takes over when the unexpected happens. Over time the advantages and disadvantages of different organizational structures tend to even out – the informal organization gets built up and unofficial ways are found around the obstacles imposed by the formal structure.

Hierarchical approach

The 'traditional' management structure is based on the concept of the *hierarchy* – each member of staff has only one manager, while a manager will have responsibility for several members of staff. Authority flows from the top down through the structure. A traditional concern has been with the *span of control* – the number of people that a manager can effectively control.

Staff versus line

Staff in organizations can often be divided into *line* workers who actually produce the end product and support *staff* who carry out supporting roles. In some organizations that produce software for the market or as a component of a larger product which is sold, the software specialists might be seen as part of the line. In a financial organization, on the other hand, the information systems department would probably be seen as part of the support staff.

Departmentalization

Differentiation concerns the departmentalization of organizations. This might be based on staff specialisms, product lines, categories of customer or geographical location.

> As will be seen later, a functional division could facilitate outsourcing.

Software development is usually organized using either a *functional* or a *task-oriented* approach. With functional departmentalization, systems analysts may be put in a separate group from the programmers. The programmers would act as a pool from which resources are drawn for particular tasks. With a task-oriented approach the programmers and systems analysts are grouped together in project teams. The project team could be gathered to implement a specific long-term project or could exist on a permanent basis to service the needs of a particular set of users.

Another variable is the degree to which individual team members are specialists with a narrow range of skills, for example only carrying out software coding, or are more multi-skilled where they are able to carry out other tasks, for example some of those associated with business and systems analysis.

> Programme management can facilitate better sharing of staff between projects.

The functional approach can lead to a more effective use of staff. Programmers can be allocated to jobs on a need basis and be released for other work when the task is completed. This avoids them being under-utilized. The functional organization will also make it easier for the programmer to have a career which is technically oriented – there will probably be a career structure within the software development department which allows programmers to rise without changing their specialism. This type of organization should also encourage the interchange of new technical ideas between technical staff and the promulgation of company-wide standards.

However, having separate departments could lead to communication problems, especially if a developer is unfamiliar with an application area. There will also be problems with software maintenance – here it is helpful to have programmers who have built up a familiarity with particular parts of the application software. Users often prefer the established project team approach because they will have a group dedicated to their needs and will not find themselves in the position of always having to fight other departments for development resources. The project team structure tends to favour a pattern of career progression where software developers eventually become business analysts.

A third method of departmentalization is based on *life-cycle phase*. Here there are separate teams for development and maintenance. Some staff can concentrate on developing new systems with few interruptions while other teams, more oriented towards service and support, deal with maintenance.

Some organizations have attempted to get the best of all worlds by having a *matrix* structure. In this case the developer would have two managers: a project leader who would give them day-to-day direction about the work in hand and a programming manager who would be concerned about such things as career development.

12.5 Coordination dependencies

Ian R. McChesney
and Séamus
Gallagher (2004)
'Communication and
co-ordination
practices in
software
engineering
projects' *Information
and Software
Technology*
46 473–89 gives a
good introduction to
these concepts and
insights into their
application.

Why and to what extent do the different units within an overall organizational structure really need to communicate? Researchers and innovators in the area of *computer-supported cooperative work* (CSCW) have been interested in identifying the types of coordination where computer tools could be of assistance. A *coordination theory* has been developed which provides a useful classification of coordination dependencies that are likely to exist in any substantial organizational undertaking. These are listed below.

- *Shared resources.* An example in software development projects is where several projects need the services of particular types of scarce technical experts for certain parts of the project. The unavailability of these experts because of commitments elsewhere could delay a project. We noted in Chapter 2 that programme management may be established at a higher level than individual projects to reduce these resources clashes.

- *Producer–customer ('right time') relationships.* A project activity may depend on a product being delivered first. For example, a business analyst may need to produce an agreed requirements document before the development of software components can begin. The Product Flow Diagram (PFD) promoted by the PRINCE2 methodology and described in Chapter 3 can help identify some of these dependencies, but the key point is that some other organizational unit, which could in fact be outside the business, is involved.

- *Task–subtask dependencies.* In order to complete a task a sequence of subtasks have to be carried out. Like the producer–customer relationships described above, this could be reflected in the PFD. Unlike the producer–customer relationship, this sequencing is forced by the technical nature of the thing being created, or the method that is being adopted, rather than by decisions about who is to do what.

- *Accessibility ('right place') dependencies.* This type of dependency is of more relevance to activities that require movement over a large geographical area. The problems of getting an available ambulance to the site of a medical emergency as quickly as possible would a prime example of this. In ICT and software development the examples are less obvious, but arranging the delivery and installation of ICT equipment might be identified as such.

- *Usability ('right thing') dependencies.* In this context, this is a broader concern than the design of user interfaces more usually associated with the term 'usability'. It relates to the general question of *fitness for purpose,* which includes the satisfaction of business requirements. In software development this could lead to activities, such as prototyping, which ensure that the system being created will meet the users' operational needs. It could also involve change management activities when users need to change requirements because of, for example, events in the business environment such as legislative changes.

- *Fit requirements.* This is ensuring that different system components work together effectively. Integration testing is one mechanism that ensures that these requirements are met. One concern of configuration management (as described in Chapter 9) is assessing whether changes made to one component will have knock-on effects on other components.

In many cases, information systems tools can support these coordination tasks. For example, project planning tools, such as Microsoft Project, can be used to help decision making about the allocation of resources both within projects and across a portfolio of concurrent projects. Such tools, through the support they give to the development, analysis and manipulation of activity networks (as we have seen in Chapters 6 and 8), can help the control of producer–customer and task–subtask dependencies. Another example of software tool support is the use of change management and configuration management databases to keep track of changes to the system under development and thus support usability and fit dependencies.

Ian McChesney and Séamus Gallagher have published a research report which analyses two real-world project environments in terms of the way coordination activities were carried out. Among some quite detailed findings, they noted the use of software tools to support some coordination activities, but also noted how a single person in the project team could have a key coordination role. This person could act as a go-between for staff who need to communicate, for example directing user enquiries to the developer best able to provide information.

E-mail was noted as a principal means of communication. The practice had been developed of copying emails to third parties who might need to be 'kept in the loop', that is, made aware of developments. It is interesting that this development was seen as invaluable – there are reports of other environments where email has become less effective as a means of communication as staff become overwhelmed by the sheer volume of emails.

12.6 Dispersed and virtual teams

We have seen how projects require a team of people to carry them out, and the members of this team could each be a specialist in a particular field. Thus, the heart of many projects is *collaborative problem solving*. The Second World War underlined the importance of cooperation between individuals and groups to execute major global operations, and encouraged research after the conflict into effective team working. At that time, group working meant, almost by definition, that the team members worked in close physical proximity. However, in recent years the concept and practice of having *dispersed* or '*virtual teams*' have emerged.

See Tom DeMarco and Timothy Lister (1999) *PeopleWare: Productive Projects and Teams*, 2nd edition, Dorset House.

We have also see how project work, especially the development of large software products, needs coordination which in turn means that team members need to communicate. Being located in the same physical space clearly assists this. However, offices can be noisy places and while software development needs communication it also needs periods of solitary concentrated effort. DeMarco and Lister describe the condition of deep concentration needed for effective creative work as 'flow', and suggest that about 15 minutes of uninterrupted effort is needed to achieve this state. Every interruption destroys flow and requires another 15 minutes for its recovery.

It was noted earlier that project managers often have little control over who will be allocated to their team. They are even less likely to have control over the physical environment in which the team will work. Many years ago, research at IBM suggested that ideally each software developer should have:

- 100 square feet of dedicated space;

- 30 square feet of work surface;

- noise protection in the form of enclosed offices or partitions at least six feet high.

For various reasons it is often difficult for software developers to be provided with this kind of accommodation, yet DeMarco and Lister found clear links between reported noise levels in the workplace and the number of defects found in the resulting software.

One answer is to send the software developers home. One recent (2004) survey found that 77% of businesses allowed at least some of their staff to work at home. Most of those working at home reported that they were more productive. The development of cheap internet-based communications, supported by broadband channels, has reduced the coordination problems that were the drawback of home working.

> The survey was carried out by the Economist Intelligence Unit and was reported on in 'Remote working boosts productivity' in *Computing*, 25 November, 2004, p. 6.

Modern communication technologies also mean that organizations can more easily form temporary teams to carry out specific projects from amongst their employees without having to relocate them. The nature of the work carried out in some projects means that the demand for certain specialist skills is intermittent. Ideally the project manager would like to have access to these skills for a short time but then be able to release them and thus avoid further costs. An example of this might be the passing need for a graphic designer to produce aesthetically pleasing designs for a web application project. This desire for flexible labour means that contract workers are often used. The internet allows these contractors to carry out well-defined tasks at their own premises without necessarily having to travel to their clients' site.

It is then only a short step to use 'off-shore' staff who live and work in a different part of the world. Hence we arrive at the dispersed or virtual team.

To recap the possible advantages of such an arrangement:

- A reduction in staff costs by using labour from developing countries where salaries are lower.

- A reduction in the overheads that arise from having your own employees on site, including costs of accommodation, social security payments, training.

- The flexible use of staff – they are not employed when they are not needed.

- Productivity might be higher.

One estimate was that 24,000 IT and software development jobs would be moved off-shore from the UK between 2003 and 2005, according to a British Computer Society working party report, *Offshoring – a challenge or opportunity for IT Professionals,* (British Computer Society 2004).

- Use of specialist staff for specific jobs, rather than more general project workers, might improve quality.
- Advantage can be taken of people working in different time zones to reduce task durations – for example, software developers can deliver new versions of code to testers in a different time zone who can test it and deliver the results back at the start of the next working day.

Some of the challenges of dispersed working are:

- The requirements for work that is distributed to contractors have to be carefully specified.
- The procedures to be followed will need to be formally expressed, where previously practices might have been picked up through observation and imitation of co-workers on site.
- Coordination of dispersed workers can be difficult.
- Payment methods may need to be modified to make them fixed price or piece-rate.
- There may be a lack of trust of co-workers who are remote and never seen.
- Assessment of the quality of delivered products will need to be thorough.
- Different time zones can cause communication and coordination problems.

12.7 Communication genres

So far we have focused on some of the reasons why men and women engaged on a common project would need to communicate, not only within work groups but with colleagues in other parts of the organization, or in some cases in partner organizations. We have also mentioned various methods of communication but have not examined communications media in a structured way.

Some work has been done to study the characteristics of various methods of communication. One approach has been to try to identify *communication genres*. These refer to something more than just the technical means of communicating. They are types of communication that people are in the habit of making and where there are some 'ground rules' about when and how such communications should be carried out. For some types of communication, such as official meetings, these rules might be quite formal. Within the general heading of 'management meetings' there could be a range of types of meeting each with their own conventions. These could be seen as genres in their own right.

Within the general heading of the email communication genre, advanced email-based applications can be developed where the content of the email is structured by preset proformas designed to fulfil a standard process, such as requesting a change to a software specification. These applications can be seen as communication genres in their own right.

A major influence on the nature of communication genres is the constraints of time and place. Modes of communication can be categorized as combinations of two opposites: same time/different time and same place/different place – see Table 12.1.

	Same place	Different place
Same time	Meetings	Telephone
	Interviews etc.	Instant messaging
Different times	Noticeboards	E-mail
	Pigeon-holes	Voicemail
		Documents

TABLE 12.1 Time/place constraints on some communication methods

The nature of the information to be conveyed also needs to be considered.

- What is the extent and complexity of the information to be conveyed? A telephone conversation may be a very quick way of conveying simple messages – but has disadvantages as a medium for large amounts of information.
- Is it easy to understand? For example, is the context well known to both the sender and the recipient? If it is likely that the recipient will need clarification of aspects of the information, then a mode of communication that is two-way would be best.
- Where the communication is personally sensitive, then face-to-face contact is the most effective form of communication, even if it can be uncomfortable or inconvenient for those concerned.

EXERCISE 12.3

What would be the best mode of communication for the following?

(a) A developer needs clarification of what is meant by a particular term used in a specification.

(b) The users of a system have found what appears to be a fault in a software application that they use.

(c) A finance director needs to ensure that a software application is changed to conform with new legal requirements.

(d) A software developer can only complete her software component if another developer finishes his component first, but he has not. The first developer is under a lot of pressure from the client to complete the work.

At different stages of a project it is likely that different communication genres will be preferred.

Early stages of a project

Charles Handy (1995) 'Trust and the virtual organization' *Harvard Business Review*, May/June 45–50.

At the start of the project, team members will need to build up their trust and confidence in their co-workers. For this same time/same place communication, actually meeting is probably best. It is argued that this is especially the case with dispersed projects: as Charles Handy has written: '*paradoxically, the more virtual an organization becomes, the more its people need to meet in person*'.

Julian Baggini (2005) 'Touched by your absence' *The Guardian* 6 January.

However, not everyone might agree with this. Julian Baggini, describing his experience of writing a textbook on philosophy with someone he had never met, argues: '*It is simply not necessary to know the whole person in order to have a good relationship with them. . . . If you get to know and dislike the way that someone behaves outside the office, that can make you uncomfortable with them in it.*'

The early stages of a project are when at least some of the team will be involved in making decisions about the overall design of the product to be delivered and the method by which it is to be created. In the preliminary stages at least, same time/same place meetings are the most effective means of progressing.

Intermediate design stages of the project

Once the overall architecture of the product has been established, detailed design on different components could well be carried out in parallel in different locations. However, some points will need to be clarified and for this, same time/different place communication could well be best, such as the use of teleconferencing.

Implementation stages of the project

Once the design is clarified and everyone knows his or her role, work can progress. Where there is a need to exchange information at this point, different time/different place communication media such as e-mail are likely to be sufficient.

M. L. Mazneski and K. M. Chudoba (2000) 'Bridging space over time global virtual team dynamics and effectivness' *Organization Science*, 11 (5).

Even at this stage some recommend regular face-to-face meetings of at least some staff as this supplies a rhythm to the project which helps coordination of the project and maintains motivation. Martha Maznevski and Katherine Chudoba observed the workings of a dispersed project and have noted '*interaction between coordination meetings was mainly in response to the previous meeting or in anticipation of the next one. The coordination meeting served as a heartbeat, rhythmically pumping new life into the team's processes . . .*'.

12.8 Communication plans

Communication is important in all projects but a vital matter in the case of dispersed projects. Because of this, consideration of the way that project stakeholders will communicate ought to be a part of the project planning process. Some have gone as far as to suggest that a specific planning document ought to address communication issues affecting the project, not just for dispersed projects but for any project with a substantial number of important stakeholders.

The first step in producing such a plan is to list the main stakeholders, with special attention to those who are participating in the development and implementation of the project – it may be recalled that the identification of stakeholders and their concerns was stressed in Chapter 1 as being fundamental to project success. Once the overall project plan has been created using a process such as that described in Chapter 3, each of the main activities and milestones is examined to see which channels and methods would be best for effective communication with these stakeholders. We have already carried out such a process in our discussion of the communication needs of the different phases of a dispersed project. Consultation with the representatives of the various groups of stakeholders would be an essential part of this process.

The results of this process could be documented in a table with the following column headings.

> This table is based on that in the Princeton Project Methodology.

- *What* This contains the name of a particular communication event, for example 'kick-off meeting', or a communication channel, for example 'project intranet site'.

- *Who/target* The target audience for the communication. 'Target audience' may not convey quite the right idea as this implies that there are passive recipients of information from a central authority. In fact the communication event or channel could be a means of eliciting information from the 'audience'.

- *Purpose* What the communication is to achieve.

- *When/frequency* If the communication by means of a single event, then a specific date can be supplied. If the event is a recurring one, such as a progress meeting, then the frequency should be indicated.

- *Type/method* The nature of the communication, for example a meeting or a distributed document.

- *Responsibility* The person who initiates the communication.

12.9 Leadership

When Amanda and Brigette first took on project management responsibilities, one of their private anxieties might well have been that staff would not take them seriously. Leadership is generally taken to mean the ability to influence others in a group to act in a particular way to achieve group goals. A leader is not necessarily a good manager or vice versa, as managers have other roles such as organizing, planning and controlling.

> See Robert Johansen et al. (1991) *Leading Business Teams*, Addison-Wesley.

Authorities on this subject have found it difficult to agree a list of the common characteristics of good leaders. It would, however, seem safe to say that they seem to have a greater need for power and achievement and have more self-control and more self-confidence than others.

Leadership is based on the idea of authority or power, although leaders do not necessarily have much formal authority. Power may come either from the person's position (*position* power), from the person's individual qualities (*personal* power) or may be a mixture of the two. Position power has been further analysed into:

> These ideas are associated with the work of J. R. P. French and B. H. Raven.

- *coercive* power, the ability to force someone to do something by threatening punishment;

- *connection* power, which is based on having access to those who have power;

- *legitimate* power, which is based on a person's title conferring a special status;

- *reward* power, where the holder can give rewards to those who carry out tasks to his or her satisfaction.

Personal power, on the other hand, can be further analysed into:

- *expert* power, which comes from being the person who is able to do a specialized task;

- *information* power, where the holder has exclusive access to information;

- *referent* power, which is based on the personal attractiveness of the leader.

EXERCISE 12.4

What kinds of power (as defined above) would the following people have?

(a) An internal auditor looking at the payroll system at Brightmouth College.

(b) A consultant who is called in to advise International Office Equipment about ways of improving software development productivity.

(c) The principal of Brightmouth College who has told staff that they must accept a new contract or face the sack.

(d) Brigette in respect to the users of the college payroll system.

(e) Amanda in respect of the people in the project team developing the annual maintenance contract application.

Leadership styles

Amanda and Brigette might be initially concerned about establishing their personal authority. Balanced against this is the need to involve the staff in decision making in order to make the best use of expertise and to gain commitment. Amanda and Brigette will need to judge when they must be authoritative and insist on things and when they must be more flexible and tolerant. Amanda, for example, may decide to be very democratic when formulating plans, but once the plans have been agreed, to insist on a very disciplined execution of the plan. Brigette, on the other hand, may find at Brightmouth College that she alone has the technical expertise to make some decisions, but, once she has briefed staff, they expect to be left alone to get on with the job as they see fit.

Attempts have been made to measure leadership styles on two axes: directive vs. permissive and autocratic vs. democratic:

This approach is associated with Rensis Likert.

- *directive autocrat:* makes decisions alone, close supervision of implementation;

- *permissive autocrat:* makes decisions alone, subordinates have latitude in implementation;

- *directive democrat:* makes decisions participatively, close supervision of implementation;

- *permissive democrat:* makes decisions participatively, subordinates have latitude in implementation.

It should be emphasized that there is no one best style of management – it depends on the situation.

Another axis used to measure management styles has been on the degree to which a manager is *task-oriented*, that is, the extent to which the execution of the task at hand is paramount, and the degree to which the manager is concerned about the people around them (*people orientation*). It is perhaps not surprising that subordinates appear to perform best with managers who score highly in *both* respects.

Work environments vary with amount of control exerted over work. Some jobs are routine and predictable (e.g. dealing with batched computer output). Others are driven by outside factors (e.g. a help desk) or are situations where future direction is uncertain (e.g. at the early stages of a feasibility study). With a high degree of uncertainty subordinates will seek guidance from above and welcome a task-oriented management style. As uncertainty is reduced, the task-oriented manager is likely to relax, becoming more people-oriented, and this will have good results. People-oriented managers are better where staff can control the work they do, without referring matters to their line managers. It is then argued that if control becomes even easier the people-oriented manager will be tempted to get involved in more task-centred questions, with undesirable results.

Research also shows that where team members are relatively inexperienced, a task-oriented approach is most effective. As group members mature, consideration for their personal needs and aspirations becomes more valued. Where maturity is very high, there is no need for a strong emphasis on either of these approaches.

EXERCISE 12.5

What in your view would be the most appropriate management style when dealing with the following subordinates?

(a) At Brightmouth College, a former member of the local authority who has dealt with the college payroll for several years and who has been employed by the college to set up and manage the new payroll section.

(b) At IOE, a new trainee analyst/programmer who has just joined Amanda's group.

(c) At IOE, a very experienced analyst/programmer in their 40s, who was recruited into the software development department some time ago from the accounts department and who has been dealing with system support for the old maintenance accounts system that is now being revised.

12.10 Conclusion

Some of the important points that have been made in this chapter are:

■ consideration should be given, when forming a new project team, to getting the right mix of people and to planning activities which will promote team building;

■ group working is more effective with some types of activity than others;

■ the people who need to communicate most with each other should be grouped together organizationally;

■ different styles of leadership are needed in different situations;

■ care should be taken to identify the most effective way of communicating with project participants at key points in the project.

12.11 Further exercises

1 To what extent is the Belbin approach to balanced teams compatible with having chief programmer teams?

2 If you have been involved recently in a group activity or project, try to categorize each participant according to the Belbin classification. Were there any duplications or gaps in any of the roles? Did this seem to have any impact on progress?

3 Three different mental obstacles to good decision making were identified in the text: faulty heuristics, escalation of commitment and information overload. What steps do you think can be taken to reduce the danger of each of these?

4 Exercise 12.5 asked you to identity the management style most appropriate for each of three different situations. Go back and consider how you as a manager would respond to each of these three situations in terms of practical things to do or avoid.

CHAPTER 13

Software quality

❖ **OBJECTIVES**

When you have completed this chapter you will be able to:

❖ explain the importance of software quality to software users and developers;

❖ define the qualities of good software;

❖ design methods of measuring the required qualities of software;

❖ monitor the quality of the processes in a software project;

❖ use external quality standards to ensure the quality of software acquired from an outside supplier;

❖ develop systems using procedures that will increase their quality.

13.1 Introduction

While quality is generally agreed to be 'a good thing', in practice what is meant by the 'quality' of a system can be vague. We need to define precisely what qualities we require of a system. However, we need to go further – we need to judge objectively whether a system meets our quality requirements and this needs measurement. This would be of particular concern to someone like Brigette at Brightmouth College in the process of selecting a package.

For someone – like Amanda at IOE – who is developing software, waiting until the system exists before measuring it would be leaving things rather late. Amanda might want to assess the likely quality of the final system while it was still under development, and also to make sure that the development methods used would produce that quality. This leads to a different emphasis – rather than concentrating on the quality of the final system, a potential customer for software might check that the suppliers were using the best development methods.

This chapter examines these issues.

13.2 The place of software quality in project planning

Quality will be of concern at all stages of project planning and execution, but will be of particular interest at the following points in the Step Wise framework (Figure 13.1).

- *Step 1: Identify project scope and objectives* Some objectives could relate to the qualities of the application to be delivered.

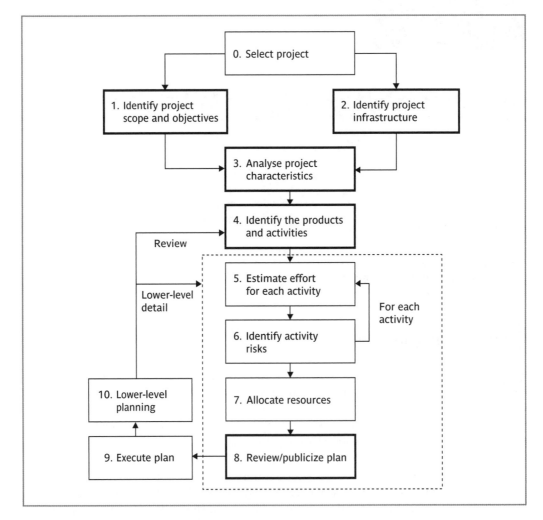

FIGURE 13.1 The place of software quality in Step Wise

- *Step 2: Identify project infrastructure* Within this step, activity 2.2 identifies installation standards and procedures. Some of these will almost certainly be about quality.

- *Step 3: Analyse project characteristics* In activity 3.2 ('Analyse other project characteristics – including quality based ones') the application to be implemented is examined to see if it has any special quality requirements. If, for example, it is safety critical then a range of activities could be added, such as *n*-version development where a number of teams develop versions of the same software which are then run in parallel with the outputs being cross-checked for discrepancies.

- *Step 4: Identify the products and activities of the project* It is at this point that the entry, exit and process requirements are identified for each activity. This is described later in this chapter.

- *Step 8: Review and publicize plan* At this stage the overall quality aspects of the project plan are reviewed.

13.3 The importance of software quality

We would expect quality to be a concern of all producers of goods and services. However, the special characteristics of software create special demands.

- *Increasing criticality of software* The final customer or user is naturally anxious about the general quality of software, especially its reliability. This is increasingly so as organizations rely more on their computer systems and software is used in more safety-critical applications, for example to control aircraft.

- *The intangibility of software* can make it difficult to know that a project task was completed satisfactorily. Task outcomes can be made tangible by demanding that the developer produce 'deliverables' that can be examined for quality.

- *Accumulating errors during software development* As computer system development comprises steps where the output from one step is the input to the next, the errors in the later deliverables will be added to those in the earlier steps, leading to an accumulating detrimental effect. In general, the later in a project that an error is found the more expensive it will be to fix. In addition, because the number of errors in the system is unknown, the debugging phases of a project are particularly difficult to control.

For these reasons quality management is an essential part of effective overall project management.

13.4 Defining software quality

In Chapter 1 we noted that a system has functional, quality and resource requirements. Functional requirements define what the system is to do, the resource requirements specify allowable costs and the quality requirements state how well this system is to operate.

> ### EXERCISE 13.1
>
> At Brightmouth College, Brigette has to select the best off-the-shelf payroll package for the college. How should she go about this in a methodical manner?
>
> One element of the approach could be the identification of criteria against which payroll packages are to be judged. What might these criteria be? How could you check the extent to which packages match these criteria?

Some qualities of a software product reflect the external view of software held by *users*, as in the case of usability. These *external qualities* have to be mapped to *internal factors* of which the *developers* would be aware. It could be argued, for example, that well-structured code is likely to have fewer errors and thus improve reliability.

Defining quality is not enough. If we are to judge whether a system meets our requirements we need to be able to measure its qualities.

The BS ISO/IEC 15939:2007 standard *Systems and software engineering – measurement process* has codified many of the practices discussed in this section.

A good measure must relate the number of units to the maximum possible. The maximum number of faults in a program, for example, is related to the size of the program, so a measure of *faults per thousand lines of code* is more helpful than *total faults in a program*.

Trying to find measures for a particular quality helps to clarify and communicate what that quality really is. What is being asked is, in effect, 'how do we know when we have been successful?'

The measures may be *direct*, where we can measure the quality directly, or *indirect*, where the thing being measured is not the quality itself but an indicator that the quality is present. For example, the number of enquiries by users received by a help desk about how one operates a particular software application might be an indirect measurement of its usability.

When project managers identify quality measurements they effectively set targets for project team members, so care has to be taken that an improvement in the measured quality is always meaningful. For example, the number of errors found in program inspections could be counted, on the grounds that the more thorough the inspection process, the more errors will be discovered. This count could, of course, be improved by allowing more errors to go through to the inspection stage rather than eradicating them earlier – which is not quite the point.

When there is concern about the need for a specific quality characteristic in a software product then a quality specification with the following minimum details should be drafted:

- *definition/description:* definition of the quality characteristic;
- *scale:* the unit of measurement;
- *test:* the practical test of the extent to which the attribute quality exists;
- *minimally acceptable:* the worst value which might be acceptable if other characteristics compensated for it, and below which the product would have to be rejected out of hand;

- *target range:* the range of values within which it is planned the quality measurement value should lie;
- *now:* the value that applies currently.

EXERCISE 13.2

Suggest quality specifications for a word processing package. Give particular attention to the way that practical tests of these attributes could be conducted.

There could be several measurements applicable to a quality characteristic. For example, in the case of reliability, this might be measured in terms of:

- *availability:* the percentage of a particular time interval that a system is usable;
- *mean time between failures:* the total service time divided by the number of failures;
- *failure on demand:* the probability that a system will not be available at the time required or the probability that a transaction will fail;
- *support activity:* the number of fault reports that are generated and processed.

EXERCISE 13.3

The enhanced IOE maintenance jobs system has been installed, and is normally available to users from 8.00 a.m. until 6.00 p.m. from Monday to Friday. Over a four-week period the system was unavailable for one whole day because of problems with a disk drive and was not available on two other days until 10.00 in the morning because of problems with overnight batch processing runs.

What were the availability and the mean time between failures of the service?

Maintainability can be seen from two different perspectives. The user will be concerned with the *elapsed time* between a fault being detected and it being corrected, while the software development managers will be concerned about the *effort* involved.

Associated with reliability is *maintainability*, which is how quickly a fault, once detected, can be corrected. A key component of this is *changeability*, which is the ease with which the software can be modified. However, before an amendment can be made, the fault has to be diagnosed. Maintainability can therefore be seen as changeability plus a new quality, *analysability*, which is the ease with which causes of failure can be identified.

13.5 ISO 9126

Currently, in the UK, the main ISO 9126 standard is known as BS ISO/IEC 9126-1:2001. This is supplemented by some 'technical reports' (TRs), published in 2003, which are provisional standards. At the time of writing, a new standard in this area, ISO 25000, is being developed.

Over the years, various lists of software quality characteristics have been put forward, such as those of James McCall and of Barry Boehm. A difficulty has been the lack of agreed definitions of the qualities of good software. The term 'maintainability' has been used, for example, to refer to the ease with which an error can be located and corrected in a piece of software, and also in a wider sense to include the ease of making any changes. For some, 'robustness' has meant the software's tolerance of incorrect input, while for others it has meant the ability to change program code without introducing errors. The ISO 9126 standard was first introduced in 1991 to tackle the question of the definition of software quality. The original 13-page document was designed as a foundation upon which further, more detailed, standards could be built. The ISO 9126 standards documents are now very lengthy. Partly this is because people with differing motivations might be interested in software quality, namely:

- *acquirers* who are obtaining software from external suppliers;
- *developers* who are building a software product;
- *independent evaluators* who are assessing the quality of a software product, not for themselves but for a community of users – for example, those who might use a particular type of software tool as part of their professional practice.

ISO 9126 has separate documents to cater for these three sets of needs. Despite the size of this set of documentation, it relates only to the definition of software quality attributes. A separate standard, ISO 14598, describes the procedures that should be carried out when assessing the degree to which a software product conforms to the selected ISO 9126 quality characteristics. This might seem unnecessary, but it is argued that ISO 14598 could be used to carry out an assessment using a different set of quality characteristics from those in ISO 9126 if circumstances required it.

The difference between internal and external quality attributes has already been noted. ISO 9126 also introduces another type of quality – *quality in use* – for which the following elements have been identified:

- *effectiveness:* the ability to achieve user goals with accuracy and completeness;
- *productivity:* avoiding the excessive use of resources, such as staff effort, in achieving user goals;
- *safety:* within reasonable levels of risk of harm to people and other entities such as business, software, property and the environment;
- *satisfaction:* smiling users.

'Users' in this context includes not just those who operate the system containing the software, but also those who maintain and enhance the software. The idea of quality in use underlines how the required quality of the software is an attribute not just of the software but also of the context of use. For instance, in the IOE scenario, suppose the maintenance job reporting procedure varies considerably, depending on the type of equipment being serviced, because different inputs are needed to calculate the cost to IOE. Say that 95% of jobs currently involve maintaining photocopiers and 5% concern maintenance of printers. If the software is written for this application, then despite good testing, some errors might still get into the operational system. As these are reported and corrected, the software would become more 'mature' as faults become rarer. If there were a rapid switch so that more printer maintenance jobs were being processed, there could be an increase in reported faults as coding bugs in previously less heavily used parts of the software code for printer maintenance were flushed out by the larger number of printer maintenance transactions. Thus, changes to software use involve changes to quality requirements.

ISO 9126 identifies six major external software quality characteristics:

■ *functionality*, which covers the functions that a software product provides to satisfy user needs;

■ *reliability*, which relates to the capability of the software to maintain its level of performance;

■ *usability*, which relates to the effort needed to use the software;

■ *efficiency*, which relates to the physical resources used when the software is executed;

■ *maintainability*, which relates to the effort needed to the make changes to the software;

■ *portability*, which relates to the ability of the software to be transferred to a different environment.

ISO 9126 suggests sub-characteristics for each of the primary characteristics. They are useful as they clarify what is meant by each of the main characteristics.

Characteristic	Sub-characteristics
Functionality	Suitability
	Accuracy
	Interoperability
	Functionality compliance
	Security

'Functionality compliance' refers to the degree to which the software adheres to application-related standards or legal requirements. Typically these could be auditing requirements. Since the original 1999 draft, a sub-characteristic called 'compliance' has been added to all six ISO external characteristics. In each case, this refers to any specific standards that might apply to the particular quality attribute.

'Interoperability' is a good illustration of the efforts of ISO 9126 to clarify terminology. 'Interoperability' refers to the ability of the software to interact with other systems. The framers of ISO 9126 have chosen this word rather than 'compatibility' because the latter causes confusion with the characteristic referred to by ISO 9126 as 'replaceability' (see below).

Characteristic	Sub-characteristics
Reliability	Maturity
	Fault tolerance
	Recoverability
	Reliability compliance

'Maturity' refers to the frequency of failure due to faults in a software product, the implication being that the more the software has been used, the more faults will have been uncovered and removed. It is also interesting to note that 'recoverability' has been clearly distinguished from 'security' which describes the control of access to a system.

Characteristic	Sub-characteristics
Usability	Understandability
	Learnability
	Operability
	Attractiveness
	Usability compliance

Note how 'learnability' is distinguished from 'operability'. A software tool could be easy to learn but time-consuming to use because, say, it uses a large number of nested menus. This might be fine for a package used intermittently, but not where the system is used for many hours each day. In this case 'learnability' has been incorporated at the expense of 'operability'.

'Attractiveness' is a recent addition to the sub-characteristics of usability and is especially important where users are not compelled to use a particular software product, as in the case of games and other entertainment products.

Characteristic	Sub-characteristics
Efficiency	Time behaviour
	Resource utilization
	Efficiency compliance
Maintainability	Analysability
	Changeability
	Stability
	Testability
	Maintainability compliance

'Analysability' is the ease with which the cause of a failure can be determined. 'Changeability' is the quality that others call 'flexibility': the latter name is a better one as 'changeability' has a different connotation in plain English – it might imply that the suppliers of the software are always changing it!

'Stability', on the other hand, does not refer to software never changing: it means that there is a low risk of a modification to the software having unexpected effects.

Characteristic	Sub-characteristics
Portability	Adaptability
	Installability
	Coexistence
	Replaceability
	Portability compliance

A new version of a word processing package might read the documents produced by previous versions and thus be able to replace them, but previous versions might not be able to read all documents created by the new version.

'Portability compliance' relates to those standards that have a bearing on portability. The use of a standard programming language common to many software/hardware environments would be an example of this. 'Replaceability' refers to the factors that give 'upwards compatibility' between old software components and the new ones. 'Downwards' compatibility is not implied by the definition.

'Coexistence' refers to the ability of the software to share resources with other software components; unlike 'interoperability', no direct data passing is necessarily involved.

ISO 9126 provides guidelines for the use of the quality characteristics. Variation in the importance of different quality characteristics depending on the type of product is stressed. Once the requirements for the software product have been established, the following steps are suggested:

1   *Judge the importance of each quality characteristic for the application* Thus reliability will be of particular concern with safety-critical systems while efficiency will be important for some real-time systems.

2   *Select the external quality measurements within the ISO 9126 framework relevant to the qualities prioritized above* Thus for reliability mean time between failures would be an important measurement, while for efficiency, and more specifically 'time behaviour', response time would be an obvious measurement.

3   *Map measurements onto ratings that reflect user satisfaction* For response time, for example, the mappings might be as in Table 13.1.

4   *Identify the relevant internal measurements and the intermediate products in which they appear* This would only be important where software was being developed, rather than existing software being evaluated. For new software, the likely quality of the final product would need to be assessed during development. For example, where the external quality in question was time behaviour, at the software design stage an

Response time (seconds)	Rating
<2	Exceeds expectation
2–5	Within the target range
6–10	Minimally acceptable
>10	Unacceptable

TABLE 13.1 Mapping measurements to user satisfaction

estimated execution time for a transaction could be produced by examining the software code and calculating the time for each instruction in a typical execution of the transaction. In our view the mappings between internal and external quality characteristics and measurements suggested in the ISO 9126 standard are the least convincing elements in the approach. The part of the standard that provides guidance at this point is a 'technical report' which is less authoritative than a full standard. It concedes that mapping external and internal measurements can be difficult and that validation to check that there is a meaningful correlation between the two in a specific environment needs to be done. This reflects a real problem in the practical world of software development of examining code structure and from that attempting to predict accurately external qualities such as reliability.

According to ISO 9126, measurements that might act as indicators of the final quality of the software can be taken at different stages of the development life cycle. For products at the early stages these indicators might be qualitative. They could, for example, be based on checklists where compliance with predefined criteria is assessed by expert judgement. As the product nears completion, objective, quantitative, measurements would increasingly be taken.

5 *Overall assessment of product quality* To what extent is it possible to combine ratings for different quality characteristics into a single overall rating for the software? A factor which discourages attempts at combining the assessments of different quality characteristics is that they can, in practice, be measured in very different ways, which makes comparison and combination difficult. Sometimes the presence of one quality could be to the detriment of another. For example, the efficiency characteristics of time behaviour and resource utilization could be enhanced by exploiting the particular characteristics of the operating system and hardware environments within which the software will perform. This, however, would probably be at the expense of portability.

It was noted above that quality assessment could be carried out for a number of different reasons: to assist software development, acquisition or independent assessment.

During the development of a software product, the assessment would be driven by the need to focus the minds of the developers on key quality requirements. The aim would be to identify possible weaknesses early on and there would be no need for an overall quality rating.

The problem here is to map an objective measurement onto an indicator of customer satisfaction which is subjective.

Response time (seconds)	Quality score
<2	5
2–3	4
4–5	3
6–7	2
8–9	1
>9	0

TABLE 13.2 Mapping response times onto user satisfaction

Where potential users are assessing a number of different software products in order to choose the best one, the outcome will be along the lines that product A is more satisfactory than product B or C. Here some idea of relative satisfaction exists and there is a justification in trying to model how this satisfaction might be formed. One approach recognizes some *mandatory* quality rating levels which a product must reach or be rejected, regardless of how good it is otherwise. Other characteristics might be *desirable* but not essential. For these a user satisfaction rating could be allocated in the range, say, 0–5. This could be based on having an objective measurement of some function and then relating different measurement values to different levels of user satisfaction – see Table 13.2.

Along with the rating for satisfaction, a rating in the range 1–5, say, could be assigned to reflect how important each quality characteristic was. The scores for each quality could be given due weight by multiplying it by its importance weighting. These weighted scores can then be summed to obtain an overall score for the product. The scores for various products are then put in the order of preference. For example, two products might be compared as to usability, efficiency and maintainability. The importance of each of these qualities might be rated as 3, 4 and 2, respectively, out of a possible maximum of 5. Quality tests might result in the situation shown in Table 13.3.

Product quality	Importance rating (a)	Product A		Product B	
		Quality score (b)	Weighted score ($a \times b$)	Quality score (c)	Weighted score ($a \times c$)
Usability	3	1	3	3	9
Efficiency	4	2	8	2	8
Maintainability	2	3	6	1	2
Overall			17		19

TABLE 13.3 Weighted quality scores

Finally, a quality assessment can be made on behalf of a user community as a whole. For example, a professional body might assess software tools that support the working practices of its members. Unlike the selection by an individual user/purchaser, this is an attempt to produce an objective assessment of the software independently of a particular user environment. It is clear that the result of such an exercise would vary considerably depending on the weightings given to each software characteristic, and different users could have different requirements. Caution would be needed here.

13.6 Product versus process quality management

The measurements described above relate to *products*. With a product-based approach to planning and control, as advocated by the PRINCE2 project management method, this focus on products is convenient. However, we saw that it is often easier to measure these product qualities in a completed computer application rather than during its development. Trying to use the attributes of intermediate products created at earlier stages to predict the quality of the final application is difficult. An alternative approach is to scrutinize the quality of the *processes* used to develop software product.

> Note that Extreme Programming advocates suggest that the extra effort needed to amend software at later stages can be exaggerated and is, in any case, often justified as adding value to the software.

The system development process comprises a number of activities linked so that the output from one activity is the input to the next (Figure 13.2). Errors can enter the process at any stage. They can be caused either by defects in a process, as when software developers make mistakes in the logic of their software, or by information not passing clearly and accurately between development stages.

Errors not removed at early stages become more expensive to correct at later stages. Each development step that passes before the error is found increases the amount of rework needed. An error in the specification found in testing will mean rework at all the stages between specification and testing. Each successive step of development is also more detailed and less able to absorb change.

Errors should therefore be eradicated by careful examination of the deliverables of each step before they are passed on. One way of doing this is by having the following *process requirements* for each step.

■ *Entry requirements*, which have to be in place before an activity can start. An example would be that a comprehensive set of test data and expected results be prepared and approved before program testing can commence.

> These requirements may be laid out in installation standards, or a *Software Quality Plan* may be drawn up for the specific project if it is a major one.

■ *Implementation requirements*, which define how the process is to be conducted. In the testing phase, for example, it could be laid down that whenever an error is found and corrected, all test runs must be repeated, even those that have previously been found to run correctly.

■ *Exit requirements*, which have to be fulfilled before an activity is deemed to have been completed. For example, for the testing phase to be recognized as being completed, all tests will have to have been run successfully with no outstanding errors.

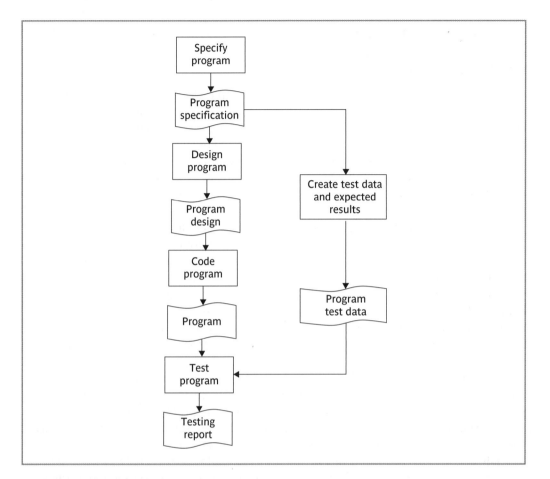

FIGURE 13.2 An example of the sequence of processes and deliverables

---

EXERCISE 13.4

In what cases might the entry conditions for one activity be different from the exit conditions for another activity that immediately precedes it?

EXERCISE 13.5

What might be the entry and exit requirements for the process *code program* shown in Figure 13.2?

13.7 Quality management systems

BS EN ISO 9001:2000

At IOE, a decision might be made to use an outside contractor to produce the annual maintenance contracts subsystem. A natural concern would be the standard of the contractor's deliverables. *Quality control* would involve the rigorous testing of all the software produced by the contractor, insisting on rework where defects are found. This would be very time-consuming. An alternative approach would focus on *quality assurance*. In this case IOE would check that the contractors themselves were carrying out effective quality control. A key element of this would be ensuring that the contractor had the right quality management system in place.

Various national and international standards bodies, including the British Standards Institution (BSI), have engaged in the creation of standards for quality management systems. The British standard is now called BS EN ISO 9001:2000, which is identical to the international standard, ISO 9001:2000. Standards such as the ISO 9000 series try to ensure that a monitoring and control system to check quality is in place. They are concerned with the certification of the development process, not of the end-product as in the case of crash helmets and electrical appliances with their familiar CE marks. Standards in the ISO 9000 series relate to quality systems in general and not just those in software development.

ISO 9000 describes the fundamental features of a quality management system (QMS) and its terminology. ISO 9001 describes how a QMS can be applied to the creation of products and the provision of services. ISO 9004 applies to process improvement.

There has been some controversy over the value of these standards. Stephen Halliday, writing in *The Observer*, had misgivings that these standards are taken by many customers to imply that the final product is of a certified standard although, as Halliday says, '*It has nothing to do with the quality of the product going out of the gate. You set down your own specifications and just have to maintain them, however low they may be.*' Obtaining certification can be expensive and time-consuming which can put smaller, but still well-run, businesses at a disadvantage. Finally, there has been a concern that a preoccupation with certification might distract attention from the real problems of producing quality products. This would be another example of means–ends inversion, discussed in Chapter 4.

Putting aside these reservations, let us examine how the standard works. First, we identify those things to be the subject of quality requirements. We then put a system in place which checks that the requirements are being fulfilled and corrective action taken when necessary.

An overview of BS EN ISO 9001:2000 QMS requirements

Remember that these standards are designed for all

The standard is built on a foundation of the following principles:

- understanding the requirements of customers so that they can be met, or even exceeded;

kinds of production – not just software development.

■ leadership to provide the unity of purpose and direction needed to achieve quality objectives;

■ involvement of staff at all levels;

■ a focus on the individual processes which create intermediate or deliverable products and services;

■ a focus on the systems of interrelated processes that create delivered products and services;

■ continuous improvement of processes;

■ decision making based on factual evidence;

■ building mutually beneficial relationships with suppliers.

These principles are applied through cycles which involve the following activities:

1 determining the needs and expectations of the customer;

2 establishing a *quality policy*, that is, a framework which allows the organization's objectives in relation to quality to be defined;

3 design of the *processes* which will create the products (or deliver the services) which will have the qualities implied in the organization's quality objectives;

4 allocation of the responsibilities for meeting these requirements for each element of each process;

5 ensuring that resources are available to execute these processes properly;

6 design of methods for measuring the effectiveness and efficiency of each process in contributing to the organization's quality objectives;

7 gathering of measurements;

8 identification of any discrepancies between the actual measurements and the target values;

9 analysis and elimination of the causes of discrepancies.

The procedures above should be designed and executed so that there is continual improvement. They should, if carried out properly, lead to an effective QMS. More detailed ISO 9001 requirements include:

■ *Documentation* of objectives, procedures (in the form of a *quality manual*), plans, and records relating to the actual operation of processes. The documentation must be subject to a change control system that ensures that it is current. Essentially one needs to be able to demonstrate to an outsider that the QMS exists and is actually adhered to.

■ *Management responsibility* – the organization needs to show that the QMS and the processes that produce goods and services conforming to the quality objectives are actively and properly managed.

■ *Resources* – an organization must ensure that adequate resources, including appropriately trained staff and appropriate infrastructure, are applied to the processes.

■ *Production* should be characterized by:
   ● planning;
   ● determination and review of customer requirements;

- effective communications between the customer and supplier;
- design and development being subject to planning, control and review;
- requirements and other information used in design being adequately and clearly recorded;
- design outcomes being verified, validated and documented in a way that provides sufficient information for those who have to use the designs;
- changes to the designs should be properly controlled;
- adequate measures to specify and evaluate the quality of purchased components;
- production of goods and the provision of services should be under controlled conditions to ensure adequate provision of information, work instruction, equipment, measurement devices, and post-delivery activities;
- measurement – to demonstrate that products conform to standards, and the QMS is effective, and to improve the effectiveness of processes that create products or services.

EXERCISE 13.6

One of the processes involved in developing software is system testing and subsequent modification to the application in the light of errors found. If a software development organization were to attempt to conform to BS EN ISO 9001:2000, how might this affect system testing?

EXERCISE 13.7

Bearing in mind the criticisms of BS EN ISO 9001 that have been mentioned, what precautionary steps could a project manager take where some work for which quality is important is to be contracted out to an organization which has BS EN ISO 9001 accreditation?

13.8 Process capability models

See H. S. Watts (1989) *Managing the Software Process*, Addison-Wesley, New York.

Rather than just checking that a system exists to detect faults, we might wish to check that a supplier uses software development methods and tools likely to produce good quality software. A customer might feel more confident, for instance, if they knew that the software supplier was using structured methods. In the United States, a number of influential *capability maturity models* (CMM) have been developed at the Software Engineering Institute (SEI), a part of Carnegie-Mellon University, of which one, SW-CMM, relates specifically to software development. The SEI originally developed CMM for the US Department of Defense to allow them to assess the capability of contractors from whom they bought software. Recently a new version of CMM, CMM Integration or CMMI, was introduced to bring together models produced for different environments into a single integrated framework. These models place organizations at one of five levels of process maturity which indicate the sophistication and quality of their production practices. These levels are defined as follows.

- *Level 1: Initial* The procedures followed tend to be haphazard. Some projects may be successful, but this tends to be because of the skills of particular individuals, including project managers. There is no level 0 and so any organization would be at this level by default.

- *Level 2: Managed* Organizations at this level will have basic project management procedures in place. However, the way individual tasks are carried out will depend largely on the person doing it.

- *Level 3: Defined* The organization has defined the way that each task in the software development life cycle should be done.

- *Level 4: Quantitatively managed* The products and processes involved in software development are subject to measurement and control.

- *Level 5: Optimizing* Improvement in procedures can be designed and implemented using the data gathered from the measurement process.

For more detail, look at the SEI website, www.cmu.edu/sei

For each of the levels, apart from the default level 1, *key process areas* (KPAs) have been identified as distinguishing the current level from the lower ones. These are listed in Table 13.4.

The assessment is done by a team of assessors coming into the organization and interviewing key staff about their practices, using a standard questionnaire to capture the information. A key objective is not just to assess, but to recommend specific actions to bring the organization up to a higher level.

Level	Key process areas
1. Initial	Not applicable
2. Managed	Requirements management, project planning and monitoring and control, supplier agreement management, measurement and analysis, process and product quality assurance, configuration management
3. Defined	Requirements development, technical solution, product integration, verification, validation, organizational process focus and definition, training, integrated project management, risk management, integrated teaming, integrated supplier management, decision analysis and resolution, organizational environment for integration
4. Quantitatively managed	Organizational process performance, quantitative project management
5. Optimizing	Organizational innovation and deployment, causal analysis and resolution

TABLE 13.4 CMMI key process areas

ISO 15504 Process assessment

ISO/IEC 15504 is a standard for process assessment that shares many concepts with CMMI. The two standards should be compatible. Like CMMI the standard is designed to provide guidance on the assessment of software development processes. To do this there must be some benchmark or *process reference model* which represents the ideal development life cycle against which the actual processes can be compared. Various process reference models could be used but the default is the one described in ISO 12207, which has been briefly discussed in Chapter 1 and which describes the main processes – such as requirements analysis and architectural design – in the classic software development life cycle.

Processes are assessed on the basis of nine process attributes – see Table 13.5.

Level	Attribute	Comments
0. Incomplete		The process is not implemented or is unsuccessful
1. Performed process	1.1 Process performance	The process produces its defined outcomes
2. Managed process	2.1 Performance management	The process is properly planned and monitored
	2.2 Work product management	Work products are properly defined and reviewed to ensure they meet requirements
3. Established process	3.1 Process definition	The processes to be carried out are carefully defined
	3.2 Process deployment	The processes defined above are properly executed by properly trained staff
4. Predictable process	4.1 Process measurement	Quantitatively measurable targets are set for each sub-process and data collected to monitor performance
	4.2 Process control	On the basis of the data collected by 4.1 corrective action is taken if there is unacceptable variation from the targets
5. Optimizing	5.1 Process innovation	As a result of the data collected by 4.1, opportunities for improving processes are identified
	5.2 Process optimization	The opportunities for process improvement are properly evaluated and where appropriate are effectively implemented

TABLE 13.5 ISO 15504 framework for process capability

When assessors are judging the degree to which a process attribute is being fulfilled they allocate one of the following scores:

Level	Interpretation
N – not achieved	0 to 15% achievement
P – partially achieved	15% to 50% achievement
L – largely achieved	50% to 85% achievement
F – fully achieved	85% achievement

In order to assess the process attribute of a process as being at a certain level of achievement, indicators have to be found that provide evidence for the assessment. For example, say the requirement analysis processes of an organization were being assessed. Assessors might wish to test whether the organization is at Level 3, which relates to there being an established process. The assessor might find a section in a procedures manual relating to the conduct of requirements. This could be evidence of the process being defined (3.1 in Table 13.5). They might also come across control documents which have been signed off as each step of the requirements analysis process has been completed. This would indicate that the defined process is actually deployed (3.2).

Implementing process improvement

The CMMI standard has now grown to over 500 pages. Without getting bogged down in detail, this section explores how the general approach might usefully be employed. To do this we will take a scenario from industry.

UVW is a company that builds machine tool equipment containing sophisticated control software. This equipment also produces log files of fault and other performance data in electronic format. UVW produces software that can read these log files and produce analysis reports and execute queries.

Both the control and analysis software is produced and maintained by the Software Engineering department. Within this department there are separate teams who deal with the software for different types of equipment. Lisa is a Software Team Leader in the Software Engineering department with a team of six systems designers reporting to her.

Her group is responsible for new control systems and the maintenance of existing systems for a particular product line. The dividing line between new development and maintenance is sometimes blurred as a new control system often makes use of existing software components which are modified to create the new software.

A separate Systems Testing Group test software for new control systems, but not fault correction and adaptive maintenance of released systems.

A project for a new control system is controlled by a Project Engineer with overall responsibility for managing both the hardware and software sides of the project. The Project Engineer is not primarily a software specialist and would make heavy demands on the Software Team Leader, such as Lisa, in an advisory capacity. Lisa may, as a Software Team Leader, work for a number of different Project Engineers in respect of different projects, but in the UVW organizational chart she is shown as reporting to the Head of Software Engineering.

A new control system starts with the Project Engineer writing a software requirement document which is reviewed by a Software Team Leader, who will then agree to the document, usually after some amendment. A copy of the requirements document will pass to the Systems Testing Group so that they can create system test cases and a systems test environment.

Lisa, if she were the designated Software Team Leader, would then write an Architecture Design document mapping the requirements to actual software components. These would be allocated to Work Packages carried out by individual members of Lisa's team.

UVW teams get the software quickly written and uploaded onto the newly developed hardware platform for initial debugging. The hardware and software engineers will then invariably have to alter the requirement and consequently the software as they find inconsistencies, faults and missing functions. The Systems Testing Group should be notified of these changes, but this can be patchy. Once the system seems to be satisfactory to the developers, it is released to the Systems Testing Group for final testing before shipping to customers.

Lisa's work problems mainly relate to late deliveries of software by her group because:

(i) the Head of Software Engineering and the Project Leaders may not liaise properly, leading to the over-commitment of resources to both new systems and maintenance jobs at the same time;

(ii) the initial testing of the prototype often leads to major new requirements being identified;

(iii) there is no proper control over change requests – the volume of these can sometimes increase the demand for software development well beyond that originally planned;

(iv) completion of system testing can be delayed because of the number of bug fixes.

We can see that there is plenty of scope for improvements. One problem is knowing where to start. However, approaches like that of CMMI can help us identify the order in which steps in improvement have to take place. Some steps need to build on the completion of others. An immediate step would be to introduce more formal planning and control. This would at least enable us to assess the size of the problems even if we are not yet able to solve them all. Given a software requirement, formal plans enable staff workloads to be distributed more carefully. The monitoring of plans would also allow managers to identify emerging problems with particular projects. Effective change control procedures would make managers more aware of how changes in the system's functionality can force project deadlines to be breached. These process developments would help an organization move from Level 1 to Level 2. Figure 13.3 illustrates how a project control system could be envisaged at the level of maturity.

The next step would be to define carefully the processes involved in each stage of the development lifecycle – see Figure 13.4. The steps of defining procedures for each development task and ensuring that they are actually carried out help to bring an organization up to Level 3.

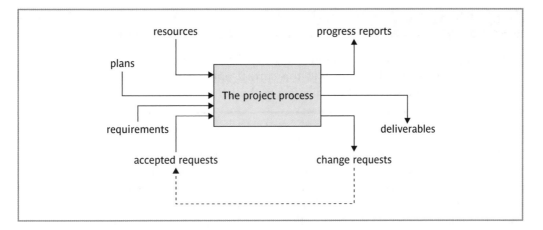

FIGURE 13.3 The project as a 'closed box'

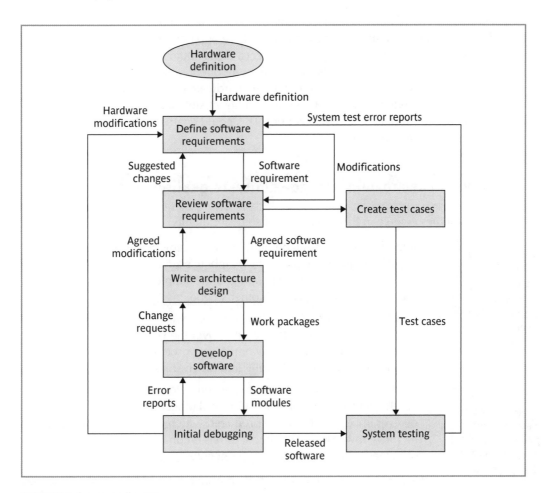

FIGURE 13.4 A process diagram

EXERCISE 13.8

The diagram in Figure 13.4 does not show the flows of information needed to indicate how managers could ensure that the correct amount of staff time is allocated to development activities. Amend the diagram to show these flows.

When more formalized processes exist, the behaviour of component processes can be monitored. We can see, for example, the numbers of change reports generated and system defects detected at the system testing phase. Apart from information about the products passing between processes, we can also collect effort information about each process itself. This enables effective remedial action to be taken speedily when problems are found. The development processes are now properly managed, bringing the organization up to Level 4.

Finally, at Level 5 of process management, the information collected is used to improve the process model itself. It might, for example, become apparent that the changes to software requirements are a major source of defects. Steps could therefore be taken to improve this process. For example, the hardware component of the system could be simulated using software tools. This could help the hardware engineers to produce more realistic designs and reduce changes. It might even be possible to build control software and test it against a simulated hardware system. This could enable earlier and cheaper resolution of technical problems.

13.9 Techniques to help enhance software quality

Three main themes emerge in this discussion of software quality:

> Gerald Weinberg (1998) *The Psychology of Computer Programming* Silver Anniversary Edition, Dorset House.

- *Increasing visibility* A landmark in the movement towards a focus on software quality was Gerald Weinberg's advocacy of 'egoless programming'. Weinberg encouraged the simple practice of programmers looking at each other's code.

- *Procedural structure* At first, programmers were left to get on with writing programs as best they could. Over the years there has been the growth of methodologies where every process in the software development cycle has carefully laid down steps.

> The creation of an early working model of a system may still be useful, as the creation of prototypes shows.

- *Checking intermediate stages* It is tempting to push forward quickly with the development of any engineered object until a 'working' model, however imperfect, has been produced which can then be 'debugged'. The move towards quality practices has emphasized checking the correctness of work at its earlier, conceptual, stages.

However, recently focus has shifted from relying solely on checking the products of intermediate stages and towards building an application as a number of smaller, relatively independent components developed quickly and tested at an early stage. This can reduce some of the problems, noted earlier, of attempting to predict the external quality of the software from early design documents. It does not preclude careful checking of the design of components.

We are now going to look at some specific techniques. The push towards more visibility has been dominated by the increasing use of *walk-throughs, inspections* and *reviews.* The movement towards a more procedural structure inevitably leads to discussion of structured programming techniques and to its later manifestation in the ideas of 'clean-room' software development.

The interest in the dramatic improvements made by the Japanese in product quality has led to much discussion of the quality techniques they have adopted, such as the use of *quality circles,* and these will be looked at briefly. Some of these ideas are variations on the theme of inspection and clean-room development.

Inspections

Inspections can be applied to documents produced at any development stage. For instance, test cases need to be reviewed – their production is usually not a high-profile task even though errors can get through to operational running because of their poor quality.

When a piece of work is completed, copies are distributed to co-workers who examine the work, noting defects. A meeting then discusses the work and a list of defects requiring rework is produced. The work to be examined could be, typically, a program listing that is free of compilation errors.

Our own experience of using this technique has been that:

> The main problem is maintaining the commitment of participants to a thorough examination of the work distributed to them after the novelty value of reviews has worn off a little.

- it is a very effective way of removing superficial errors;
- it motivates developers to produce better structured and self-explanatory software;
- it helps spread good programming practices as the participants discuss specific pieces of code;
- it can enhance team spirit.

> This is sometimes called 'peer review', where 'peers' are people who are equals.

The item will usually be reviewed by colleagues who work in the same area, so that software developers, for example, will have their work reviewed by fellow developers. To reduce the problems of communication between different stages, there may be representatives from the stages preceding and following the one which produced the work under review.

IBM made the review process more structured and formal, producing statistics to show its effectiveness. A Fagan inspection (named after the IBM employee who pioneered the technique) is led, not by the author of the work, but by a specially trained 'moderator'.

The general principles behind the Fagan method

See M. E. Fagan's (1976) article 'Design and code inspections to reduce errors in program development' *IBM Systems Journal* 15(3).

- Inspections are carried out on all major deliverables.
- All types of defect are noted – not just logic or function errors.
- Inspections can be carried out by colleagues at all levels except the very top.
- Inspections are carried out using a predefined set of steps.
- Inspection meetings do not last for more than two hours.

- The inspection is led by a *moderator* who has had specific training in the technique.
- The other participants have defined roles. For example, one person will act as a *recorder* and note all defects found, and another will act as *reader* and take the other participants through the document under inspection.
- Checklists are used to assist the fault-finding process.
- Material is inspected at an optimal rate of about 100 lines an hour.
- Statistics are maintained so that the effectiveness of the inspection process can be monitored.

EXERCISE 13.9

Compare and contrast the peer review process described above with pair programming which is advocated as part of extreme programming (XP).

Structured programming and clean-room software development

E. W. Dijkstra in 1968 wrote a letter to a learned computing journal which was entitled 'Go To Statement Considered Harmful'. This unfortunately led to the common idea that structured programming was simply about not using GO TOs.

In the late 1960s, software was seen to be getting more complex while the capacity of the human mind to hold detail remained limited. It was also realized that it was impossible to test any substantial piece of software completely given the huge number of possible input combinations. Testing, at best, could prove the presence of errors, not their absence. Thus Dijkstra and others suggested that the only way to reassure ourselves about the correctness of software was by examining the code.

The way to deal with complex systems, it was contended, was to break them down into components of a size the human mind could comprehend. For a large system there would be a hierarchy of components and sub-components. For this decomposition to work properly, each component would have to be self-contained, with only one entry and exit point.

The ideas of structured programming have been further developed into the ideas of clean-room software development by people such as the late Harlan Mills of IBM.

With this type of development there are three separate teams:

Usage profiles reflect the need to assess *quality in use* as discussed earlier in relation to ISO 9126. They will be further discussed in the Section 13.10 on testing below.

- *a specification team*, which obtains the user requirements and also a *usage profile* estimating the volume of use for each feature in the system;
- *a development team*, which develops the code but which does no machine testing of the program code produced;
- *a certification team*, which carries out testing.

Any system is produced in increments – recall Section 4.10 – each of which should be capable of actual operation by the end-user. The development team does no debugging; instead, all software has to be verified by them using mathematical techniques. The argument is that software which is constructed by throwing up a crude program, which then has test data thrown at it and a series of hit-and-miss amendments made to it until it works, is bound to be unreliable.

The certification team carry out the testing, which is continued until a statistical model shows that the failure intensity has been reduced to an acceptable level.

Formal methods

Clean-room development, mentioned above, uses mathematical verification techniques. These techniques use unambiguous, mathematically based, specification languages of which Z and VDM are examples. They are used to define *preconditions* and *postconditions* for each procedure. Preconditions define the allowable states, before processing, of the data items upon which a procedure is to work. The postconditions define the state of those data items after processing. The mathematical notation should ensure that such a specification is precise and unambiguous. It should also be possible to prove mathematically (in much the same way that at school you learnt to prove Pythagoras' theorem) that a particular algorithm will work on the data defined by the preconditions in such a way as to produce the postconditions. Despite the claims of the effectiveness of the use of a formal notation to define software specifications for many years now, it is rarely used in mainstream software development. This is despite it being quite widely being taught in universities. A newer development that may meet with more success is the development of Object Constraint Language (OCL). It adds precise, unambiguous, detail to the UML models, for example about the ranges of values that would be valid for a named attribute. It uses an unambiguous, but non-mathematical, notation which developers who familiar with Java-like programming languages should grasp relatively easily.

Software quality circles

Much interest has been shown in Japanese software quality practices. The aim of the 'Japanese' approach is to examine and modify the activities in the development process in order to reduce the number of errors that they have in their end-products. Testing and Fagan inspections can assist the removal of errors – but the same types of error could occur repeatedly in successive products created by a faculty process. By uncovering the source of errors, this repetition can be eliminated.

Staff are involved in the identification of sources of errors through the formation of *quality circles*. These can be set up in all departments of an organization, including those producing software where they are known as software quality circles (SWQC).

A quality circle is a group of four to ten volunteers working in the same area who meet for, say, an hour a week to identify, analyse and solve their work-related problems. One of their number is the group leader and there could be an outsider, a *facilitator*, who can advise on procedural matters. In order to make the quality circle work effectively, training needs to be given.

Together the quality group select a pressing problem that affects their work. They identify what they think are the causes of the problem and decide on a course of action to remove these causes. Often, because of resource or possible organizational constraints, they will have to present their ideas to management to obtain approval before implementing the process improvement.

EXERCISE 13.10

What are the important differences between a quality circle and a review group?

Associated with quality circles is the compilation of *most probable error lists*. For example, at IOE, Amanda might find that the annual maintenance contracts project is being delayed because of errors in the requirements specifications. The project team could be assembled and spend some time producing a list of the most common types of error that occur in requirements specifications. This is then used to identify measures which can reduce the occurrence of each type of error. They might suggest, for instance, that test cases be produced at the same time as the requirements specification and that these test cases should be dry run at an inspection. The result is a checklist for use when conducting inspections of requirement specifications.

Lessons learnt reports

Another way by which an organization can improve its performance is by reflecting on the performance of a project at its immediate end when the experience is still fresh. This reflection may identify lessons to be applied to future projects. Project managers are required to write a *Lessons Learnt* report at the end of the project. This should be distinguished from a *Post Implementation Review* (PIR). A PIR takes place after a significant period of operation of the new system, and focuses on the effectiveness of the new system, rather than the original project process. The PIR is often produced by someone who was not involved in the original project, in order to ensure neutrality. An outcome of the PIR will often be changes to enhance the effectiveness of the installed system.

The Lessons Learnt report, on the other hand, is written by the project manager as soon as possible after the completion of the project. This urgency is because the project team is often dispersed to new work soon after the finish of the project. One problem that is frequently voiced is that there is often very little follow-up on the recommendations of such reports, as there is often no body within the organization with the responsibility and authority to do so.

13.10 Testing

The final judgement of the quality of a software application is whether it actually works correctly when executed. This section looks at aspects of the planning and management of testing. A major headache with testing is estimating how much testing remains at any point. This estimate of the work still to be done depends on an unknown, the number of bugs left in the code. We will briefly discuss how we can deal with this problem.

In Chapter 4, the *V-process model* was introduced as an extension to the waterfall process model. Figure 13.5 gives a diagrammatic representation of this model. This stresses the necessity for validation activities that match the activities creating the products of the project.

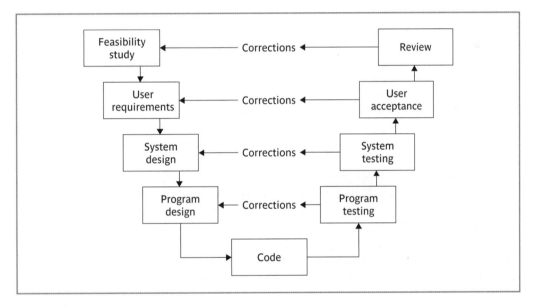

FIGURE 13.5 The V-process model

The V-process model can be seen as expanding the activity box 'testing' in the waterfall model. Each step has a matching validation process which can, where defects are found, cause a loop back to the corresponding development stage and a reworking of the following steps. Ideally this feeding back should occur only where a discrepancy has been found between what was specified by a particular activity and what was actually implemented in the next lower activity on the descent of the V loop. For example, the system designer might have written that a calculation be carried out in a certain way. A developer building code to meet this design might have misunderstood what was required. At system testing stage, the original designer would be responsible for checking that the software is doing what was specified and this would discover the coder's misreading of that document.

Using the V-process model as a framework, planning decisions can be made at the outset as to the types and amounts of testing to be done. An obvious example of this would be that if the software were acquired 'off-the-shelf', the program design and code stages would not be relevant and so program testing would not be needed. User requirements would still be produced so user acceptance tests would still be valid.

Black box and *glass box* testing can be distinguished. Acceptance testing is an example of black box testing where the testers would not know about the internal software structure. They would simply input typical business transactions and see if the software responds in a way compatible with the user requirements. With glass box testing the tester is aware of the internal structure and would as a consequence be able to create test cases that check particular paths through the code. The initial program testing could be like this. Another distinction is between verification and validation. Verification focuses on the 'truth' or correctness of the application, that is, the extent to which it follows its specification. Validation focuses more on 'value' – does it do the job for which it was intended? Program testing may find a perfect match between the code and its specification. Even so, acceptance testing might find that a 'correct' program is useless because of an incorrect interpretation of the requirements by the designer who drafted the specification.

Another question to be settled at the planning stage is who carries out testing. Many organizations have separate system testing groups providing an independent assessment of the correctness of software before its release. In other organizations, staff are allocated to a purely testing role but work alongside the developers rather than in a separate group. While an independent testing group can provide a final quality check, it has been argued that developers may take less care in their work if they know of the existence of this safety net.

Having identified the types of testing to be done and who is to do it, the next stage is to draft a *test plan*. Part of this will describe how the *testing environment* will be set up. This would be of particular concern where the new software is to control some equipment. In these cases a hardware configuration would need to be set up. *Test cases* would need to be drafted, based on documentation of the functionality produced during the development cycle. The document used as the basis for testing would depend on the type of testing being done. For system testing it could be the system specification.

John D. Musa and A. Frank Ackerman (1989) 'Quantifying software validation: when to stop testing' *IEEE Software* May 19–27.

In addition to a description of the functionality a *usage profile* might also be taken into account. Research has established that errors in the most heavily used components tend to be the first to cause failures. John Musa, when he worked at AT&T Bell Laboratories, showed how this could be exploited to reduce operational failure rates by assessing the amount of use each part of the software application was likely to have. The more heavily used components could then be subjected to more rigorous testing.

For each transaction a set of sample inputs and the outputs that would be expected are drafted. If an error survives through to operational running it means that the software developers have made a mistake in some part of the code. It also means that the testers have failed to devise a test case that would have detected that error. Thus test cases are themselves a valuable asset that should be reviewed with the same level of scrutiny applied to the software code. The value of this asset can be further enhanced by encoding the test inputs into a script to be executed by an automatic testing tool that simulates a user entering data at a workstation. The simulator can also check the actual outputs against those recorded as expected.

When the test cases are run, the tester may raise *issues*, that is, reports of discrepancies between the expected and what was found. A means of formally recording these issues and their subsequent history is needed. A review body adjudicates on the issues. The outcome of this scrutiny would be one of the following:

- The issue is dismissed on the grounds that there has been a misunderstanding of a requirement by the tester.

- The issue is identified as a fault which the developers need to correct – where development is being done by contractors then they would be expected to cover the cost of the correction.

- It is recognized that the software is behaving as specified, but the requirement originally agreed is in fact incorrect – remedying this means adding a new requirement and a contractor could expect to receive payment for the additional work.

- The issue is identified as a fault but is treated as an *off-specification* – it is decided that the application can be made operational with the error still in place.

When corrections are made, tests will need to be repeated. This is where the additional effort in creating automated test scripts can pay off. A danger is that a change introduced to correct an error could actually introduce errors in processes that were previously running correctly. When code changes are made, all tests previously carried out should be rerun. This is known as *regression testing*.

Earlier, we noted the problem of estimating the number of errors left in an application under test. At the start of testing, there is one relatively straightforward way of estimating the number of errors in code. Simply put, bigger programs are likely to have more errors. If you have collected error data from past projects, you can arrive at the historic number of errors per 1000 lines of code. This can then be used to arrive at a reasonable estimate of the number of the errors likely to be found in a new system development of a known size.

This estimate could be confirmed during the actual testing. One suggestion is that known errors can be seeded in the software. This seeding could be done by having one or more people doing a desk-check of code, but then leaving any errors found in the code. Say 10 such errors are found. Then suppose that after the first set of tests 30 errors were found of which six were known errors, that is 60% of the seeded errors. This suggests that around 40% of the errors have still be to detected, that is 20 errors (of which four are already known). The method of calculating an estimate of the errors in the software is

(total errors found)/(seeded errors found) × (total number of seeded errors)

You may be thinking that deliberately putting (or leaving) known errors in software is a bit sneaky. It might be more acceptable to use a slightly different approach originally suggested by Tom Gilb. Two different reviewers, or groups of reviewers, are asked to inspect or test the same code. They must be completely independent of one another. Three counts are collected:

Tom Gilb (1977)
Software Metrics
Winthrop Publishers,
Cambridge, MA.

- n1, the number of valid errors found by A
- n2, the number of valid errors found by B
- n12, the number of cases where the same error is found by both A and B.

The smaller the proportion of errors found by both A and B compared to those found by only one reviewer, the larger the total number of errors likely to be in the software. An estimate of the total number of errors (n) can be calculated by the formula:

$$n = (n1 \times n2)/n12$$

For example, A finds 30 errors and B finds 20 errors of which 15 are common to both A and B. The estimated total number of errors would be:

$$(30 \times 20)/15 = 40$$

13.11 Quality plans

Some organizations produce *quality plans* for each project. These show how the standard quality procedures and standards laid down in an organization's *quality manual* will actually be applied to the project. If an approach to planning such as Step Wise has been followed, quality-related activities and requirements will have been identified by the main planning process with no need for a separate quality plan. However, where software is being produced for an external client, the client's quality assurance staff might require that a quality plan be produced to ensure the quality of the delivered products. A quality plan can be seen as a checklist that all quality issues have been dealt with by the planning process. Thus, most of the content will be references to other documents.

A quality plan might have entries for:

This contents list is based on a draft IEEE standard for software quality assurance plans.

- purpose – scope of plan;
- list of references to other documents;
- management arrangements, including organization, tasks and responsibilities;
- documentation to be produced;
- standards, practices and conventions;
- reviews and audits;
- testing;
- problem reporting and corrective action;
- tools, techniques and methodologies;
- code, media and supplier control;
- records collection, maintenance and retention;
- training;
- risk management – the methods of risk management that are to be used.

13.12 Conclusion

Important points to remember about software quality include the following.

- Quality by itself is a vague concept and practical quality requirements have to be carefully defined.
- There have to be practical ways of testing for the relative presence or absence of quality.
- Most of the qualities that are apparent to the users of software can only be tested for when the system is completed.
- Therefore ways are needed of checking during development what the quality of the final system is likely to be.
- Some quality-enhancing techniques concentrate on testing the products of the development process, while others try to evaluate the quality of the development processes used.

13.13 Further exercises

1 An organization is contemplating the purchase of a project planning software tool, such as MS Project, and has decided to draw up quality specifications for the package. The features that they are particularly concerned with are:
- setting up details of new projects;
- allocating resources to project tasks, taking account of the need for resource smoothing;
- updating the project details with information about actual tasks completed;
- the effective presentation of plans.

Draw up quality specifications in respect of the qualities of:
- usability
- reliability
- recoverability.

2 The following is an excerpt from a report generated from a help-desk logging system.

Module	Date fault reported	Fault corrected	Effort (hours)
AA247	1.4.2004	2.4.2004	5
AA247	10.4.2004	5.5.2004	4
AA247	12.4.2004	5.5.2004	3
AA247	6.5.2004	7.5.2004	2

Assess the maintainability of module AA247 from the point of view of:

- the user management;
- the developer management.

3 Discuss how meaningful the following measurements are.

(a) The number of error messages produced on the first compilation of a program.
(b) The average effort to implement changes requested by users to a system.
(c) The percentage of lines in program listings that are comments.
(d) The number of pages in a requirements document.

4 How might you measure the effectiveness of a user manual for a software package? Consider both the measurements that might be applicable and the procedures by which the measurements might be taken.

5 What might the entry, implementation and exit requirements be for the process *design program structure*?

6 Identify a task that you do as part of your everyday work. For that task identify entry, process and exit requirements.

7 What BS EN ISO 9001 requirements have a bearing on the need for an effective configuration management system?

Appendix A:
PRINCE2 – an overview

A.1 Introduction to PRINCE2

The OGC is the Office of Government Commerce, which has replaced the CCTA, the Central Computer and Telecommunications Agency.

PRINCE stands for 'PRojects IN Controlled Environments'.

Large organizations can have a number of software and other projects being executed at the same time. Some of these might use external suppliers of products and services. In such an environment it would be helpful if the procedures by which each project were run were standardized rather than having to be continually reinvented. However, each project will make different demands on management: some, for example, might be more technically challenging, might affect particularly critical areas of the business or might involve larger numbers of different types of users. Because the adoption of a management method is not cost-free, the degree of control that will be cost-effective will vary from project to project. Hence any standard approach should incorporate mechanisms to tailor management procedures and structures to suit localized needs. In the UK, the government has sponsored, through the OGC, a set of such procedures, called PRINCE, which has, after several years, been revised as PRINCE2.

The precursor to PRINCE was a project management method called PROMPT, which suffered from the defect that it was not flexible enough to deal adequately with all types of project. This was followed by the first version of PRINCE, which was designed primarily for an ICT development environment so that, for example, it was made to have a good fit with SSADM. It soon became apparent, however, that the method was applicable to projects outside the strictly ICT domain and PRINCE2 makes no specific references to ICT development.

It is now possible to take examinations in PRINCE2 and to be thus recognized as a PRINCE2 practitioner.

A.2 The components of PRINCE2

The method does not claim to cover all aspects of project management. It has the following components:

- organization;
- planning;
- controls;
- stages;
- management of risk;

- quality;
- configuration management;
- change control.

The following list provides a convenient structure that we will use to explain PRINCE2:

- techniques;
- organization;
- documentation;
- procedures.

This appendix will not explore the supplementary techniques where the PRINCE2 manual lays down some basic requirements. We do not describe these areas in detail since there is sufficient material elsewhere in this book. They include:

- risk management;
- quality management;
- configuration management;
- change control.

Below, we will outline the general approach to planning that PRINCE2 advocates. It will be noted that PRINCE2, compared, for example, to SSADM, is rather light in its description of techniques. It is stronger in its rules for the project management structures that should be adopted. In our view, its main focus is on the project as an information system. Project management information is identified and the procedures by which the various elements of this information are created, processed and used are described at some length. This project information is mainly associated with the delivery of *products*, in a controlled environment, resulting in benefits to the business.

A.3 PRINCE planning technique

The Step Wise approach was outlined in Chapter 3, while risk was discussed in Chapter 7.

Figure A.1 shows the stages in the planning process that are suggested by PRINCE2. The first of these – *Design a plan* – is essentially deciding what kind of information is to go into the plan, particularly at what level of detail the plan is to be drawn. The remaining steps are very similar to the Step Wise approach to planning that was outlined in Chapter 3, except that in the Step Wise approach the risk analysis was carried out immediately after the estimation of effort for each activity. This was because in our view risk identification follows on naturally from estimation: you work out how long you think it will take to do an activity and then you consider what factors could work to make that estimate incorrect. Also, the identification of risks can lead to new activities being introduced to avoid the risks occurring and this is conveniently done before the schedule is put together by allocating resources. However, the Step Wise approach is not necessarily at odds with PRINCE2 as PRINCE2 does emphasize the iterative nature of risk analysis.

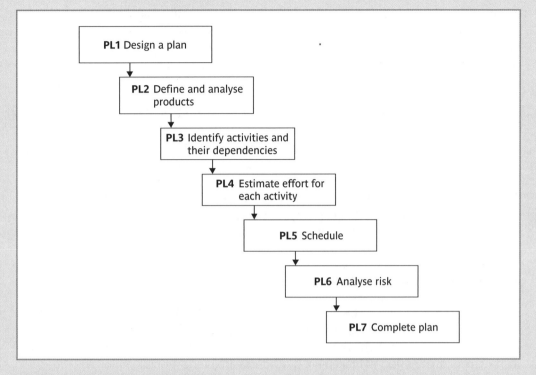

FIGURE A.1 PRINCE2 approach to planning

Like Step Wise, PRINCE2 is very product-based. In the second planning phase, PL2 in Figure A.1, all the business products, plus the management and quality documents needed to control their delivery, are identified.

This sequence of steps can be used in several places in the PRINCE2 procedural framework to produce a variety of different types of plan.

A.4 PRINCE2 project organization

PRINCE2 identifies roles rather than jobs. Depending on the circumstances, a role could, in fact, be carried out by more than one person, or a single person could assume more than one role.

PRINCE2 is based on the perception that the project will involve *users* of the products of the project, on the one hand, and *suppliers* of goods and services needed by the project on the other. While the users and suppliers could in fact belong to the same organization, for management and control purposes the two sides need to be carefully distinguished. Furthermore, on the customer side, two management roles exist. Any development project is carried out, not for its own sake, but to do something useful for the customer organization. The *Executive* role has the responsibility of ensuring that the project continues to meet these business requirements. A danger, for example, is that development costs might grow in such a way that they exceed any benefits of the completed project. The customer side will also, of course, contain the community who will actually use the completed system on a day-to-day basis. Although we have talked about the supplier and customer sides, it could also be argued that the suppliers who will provide the system and the users who will operate it need to cooperate to ensure that the operational system provides the benefits sought after by their customer, the 'Executive'.

PRINCE2 specifies that the three roles of *Executive*, *Supplier* and *User* are represented on a *Project Board* which has overall accountability for the success of the project and responsibility for the commitment of resources.

Note that we have followed the convention of indicating specific PRINCE2 terms by initial capital letters, Project Board, for example. All these terms are as in the PRINCE2 manual, which has Crown copyright.

The senior staff carrying out the respective roles will be responsible officers within their respective organizations and the oversight of the project will probably be only one of many responsibilities. Hence, the task of managing the project on a day-to-day basis will be delegated by the Project Board to a *Project Manager*. On a large project it could be necessary for the Project Manager to delegate the managing of certain aspects of the project to specialist *Team Managers*.

Conscientious and motivated staff will inevitably focus on meeting user requirements and give a lower priority to dealing with what they might see as project management 'red tape'. It could even be that the Project Manager with the daily burden of pushing the project forward might not be immune to this. However, this 'red tape' is needed to ensure that the project remains under control and that it continues to meet its business justification. Thus, some assurance is needed, independent of project management, that project management procedures are being properly followed. The ultimate responsibility for this assurance resides with the Project Board, but in practice detailed project assurance could be carried out by staff, independent of the team executing the project, who report to the Project Board members. Different types of project assurance specialists might be employed to ensure the business justification of the project is maintained, that the users' needs are being met and that the necessary technical requirements are being adhered to by the suppliers.

Project support

The Project Board, Project Manager, Team Leaders and project assurance and support staff are known collectively in PRINCE2 as the Project Management Team.

The Project Manager can require day-to-day support with the administration of the project. This might involve such tasks as processing time sheets or updating a computer-based project management tool such as Microsoft Project. It could be convenient for one group within an organization to supply this support to a number of projects. A key member of the project support team will be the Configuration Librarian, who will keep track of the latest versions of the products and documents generated by the project.

A.5 Project Stages

It is sensible to divide large projects into more manageable segments. PRINCE2 caters for this through the idea of *Stages*. These are subsets of the project activities and are managed as a sequence of individual units. Normally, the Project Manager will, at any one time, be authorized by the Project Board to execute only the current Stage. The Project Manager will be able to start the next Stage only when the Project Board has met to give its approval for the plans for that Stage. The end of a Stage signals a decision point when the Project Board will review the progress to date and reassure itself that the project is still viable from a business point of view – in particular, that the expected benefits are still likely to justify the projected costs.

The typical system development life cycle contains a number of phases, where each phase makes use of different specialist techniques. These technical phases might be the typical steps outlined in Chapter 1: requirements analysis and specification, logical design, physical design, build, testing and installation. It is convenient in many cases for the management Stages specified by PRINCE2 to be mapped onto these technical phases, but the PRINCE2 standards are at pains to stress that it is not always convenient to do this – for instance the project might be more manageable if more than one technical phase were combined to create a Stage.

As will be explained in more detail in Section A.8 on 'Starting a project', at the beginning of a project a *Project Plan* will be created which will give the envisaged Stages. Only the first of these Stages will need to have a detailed *Stage Plan* immediately available. For the later stages, it is better to complete the detailed Stage Plan just a little while before the Stage is due to start. In that way, the Stage Plan can take account of a more complete picture of the project: at the beginning of the project, for example, it would be impossible to plan the system building stage in detail when the system requirement has not yet been clearly defined.

Once the Stage has been authorized and its execution has been embarked upon, the Project Board should not need to meet as long as any deviations from planned time and cost are only minor and are within laid-down project tolerances. It should be sufficient for members of the Project Board to receive regular reports from the Project Manager. If these tolerances are likely to be exceeded, then the Project Manager has a responsibility to produce an Exception Report for the Project Board. If the problems are serious enough to undermine the Stage Plan, then the Project Manager might be required to produce a modified Stage Plan, or more properly an Exception Plan, which the Project Board will need to approve formally. In extreme circumstances the Project Board might at this point decide to terminate the project prematurely.

A.6 Project procedures

Table A.1 lists the main project management processes for which PRINCE2 lays down procedures to deal with the various events that the Project Management Team might encounter.

The levels of staff who are involved with each of the groups of project management processes in Table A.1 are indicated in Figure A.2. The general planning process PL is not shown as this can take place at various times and places for different reasons. For example, it could take place during the 'Initiating a project' (IP) process to create the Project Plan, or during 'Managing stage boundaries' (SB) when a Stage Plan for the next Stage is constructed or when an Exception Plan needs to be produced.

PRINCE ID	Major processes
SU	Starting up a project
IP	Initiating a project
DP	Directing a project
CS	Controlling a stage
MP	Managing product delivery
SB	Managing stage boundaries
CP	Closing a project
PL	Planning

TABLE A.1 Major PRINCE2 processes

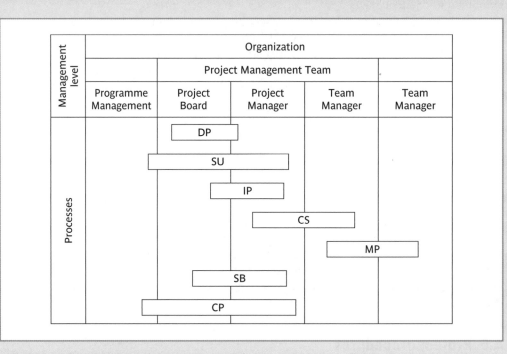

FIGURE A.2 Project management roles (see Table A.1 for key)

A.7 Directing a project

The main points where the Project Board have to be active are covered by the DP processes – *Directing a project*. These points are:

- authorizing initiation – agreeing to the start of detailed planning of a project;
- authorizing a project – agreeing, after the planning has been completed, that the project can go ahead;

- authorizing a Stage or Exception Plan;
- giving ad hoc direction;
- closing a project.

A.8 Starting up a project

With the first version of PRINCE there were sometimes difficulties knowing at which point the project had really started. The separate processes of Start Up and Initiation could avoid this.

As we noted in Chapter 2, the decision to undertake a project does not spring out of thin air. Where a customer organization has a coherent strategy, it is likely that there will be a layer of *programme management* where the 'programme' is a group of projects that are coordinated to meet an integrated set of business requirements. The current project could therefore be triggered by the programme managers. In any case, PRINCE2 envisages that the project cycle will be sparked by some kind of *Project Mandate*, which will identify the customer and the general subject of the project. The PRINCE2 Start Up process is essentially concerned with getting into a position where detailed planning of the proposed project can begin.

As a starting point, this will need the recruitment of people to the various roles in the Project Management Team. The Project Mandate, which could be a rather insubstantial or imprecise document, might need to be refined and expanded into a *Project Brief*, which defines the objectives of the project. Based on this, the general technical approach to be adopted to meet these objectives needs to be decided upon and documented in the *Project Approach*. The kinds of issue raised in Chapter 4 will need to be considered at this point. This could involve decisions about whether an off-the-shelf package can be bought or whether a bespoke package is required, and, if so, whether its development is to be carried out 'in-house' or by external contractors. All these activities lead to the formulation of a general plan of how the detailed planning is to be carried out.

A.9 Initiating the project

Having completed the Start Up Process, the Project Board can now decide that there are sufficient grounds to go on to more detailed planning. This begins with the consideration of a *Project Quality Plan*. Despite what some books suggest, quality levels do have cost implications. Different projects will have different quality requirements – faults in a college timetabling system are annoying but do not have the same consequences as the failure of a system controlling the flight of a passenger aeroplane. These quality requirements will have an effect on the activities that will have to be scheduled and the resources that will have to be found. This Project Quality Plan, plus the information in the Project Brief and Project Approach documents, now allow a *Project Plan* to be drafted. This will contain:

- the major products to be created;
- the main activities to be undertaken;
- project risks and their counter-measures;
- effort requirements;

- timescales;
- key decision points.

We now have a much clearer idea of the overall cost of the project than we did at the time of the original Project Mandate. The business case can now be reviewed to see whether the proposed project is still viable. The reliability of the business case will depend on the validity of the assumptions upon which it is based. The possibility that particular assumptions are incorrect is assessed and documented in a *Risk Log*. The final parts of project initiation are specifying how the project is to be controlled in terms of reporting and decision-making responsibilities and the setting up of project files.

The culmination of Initiating a Project is the putting together of a *Project Initiation Document*, which brings together the documentation generated by the Start Up and Initiation processes. If the Project Board can approve this document then the first proper Stage of the project can start.

A.10 Controlling a Stage

Once a Stage has been initiated, the Project Manager should be able to get on with the direction of the Stage without having to organize regular formal meetings with the Project Board.

Table A.2 shows the actions that the Project Manager might have to carry out while the Stage is being executed and for which the originators of PRINCE2 have laid down procedural guidelines.

The Project Manager will have to authorize *Work Packages* (CS1), tasks that have to be carried out to create the products that should be the desired outcome of the project, such as software modules. On a substantial project, these authorizations will be passed not directly to the people who will do the work but to Team Managers.

Once the work has been authorized, the Project Manager will then need to find out how that work is progressing (CS2). This involves the kinds of task touched on in Chapter 9

PRINCE ID	Controlling Stages (CS) processes
CS1	Authorize Work Package
CS2	Assess progress
CS3	Capture Project Issues
CS4	Examine Project Issues
CS5	Review Stage status
CS6	Report highlights
CS7	Take corrective action
CS8	Escalate project issue
CS9	Receive completed Work Package

TABLE A.2 PRINCE2 processes when controlling a Stage

on project control. For instance, progress information will have to be gathered to see if tasks are likely to be completed on time; feedback on recent quality-checking activities will also be needed to ensure that apparent progress is not being made by releasing products before they are really ready. Eventually, for each Work Package the Project Manager will be informed that the work can be signed-off as completed (CS9). This progress data will be used to add actual completion dates to the details of planned activities that have been recorded in the Stage Plan.

A major part of a Project Manager's job during the execution of a Stage is bound to be 'fire-fighting' – dealing with the unexpected problems that are certain to occur. PRINCE2 lays down a procedure (CS3 *Capturing Project Issues*) to ensure that these 'issues' are properly recorded. The 'issues' could be changes to requirements, changes to the environment such as new legal obligations, and other problems that might or might not have been foreseen by the risk analysis for the project. All these issues should be logged. Another PRINCE2 procedure (CS4) is designed to ensure that all these issues are dealt with in an effective way. Outcomes can include a *Request for Change* to modify the user requirement or an *Off-Specification*, which records known and accepted errors and omissions in the product to be delivered.

The process of assessing progress (CS2) requires the Project Manager to look at the individual strands of work going on in his or her area of responsibility. PRINCE2 envisages a separate but related activity where having gathered this progress information and also any outstanding Project Issues, the Project Manager checks the health of the Stage as a whole (CS5). In particular, the Project Manager will want to be reassured that the project as a whole is still progressing within its *tolerances*, the boundaries within which the Project Manager is allowed to manoeuvre without having to obtain clearance from the Project Board. One outcome of CS5 could be the carrying out of corrective action (CS7) that might include authorizing new Work Packages to deal with specific problems. Where work is progressing so that Project Issues are being kept under control and the Stage is within tolerances, then it will be enough to communicate progress to the Project Board by means of *Highlight reports* (CS6). In some cases the Project Manager might feel unable to progress with a matter without guidance from higher management and will request advice. Where activities have taken longer than planned or have taken up more resources than were budgeted so that the Project Manager is in danger of having to act outside the tolerances laid down in the Stage Plan, the Project Manager might have to 'escalate' a particular issue (CS8) by drafting an *Exception Report* to be considered by the Project Board. This should not only explain why the Stage has gone adrift from its original plan, but also detail possible options for recovering the situation and make a specific recommendation to the Project Board.

A.11 Managing product delivery

The processes described in 'Controlling a Stage' all assume that the work needed to complete a Stage is under the direct control of the Project Manager. Of course, it could be the case that, as described in Chapter 10 on contract management, some of the work is to be carried out by third party suppliers, that is, by an external organization that is not the primary supplier in direct contact with the customer, but a sub-contractor who carries out

PRINCE ID	Managing product delivery (MP) processes
MP1	Accept Work Package
MP2	Execute Work Package
MP3	Deliver Work Package

TABLE A.3 PRINCE2 processes when managing product delivery

work on behalf of the supplier. These sub-contractors might not be using PRINCE2. Hence the situation could need careful handling and PRINCE2 provides some guidelines to help this – see Table A.3.

Once the Project Manager has authorized a Work Package (CS1), as described in the 'Controlling a Stage' section, the person who is to be responsible for the execution of the Work Package needs to check the requirements of the Work Package to ensure that there is common understanding on what exactly is to be delivered, the constraints that might apply to the work and the requirements of any interfaces with other work (MP1). The Team Manager who is accepting the work must be confident that the targets can be realistically achieved. This could involve working out a *Team Plan* detailing how the work is to be done.

Once the work has been accepted, work can start on executing the Work Package (MP2). As this could be done by a sub-contractor who does not use PRINCE2, PRINCE2 lays down the general requirement that the responsible Team Manager should have the information ready to hand to report back to the Project Manager on progress as laid down in the authorized Work Package document. Finally, the need to define and agree the process by which completed Work Packages are handed over to the Project Manager is identified (MP3).

A.12 Managing Stage boundaries

The transition from one Stage to another will involve the processes shown in Table A.4.

A key PRINCE2 principle is to avoid too detailed planning at too early a stage. At the beginning of the project, for instance, the overall Project Plan is produced, but the more detailed Stage Plan is only produced for the first Stage. Towards the end of a Stage, the detailed plan for the next Stage can be mapped out as a clearer idea of the project requirements emerges (SB1). The creation of the Stage Plan for the next Stage could show up inadequacies in the overall Project Plan, which might need to be updated. For example, the design Stage of a project might reveal that the functionality of the system is greater than was foreseen when the first Project Plan was produced. More time might therefore be needed at the build Stage and this needs to be reflected in the Project Plan (SB2).

More time needed at build Stage will almost certainly mean that the date by which the project will be finally completed will be put back. This will lead to increasing development costs and the deferment of any income from the implemented system. At this point we need a process that checks that the project is still viable, that is, that the benefits of the delivered system will still outweigh the costs (SB3).

PRINCE ID	Managing Stage boundaries
SB1	Planning a Stage
SB2	Updating the Project Plan
SB3	Updating the project business case
SB4	Updating the Risk Log
SB5	Reporting a Stage End
SB6	Producing an Exception Report

TABLE A.4 PRINCE2 processes when managing Stage boundaries

The situation with regard to risks might also have changed and this too needs to be reviewed (SB4). For example, as the project moves from design to build, some risks will disappear – if users were heavily involved in a design phase based around prototyping, a risk such as the non-availability of users for prototype evaluation will no longer be applicable and can be struck out. Other risks might, however, have materialized – a new version of the software building tool to be used could have been imposed by the organization and there is the possibility that developers might have technical difficulties adapting to the new product.

When all these things have been done, the new Stage will still need to wait for the successful completion of the last Stage. When this happens, the Project Manager can report the completion of the Stage (SB5) and the approval of the Project Board for the new Stage Plan can be requested.

A.13 Closing the project

PRINCE2 divides the closing of a project into three separate processes:

- decommissioning a project (CP1);
- identifying follow-on actions (CP2);
- evaluating the project (CP3).

One follow-on action will be to plan for the Post Project Review which evaluates the effectiveness of the installed system after a set period of operation.

Decommissioning is mainly ensuring that all the loose ends are tied up. All Project Issues should either have been resolved or have been recorded as requiring *Follow-on Actions*. All the planned project products should have been accepted by the client and the requested operational and maintenance arrangements should be in place. Project files will have to be stored away into an archive and all parties involved should be notified that the project is now closed. PRINCE2 does not specify that team members and key users should have a celebratory drink, but now might be the time to consider this. Decommissioning might have been caused by an ad hoc direction (DP4) to terminate a project prematurely as it is no longer required and in this case a wake could be more appropriate.

In organizations where development resources are scarce, there might appear to be little time available to reflect on practice and to dwell on past mistakes. However, if this is not done, time will be wasted in dealing with recurrent problems. PRINCE2 recognizes this by specifying that at this point a *Project End Report* should be produced, documenting the extent to which the project has met the objectives set out in the Project Initiation Document, and also a *Lessons Learnt Report*, which should make suggestions about how problems could be avoided in future projects.

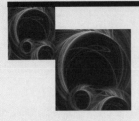

Appendix B:
Answer pointers

Chapter 1

1.1 Examples of projects

The order you put these projects in is, of course, to a large degree subjective. Here is one example of a possible ordering.

1 **Putting a robot vehicle on Mars to search for signs of life** Almost everybody puts this one first. The huge scale of the task, the relative novelty of the project, all the different specialisms involved and the international nature of the project make it special. Note that the successful achievement of the project from the engineering point of view is the safe landing of the robot, not the discovery of signs of life.

2 **Writing an operating system** This is a prime example of a software development project.

3 **Amending a financial system to deal with a common European currency** This project is modifying an existing system rather than creating a new one from scratch. Many software projects have this characteristic and it does not make them any less a software project.

4 **Installing a new version of a word processing package in an organization** Although no software is being produced or modified, many of the stages that are associated with software projects will be involved and the techniques of software project management would be appropriate.

5 **Investigation into the reasons why a user has a problem with a computer system** This will have many of the stages common to software projects, although the precise nature of the end result is uncertain at the outset. It could be that the user needs some simple remedial training. On the other hand, it could turn out to be quite a considerable software modification task.

6 **Getting married** There should be lots of arguments about this one! Some will be reluctant to give a high rating to this because of its personal nature. The degree to which this is 'project-like' will depend very much upon the cultural milieu in which it takes place. Very often it requires a high degree of planning, involves lots of different people and, for most people, is a non-routine operation.

7 **A research project into what makes a good human–computer interface** Compared to some of the projects above, the objectives of the research project are more open-ended and the idea of a specific client for the end-product may be less well defined. Research projects are in some ways special cases and the approach to their planning needs a rather different approach, which is outside the scope of this book.

8 **Producing an edition of a newspaper** In some ways this has all the characteristics of a project. There are lots of different people with lots of different specialisms whose work needs to be coordinated in order to produce an end-product under very tight time constraints. What argues against this as a typical project is that it is repeated. After a while, everyone knows what he or she needs to do and most of the problems that arise are familiar and the procedures to deal with them are well defined.

9 **A second-year programming assignment for a computing student** This is not being done for a customer, although it could be argued that the tutor responsible for setting and assessing the assignment is, in effect, a surrogate client. Not all the stages of a normal project will be gone through.

1.2 Brightmouth College payroll: Stages of a project

1 **Project evaluation** All the costs that would be incurred by the college if it were to carry out its own payroll processing would need to be carefully examined to ensure that it would be more cost-effective than letting the local authority carry on providing the service.

2 **Planning** The way that the transfer to local processing is to be carried out needs to be carefully planned with the participation of all those concerned. Some detailed planning would need to be deferred until more information was available, for example which payroll package was to be used.

3 **Requirements elicitation and analysis** This is finding out what the users need from the system. To a large extent it will often consist of finding out what the current system does, as it may be assumed that in general the new system is to provide the same functions as the old. The users might have additional requirements, however, or there might even be facilities that are no longer needed.

4 **Specification** This involves documenting what the new system is to be able to do.

5 **Design/coding** As an 'off-the-shelf' package is envisaged, these stages will be replaced by a package evaluation and selection activity.

6 **Verification and validation** Tests will need to be carried out to ensure that the selected package will actually do what is required. This task might well involve parallel running of the old and new systems and a comparison of the output from them both to check for any inconsistencies.

7 **Implementation** This would involve such things as installing the software, setting system parameters such as the salary scales, and setting up details of employees.

8 **Maintenance/support** This will include dealing with users' queries, liaising with the package supplier and taking account of new payroll requirements.

1.3 Estimation of the height of the building you are in

We will not spoil the fun by suggesting a particular method.

1.4 The nature of an operating system

Many large organizations that are committed to computer-based information systems have specialists responsible for the maintenance of operating systems. However, as an operating system is primarily concerned with driving the hardware, it is argued that it has more in common with what we have described as embedded systems.

1.5 Brightmouth College payroll: objectives-driven vs. product-driven

This project is really driven by objectives. If in-house payroll processing turns out not to be cost-effective, then the project should not try to implement such a solution. Other ways of meeting the objectives set could be considered: for example, it might be possible to contract out the processing to some organization other than the local authority at a lower cost.

1.6 Brightmouth college payroll: stakeholders

Major stakeholders would include:

- the finance department;
- the human resources department, who would need to supply most of the employee details needed;
- heads of departments, who would need to submit details of hours worked for part-time staff;
- staff, who would naturally be concerned that they are paid correctly;
- site management: the new arrangements may mean that the office layout has to be rearranged physically;
- software and hardware vendors.

One group of stakeholders that might not be readily identified at first is the local government authority and its staff. It might seem strange to list the people who used to do the job, but who are no longer required. The project manager's job will be made a lot easier if their cooperation and help can be obtained. The project manager would do well to sound out tactfully how the local authority staff feel about losing this work. It could be that they are pleased to be shot of the workload and hassle involved! Arrangements that take into account existing local authority staff might be possible. For example, if the college needs to recruit new staff to deal with payroll, it might smooth things to give the job to a member of the local authority staff who already deals with this area.

1.7 Defining objectives

Among the comments and queries that could be made in each case are:

(i) Have the actual time and the amount of the budget been specified somewhere? Deadline and budget constraints normally have to be set against the scope and the quality of the functions to be delivered. For example, if the deadline were not achieved, would the customer rather have the full set of functionality at a later date, or an essential sub-set of the functionality on the deadline date?

(ii) 'The fewest possible software errors' is not precise. Removing errors requires effort and hence money. Can developers spend as much money and time as they like if this reduces errors?

(iii) What does 'user-friendly' really mean? How is it measured? Normally 'ease of use' is measured by the time it takes for a beginner to become proficient in carrying out standard operations.

(iv) What does 'full documentation' mean? A list of the types of document to be produced, perhaps with an indication of the content layout, would be more useful.

1.8 Brightmouth college payroll: objectives, goals and measures of effectiveness

The original objective might have been formulated as: '*To carry out payroll processing at less cost while maintaining the current scope and quality of services*'.

In order to achieve this, sub-objectives or goals will usually have been identified, for example:

■ to transfer payroll processing to the college by 1 April;

■ to implement in the new system those facilities that exist in the current system less those identified in the initial report as not being required;

■ to carry out the implementation of the payroll processing capability within the financial constraints identified in the initial report.

It should be noted that the objectives listed above do not explicitly mention such things as putting into place ongoing arrangements to deal with hardware and software maintenance, security arrangements and so on. By discussing and trying to agree objectives with the various people involved, the true requirements of the project can be clarified.

Measures of effectiveness for the sub-objectives listed above might include the following:

■ *Date of implementation* Was the new system being used operationally by the agreed date?

■ *Facilities* In parallel runs, were all the outputs produced by the old system and still required also produced by the new system?

■ *Costs* How did the actual costs incurred compare with the budgeted costs?

1.9 A day in the life of a project manager

Planning:

■ staffing requirements for the next year.

Representing the section:

■ at the group meeting;

■ when communicating with the human resources manager about replacement staff;

■ when explaining about the delay to users.

Controlling, innovating, directing:

- deciding what needs to be done to make good the progress that will be lost through temporarily losing a member of staff.

Staffing:

- deciding which member of staff is to do what;
- discussion with human resources about the requirement for temporary staff;
- planning staffing for the next year.

Note: the same activity can involve many different roles.

1.10 Collecting control data

The project seems to have two major components: training and document transfer. If trainers were expected to tour offices giving training then one would expect there to be a schedule indicating when each office was to receive training. The following information about the progress of the information might therefore be collected:

- the number of offices that had received training – this could be compared with the schedule;
- the number of staff who had received training – to ensure that all staff were attending;
- feedback from staff on the perceived quality of training – for example, by post-training evaluation forms.

For the document transfer aspect, the following might be usefully collected for each office on a regular basis during the transfer process:

- number of documents transferred;
- estimated number of documents still needing to be transferred;
- number of staff-hours spent on transferring documents – to monitor the budget and transfer productivity;
- number of staff involved in the transfer.

When all documents have been transferred, performance tests to check response times might be required.

Chapter 2

2.1 Costs and benefits for the Brightmouth College payroll system

Table B.1 lists costs and benefits for the proposed Brightmouth HE College payroll system. It is not comprehensive but illustrates some of the types of items that you should have listed.

Category	Cost/benefit
Development costs	Software purchase – software cost plus selection and purchasing cost
	Project team employment costs
Setup costs	Training includes costs of trainers and operational staff time lost while training Staff recruitment
	Computer hardware and other equipment which might have a residual value at end of projected life
	Accommodation – any new/refurbished accommodation and furniture required to house new system
	Initial systems supplies – purchase of stationery, disks and other consumables
Operational costs	Operations staff – full employment costs
	Stationery – purchase and storage
	Maintenance and standby – contract or estimation of occurrence costs
	Accommodation, including heating, power, insurance etc.
Quantified and valued	Saving on local authority fees
	Later payment – increase interest income through paying salaries later in the month
Quantified but not valued	Improved accuracy – the number of errors needing to be corrected each month
Identified but not easily valued	Improved management information – this should lead to improved decision making but it is very difficult to quantify the potential benefits

TABLE B.1 Costs and benefits for the Brightmouth College payroll system

2.2 Ranking project cash flows

Obviously you will have your own views about which have the best and worst cash flows. You should, however, have considered the following points: project 2 requires a very large investment compared to its gain – in fact we could obtain £100,000 by undertaking both projects 1 and 3 for a lower cost than project 2. Both projects 1 and 4 produce the bulk of their incomes relatively late in their lives compared with project 3, which produces a steady income over its life.

2.3 Calculating payback periods

The payback periods for each of the projects will occur during the year indicated: project 1, year 5; project 2, year 5; project 3, year 4 and project 4, at the end of year 4.

We would therefore favour project 3 or 4 over the other two. Note that, in reality, with relatively short-term projects such as these we would produce a monthly (or at least quarterly) cash flow forecast and it is therefore likely that project 3 would be seen more clearly to have a shorter payback period than project 4.

2.4 Calculating the return on investment

The return on investments for each of the projects is: project 1: 10%, project 2: 2%, project 3: 10% and project 4: 12.5%. Project 4 therefore stands out as being the most beneficial as it earns the highest return.

2.5 Calculating the net present value

The net present value for each of the projects is calculated as in Table B.2. On the basis of net present value, project 4 clearly provides the greatest return and project 2 is clearly not worth considering.

Year	Discount factor	Discounted cash flow (£)		
		Project 2	Project 3	Project 4
0	1.00	−1,000,000	−100,000	−120,000
1	0.90	181,820	27,273	27,273
2	0.82	165,280	24,792	24,792
3	0.75	150,260	22,539	22,539
4	0.68	136,600	20,490	20,490
5	0.62	186,270	18,627	46,568
NPV		−179,770	13,721	21,662

TABLE B.2 Calculating the net present value of projects 2, 3 and 4

2.6 Calculating the effect of discount rates on NPV

Table B.3 illustrates the effect of varying discount rates on the NPV. In each case the 'best' project is indicated in bold. In this somewhat artificial example, which project is best is very sensitive to the chosen discount rate. In such a case we must either have a very strong reason to use a particular discount rate or take other criteria into account when choosing among the projects.

2.7 Project evaluation using cost–benefit analysis

Expected sales of £500,000 per year over four years would generate an expected net income of £1.2m (after allowing for annual costs of £200,000), which, by almost any criteria, would provide a good return on an investment of £750,000. However, if sales are low, and there is a 30% chance of this happening, the company will lose money – it is unlikely that any company would wish to take such a risk knowingly.

This example illustrates one of the basic objections to using this approach for one-off decisions. Were we to repeat the project a large number of times we would expect, *on average*, an income of £500,000 per annum. However, the company is developing this package only once – they can't keep trying in the hope of, on average, generating a respectable income. Indeed, a severe loss on this project could mean it is the last project they are able to undertake.

Year	Cash flow values (£)		
	Project A	**Project B**	**Project C**
0	−8,000	−8,000	−10,000
1	4,000	1,000	2,000
2	4,000	2,000	2,000
3	2,000	4,000	6,000
4	1,000	3,000	2,000
5	500	9,000	2,000
6	500	−6,000	2,000
Net Profit	£4,000	£5,000	£6,000
NPV @ 8%	£2,111	£2,365	**£2,421**
NPV @ 10%	£1,720	**£1,818**	£1,716
NPV @ 12%	**£1,356**	£1,308	£1,070

TABLE B.3 The effect on net present value of varying the discount rate

Chapter 3

3.1 External stakeholders in IOE accounts system

The main stakeholders who need to be considered are the IOE customers. It will be worth consulting some representative customers about the attractiveness of the new annual maintenance contract scheme. IOE might have a partnership arrangement with the manufacturers of the equipment it maintains whereby it is recognized as approved to carry out repairs. It might therefore need to consult the equipment providers about the new scheme. The suppliers might, for example, be willing to promote the scheme on a commission basis. It is possible with annual maintenance contract schemes of this nature to outsource their financing to an insurance company. Essentially, in return for an annual premium, the insurance company would pay IOE every time a maintenance job is carried out under this scheme.

3.2 Product description for acceptance test cases

An example of a possible product description for acceptance test cases is shown below:

Name/identity	Acceptance test case
Purpose	To record the individual tests that will be carried out during the acceptance testing. It will ensure that testing is comprehensive i.e. that all user requirements are tested.
Derivation	The user requirements report
Composition	For each test case the following will be recorded:
	(i) cross-reference to user requirements;
	(ii) preconditions – including items that would need to be set up on the database before the test can be executed;
	(iii) input data;
	(iv) expected results.
Form	A word-processed document created using a template
Quality criteria	Independently reviewed against the requirements document to ensure that all requirements are covered. Internal consistency checked, including whether pre-conditions are complete and expected results correctly calculated.

Note: Other products – such as a testing plan – would also have to be created in order to document the acceptance testing phase.

3.3 Creating an invitation to tender (ITT) – Product Flow Diagram

Figure B.1 illustrates a Product Flow Diagram for the products needed to create an invitation to tender for Brightmouth College payroll.

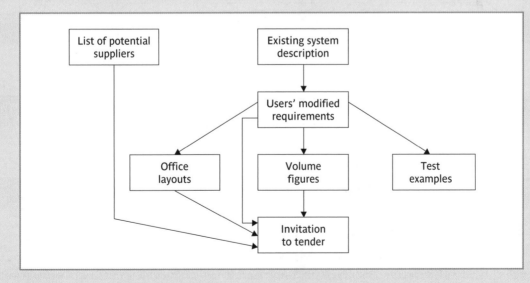

FIGURE B.1 Product Flow Diagram for the creation of an 'invitation to tender'

Different PFDs could be produced depending on the policy decisions made about how the process is to be carried out. This is one way in which it could be done. A person acting as an analyst investigates the current way of doing payroll in order to find out the basic functions that the new system must have. This document may prompt the user management to come up with some new functions that would let them do things with the new system that they could not do before. Once it is known, for example, what types of record the new system will hold, and the functions the new system will have, the size of the database and the number and size of transactions to be carried out can then be estimated. This will indicate the size and power needed for the hardware platform on which the application will run. The hardware will need to be housed within a particular physical layout governed by the office space available at the college and contractors may need to take this into account. The invitations to tender (ITTs) will need to be sent to suitable potential suppliers and some research will be needed to decide who these suppliers will be. The documented requirements are the basis for a set of procedures to evaluate the proposals, including some test cases.

3.4 Invitation to tender activity network

Figure B.2 illustrates the activity network, showing the activities needed to create an invitation to tender for the Brightmouth College payroll.

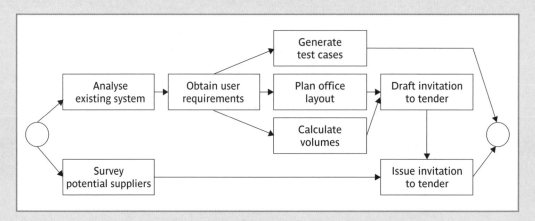

FIGURE B.2 Brightmouth College payroll project activity network fragment

3.5 Including a checkpoint

Figure B.3 illustrates the inclusion of a checkpoint in Amanda's activity network.

3.6 Quality checks on user requirements

The users will need at least to read and approve the system specification. This might be rather late to make major changes, so user approval of earlier documents such as interview notes would be helpful.

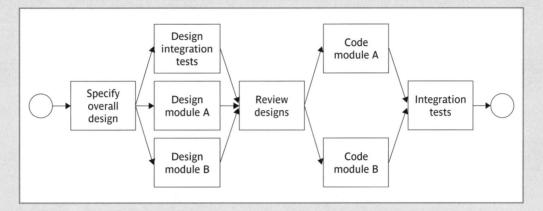

FIGURE B.3 An activity network for a software development task, modified to include a checkpoint

3.7 Cross-reference of a planning document to Step Wise activities

Table B.4 suggests the Step Wise activities needed to create the different sections of a plan.

Section of plan	Step Wise activities	
Introduction		
Background	1.3	Identify stakeholders
	2.1	Establish relationship between project and strategic planning
Project objectives	1.1	Identify objectives and measures of effectiveness
	1.4	Modify objectives in the light of stakeholder analysis
Constraints	1.1	Identify objectives and measures of effectiveness
	2.2	Identify installation standards and procedures
Methods	3.	Analyse project characteristics
	4.2	Document generic product flows (this could help establish a methodology)
Project products	4.1	Identify and describe project products
Activities to be carried out	4.4	Produce ideal activity network
	4.5	Modify ideal activity network
Resources to be used	3.6	Review overall resource estimates
	5.1	Carry out bottom-up estimates
	7.	Allocate resources
Risks to the project	3.3	Identify high-level project risks
	6.	Identify activity risks
Management of the project	1.2	Establish project authority
	1.5	Establish methods of communication with all parties
	2.3	Identify project team organization

TABLE B.4 Sections of a plan cross-referenced to Step Wise activities

Chapter 4

4.1 Classification of systems

(a) A payroll system is a data-oriented or information system that is application specific.

(b) The bottling plant system is a process control or industrial system which contains embedded software.

(c) This looks like an information system that may make use of computer graphics. The plant itself might use control software which might be safety critical but this is not the subject of the project under consideration.

(d) Project management software tools are often categorized as general packages. There would be a considerable information systems element to them.

(e) This could use an information retrieval package that is a general software package. It is also a strong candidate for a knowledge-based system.

4.2 Identification of risks

The user staff could, arguably, be regarded as a project resource. The writers' view is that it is useful to add a fourth category of risk – those belonging to the *environment* in which the system is to be implemented.

Among the risks that might be identified at Brightmouth College are:

- conflict of views between the finance and personnel departments;
- lack of staff acceptance for the system, especially among personnel staff;
- lack of cooperation by the local authority that used to carry out payroll work;
- lack of experience with running payroll at the college, leading to errors and delays in processing;
- lack of administrative computing expertise at the college;
- possible inadequacy of the chosen hardware;
- changes to the payroll requirements.

4.3 Selection of project approaches

(a) This would appear to be a knowledge-based system that is also safety critical. Techniques associated with knowledge-based systems could be used for constructing the system. Testing would need to be very carefully conducted. A lengthy parallel run where the system is used to shadow the human decisions made in real cases and the results compared could be considered. Another approach would be to develop two or more systems in parallel so that the advice offered could be cross-checked.

(b) This is an information system that will be on a relatively large scale. A structured approach designed for information systems applications, such as SSADM, would be justified. When student loans were first introduced there was no existing system and so there might have been some scope for a prototype.

(c) This is an embedded system that is safety-critical. Measures that might ensure the reliability of the system include:
- use of mathematics-based specification languages to avoid ambiguity;
- developing parallel versions of the same software so that they can be cross-checked;
- statistical control of software testing to allow for the estimation of the reliability of the software.

4.4 Stages of a project where a prototype can be appropriate

(a) A prototype could be useful as part of the feasibility study. A mock-up of an executive information system loaded with current management information could be set up manually and then be tried out by the managers to see how easy and useful they found it.

(b) A prototype could be used to assist in the design of the user dialogues. Structured approaches like SSADM often allow for prototypes for this purpose as part of requirement specification.

(c) A prototype of the most response-critical transactions could be made at the physical design stage to see whether Microsoft Access could produce software that gave a satisfactory performance.

Chapter 5

5.1 Calculating productivity rates and using productivity rates to project effort

Tables B.5 and B.6 illustrate productivity rates and estimated project effort.

Project	Work-months	SLOC	Productivity (SLOC/month)
a	16.7	6,050	362
b	22.6	8,363	370
c	32.2	13,334	414
d	3.9	5,942	1,524
e	17.3	3,315	192
f	67.7	38,988	576
g	10.1	38,614	3,823
h	19.3	12,762	661
i	59.5	26,500	445
Overall	249.3	153,868	617

TABLE B.5 Productivity rates

Project	Estimated work-months	Actual	Difference
a	6050/617 = 9.80	16.7	6.90
d	5942/617 = 9.63	3.9	−5.73

TABLE B.6 Estimated effort

There would be an under-estimate of 6.9 work-months for project a and an over-estimate of 5.7 for project d.

5.2 Agile methods and the problems of estimating

Points that might be discussed include the following.

- *Diseconomies of scale with larger projects.* It is recommended that the programming team does not contain more than ten people in order assist easy team communication.

- *Threats to quality of tight deadlines.* Time-boxing can help here. There are four sets of project outcomes that can be traded off: scope of the functionality, quality, project duration and cost. The XP approach argues that quality, project duration, and cost can be controlled by the business management, but scope must be controlled by the development team. If the project comes under time pressure, some low-priority deliverables may need to be held over to the next release, but something will still be released on time, and the quality of this will not have been compromised.

- *Substandard work not being apparent until late in the project.* Testing is done as an integral part of the design/code process and is not put off as a task to be done by another group, such as a system testing group, at a later stage in the project.

5.3 Course staff costs program – activities required

A list of activities might include:

- obtaining user requirements;
- analysis of the structure of the data already held;
- design of the report layout;
- writing the user proposal;
- planning test cases;
- technical specification;
- design of the software structure;
- software coding;
- testing software;
- writing the operating instruction;
- acceptance testing.

The most difficult tasks to estimate are often those that are most sensitive to the size and the complexity of the software to be produced, in this case the design, writing and testing of the software. Writing the technical specification can also be difficult because of this, but estimating problems tend to be concealed here as deadlines can be met by omitting detail that can be added later when deficiencies are found.

The duration of activities that are to be carried out by users may also present problems, as this might depend upon their sense of priorities.

5.4 SLOC estimate for customer insertion program

Figure B.4 gives an outline program structure using a Jackson structured diagram. The numbers in circles are our estimates of the lines of 'generic' code needed to implement each sub-process in the program. They should add up to 95 SLOC.

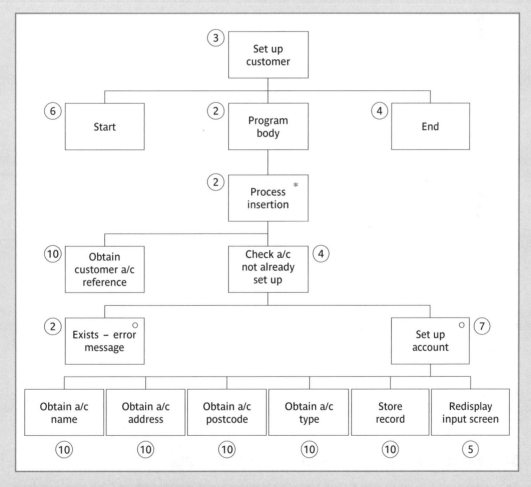

FIGURE B.4 Outline program structure for 'set up customer' transaction
* means the process is repeated; o means the processes are alternatives.

5.5 Effort drivers for a student assignment

The most obvious effort driver would seem to be the number of words required. Difficulty factors might include:

■ *availability of material*, for example in the library;

■ *familiarity* of the student with the topic;

■ *breadth/depth required*, that is, a broad survey of a wide field or an in-depth study of a narrow area;

■ *technical difficulty* – some topics are easier to explain than others.

It could be argued that time available is the constraint. The student just does what can be done in the time available (see 'design to cost').

5.6 Calculating Euclidean distance

The Euclidean distance between project B and the target case is the square root of $((7 - 5)^2 + (15 - 10)^2)$, that is, 5.39. Project A is therefore a closer analogy.

5.7 Albrecht function points

External input types	none
External output types	the report, that is, 1
Logical internal file types	none
External interface file types	payroll file, staff file (timetabling), courses file (timetabling), that is, 3
External inquiry types	none

The function point counts are as follows:

External enquiry types	none
External output types	$1 \times 7 = 7$
Logical internal file types	none
External interface types	$3 \times 7 = 21$
External inquiry types	none
Total	28

5.8 Calculation of SLOC from Albrecht function points

The estimated lines of Java = $28 \times 53 = 1484$. With a productivity rate of 50 SLOC per day, this gives an estimated effort of 1484/50, that is, approximately 30 days.

5.9 Mark II function points

The function types are:

Input data types	6
Entities accessed	1
Output data types	1

Unadjusted function points = $(0.58 \times 6) + (1.66 \times 1) + (0.26 \times 1) = 5.4$

5.10 Data movements

Data movement	Type
Incoming vehicle sensed	E
Access vehicle count	R
Signal barrier to be lifted	X
Increment vehicle count	W
Outgoing vehicle sensed	E
Decrement vehicle count	W
New maximum input	E
Set new maximum	W
Adjust current vehicle count	E
Record adjusted vehicle count	W

Note that different interpretations of the requirements could lead to different counts. The description in the exercise does not, for example, specify that the system should output a message that the car park is full or has spaces, although this might be expected.

5.11 COCOMO – calculating the exponent scale factors

Table B.7 shows scale factors for the example.

Factor	Rating	Value
PREC	nominal	3.72
FLEX	high	2.03
RESL	very low	7.07
TEAM	very high	1.10
PMAT	low	6.24

TABLE B.7 Assessing the scale factors

(i) The overall scale factor would be $0.91 + 0.01 \times (3.72 + 2.03 + 7.07 + 1.10 + 6.24)$
$$= 0.91 + 0.01 \times 20.16$$
$$= 1.112$$

(ii) The estimated effort would be $2.94 \times 2^{1.112} = 6.35$ staff-months

5.12 COCOMO II Applying effort multipliers

Factor	Description	Rating	Effort multiplier
RCPX	product reliability and complexity	vh	1.91
RUSE	reuse	vh	1.15
PDIF	platform difficulty	l	0.87
PERS	personnel capability	vh	0.63
PREX	personnel experience	nominal	1.00
FCIL	facilities	nominal	1.00
SCED	required development schedule	nominal	1.00

TABLE B.8 Effort multipliers

The combined effort modifier would be

$$(1.91 \times 1.15 \times 0.87 \times 0.63 \times 1.00 \times 1.00 \times 1.00) = 1.20$$

The modified estimate would be $200 \times 1.20 = 240$ staff months

Chapter 6

6.1 Drawing a CPM network

A solution is given in Figure 6.14. If your solution is not exactly the same as this, do not worry. Just check that it is *logically* the same and that it follows the precedence network conventions of layout and labelling etc.

6.2 The precedence network

Figure B.5 illustrates a precedence network for Amanda's project, showing an earliest completion date of day 104.

6.3 Calculating activity floats

Free float and interfering float for each of the activities are shown in Table B.9. Note that activity A has no free float since any delay in its completion will delay the start of activity C. Float must be regularly monitored as a project progresses since a delay in any activity beyond its free float allowance will eat into the float of subsequent activities.

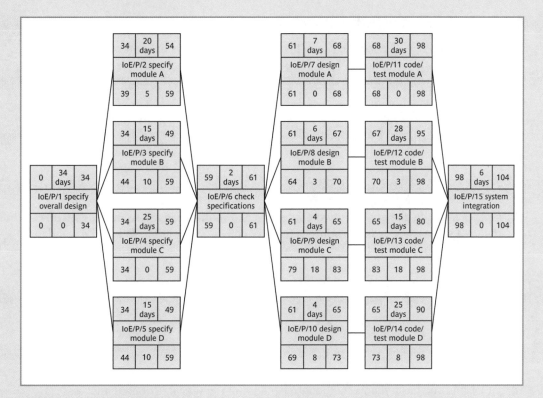

FIGURE B.5 Amanda's precedence network

Activity	Total float	Free float	Interfering float
A	2	0	2
B	3	0	3
C	2	0	2
D	3	1	2
E	3	3	0
F	0	0	0
G	0	0	0
H	2	2	0

TABLE B.9 Activity floats

6.4 Shortening a project duration

Shortening activity F to 8 weeks will bring the project completion date forward to week 11 – that is, it will save 2 weeks on the duration of the project. However, there are now two critical paths, start–F–G–finish and start–A–C–H–finish, so that reducing the duration of activity F any further will not shorten the project duration any further. If we wish to complete the project earlier than week 11 we must save time on both of these critical paths.

6.5 Errors drawing activity networks

(a) Activity D dangles, giving the project two 'end events'. This network should be drawn as below. To aid comparison with the original, the nodes have not been renumbered, although we would normally do so.

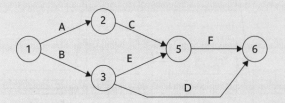

(b) Once again, this network has two end nodes, but in this case the solution is slightly different since we should introduce a dummy activity if we are to follow the standard CPM conventions.

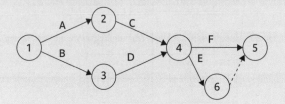

(c) Either this one has a dangle (although, because of the way it is drawn, it is less obvious) or activity E has its arrow pointing in the wrong direction. We need a bit more information before we can redraw this one correctly.

(d) Strictly speaking, there is nothing wrong with this one – it is just badly drawn and the nodes are not numbered according to the standard conventions. It should be redrawn as in the following example.

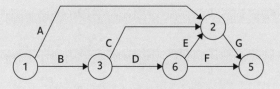

In this diagram the nodes have retained their original numbers (to aid identification), although they should of course be renumbered sequentially from left to right.

(e) This one contains a loop – F cannot start before G has finished, G cannot start before E has finished and E cannot start before G has finished. One of the arrows is wrong! It is probably activity F that is wrong but we cannot be sure without further information.

6.6 Drawing Brigette's activity network as a CPM network

Brigette's payroll CPM network should look like the diagram shown in Figure B.6. If your diagram is not exactly the same as this, check that it is logically the same.

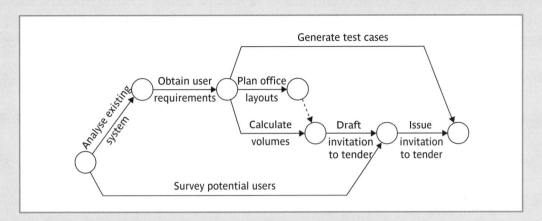

FIGURE B.6 Brigette's CPM network

Chapter 7

7.1 Matching causes and effects

There is no one correct answer to this. An example of a possible answer is provided below.

(a) i and ii. Staff inexperience leads to code that has many errors in it and which therefore needs additional testing time. Inexperienced staff will take longer to carry out development in any case.

(b) iv. If top management do not have a strong commitment to the project they will not act with a sense of urgency.

(c) ii. New technology takes time to get used to.

(d) iii. If users are uncertain of their requirements then they are likely to identify new requirements as the project progresses.

Exercise 7.2 Identifying risks

Once again the answer below can only be indicative – there is no one correct answer.

Domain	IOE	Brightmouth payroll
Actors	Possible user resistance – see the Section 3.5 case study example	Lack of experience running payroll – see answer to Exercise 4.2
Structure	Not all stakeholders are represented on the Project Board – see Section 3.3	Lack of cooperation between the local authority and the college
Tasks	Uncertainty about time needed to change existing software – see Section 3.8	Evaluation of packages – software may be difficult to access to carry out evaluation testing
Technology	Existing hardware is not adequate to deal with new application	Existing hardware is not adequate to deal with new application

Exercise 7.3 Conditions needed for successful pooling arrangement

Among the conditions would be the following.

- The chance of fire is precisely 1 in 1000. As this is only an estimate of an average, this could not be guaranteed. If a fire happened at a second location, the pool would already have been exhausted. Having a larger number of contributors and a larger pool would reduce, but not eliminate, this risk.

- The sites would have to be at completely different locations so that a fire at one site does not affect the others.

- Each site has the same chance of fire. If the people at a site were aware that the chance of fire was a lot less in their location, they might object to having to effectively subsidize other sites.

- The amount of damage caused is always the same.

Exercise 7.4 Pre-conditions to facilitate contingency actions

Staff illness is just one of several reasons why you might need to transfer staff between job roles in the middle of an activity. Such transfers would be made easier if:

- there was a standard methodology for the way that the work was carried out;
- intermediate steps were well documented;
- other staff were involved in reviewing products at regular intervals;
- job descriptions were flexible.

It is interesting to note that in an extreme programming environment, the recommended approach of pair programming should provide an alternative way of dealing with this problem.

The factors to be taken account of could include costs and human factors. The structured approach to development that the bullet points above imply would involve costs in selecting the right methodology, training and other aspects of implementation and management of the process to ensure that staff adhere to the requirements of the methodology. Very flexible staffing arrangements where staff could be switched between jobs at short notice could have implications for morale (which might be positive as well as negative).

7.5 Calculating expected activity durations

Table B.10 shows the activity duration estimates from Table 7.6 along with the calculated expected durations, t_e.

7.6 The forward pass to calculate expected completion date

The expected duration and the expected dates for the other project events are shown in Figure 7.6. An expected duration of 13.5 weeks means that we expect the project to be completed halfway through week 14, although since this is only an expected value it could finish earlier or later.

Activity	Activity durations (weeks)			
	Optimistic (*a*)	Most likely (*m*)	Pessimistic (*b*)	Expected (*t_e*)
A	5	6	8	6.17
B	3	4	5	4.00
C	2	3	3	2.83
D	3.5	4	5	4.08
E	1	3	4	2.83
F	8	10	15	10.50
G	2	3	4	3.00
H	2	2	2.5	2.08

TABLE B.10 Calculating expected activity durations

7.7 Calculating standard deviations

The correct values are shown in Figure 7.7. Brief calculations for events 4 and 6 are given here.

Event 4:   Path A + C has a standard deviation of $\sqrt{(0.50^2 + 0.17^2)} = 0.53$

Path B + D has a standard deviation of $\sqrt{(0.33^2 + 0.25^2)} = 0.41$

Node 4 therefore has a standard deviation of 0.53.

Event 6:   Path 4 + H has a standard deviation of $\sqrt{(0.53^2 + 0.08^2)} = 0.54$

Path 5 + G has a standard deviation of $\sqrt{(1.17^2 + 0.33^2)} = 1.22$

Node 6 therefore has a standard deviation of 1.22.

7.8 Calculating *z* values

The *z* value for event 5 is $\dfrac{10 - 10.5}{1.17} = -0.43$, for event 6 it is $\dfrac{15 - 13.5}{1.22} = 1.23$.

7.9 Obtaining probabilities

Event 4:   The *z* value is 1.89 which equates to a probability of approximately 3%. There is therefore only a 3% chance that we will not achieve this event by the target date of the end of week 10.

Event 5:   The *z* value is −0.43 which equates to a probability of approximately 67%. There is therefore a 67% chance that we will not achieve this event by the target date of the end of week 10.

To calculate the probability of completing the project by week 14 we need to calculate a new *z* value for event 6 using a target date of 14. This new *z* value is

$$z = \frac{14 - 13.5}{1.22} = 0.41$$

This equates to a probability of approximately 35%. This is the probability of not meeting the target date. The probability of meeting the target date is therefore 65% (100% − 35%).

Chapter 8

8.1 Smoothing resource demand

Smoothing analyst/designer demand for stage 4 is reasonably easy. The design of module D could be scheduled after the design of module C. Stage 2 is more problematic as scheduling the specification of module D to start after the completion of B would delay the project. Amanda might consider doing this if whoever is specifying module A could also be allocated to module D for the last six days – although she may well decide that drafting an extra person into a specification activity is unsatisfactory.

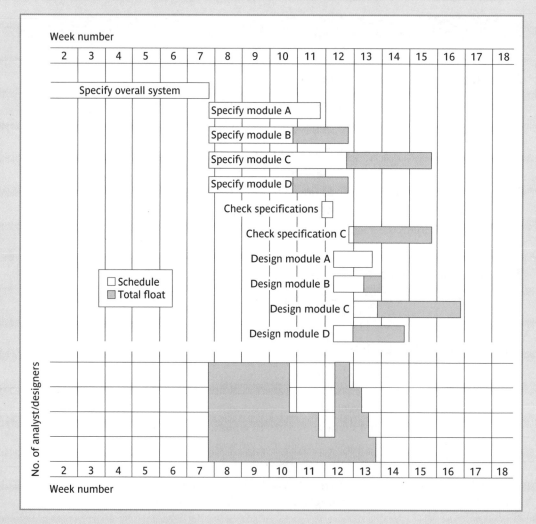

FIGURE B.7 Amanda's revised bar chart and resource histogram

8.2 Drawing a revised resource histogram

In Figure B.7 activities start at their earliest dates. The shaded area of each bar is the activity's total float. If an activity starts later than its earliest date, part of its float is 'used up'. In Figure B.8 this is shown by the shaded area of some bars moving to the left.

If the activities are scheduled at the earliest dates, then the plan still calls for four analyst/designers as shown in Figure B.7. By delaying the start of some activities, however, Amanda is able to ensure that using three analyst/designers is sufficient except for a single day. This is shown in Figure B.8.

Note that if the specification of module C were to be delayed for a further day, the project could be completed with only three analyst/designers, although its completion day would, of course, be delayed.

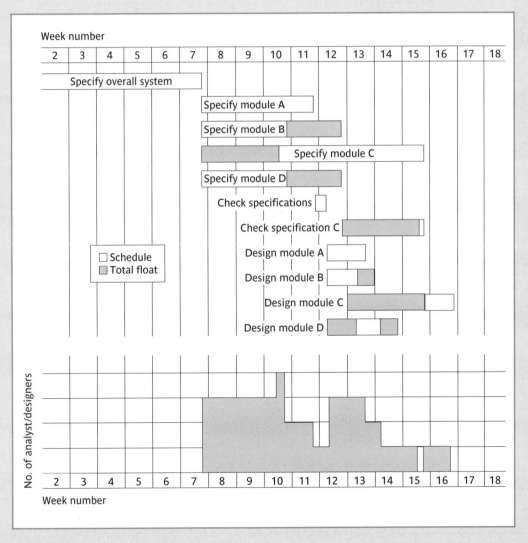

FIGURE B.8 The effect of delaying some activity starts

8.3 Identifying critical activities

The critical path is now as shown in Figure B.9. Note the lag of 15 days against activity IoE/P/4, ensuring that its start is delayed until an analyst/designer is expected to be available.

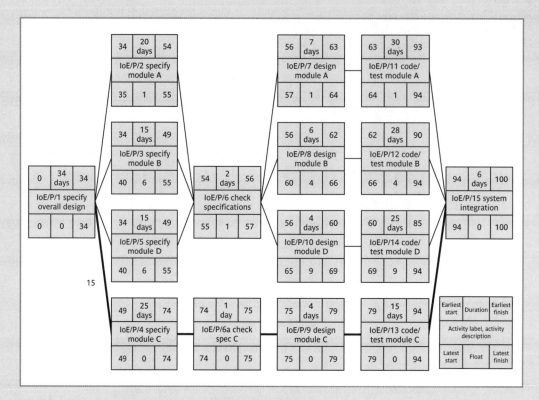

FIGURE B.9 The critical activities after delaying the start of module C

However, the availability of an analyst/designer for IoE/P/4 is dependent upon IoE/P/3 or IoE/P/5 being completed on time – these two activities are therefore also now critical in the sense that a delay in both of them would delay IoE/P/4, which is on the normal critical path. These two activities, although not on the critical path, are, in that sense, critical.

8.4 Assigning staff to activities

Belinda must specify module B as she will then be available in time to start the specification of module C. This leaves Daisy for the specification and design of module A. Belinda cannot do the design of module B as she will still be working on the module C specification when this needs to be done (6 days between days 56 and 66). This will have to be left to Tom, as he should be free on day 60.

Can you think of any other way in which she might have allocated the three team members to these activities?

8.5 Calculating project costs

The easiest way to calculate the total cost is to set up a table similar to Table B.11.

Calculating the distribution of costs over the life of the project is best done as a per week or per month figure rather than as daily costs. The expenditure per week for Amanda's project is shown as a chart in Figure 8.9.

Analyst	Daily cost (£)	Days required	Cost (£)
Amanda	300	110^2	33,000
Belinda	250	50	12,500
Tom	175	25	4,375
Daisy	225	27	6,075
Gavin	150	30	4,500
Purdy	150	28	4,200
Justin	150	15	2,250
Spencer	150	25	3,750
Daily on-cost	200	100	20,000
Total			90,650

TABLE B.11 Calculating the cost of Amanda's project
[2] This includes 10 days for pre-project planning and post-project review.

Chapter 9

9.1 Lines of code as a partial task completion indicator

There are many reasons why the proportion of lines coded is not a good indicator of completeness. In particular, you should have considered the following:

- the estimated total number of lines of code might be inaccurate;
- the lines of code so far might have been easier, or harder, than those to follow – for example, reuse of existing components might speed up development;
- a program is not generally considered complete until it has been tested – testing and debugging the code could take considerable time once the code has been written.

With more knowledge of what has been done and what is left to complete it might be possible to make a reasonable estimate of completeness. Breaking the development task into smaller sub-tasks such as software design, coding and unit testing might be of some assistance here.

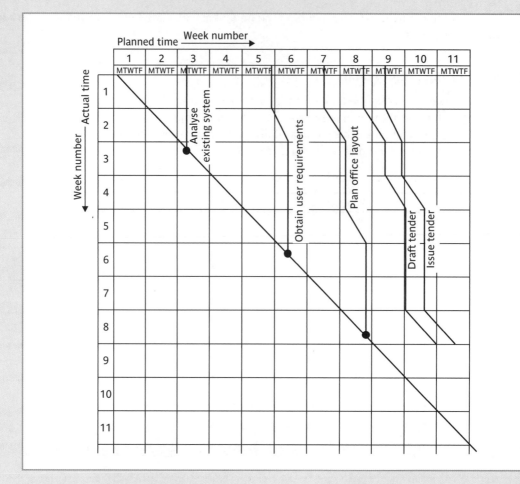

FIGURE B.10 The revised timeline chart

9.2 Revising the timeline chart

At the end of week 8, the scheduled completion dates for drafting and issuing the tender need to be revised – note that both need to be changed since they are both on the critical path (Figure B.10).

Subsequently, Brigette needs to show only the completion of each of these two remaining activities on the timeline chart – the project being completed by the Thursday of week 11 (Figure B.11).

9.3 Amanda's earned value analysis

It should be apparent from Figure 9.11 that the initial activity, 'specify overall system', has slipped by one day. It may not be quite so obvious from Figure 9.11 alone what else has happened to her project – inspection of Figure 9.11 and Table 9.2 should, however,

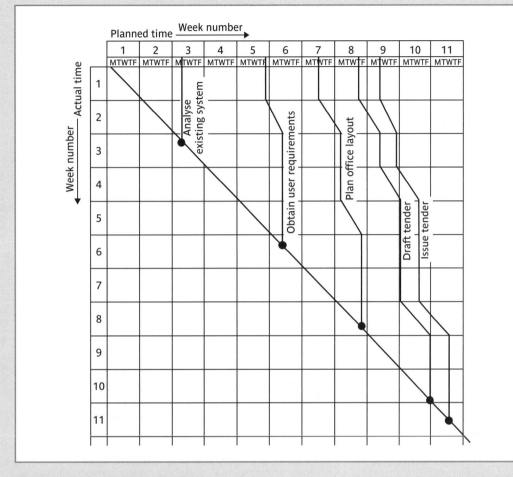

FIGURE B.11 The completed timeline chart

make it possible to deduce that one of the activities 'specify module B' and 'specify module D' has taken 2 days longer than forecast and the other has taken 5 days longer. In addition, 'specify module A' should have been completed by day 54 but has not. Thus, the project has earned 34 workdays by day 35, 49 workdays by day 52 and 64 workdays by day 55.

From Figure 9.11 it is not possible to deduce the underlying causes of the slippage or to forecast the consequences for the project. The use of earned value analysis for forecasting is described later in Section 9.6.

9.4 The effects of specification changes

Among the items most likely to be affected by the change are test data, expected results and the user handbooks.

9.5 Control procedures for development systems

Stages 1 to 6 will be basically the same except that an estimate on the effect of the project's timescale will need to be included in steps 3 and 4. Step 7 might not be required as system acceptance might not have taken place yet and acceptance testing of the changes will be included in that.

The release of software in step 8 will not be needed if the system is not yet operational, although master copies of products will need to be updated.

9.6 Reasons for scope creep

As well as user requests for extra features, developers will find that additional code may be needed to deal with exceptional circumstances that become apparent during detailed design. Additional functionality could also occur because of the need to coordinate components.

Chapter 10

10.1 Choice of type of package at IOE

The problem for Amanda at IOE would be that the new annual maintenance contracts subsystem would essentially be an extension to and enhancement of the existing maintenance accounting system, so that the interfacing of an off-the-shelf package might involve quite a few difficulties. This seems to indicate that bespoke development is needed. An alternative approach might be to consider replacing the whole of the maintenance accounting system with a new off-the-shelf application.

10.2 Calculation of charges for a project

For the first 2000 FPs	$967 \times 2,000$	= $1,934,000
For the next 500 FPs	$1,019 \times 500$	= $509,500
For the next 500 FPs	$1,058 \times 500$	= $529,000
For the last 200 FPs	$1,094 \times 200$	= $218,800
Charge for all 3,200 FPs		$3,191,300

10.3 Calculating the cost of additional functionality

For changed FPs	$500 \times 600 \times (150/100)$	= $450,000
For additional FPs	200×600	= $120,000
Total charge		$570,000

10.4 Advantage to customer of variable cost charges

The supplier will need to quote a price that will include a margin to cater for possible increases in equipment prices. It might turn out that actual prices do not increase as much as was estimated – in the case of ICT equipment some prices are likely to go down – but the customer would still have to pay the additional margin. If the contract specifies a fixed charge plus the actual cost of materials and equipment, then the customer in this case would be better off.

10.5 Calculating value for money

System X savings would be £20 × 20 hours × 4 years = £1,600, for the automatic scale point adjustment facility, and £20 × 12 hours × 2 times a year × 4 years = £1,920, for the bar-chart production facility. In total the saving for system X would be £3,520.

For system Y, the saving would be £300 × 0.5 (to take account of the probability of change). That is, £150.

Even though system X costs £500 more, it will still give better value for money.

Note that discounted cash flow calculations could be applied to these figures.

10.6 Evaluation methods

i.   The usability of an existing system could be evaluated by such means as the examination of user handbooks, the observation of demonstrations and practical user trails.

ii. This is clearly tricky. One would have to evaluate the methods that the developers intend to use to see whether they adhere to good interface design practice. One might also examine any interface standards that are in use by the supplier.

iii. Note that the question focuses on the costs of maintenance, rather than that of reliability. The cost of unexpected maintenance could be reduced, at least for a short time, by passing this risk to the supplier if there is a comprehensive warranty. The warranties provided by suppliers would therefore need to be scrutinized. Discussion with reference sites might also be helpful.

iv. Once again guarantees could be put in place by suppliers concerning this. The nature of these guarantees could be examined. Discussion with reference sites could once again be helpful.

v.   Training materials could be examined. The training staff could be interviewed and their CVs examined. Reference sites that have already used the supplier's training services could be approached for their views.

Chapter 11

11.1 Tasks and responsibilities of an analyst/programmer

Analyst/programmers are expected to be able to carry out both analysis and programming tasks. It is likely, however, that the kinds of analysis tasks undertaken will be restricted. They may, for example, do the analysis work for enhancements to existing systems but not of completely new applications. Making this broad assumption, a list of tasks and responsibilities might be as follows:

- carry out detailed investigations of new requirements for existing computer applications;
- analyse the results of investigations and review the solutions to problems experienced, including the estimation of relevant costs;
- prepare systems specifications in accordance with organizational standards;
- conduct appropriate systems testing;
- prepare functional module specifications;
- produce and modify module structure diagrams;
- code and amend software modules;
- carry out appropriate unit testing;
- produce and amend user documentation;
- liaise with users, carrying out appropriate training in the use of computer applications where required.

11.2 Rewarding reuse

A problem here is that the software developers who make most use of reused components will, as a consequence, be producing less code themselves. You also want to encourage programmers to produce software components that other people can use: this might help the productivity of the organization but not that of the current project that they are working on!

You need to have a method, like function point analysis, which measures the functions and features actually delivered to the user. You also need to have some way of measuring the code used in the application that has been taken from elsewhere. Percentage targets of the amount of reused code to new code could be set and staff rewarded if the targets are met. As an alternative, the savings made by reuse could be measured and a profit-sharing scheme could be operated.

Programmers could be encouraged to produce and publish reusable components by a system of royalties for each time a software component is reused.

11.3 Financial incentives for top executives

This exercise was designed to be thought-provoking. Some thoughts that have come out of discussion on this topic are given below.

■ To some extent, material wants and, therefore, the motivation to obtain more money to satisfy these wants can be generated through the marketing and advertising of new types of goods and services – but how likely is this to be at the very top?

■ Large salaries are associated with status, esteem and success. It could be that these are the real reward.

■ Historically, wealth has been associated with power, such as the ownership of land.

The essential point is that for many people money is not just a means of satisfying material wants.

11.4 High and low motivational incidents

This will obviously depend on individual experiences.

11.5 Possible objections to the stockholder ethical model

The purpose of this exercise is to stimulate debate, but some possible discussion points could be:

■ The model implies that employees and customers exist simply to maximize the profits of the stockholders/shareholders. This suggests that the whole purpose of the business is this generation of profits. But as has been shown in the recent global financial crisis, businesses carry out functions that are important for society as a whole, for example, when it appeared that some high street banks might cease to operate, the UK and other governments stepped in and took over ownership in order to support the economy as a whole. This suggests that the capital provided by shareholders can be seen as a means of enabling the main business of the enterprise rather than the other way around.

■ If commercial organizations are amoral in that their only concern is the generation of profits to the possible detriment of other stakeholders, then this is an argument for the public ownership of organizations such as energy suppliers upon whom society depends.

■ If we expect individuals as individuals to be socially responsible and ethical, then when these individuals are also shareholders we might expect them to be socially responsible in that role as well.

■ Paradoxically, acting in a socially responsible way may be a way of fostering goodwill in the community, winning new business and contributing eventually to shareholder value.

Chapter 12

12.1 Social loafing

Among other ideas, the effects of social loafing can be reduced by:

■ making the work of each performer individually identifiable;

■ involving and interesting group members in the outcome of group efforts;

■ rewarding individuals for their contributions to the group effort (rather like sports teams who pick out a 'club player of the year').

12.2 Effect of ICT on the Delphi technique

Developments in ICT that assist cooperative working, especially the advent of electronic mail and groupware such as Lotus Notes, will cut quite considerably the communication delays involved in the Delphi technique.

12.3 Modes of communication

Once again, there is no one correct set of answers. Discussion points might be:

(a) The developer might not be familiar with the context of the application domain – for example the terminology employed by the users. Ideally, clarification should be via same time/same place or same time/different place (e.g. telephone), as the business analyst and developer could go through a cycle of questions and answers quickly, and follow-up questions could be posed where answers were not completely clear.

(b) To start with, same time/different place (e.g. a call to a help desk) might be most appropriate as the problem might be a simple misunderstanding. If a fault in the software was actually found then a different time/different place mode of communication would be needed to record the fault report so that it could be dealt with by the software maintenance team.

(c) The requirement could be very complex and need considerable analysis, so initially different time/different place communication involving studying and writing documents might be best. Different options might need to be considered by the business and for this a same time/same place meeting might be expedient.

(d) There might be good reasons why the second developer is late. For example, he might have been on sick leave. It might also be that he is unaware of the urgency of the task. Informal communication, ideally face to face, might be appropriate, at least initially.

12.4 Classification of types of power

More than one type of power can be involved in each case.

i. Some *expert* power is involved here, but for those who are subject to the audit, the main type of power is *connection* power as the auditor will produce a report that will go to higher management. External auditors often have *coercive* power.

ii. Here, power will mainly be *expert-* and *information-based*, but as the consultant will report to higher management, *connection* power also exists.

iii. This sounds pretty *coercive*.

iv. Brigette has some *connection* power. The technical expertise that is involved in her job means she has some *expert* power. She has little or no *coercive* power as she is not the manager of the staff involved. She might be able to exert some *reward* power as she can satisfy some of the staff's need for ICT support.

v. Amanda is unlikely to have direct *coercive* power although she might be able to institute disciplinary procedures. Through the system of annual reviews common to many organizations, she might have some *reward* power. *Connection* power, through her access to higher management, is also present. Her access to users means she has *information* power. If she brings specific expertise to the project (such as analysis skills) she might have some *expert* power. By acting as a role model that other project team members might want to emulate she may even be displaying *referent* power.

12.5 Appropriate management styles

i. The clerk will know much more than anyone else about the practical details of the work. Heavy *task-oriented* supervision would therefore not be appropriate. As the clerk is working in a new environment and forging new relationships, a considerable amount of people-oriented supervision/support might be needed initially.

ii. Both task-oriented and people-oriented management would be needed with the trainee.

iii. The experienced maintenance programmer has probably had considerable autonomy in the past. The extensions to the systems could have a considerable, detailed, impact on this person's work. A very carefully judged increase in task-oriented management will be required for a short time.

Chapter 13

13.1 Selection of payroll package for college

(a) Carry out an investigation to find out what the users' requirements really are. This might uncover that there are different sets of requirements for different groups of users.

(b) Organize the requirements into groups relating to individual qualities and attributes. These might be, for example, functionality (the range of features that the software has), price, usability, capacity, efficiency, flexibility and reliability.

(c) Some of these requirements will be of an absolute nature. For example, an application will have to hold records for up to a certain maximum number of employees. If it cannot, it will have to be immediately eliminated from further consideration.

(d) In other cases the requirement is relative. Some of the relative requirements are more important than others. A low price is desirable but more expensive software cannot be ruled out straightaway. This can be reflected by giving each of the requirements a rating, a score out of 10, say, for importance.

(e) A range of possible candidate packages needs to be identified. If there are lots of possibilities, an initial screening, for instance, by price, can be applied to reduce the contenders to a manageable shortlist.

(f) Practical ways of measuring the desired qualities in the software have to be devised. In some cases, for example with price and capacity, sales literature or a technical specification can be consulted. In other cases, efficiency for instance, practical trials could be conducted, while in yet other cases a survey of existing users might provide the information required.

(g) It is likely that some software is going to be deficient in some ways, but that this will be compensated by other qualities. A simple way of combining the findings on different qualities is to give a mark out of 10 for the relative presence/absence of the quality. Each of these scores can be multiplied by a score out of 10 for the importance of the quality (see (d)) and the results of all these multiplications can be summed to give an overall score for the software.

13.2 Possible quality specifications for word processing software

There are many that could be defined and just two examples are given below. One point that may emerge is that the software might be best broken down into a number of different functional areas, each of which can be evaluated separately, such as document preparation, presentation, mail merging and so on. For example:

- *quality:* ease of learning;
- *definition:* the time taken, by a novice, to learn how to operate the package to produce a standard document;
- *scale:* hours;
- *test:* interview novices to ascertain their previous experience of word processing. Supply them with a machine, the software, a training manual and a standard document to set up. Time how long it takes them to learn how to set the document up;
- *minimally* acceptable: > 2.5 to 4 hours;
- *target range:* 1 to 2.5 hours;
- *now:* 3 hours;

or

- *quality:* ease of use;
- *definition:* the time taken for an experienced user to produce a standard document;
- *scale:* minutes;
- *test:* time user who has experience of package to produce the standard document;
- *minimally acceptable:* 40 to 45 minutes;
- *target range:* 30 to 40 minutes;
- *current:* 45 minutes.

This topic of evaluation is an extensive one and the pointers above leave all sorts of unanswered questions in the air. Readers who wish to explore this area should read one of the more specialist books on the topic.

13.3 Availability and mean time between failures

Each day the system should be available from 8 a.m. to 6 p.m., that is 10 hours.

Over four weeks that should be $10 \times 5 \times 4$ hours = 200 hours.

It was unavailable for one day, i.e. 10 hours.

It was unavailable until 10.00 on two other days = 4 hours.

The hours available were therefore $200 - 10 - 4 = 186$ hours.

Availability would therefore be $186/200 \times 100 = 93\%$.

Assuming that three failures are counted, mean time between failures would be $186/3 = 62$ hours.

13.4 Entry requirements for an activity different from the exit requirements for another activity that immediately precedes it

It is possible for one activity to start before the immediately preceding activity has been completely finished. In this case, the entry requirement for the following activity has been satisfied, even though the exit requirement of the preceding activity has not. For example, software modules could be used for performance testing of the hardware platform even though there are some residual defects concerning screen layouts.

Another situation where the entry requirements could vary from the preceding exit requirements is where a particular resource needs to be available in order for the new activity to start.

13.5 Entry and exit requirements

- *Entry requirements* A program design must have been produced that has been reviewed and any rework required by the review must have been carried out and been inspected by the chair of the review group.

- *Exit requirements* A program must have been produced that has been compiled and is free of compilation errors; the code must have been reviewed and any rework required by the review must have been carried out and been inspected by the chair of the review group.

It should be noted that the review group could use checklists for each type of product reviewed and these could be regarded as further entry/exit requirements.

13.6 Application of BS EN ISO 9001 standards to system testing

There would be a need for a documented procedure that governs system testing.

The quality objective for system testing might be defined as ensuring that the software conforms to the requirements laid down in the user specification.

Processes to ensure this could include documented cross-references from test cases to sections of the specification.

The results of executing test cases would need to be recorded and the subsequent remedying of any discrepancies would also need to be recorded.

13.7 Precautionary steps when work is contracted out

The project manager could check who actually carried out the certification. They could also discover the scope of the BS EN ISO 9001 certification that was awarded. For example, it could be that certification only applied to the processes that created some products and not others.

Perhaps the most important point is that the project manager will need to be reassured that the *specification* to which the contractors will be working is an adequate reflection of the requirements of the client organization.

13.8 Information flows for staff allocation

When the *architecture design* process which creates work packages is taking place, there could be a further output, namely the effort estimation for each software component. These could be passed to a management process which allocates staff to the *develop software* process. The develop software process would need to pass back information about the actual effort being used as this would allow adjustments to resource allocations to be made as necessary.

13.9 Comparison of peer review and pair programming

Here are some ways in which they might be contrasted:

Pair programming	Peer review
Works on the principle that two heads are better than one	Peer review groups could be made up of more people.
Driver and navigator are jointly responsible for producing the software product	Developer solely responsible for the initial creation of the product which is then reviewed.
Discussion of the rationale for the design as it is being produced	Reviewers see the final product only, not the reasoning behind it unless design documentation provides the rationale.
Real-time interaction between participants	Batch orientation with focus on the documents.
Development effort doubled	The time of several members of staff needed to study documents and then attend the review meeting.

There could be further discussion of the respective advantages and disadvantages of each approach.

13.10 The important differences between a quality circle and a review group

The quality circle would be looking at the process in general while the review group would look at a particular instance of a product. The use of review groups alone could be inefficient because they could be removing the same type of defect again and again rather than addressing, as the quality circle does, the task of stopping the defects at their source.

Further reading

General books on project management – not IS specific

Field, Mike and Laurie Keller, *Project Management*, London, International Thomson Business Press, 1998.

Haynes, Marion E., *Project Management: Practical tools for success*, Mento Park, CA, Crisp Publications, 2002.

Lock, Dennis, *Project Management* (9th edition), Aldershot, Gower, 2007.

Lockyer, Keith and James Gordon, *Project Management and Project Network Techniques* (7th edition), London, Financial Times Prentice Hall, 2005.

Nickson, David and Suzy Siddons, *Managing Projects*, Made Simple Books, Oxford, Butterworth-Heinemann, 1997.

General books on software and IS management

Bennatan, E. M., *On Time Within Budget: Software project management practices and techniques*, Chichester, Wiley, 2000.

Cadle, James and Donald Yeates, *Project Management for Information Systems* (5th edition), London, FT Prentice Hall, 2007.

Hughes, Bob (editor) *Project Management for IT-related Projects*, London, The British Computer Society, 2004.

Schwalbe, Kathy, *IT Project Management* (5th edition), London, Thomson Course Technology, 2007.

Other books worth looking at

Frederick Brooks, *The Mythical Man-Month: Essays on Software Engineering*, Anniversary Edition, Reading, MA, Addison-Wesley, 1995. A slightly dated but classic exposition of the central issues of software project management from the man who was in charge of the IBM 360 Operating System development project. You should try to look at it at some time.

Chris Kemerer (ed) *Software Project Management – Readings and Cases*, Chicago, Irwin, McGraw-Hill, 1997. A collection of classic papers on topics such as estimation, risk management, life cycles, reuse and process improvement. Strongly recommended.

Strategic planning and programme management

Office of Government Commerce, *Managing Successful Programmes*, London, The Stationery Office, 2007.

Office of Government Commerce, *For Successful Programme Management: Think MSP*, London, The Stationery Office, 2007. An abridged guide to MSP.

Ould, Martyn, *Managing Software Quality and Business Risk*, Chichester, Wiley, 1999.

Reiss, Geoff, Malcolm Anthony, John Chapman, Geoff Leigh, Paul Rayner and Adrian Pyne Gower, *Book of Programme Management*, Aldershot, Gower Publishing, 2006.

Project process models

DSDM Consortium, *DSDM Atern Pocket Book* Ashford, DSDM Consortium 2007.

Beck, Kent with Cynthia Andreas, *Extreme Programming Explained: Embrace change* (2nd edition), Harlow, Addison-Wesley, 2004.

Booch, Grady, *Object Solutions: Managing the object oriented project*, Reading, MA, Addison-Wesley, 1996.

Gilb, Tom and Susannah Finzi, *Principles of Software Engineering Management*, Wokingham, Addison-Wesley, 1988. Among other things, this book was one of the first to introduce to a wider audience many of the ideas that have subsequently been codified in approaches such as DSDM.

Wood, Jane and Denise Silver, *Joint Application Development*, New York, Wiley, 1995.

PRINCE2

Office of Government Commerce, *Managing Successful Projects with PRINCE2*, London, The Stationery Office, 2005.

Office of Government Commerce, *For Successful Project Management: Think PRINCE2*, London, The Stationery Office, 2007. A condensed description of PRINCE2.

Office of Government Commerce, *People Issues and PRINCE2*, London, The Stationery Office, 2002.

Estimation

Boehm, Barry W. et al., *Software Estimation with COCOMO II*, Upper Saddle River, NJ, Prentice Hall, 2002.

Boehm, Barry W., *Software Engineering Economics*, Prentice Hall, 1981. Along with Brooks' *Mythical man-month*, one of the most frequently cited books on software project management.

Common Software Measurement International Consortium (COSMIC), *COSMICFFP Measurement Manual* (www.1rg1.uqam.ca/cosmic-ffp/manual.html).

DeMarco, Tom, *Controlling Software Projects: Management, measurement and estimation*, Englewood Cliffs, NJ, Yourdon Press, 1982.

Hughes, Bob, *Practical Software Measurement*, London, McGraw-Hill, 2002. Clearly we have an interest here! Could be seen as a companion book to this one.

Symons, Charles R., *Software Sizing and Estimating Mk II FPA (Function Point Analysis)*, Chichester, Wiley, 1991. A book by the inventor of Mark II function points.

Control, risk and quality

Boehm, Barry W., *Software Risk Management*, IEEE Computer Society Press, 1989.
DeMarco, Tom and Timothy Lister, *Waltzing with Bears: Managing Risk on Software Projects*, New York, Dorset House, 2003.
Down, Alex, Michael Coleman and Peter Absolon, *Risk Management for Software Projects*, Maidenhead, McGraw-Hill, 1994.
Grey, Stephen, *Practical Risk Assessment for Project Management*, Chichester, Wiley, 1995.
Humphrey, Watts S., *Managing the Software Process*, Reading, MA, Addison-Wesley, 1990.
Leach, L. P., *Critical Chain Project Management*, Norwood, MA, Artech House, 2000.
Manns, Tom and Michael Coleman, *Software Quality Assurance* (2nd edition), Basingstoke, Macmillan, 1996.

People management

Arnold, John, Cary Cooper and Ivan Robertson, *Work Psychology: Understanding human behaviour in the workplace* (4th edition), London, FT Prentice-Hall, 2004.
Belbin, Nigel, *The Belbin Guide to Succeeding at Work*, Cambridge, Belbin, 2008.
Belbin, R. Meredith, *Management Teams: Why they succeed or fail* (2nd edition), Oxford, Elsevier, 2003.
Belbin, R. Meredith, *Team Roles at Work*, Oxford, Butterworth-Heinemann, 1996.
DeMarco, Tom, Peter Hruschka, Tim Lister, Steve McMenamin, James Robertson and Suzanne Robertson, *Adrenaline Junkies and Template Zombies: Understanding Patterns of Project Behavior*, New York, Dorset House, 2008.
Handy, Charles B., *Understanding Organizations* (4th edition), London, Penguin, 1993.
Weinberg, G. M., *The Psychology of Computer Programming*, Silver Anniversary Edition, New York, Dorset House, 1998.
Yourdon, Edward, *Death March* (2nd edition), Englewood Cliffs, NJ, Yourdon Press, 2003. We have reservations about some aspects of this book, but it is certainly worth looking at.

Ethical and legal issues

Bainbridge, David, *Introduction to Computer Law* (6th edition), Harlow, Longman, 2007.
Bott, Frank, *Professional Issues in Information Technology*, London, The British Computer Society, 2005.
Holt, Jeremy and Jeremy Newton, *A Manager's Guide to IT Law*, London, The British Computer Society, 2004.
Burnett, Rachel, *IT Legal Risk Management*, London, Institute for the Management of Information Systems, 2003.

Project management and other standards

Association for Project Management, *APM Body of Knowledge* (5th edition), High Wycombe, Association for Project Management, 2006.

British Standards Institution, *BS 6079-1:2002 Guide to Project Management*, London, BSI, 2002.

British Standards Institution, *TickIT Guide (5.5) A Guide to Software Quality Management System Construction and Certification to ISO 9001:2000*, London, BSI, 2007.

ISO/IEC 12207:1995 Information technology: software lifecycle processes (amended 2002 and 2004).

ISO/IEC 15504-1:2004 Information technology: process assessment Part 1 Concepts and vocabulary.

ISO/IEC 15504-2:2004 Information technology: process assessment Part 2 Performing and assessment.

ISO/IEC 15504-3:2004 Information technology: process assessment Part 3 Guidance on performing an assessment.

ISO/IEC 15504-4:2004 Information technology: process assessment Part 4 Guidance on use for process improvement and process capability determination.

ISO/IEC 14598-1:1999 Information technology: software product evaluation Part 1 General overview.

ISO/IEC 14598-2:2000 Information technology: software product evaluation Part 2 Planning and management.

ISO/IEC 9126-1:2001 Information technology: software product quality Part 1 Quality model.

ISO/IEC TR 9126-2:2003 Software engineering: product quality Part 2 External metrics.

ISO/IEC TR 9126-3:2003 Software engineering: product quality Part 3 Internal metrics.

ISO/IEC TR 9126-4:2004 Software engineering: product quality Part 4 Quality in use metrics.

Project Management Institute and PMI Standards Committee, *A Guide to the Project Management Body of Knowledge*, Upper Derby, PA, PMI, 1996, www.pmi.org

Software Engineering Institute, *CMMI for Development 1.2*, Pittsburgh, SEI, 2006, www.sei.cmu.edu

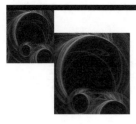

Index

(n.b. References to margin notes are denoted by 'n' following the page number)